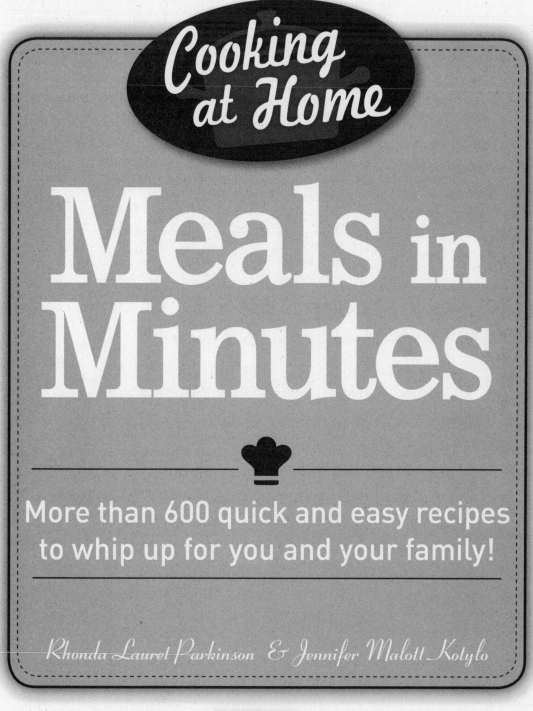

Cooking at Home

Meals in Minutes

More than 600 quick and easy recipes
to whip up for you and your family!

Rhonda Lauret Parkinson   &   Jennifer Malott Kotylo

JG
PRESS

Published by World Publications Group, Inc.
140 Laurel Street, East Bridgewater, MA. 02333
www.wrldpub.com

ISBN 10: 1-57215-754-2
ISBN 13: 978-1-57215-754-5

Printed and bound in the United States of America.

10 9 8 7 6 5 4 3 2 1

Previously published as *The Everything® Quick Meals Cookbook*
and *The Everything® Quick and Easy 30-Minute, 5-Ingredient Cookbook.*

Contents

Quick and Easy 30-Minute, 5-Ingredient Recipes

Introduction

In today's busy world, it seems that no one has time to cook anymore. At the end of a busy workday, few people have the inclination to pour over recipe books trying to decide what to make for dinner, let alone to prepare and cook it. It's all too easy to join the growing trend of "fast-food families" who rely on the corner drive-through restaurant for their meals.

Why should you prepare home-cooked meals? For one thing, they're healthier. A steady diet of burgers, French fries, and other fast-food standbys has a high nutritional cost. Despite the best efforts of fast-food and family restaurant chains, the average take-out meal is loaded with excess fat, sodium, and calories. Enjoying the occasional Sunday breakfast or celebration dinner at a restaurant is one thing, but eating out regularly can wreak havoc with your waistline, and lead to long-term health problems.

Studies show that children of families that frequently eat fast-food dinners also tend to make poor food choices at home, favoring chips and soda over fresh fruit and vegetables. This can signal the start of a lifelong struggle with obesity and the health problems associated with being overweight.

Cooking at home saves money. True, it's easy to splurge when you're inspired to create a special meal on the spur of the moment; a trip to the farmer's market for organic vegetables, to the butcher for a special cut of meat, and finally to the supermarket for ingredients to make that special sauce all add up. But the meal's high price tag comes from making numerous one-time purchases, with no plans for using up excess ingredients or leftovers. Instead of discarding that unused half cup of canned herbed tomatoes, why not incorporate it into another meal? Planning in advance enables you to get the most for your food dollar.

Believe it or not, cooking at home saves time. Once you develop a regular routine—writing up a grocery list, taking a spare hour to do advance prep work on the weekend, and planning for leftovers—you'll find it's easy to quickly pull together a meal. From start to finish, dinner can be on the table in under thirty minutes (frequently under twenty). That's less time than it takes for a pizza to arrive during the busy dinner hour.

Besides, having a plan and sticking to it—instead of struggling to throw something together—may help you to discover cooking's therapeutic side. Preparing a nutritious home-cooked meal for your family is a great way to unwind at the end of the day.

Finally, preparing home-cooked meals can help bring back family mealtime. Numerous studies demonstrate the benefits of regularly eating together, from stronger family bonds to improved socialization and communication skills for children. But we all lead such active lives that this can be hard to arrange. Some stressed-out parents see the fast-food restaurant as a convenient solution, allowing them to spend time with their children while avoiding the hassles of cooking and cleanup. Being able to whip up a meal in under thirty minutes will give back that extra time you need to sit down for a family meal before rushing off to other activities. And you'll feel better knowing that you are helping your children establish healthy eating habits that will last a lifetime.

Chapter 1
Quick-Cooking Essentials

One of the biggest challenges for today's cooks is figuring out how to prepare meals that are quick, easy, and healthy. The lure of the local takeout restaurant can be strong, especially on busy weeknights. However, you do have alternatives. There are many timesaving strategies and tips that can help turn cooking family meals from a seemingly impossible chore into a joy—without requiring too much time in the kitchen!

Shopping for the Week

In response to the needs of a fast-paced society, there are numerous culinary shows dedicated to showing you how to whip up a meal in minutes. While celebrity chefs such as Rachael Ray make it seem easy, it takes a bit of advance planning to put together fast and healthy meals every night of the week. It all begins with the weekly trip to the supermarket.

Smart Shopping with a List

Never go grocery shopping without a list. There's nothing worse than having to make repeated trips to an overcrowded supermarket for a few items. A list also helps eliminate impulse purchases, which inflate your shopping bill and, worse, may end up forgotten in the vegetable crisper or back of the pantry shelf.

Before you begin writing a list, plan your meals for the week. Don't forget to take previously frozen food and leftovers into account. For example, if you're making Quick Tuna with Marinara Sauce (page 134), you could prepare a double batch of the sauce to use for soup. Those cooked chicken breasts you froze earlier can be thawed and used to make Leftover Coconut Chicken (page 198). For lettuce and other highly perishable vegetables, buy as much as you need to last a few days and then plan a return trip to stock up in the middle of the week.

Consider the supermarket layout when formulating your list. Most supermarkets (including ethnic groceries) tend to work from the outside in, placing the fresh produce and perishable items around the perimeter, and the dried goods in the aisles in the middle. Organize the list so that the items are placed in the order you would find them in the store. This will prevent wandering back and forth between aisles, and shorten your total shopping time.

Let Your Computer Do the Work

A computer can be an invaluable aid in preparing a grocery list. When working out a meal plan, it's easy to forget staples (both food and nonfood items) that need replacing on a regular basis, such as cereal or soap. Keeping a basic list of items on file, and adding or subtracting from it each week as needed, will make this task much easier and help prevent repeated trips to the supermarket. Besides, a printed list is often much easier to read!

Quick-Cooking Tips

Organization is key when it comes to quick cooking. Professional chefs follow a philosophy called *mise en place*. Literally meaning "everything in its place," it refers to a system of advance preparation that is designed to help the cooking process unfold more smoothly. The quick cook's version of *mise en place* includes advance preparation, making use of convenience foods, and incorporating leftovers.

Thinking Ahead: Advance Preparation

At home, get a head start on meal preparation by chopping vegetables and cooking rice or noodles to use during the week. How much advance prep work you do will depend on how much time you have during the week, as well as whether or not you enjoy it. If the thought of peeling and chopping onions after a long workday is enough to send you out the door to the nearest restaurant, do the prep work on the weekend when you're not so stressed. Store the amount you need for each meal in a resealable plastic bag and refrigerate until needed.

Saving Time with Leftovers

Incorporating leftovers into your meal plan is a great way to speed up cooking time during the week. When preparing pasta or rice for dinner, it's just as easy to cook a double portion and store half to use later. (This is a particularly good idea if you're not a fan of instant rice.) Similarly, it's easy to broil or grill an extra chicken breast, piece of beef, or seafood steak. Besides saving time later, preparing a double portion of sauce may actually add extra flavor to your meals, since the sauce ingredients will have more opportunity to blend together. Just be sure to always follow basic food hygiene rules for storing and reheating food.

Many leftovers can be frozen until needed. Wrap the food in individual portions in freezer bags, label with the date, and store until needed. When it comes time to cook, simply reheat the frozen food in the microwave, oven, or stovetop as required.

A Matter of Convenience

Be sure to take advantage of your supermarket's selection of convenience items. Cooked deli chicken, precut vegetables from the salad bar, and prepared fruit (such as cored pineapple) are great timesavers. Just bag them into individual meal portions when you get home, store in the refrigerator, and you're all set! Thanks to growing demand from consumers, many supermarkets are expanding their offerings of prepared canned and bottled foods—it's becoming easier to find everything from canned squid to bottled minced garlic. Greater awareness of the need to eat healthy meals means that many of these foods are low in fat and sodium.

The freezer section of your supermarket is a great resource for prepped foods—such as precut vegetables—along with specialty items such as frozen cooked meatballs. Regularly incorporating frozen foods into your meal plan will reduce preparation and cooking times. And if you're concerned about the nutritional value of frozen foods, relax: freezing is the healthiest form of food preservation. Studies have shown that the nutritional value of frozen vegetables is equal to, and sometimes even surpasses, that of fresh vegetables.

Stocking the Kitchen

Just because your cooking time is limited doesn't mean you should skimp when it comes to purchasing quality cooking equipment. It's easier to work quickly and efficiently in a well-organized, properly equipped kitchen. For the cook whose main goal is to prepare quality home-cooked meals in a hurry, there are a few appliances that are essential.

Microwave Magic

Cooking food in a microwave oven (instead of in a conventional oven or on the stovetop) has several advantages: it reduces cooking time, uses less energy, and doesn't heat up the kitchen. Nonetheless, despite the fact that the microwave oven celebrated its sixtieth birthday in 2007, in many homes it is still used primarily to reheat leftovers, or cook fast food such as pizza. However, a microwave can dramatically shorten cooking times at every meal.

A microwave oven cooks food when the microwaves hit the food, causing water molecules in the food to vibrate and produce heat. This makes it perfect for cooking food with a high liquid content, such as soups and casseroles, or for boiling rice and vegetables. And nothing beats a microwave for making chocolate-based desserts such as Microwave Fudge (page 268) or Fast Chocolate Fondue (page 264). It's so much easier to melt heat-sensitive chocolate in the microwave, stirring occasionally, than to stand over the stovetop constantly stirring and adjusting the temperature to prevent the chocolate from scorching.

A microwave will help with the preliminary stages of cooking a meal, such as thawing or defrosting frozen food, blanching vegetables, quickly boiling water, or reheating rice. Within certain limits, you can even prepare complete meals in a microwave. Just remember that, since the microwave cooks food from the outside inward, it's important to make sure that meat, poultry, and seafood are thoroughly cooked.

The precise cooking times needed to microwave food will depend on the model of microwave you are using—everything from the wattage level to the microwave stirrer can affect the amount of time it takes for food to cook. There can even be differences in cooking times between two microwaves of the same make and model, as "hot spots" develop over time. When a recipe calls for cooking food in the microwave, always start with the minimum cooking time given, and then continue cooking at shorter intervals as needed until the food is cooked.

Mixing and Processing Food

A blender is the ultimate timesaving device, used for everything from chopping onions to crushing ice and puréeing vegetables for soup. As with the microwave, the culinary possibilities of the blender are sometimes overlooked. While the blender's main claim to fame is liquefying ingredients for smoothies and mixed drinks, it can also be used to make sauces (such as Italian pesto or cold tomato sauce) and cold soups.

Another useful tool is a mini food processor. Much less expensive than higher-end models designed to perform complex tasks such as making bread dough, a mini food processor is excellent for mincing garlic, chopping herbs, grating cheese, and crushing bread crumbs. The size and shape of its work bowl makes a mini food processor more efficient than a blender at performing these tasks when you're only using a small quantity of food.

Essential Cooking Utensils

Quality, not quantity, is what counts when it comes to buying cooking utensils. A basic supply of high-quality pots, pans, bakeware, and other assorted kitchen utensils—many nonstick and dishwasher safe—will making cooking easier and cleanup time shorter. Here is a basic list of tools that every busy cook should have:

- **Nonstick baking sheets:** Be sure to buy two or more.
- **Complete set of pots and pans:** Be sure to include a large pot for cooking noodles.
- **Complete set of plastic mixing bowls:** For sifting and mixing ingredients.
- **Pepper mill:** It takes only seconds to grind a few peppercorns in the mill, giving you fresh ground pepper with significantly more flavor than store-bought.
- **A metal whisk:** Sometimes called a balloon whisk, a small metal whisk is perfect for mixing sauces.
- **Plastic cutting boards for cutting and chopping food:** Plastic boards are easier to clean than traditional wood chopping boards.
- **Heatproof rubber spatula:** Use to stir and turn food during cooking.
- **Measuring cups and spoons:** Along with a complete set of regular measuring cups for liquid ingredients, be sure to buy a set of nested measuring cups that can be easily leveled off for measuring flour and other dry ingredients. Try to find liquid measuring cups that are microwave-safe—these are very convenient for quickly heating specific amounts of water or sauces in the microwave.
- **A complete set of knives:** Buy the best that you can afford and have them sharpened regularly.
- **A metal steamer:** For steaming vegetables quickly.
- **Strainer and colander:** Look for metal or silicone colanders that are heat-resistant to high temperatures.

- **Containers for storing dry goods:** Plastic is fine; just make sure there is a tight seal between the container body and the lid.
- **Microwave accessories:** Microwave-safe plastic wrap and wax paper are frequently used in recipes that call for covering food while it is cooking.

Staple Ingredients

Stocking the pantry is a key strategy in preparing home-cooked meals fast. Whether you're cooking for friends, family, or just yourself, having to repeatedly make emergency trips to the supermarket for that one essential ingredient you forgot to buy will lower your enthusiasm for cooking considerably. This isn't meant to be an exhaustive list of what every kitchen should have, but rather a rundown of staples that should always be on hand:

- **Flour:** All-purpose flour is a blended wheat flour that can be used for most types of baking.
- **Baking powder and baking soda:** Staples in any kitchen, these are essential for baking recipes such as quick breads.
- **Sugar:** Keep both granulated and brown sugar on hand for use as sweeteners in sauces and for baking.
- **Olive oil:** Use extra-virgin olive oil—the healthiest type of olive oil —for marinades and salad dressings. For sautés, use pure olive oil (also called simply olive oil).
- **Vegetable oil:** While pure olive oil is acceptable for most stir-fries, at times it may contrast with the flavors in a dish. To avoid potential problems, stick with a vegetable oil, such as canola oil, for stir-fries.
- **Bottled minced garlic and ginger:** These are great timesavers on nights when you just don't feel up to peeling and mincing.
- **Dried spices:** Spices are perfect for enhancing flavor without adding fat and calories. While literally hundreds of spices exist, there are certain ones you'll find yourself using regularly. These include dried basil, dried parsley, dried oregano, ground cinnamon, ground nutmeg, paprika, red pepper flakes, and chili powder.

- **Instant rice:** Instant rice is a great timesaver for nights when you don't have time to cook rice on the stovetop or in a rice cooker. While instant white rice can taste rather bland, a number of other varieties, such as quick-cooking brown and jasmine rice, can be found in many supermarkets or purchased online.
- **Regular rice:** Be sure to also keep regular long-grain white rice and scented jasmine rice on hand to cook ahead of time and reheat, or for nights when you have at least thirty minutes to cook dinner.
- **Pasta:** You'll want to keep a selection of small-shaped pasta, such as penne and macaroni, in the cupboard. Smaller pastas come in a variety of unusual shapes that enhance the appearance of a dish. Better still, they cook more quickly than longer pastas!
- **Asian rice noodles:** Available in a variety of different widths and sizes, rice noodles add a different texture and flavor to a dish. An added plus is that they are gluten-free. Round rice-paper wrappers (used to make Asian spring rolls) only require a quick dip in water before being ready to use.
- **Canned beans:** High in fiber and loaded with vitamins and minerals, beans are the healthiest type of plant food. Most stores carry a wide selection of beans, including red, black, white, navy, and chickpeas.
- **Canned tomatoes:** Canned chopped or diced tomatoes will save preparation time.

Safe Storage

Since a major part of your cooking strategy depends on advance preparation, you'll need to have necessary supplies for storing food. Be sure to have small and large resealable bags for storing leftovers at room temperature or in the refrigerator—these are also ideal for marinating food. For freezing, containers, bags, and paper specifically designed for the freezer will keep out excess moisture and vapor that can cause freezer burn. The ultimate all-purpose food storage wrapper, aluminum foil, molds easily to the shape of the food and can withstand extreme temperatures.

Shelf Life

Using dry ingredients that are past their prime can affect flavor, or even cause a recipe not to turn out properly. Cookies and other baked goods don't taste the same; older rice needs more water, which increases the cooking time. Be sure to store staples such as flour, rice, and sugar in tightly sealed canisters in a cool, dry place. Here is a chart showing the maximum shelf life for staples commonly used in cooking:

Ingredient	Maximum Storage
Flour	1 year
Baking powder	1 year
Baking soda	1 year
Granulated sugar	18 months
Brown sugar	6 months
Rice	2 years
Dried spices	2 years

While it's becoming increasingly rare, it is possible that a bag of flour or rice you bring home from the grocery store may be infected with weevils or other small pests. Once the bugs find their way out of the bag and into your kitchen cupboard, they can be extremely difficult to get rid of. To guard against an infestation, freeze all dry ingredients for forty-eight hours before storage. This will kill both the bugs themselves and any eggs that may be residing in the food.

Speedy Cooking Techniques: Sautéing, Steaming, and Stir-Frying

Quick-cooking techniques such as stir-frying and steaming are very easy to learn. An added plus is that they are healthier than longer cooking techniques: shorter cooking time means that the food retains more of its nutrients.

Stir-Frying

Invented by the Chinese to cope with a shortage of oil, stir-frying consists of cooking food by stirring it rapidly at high heat in a small amount of oil. Traditionally, Chinese stir-fries are prepared in a bowl-shaped utensil called a wok, but a deep-sided skillet makes an acceptable substitute. Stir-frying requires more advance preparation than other cooking methods. However, the short cooking time more than makes up for the extra prep work, as the average stir-fry dish takes less than ten minutes to make.

Here are the basic steps needed to prepare a stir-fry:

- **Prepare all the ingredients:** Cut the meat and vegetables into bite-size pieces and place on a dish near the stove.
- **Preheat the pan:** Heat the pan on medium-high heat before adding the oil.
- **Heat the oil for stir-frying:** Add vegetable or peanut oil, tilting the pan so that the oil coats the bottom and halfway up the sides of the pan.
- **Test the oil to see if it is hot:** The easiest way is to drop a piece of fresh gingerroot into the hot oil. If it starts sizzling immediately, the oil is ready.
- **Add the first set of ingredients:** Usually the meat, poultry, or seafood is added first. Lay the meat out flat and let it sear for about thirty seconds before you begin stirring.
- **Add the second set of ingredients:** Usually these are the vegetables. Unlike meat, vegetables need to be stir-fried continually to prevent burning.
- **Add a sauce:** The sauce is normally added near the end of stir-frying.

Sautéing

Like stir-frying, sautéing consists of cooking food in a small amount of oil over high heat. However, sautéed food doesn't need the constant stirring required for stir-frying (although it will need to be turned over to ensure that each side is browned and cooked through). Furthermore, the food does not need to be cut into bite-size pieces, but can be cooked whole.

Both sautéing and stir-frying have their advantages. Stir-frying takes less time, as cutting food into bite-size pieces makes it cook more quickly. On the other hand, there is less preparatory work required to sauté food.

Steaming

Generally considered to be the healthiest cooking technique, steaming consists of using moist heat, commonly called steam, to cook food. Unlike stir-frying, grilling, and other quick-cooking methods, steaming does not destroy important nutrients in the food. Even a simple method such as cooking food in boiling water is less healthy, since you lose many nutrients when you drain the cooking water. Furthermore, steaming does a better job of coaxing out the subtle flavors of the food.

The only potential disadvantage of steaming is that it can sometimes (although not always) take longer than other cooking methods. Still, even cooks in a hurry will find it's a great way to cook many types of food, particularly fish and vegetables.

Whether you're using traditional Chinese bamboo steamer baskets placed in a wok or a simple metal steamer inserted into a saucepan, steaming is easy if you follow a few simple steps:

- When using a bamboo steamer, place a bamboo base into a Chinese wok, making sure it doesn't fit too snugly.
- When steaming larger items (such as fish) in a bamboo steamer, place the food on a heatproof dish. For smaller items, you can use a bamboo steaming basket placed on top of the base.
- Pour enough boiling water in the sides of the wok so that the water comes within an inch of the food.
- When using a metal steamer insert, add water to a medium-sized saucepan, and then add the insert. The water should come within an inch of the food.
- Whatever type of steamer you are using, it's important to make sure the water doesn't touch the food. Let the steam cook the food.

- Keep the water at a rolling boil while cooking the food. Add more boiling water as needed.

To steam vegetables, cook over the boiling water until they are tender but still crisp when pierced with a fork (about two to three minutes for most vegetables). To steam poultry, cook until the chicken is tender and the juices run clear when pierced with a fork. To steam fish, cook until the fish flakes easily with a fork.

Chapter 2
Breakfast

Bagel and Cream Cheese with Italian Seasonings

Serves 4

Preparation time:
5 minutes

4 plain bagels
½ cup plain cream
    cheese
½ teaspoon dried
    oregano leaves
½ teaspoon dried basil
    leaves
¼ teaspoon garlic salt
4 teaspoons lemon juice
1 teaspoon balsamic
    vinegar

Here's an easy way to spice up plain cream cheese, using ingredients on hand in the cupboard. If you like, feel free to replace the dried oregano and basil with an equal amount of Italian seasoning mix, which contains a blend of several herbs, including rosemary, thyme, marjoram, basil, and oregano.

1. Cut the bagels in half and place in an 8-slice toaster.

2. While the bagels are toasting, prepare the cream cheese: in a bowl, stir the oregano, basil, garlic salt, lemon juice, and balsamic vinegar into the cream cheese, blending thoroughly.

3. Use a knife to spread about 1 tablespoon of the cream cheese mixture on each bagel half.

Ten-Minute Yogurt and Rice Pudding

Serves 4

Preparation time:
2–3 minutes
Cooking time: 10 minutes

1 cup coconut milk
1 cup water
2 cups instant rice
¼ teaspoon salt
½ cup raisins
2 cups peach-flavored
    yogurt

Using instant rice means this simple pudding takes just over 10 minutes to make. Feel free to replace the peach yogurt with your favorite variety of yogurt, or to spice up the pudding by adding ½ teaspoon of ground cinnamon or nutmeg.

1. Bring the coconut milk and water to boil in a medium saucepan.

2. Stir in the rice, making sure it is thoroughly wet. Stir in the salt.

3. Cover the saucepan and let stand for 5 minutes, or until the water is absorbed. Fluff up with a fork.

4. In a large bowl, combine the cooked rice with the raisins and peach-flavored yogurt. Serve immediately, or chill until ready to serve.

Instant Granola

Be sure that the melted margarine covers the bottom of the cooking dish, and to spread out the granola mixture so that it doesn't burn. You can increase the brown sugar to 3 tablespoons if desired.

Serves 2

Preparation time:
5 minutes
Cooking time:
2–3 minutes

3 tablespoons margarine
1 cup quick-cooking oats
¼ cup vegetable oil
2 tablespoons brown
   sugar
2 tablespoons apple juice
½ cup dried fruit and nut
   mix

1. Place the margarine in a 1-quart microwave-safe casserole dish.

2. Heat the margarine in the microwave on high heat for 15 seconds, or until it is melted.

3. In a medium mixing bowl, stir together the quick-cooking oats, vegetable oil, and brown sugar. Spoon the oat mixture into the dish, spreading it out evenly.

4. Microwave on high heat for 1 minute. Add the apple juice and the dried fruit and nut mixture, stirring to mix thoroughly into the oats.

5. Give the dish a quarter turn and microwave on high heat for 1 more minute, then another 30 seconds if needed, until the granola is cooked, stirring the granola and making another quarter turn. Be sure not to overcook the fruit. (Do not worry about foaming at the top of the granola.)

Marvelous Muesli

The uncooked version of granola, muesli is a nutritious dish combining fruit and nuts with oats. While the exact origins of muesli are unknown, the modern version was invented by Dr. Maximilian Bircher-Benner, who wanted to provide a healthy meal for patients in his sanatorium. Using oats makes this dish high in fiber, while the fruit provides a healthy source of sucrose.

Easy Cheese Frittata

Serves 4

Preparation time:
5 minutes
Cooking time: 15 minutes

6 eggs
¼ teaspoon nutmeg
Salt and black pepper to taste
2 cups shredded cheese, divided
2 teaspoons olive oil

The Italian version of an omelet, a frittata is served open-faced instead of folded over. A blend of shredded Italian cheeses would be ideal for this recipe.

1. In a large bowl, whisk the eggs with the nutmeg, salt, and pepper. Stir in 1½ cups cheese.

2. Heat a medium-sized skillet over medium-high heat. Add the oil, tilting so that it covers the bottom of the pan. Pour the egg mixture into the pan. Cook the frittata on low-medium heat, using a heatproof turner to lift the edges occasionally so that the uncooked egg flows underneath.

3. When the frittata is firm on top, remove from the pan, turn it, and slide it back into the pan.

4. Sprinkle the remaining cheese on top and cook for a few more minutes, until the cheese is melted and the frittata cooked through.

Flipping a Frittata

Traditionally, a frittata is flipped over before adding the cheese topping. To flip over the frittata, cover the frying pan with a plate, and then turn the pan over so that the frittata falls on the plate. Set the skillet back on the stove element, and carefully slide the frittata off the plate and back into the pan. Sprinkle the cheese over the top. Cook for 1 to 2 more minutes, until the cheese has melted.

Fast Frittata with Beans

For an extra touch, serve the frittata with a flavorful red or green salsa.

1. In a small bowl, beat the eggs with the salt and pepper.

2. Stir in the minced onion, vegetables, milk, and garlic. Stir in the beans.

3. Pour the egg mixture into the pan. Cook the frittata on low-medium heat, using a heatproof turner to lift the edges occasionally so that the uncooked egg flows underneath.

4. When the frittata is firm on top, remove it from the pan, turn it, and slide it back into the pan.

5. Sprinkle the cheese on top and cook for a few more minutes, until the cheese is melted and the frittata cooked through.

Serves 4

Preparation time: 10 minutes
Cooking time: 10 minutes

4 large eggs
¼ teaspoon salt
⅛ teaspoon black pepper
2 tablespoons minced onion
1 cup frozen vegetables, thawed
½ cup fat-free evaporated milk
1 teaspoon bottled minced garlic
¾ cup drained canned black beans
¾ cup drained white beans
½ cup shredded Cheddar cheese

Simple Cinnamon Toast

The combination of ground cinnamon and granulated sugar is the secret behind this simple, fragrant breakfast treat.

1. In a small bowl, stir together the sugar and ground cinnamon.

2. Toast the bread. Spread 2 teaspoons margarine over one side of each slice of bread.

3. Sprinkle the cinnamon and sugar mixture on top of each slice of bread (2 to 2½ teaspoons for each slice).

Serves 4

Preparation time:
5–10 minutes

2 tablespoons granulated sugar
1 tablespoon ground cinnamon
4 slices bread
8 teaspoons margarine

Basic Banana Muffins

Fresh-baked banana muffins have a sweet flavor. For an extra touch of flavor, add 2 to 3 tablespoons of sweetened coconut flakes to the muffin batter.

Yields 12 muffins

Preparation time:
10 minutes
Cooking time:
20–25 minutes

1 cup milk
1 large egg
⅓ cup vegetable oil
1 teaspoon vanilla extract
3 medium bananas,
*   peeled and mashed*
2 cups all-purpose flour
½ teaspoon baking soda
1¼ teaspoons baking
*   powder*
½ cup granulated sugar
½ teaspoon salt
½ teaspoon ground
*   cinnamon*

1. Preheat the oven to 375°F. Grease one muffin tin.

2. In a medium mixing bowl, whisk together the milk, egg, vegetable oil, vanilla extract, and mashed banana.

3. In a large mixing bowl, stir together the flour, baking soda, baking powder, sugar, salt, and ground cinnamon, mixing well.

4. Pour the milk mixture into the dry ingredients. Stir until the mixture is just combined and still a bit lumpy (do not overbeat).

5. Fill each muffin cup about two-thirds full with muffin batter. (If you have leftover muffin batter, refrigerate and use within a few days.) Bake the muffins for 20 to 25 minutes, until they are a light golden brown and a toothpick inserted in the middle comes out clean.

Muffin Cooking Tips

Muffins are easy to make if you follow a few simple steps. Don't over-beat the batter—a good muffin batter has a few lumps. Once the batter is mixed, fill the cups and put the muffins in the oven immediately. Be sure not to fill the cups over two-thirds full, or the muffins will have an uneven shape. Remove the muffins from the oven when a toothpick inserted in the middle of a muffin comes out clean.

Chocolate Chip Muffins

Easy-melting semisweet chocolate chips are perfect for baked goods.

1. Preheat the oven to 375°F. Grease one muffin tin.

2. In a medium mixing bowl, whisk together the milk, egg, and vegetable oil.

3. In a large mixing bowl, stir together the flour, sugar, salt, and baking powder, mixing well. Gently stir in the chocolate chips.

4. Pour the milk mixture into the dry ingredients. Stir until the mixture is just combined and still a bit lumpy (do not overbeat).

5. Fill each muffin cup about two-thirds full with muffin batter. (If you have leftover muffin batter, refrigerate and use within a few days). Bake the muffins for 20 to 25 minutes, until they turn a light golden brown and a toothpick inserted in the middle comes out clean.

Yields 12 muffins

Preparation time:
10 minutes
Cooking time:
20–25 minutes

1 cup milk
1 large egg
⅓ cup vegetable oil
2 cups all-purpose flour
⅓ cup granulated sugar
½ teaspoon salt
2 teaspoons baking
   powder
1 cup semisweet
   chocolate chips

Tofu Breakfast Shake

Serves 2

Preparation time:
7–10 minutes

1 (12-ounce) package soft
    tofu
1 banana
1 cup raspberries, fresh
    or frozen
½ cup orange juice
1 cup soymilk
2 tablespoons liquid
    honey

The soft texture of silken tofu makes it perfect for everything from shakes or smoothies to custards and puddings. For an interesting twist (and to increase the health benefits of this nutritious breakfast even further), try adding 2 tablespoons of brewed green tea.

1. Carefully remove the tofu from the package and cut into loose chunks. Cut the banana into chunks.

2. Combine all the ingredients in a blender. Process until smooth.

Tofu By Any Other Name

Originating in Japan, silken tofu is made by a process similar to yogurt making. This gives it a creamier, more custardy texture than regular tofu—perfect for puddings, smoothies, dressings, and other blended dishes.

Make-Ahead Muffin Batter

Nothing beats enjoying fresh muffins in the morning without having to do any stirring or mixing! When preparing make-ahead muffin batter, it's even more important than usual to not overbeat the batter. Refrigerate the batter and use within one week.

1. In a medium mixing bowl, whisk together the buttermilk, egg, vegetable oil, and vanilla extract.

2. In a large mixing bowl, stir together the flour, sugar, salt, baking soda, and baking powder, mixing well.

3. Pour the buttermilk mixture into the dry ingredients. Stir until the mixture is just combined and still a bit lumpy (do not overbeat).

4. Fold in the chocolate chips. Cover the bowl and store in the refrigerator until ready to use.

5. When ready to bake the muffins, fill greased muffin cups about two-thirds full with the muffin batter. Bake the muffins in a 375°F oven for 20 to 25 minutes, until they turn a light golden brown and a toothpick inserted in the middle comes out clean.

Yields 12 muffins

Preparation time:
10 minutes
Cooking time:
20–25 minutes

1 cup buttermilk
1 large egg
⅓ cup vegetable oil
1 teaspoon vanilla extract
2 cups all-purpose flour
½ cup granulated sugar
½ teaspoon salt
½ teaspoon baking soda
1½ teaspoons baking powder
¾ cup semi-sweet chocolate chips

Basic Blender Pancakes

Serves 12

Preparation time:
10 minutes
Cooking time:
5–6 minutes per pancake

2 cups plain yogurt
2 large eggs
3 tablespoons vegetable
     oil
2 tablespoons granulated
     sugar
2 tablespoons brown
     sugar
2 cups all-purpose flour
½ teaspoon salt
4 teaspoons baking
     powder
Water, as needed

If desired, you can replace the yogurt with 2½ cups of either small curd cottage cheese or ricotta cheese.

1. Preheat a griddle or skillet over medium-high heat.

2. In a blender or food processor with knife blade attached, blend the yogurt, eggs, and vegetable oil. Add the sugars, flour, salt, and baking powder. Blend until smooth, adding as much water as needed until you have a pancake batter that is neither too thick nor too runny.

3. Grease the griddle or skillet as needed.

4. Pour the batter in ¼ cup portions into the pan. Cook the pancakes until they are browned on the bottom and bubbles start forming on top. Turn the pancakes over and cook the other side.

5. Continue cooking the remainder of the pancakes, adding more oil or margarine to grease the pan as needed.

How to Freeze Pancakes

Got leftover pancakes? To freeze, place a sheet of wax paper between each pancake to keep them separate, and wrap in a resealable plastic bag. To reheat the pancakes, unwrap, remove the wax paper, and cook the pancakes in stacks of two in a microwave on high heat for 1 to 1½ minutes, or in a 375°F oven for 10 to 15 minutes.

High Protein Peanut Butter Pancakes

The total cooking time for pancakes will depend on the size of the skillet and how many pancakes you can cook at a time.

Serves 6

Preparation time:
10 minutes
Cooking time:
5–6 minutes per pancake

1 cup all-purpose flour
2 tablespoons brown
    sugar
¼ teaspoon salt
2 teaspoons baking
    powder
1 large egg
1 cup coconut milk
2 tablespoons melted
    butter
⅓ cup peanut butter
4 tablespoons water, or
    as needed

1. In a medium mixing bowl, stir together the flour, brown sugar, salt, and baking powder.

2. In a large mixing bowl, beat together the egg, coconut milk, melted butter, and peanut butter.

3. Grease a griddle or skillet and heat over medium-high heat. Combine the dry and wet ingredients, stirring until they are just combined. Add as much water as needed until you have a batter that is neither too thick nor too runny. Don't overbeat the batter, and don't worry if there are a few lumps.

4. Pour the batter in ¼ cup portions into the pan. Cook the pancakes until they are browned on the bottom and bubbles start forming on top. Turn the pancakes over and cook the other side.

5. Continue cooking the remainder of the pancakes, adding more oil or margarine to grease the pan as needed.

Perfect Pancake Toppings

Maple syrup is the traditional pancake topping, but if you're not a fan there are other options. For a more nutritious dish, top the pancakes with fresh fruit that is mixed with either plain yogurt or cottage cheese. When you want something a little more decadent, melted butter mixed with sugar, warmed fruit preserves, or even icing sugar are all good choices.

Microwave Scrambled Eggs

This recipe makes a very light, fluffy scrambled egg. The paprika adds extra flavor, but doesn't overpower the other ingredients.

Serves 2

Preparation time:
5 minutes
Cooking time:
1–2 minutes

3 large eggs
3 tablespoons milk
¼ teaspoon salt
⅛ teaspoon black pepper
⅛ teaspoon paprika
1 tablespoon margarine

1. In a small bowl, lightly beat the eggs with the milk, salt, pepper, and paprika.

2. Place the margarine in a microwave-safe bowl. Microwave on high heat for 30 seconds, and then for 5 seconds at a time until the margarine melts (total cooking time should be 30 to 45 seconds).

3. Pour the egg mixture into the bowl, stirring.

4. Microwave the egg on high heat for 45 seconds. Stir to break up the egg a bit, then continue microwaving for 30 seconds, and then for 15 seconds at a time, stirring each time, until the egg is just cooked through. Serve immediately.

Scrambled Egg Variations

A few additions can transform basic scrambled eggs into a hearty meal that will easily serve as a lunch or light dinner. For cheesy eggs, add ½ cup shredded American or other processed cheese to the eggs after they have begun to thicken. For a heartier dish, add ½ pound of cooked and drained bulk sausage to the thickening egg mixture. And to create Denver-style scrambled eggs, cook ⅓ cup chopped onion, ⅓ cup diced green pepper, and ⅓ cup diced ham in the melted butter before adding the eggs to the bowl.

Vegetarian "Egg" Scramble

Most of the preparation time for this vegetarian version of scrambled eggs comes from draining the tofu. If you drain the tofu ahead of time (storing it in the refrigerator), this easy dish can be ready in under 10 minutes.

Serves 4

Preparation time:
20 minutes
Cooking time:
5–7 minutes

12 ounces extra-firm tofu
1 teaspoon turmeric
1 teaspoon dried dill
¼ teaspoon garlic powder
1 teaspoon salt
½ teaspoon black pepper
2 tablespoons nutritional
  yeast
1 teaspoon bottled
  minced ginger
2 tablespoons minced
  onion
1 tablespoon vegetable oil
2 tablespoons soymilk

1. Drain the tofu and cut into ½-inch cubes. Place the cubes in a bowl and use your fingers to crumble and break them up until the tofu has the texture of scrambled egg.

2. Stir in the turmeric, dried dill, garlic powder, salt, pepper, nutritional yeast, minced ginger, and minced onion.

3. Heat the oil in a skillet over medium-high heat. Add the crumbled tofu. Cook, stirring the tofu continually, for about 2 minutes, then stir in the milk.

4. Continue stirring until the tofu has a light, fluffy texture, adding more oil as needed.

The Vegetarian Version of Scrambled Eggs

The two key ingredients in vegetarian scrambled eggs are nutritional yeast and turmeric. An inactive yeast fortified with vitamins, nutritional yeast adds a savory cheese and nutty flavor to the dish. Turmeric, a spice frequently used in Southeast Asian cooking, gives the scrambled tofu a golden yellow color similar to regular scrambled eggs.

French Toast

Crusty French or sourdough bread, sliced 1-inch thick,
is ideal for making French toast.

Serves 4

Preparation time:
5–10 minutes
Cooking time: 15 minutes

4 eggs
1 cup milk
¼ teaspoon salt
⅛ teaspoon ground
nutmeg
2 tablespoons margarine
8 slices bread
¼ cup brown sugar,
optional
½ cup maple syrup, or as
needed

1. In a medium-sized bowl, whisk the eggs with the milk, salt, and ground nutmeg.

2. Heat the margarine in a skillet on medium to low-medium heat.

3. Dip one of the pieces of bread in the egg mixture, coating well. Continue with the remaining pieces of bread, but only dip as many pieces of bread in the mixture as you are cooking at one time.

4. Lay the soaked bread in the skillet. Cook on one side for about 2 minutes until browned, then turn over and cook the other side.

5. Serve the French toast with the brown sugar and maple syrup.

The Best French Toast

French toast should be firm enough to cut into, and not too soggy. For best results, use a good crusty bread such as French bread, or white bread that is several days old.

Fun French Toast Sticks with Cinnamon

Kids love making this fun twist on traditional French toast. While maple syrup is the traditional French toast topping, these also taste delicious topped with jam or powdered sugar.

Serves 4

Preparation time:
5–10 minutes
Cooking time: 15 minutes

8 slices raisin bread
4 eggs
1 cup milk
¼ teaspoon salt
¼ teaspoon ground
    cinnamon
½ teaspoon vanilla extract
2 tablespoons margarine
½ cup maple syrup, or as
    needed

1. Cut each piece of bread lengthwise into four equal pieces.

2. In a small bowl, whisk the eggs with the milk, salt, cinnamon, and vanilla.

3. Heat the margarine in a skillet on medium to low-medium heat.

4. One at a time, dip the bread slices in the egg mixture, coating well. Only dip as many pieces of bread in the mixture as you are cooking at one time.

5. Lay the soaked bread pieces in the skillet. Cook on one side for about 2 minutes until browned, then turn over and cook the other side.

6. Serve the French toast sticks with the maple syrup.

Marshmallow Breakfast Bars

Breakfast bars make a fun change from regular breakfast cereal. Be sure to keep an eye on the marshmallow mixture so that it doesn't burn.

Serves 6

Preparation: 5–8 minutes
Cooking time:
10–15 minutes

4 tablespoons margarine
½ cup peanut butter
2 cups mini marshmallows
½ cup sugar
½ cup milk
2 cups quick-cooking
    oats
½ cup raisins
¼ cup dried cranberries

1. In a heavy medium-size saucepan, melt the margarine on low-medium heat. Add the peanut butter, stirring. Turn the heat down to low and add the marshmallows. Continue cooking over low heat, stirring occasionally, until the peanut butter and marshmallows are almost melted.

2. While melting the marshmallow and peanut butter, heat the sugar and milk to boiling in a separate small saucepan, stirring to dissolve the sugar.

3. Stir the oats into the melted marshmallow and peanut butter mixture. Stir in the heated milk and sugar, raisins, and cranberries.

4. Spread the mixture in a greased 9" x 9" pan, using a spatula or your hands to press it down evenly.

5. Chill for at least 15 minutes. Cut into bars.

Replacing Marshmallows with Mini Marshmallows

Replacing regular-size marshmallows with mini marshmallows gives you a greater assortment of colors. Use 10 mini marshmallows for every regular-size marshmallow called for in a recipe.

Chapter 3
Midday Meals

Leftover Meat Loaf Sandwich

This recipe would also work well with leftover Sweet-and-Sour Meat Loaf (page 102)—instead of honey mustard, use fiery hot mustard.

Serves 1

Preparation time:
3–5 minutes
Cooking time: 7–8 minutes

2 tablespoons margarine, divided
2 slices crusty Italian or French bread
2 teaspoons honey mustard
1 slice provolone or mozzarella cheese
1 leaf romaine lettuce, washed
1 slice leftover Five-Ingredient Meat Loaf (page 101), about ½-inch thick

1. Spread 1 tablespoon margarine over the inside of one slice of bread and the mustard over the inside of the other slice.

2. Lay a slice of cheese and the lettuce leaf on the inside of one bread slice. Add the meat loaf on the inside of the other bread slice. Close up the sandwich.

3. Heat a frying pan on medium heat. Melt the remaining tablespoon of margarine in the frying pan, tilting the pan so that the margarine coats the bottom.

4. Place the sandwich in the frying pan. Cook until the bottom is golden brown, then turn and coat the other side. Add more margarine to the pan if needed. Serve hot.

Swiss Cheese and Ham Sandwich

Adding a spice or combination of spices is a great way to create your own gourmet mayonnaise. In addition to cayenne pepper, good choices include curry powder, prepared Italian pesto sauce, or even sweet Thai chili sauce.

Serves 1

Preparation time:
5 minutes

1½ tablespoons mayonnaise
¼ teaspoon cayenne pepper, or to taste
2 slices rye bread
2 slices processed Swiss cheese
2 teaspoons mustard
1 slice cooked ham
½ medium tomato, thinly sliced

1. In a small bowl, combine the mayonnaise and cayenne pepper.

2. Spread the mayonnaise on the inside of one slice of bread and place the Swiss cheese on top.

3. Spread the mustard on the inside of the other slice of bread and add the sliced ham. Add the sliced tomato. Close up the sandwich.

Fast Chicken Fajitas

Deli chicken and packaged coleslaw mix take a lot of prep work out of this recipe. Instead of deli chicken, you can also use stir-fry chicken strips—stir-fry the chicken strips with the lime juice and paprika until they turn white and are nearly cooked through. If you like, top each fajita with 2 tablespoons of shredded cheese before rolling it up.

1. Heat the vegetable oil in a skillet over medium-high heat. Stir in the chili powder. Add the deli chicken and cook for a minute, stirring to heat through. Stir in the lime juice while cooking the chicken.

2. Add the packaged coleslaw mix. Stir in the salt. Cook, stirring frequently, until the packaged coleslaw mix is heated through (1 to 2 minutes). Splash with the apple juice while cooking.

3. Stir in the black beans. Cook briefly, stirring to mix everything together.

4. Lay a tortilla wrap in front of you. Spoon ¹⁄₆th of the chicken and bean mixture in the center of the tortilla wrap, taking care not to come too close to the edges. Fold in the left and right sides and roll up the wrap. Repeat with the remainder of the tortillas.

Fantastic Fajitas

Originally conceived of as a creative way to add extra flavor to a tough cut of beef, fajitas are now one of the most popular items on Mexican restaurant menus. Traditionally, fajitas are made with skirt steak. In this recipe the beef is replaced with chicken from the delicatessen.

Serves 6

Preparation time:
5 minutes
Cooking time: 5 minutes

1 tablespoon vegetable oil
½ teaspoon chili powder
1 cup cooked deli
　chicken, shredded
1 tablespoon lime juice
1 cup packaged coleslaw
　mix
½ teaspoon salt
1 tablespoon apple juice
½ cup canned black
　beans, drained
6 tortilla wraps

Herbed Cottage Cheese Wrap

Serves 2

Preparation time:
10 minutes

1 cup cottage cheese
1 tablespoon low-fat
    French dressing
¼ cup chopped chives
¼ teaspoon salt, or to
    taste
Black pepper, to taste
4 tortilla wraps

*Chives are a great way to add extra flavor to cottage cheese—
besides adding onion flavor, they are low in fat and calories.
Feel free to use a flavored tortilla wrap, such as spinach or
red pepper.*

1. In a medium bowl, combine the cottage cheese, French dressing, chopped chives, salt, and pepper, stirring to mix well.

2. Lay out a tortilla wrap in front of you. Spread one-quarter of the cottage cheese mixture on the bottom half of the wrap, taking care not to come too close to the edges. Roll up the wrap.

3. Fill the rest of the wraps. Serve immediately or store in a resealable plastic bag in the refrigerator until ready to serve.

Spicy Cottage Cheese

The mild flavor of cottage cheese pairs nicely with many types of herbs and spices. Instead of French dressing and chives, try adding a pinch of ground cinnamon and ½ teaspoon of vanilla extract. For more heat, blend the cottage cheese with a pinch of cayenne pepper and 1 tablespoon of lemon juice.

Hot and Spicy Cucumber Sandwich

Paprika adds extra heat to the traditional cucumber sandwich, while cream cheese turns it from an afternoon snack into a nutritious midday meal.

Serves 2

Preparation time:
10 minutes

1½ teaspoons lemon juice
4 tablespoons cream
    cheese, softened
¼ teaspoon paprika, or to
    taste
1½ teaspoons chopped
    red onion
4 slices bread
4 teaspoons margarine, or
    as needed
½ medium cucumber,
    thinly sliced

1. In a small bowl, stir the lemon juice into the cream cheese. Stir in the paprika and chopped red onion.

2. Lay two slices of bread out in front of you. Spread 2 teaspoons of margarine on the inside of one slice of bread. Lay out half of the cucumber slices on top.

3. Spread half the cream cheese mixture on the inside of the other slice of bread.

4. Close up the sandwich. Cut in half or quarters as desired.

5. Repeat with the remaining two slices of bread.

Deviled Egg Sandwich

Serves 2

Preparation time:
10 minutes

3 hard-boiled eggs
1½ tablespoons cream
  cheese
¼ teaspoon paprika, or to
  taste
1½ teaspoons lemon
  juice, or as needed
1 tablespoon chopped
  red onion
4 slices bread
4 teaspoons honey
  mustard
2 lettuce leaves
1 medium tomato, sliced

Using cream cheese instead of mayonnaise makes a healthier version of classic deviled eggs. If you like, use a small amount of juice from the tomato instead of lemon juice to moisten the mashed egg mixture.

1. Carefully peel the hard-boiled eggs and chop. Place the eggs in a medium bowl and mash with the cream cheese. Stir in the paprika, lemon juice, and red onion, until everything is mixed together.

2   Toast the bread.

3. Lay two slices of toast in front of you. Spread 2 teaspoons honey mustard over one side of a slice of bread. Add a lettuce leaf and half the sliced tomato. Spread half the deviled egg mixture over the inside of another slice of bread. Place on top of the other slice and close. Cut diagonally in half.

4. Repeat with the remaining two slices of bread.

Make-Ahead Hard-Boiled Eggs

Eggs can be hard-boiled ahead of time and used as needed during the week. Store the eggs in their original container in the refrigerator. The eggs will last for about seven days.

Grilled Cheese Sandwich

You can add extra protein to this simple sandwich by adding a thin slice of ham or leftover cooked chicken.

1. Spread 1 tablespoon margarine over the inside of one slice of bread. Spread the mustard on the inside of the other slice and sprinkle the paprika over it. Add the Swiss cheese and close up the sandwich.

2. Heat a frying pan on medium heat. Melt 1 tablespoon of margarine in the frying pan, tilting the pan so that the margarine coats the bottom.

3. Place the sandwich in the frying pan. Cook until the bottom is golden brown, then turn and coat the other side. Add more margarine to the pan if needed. Serve hot.

Serves 1

Preparation time:
2 minutes
Cooking time:
7–8 minutes

2 tablespoons margarine, divided
2 slices sourdough bread
2 teaspoons prepared mustard, or as needed
⅛ teaspoon paprika, or to taste
2 slices Swiss cheese

Leftover Chicken with Bruschetta

If you don't have a microwave, heat the sandwich in a 250°F oven for 5 minutes, or until it is browned.

1. Spread the softened goat cheese over the inside of both slices of bread.

2. Lay the marinated artichoke hearts on top of the cheese on one slice of bread. Spread the Italian-Inspired Bruschetta over the inside of the other slice.

3. Add the shredded chicken and close up the sandwich.

4. To heat the sandwich, place on a microwave-safe plate and microwave on high heat for 20 seconds, then for 5 seconds at a time until it is heated.

Serves 1

Preparation time:
5–7 minutes
Cooking time: 1 minute

2 ounces goat cheese, softened
2 slices crusty French or Italian bread
2 Marinated Artichoke Hearts (page 227), sliced
2 tablespoons leftover Italian-Inspired Bruschetta (page 233)
½ cup leftover grilled chicken breast, shredded

Thai Chicken and Rice Wraps

Serves 4

Preparation time:
5 minutes

4 tortilla wraps
¼ cup peanut sauce
½ cup Steamed Coconut
*   Rice (page 151)*
1 cup cooked chicken,
*   chopped*

Peanut sauce is available in Asian markets, or in the international section of many supermarkets. Feel free to load up the wrap by adding shredding carrots and sliced cucumber.

1. Lay a tortilla wrap out flat. Spread 1 tablespoon of the peanut sauce over the inside of the wrap.

2. Spread 2 tablespoons of the coconut rice onto the tortilla, taking care not to go too close to the edges. Add ¼ cup of the chopped chicken on top. Roll up the wrap.

3. Continue with the remainder of the tortilla wraps.

Make Your Own Peanut Sauce

It's easy! In a small bowl, whisk together ½ cup peanut butter and ¼ cup coconut milk. Add 2 teaspoons lime juice, 1 teaspoon fish sauce or soy sauce, 1 teaspoon brown sugar, and red curry paste to taste.

Easy Enchiladas

Preparing enchiladas in the microwave instead of baking them in the oven substantially reduces the cooking time. To speed things up even further, use leftover cooked ground beef and reheat in the microwave.

Serves 4

Preparation time:
5 minutes
Cooking time:
10–15 minutes

1 cup ground beef
¼ teaspoon ground cumin
¼ teaspoon salt, or to
   taste
⅛ teaspoon black pepper,
   or to taste
8 corn tortillas
2 cups store-bought
   enchilada sauce
1 cup shredded Cheddar
   cheese

1. In a bowl, season the ground beef with the cumin, salt, and pepper, using your fingers to mix it in. Let the ground beef stand while you are preparing the tortillas and sauce.

2. Place the corn tortillas on a microwave-safe plate. Microwave at high heat for 30 seconds, and then for 10 seconds at a time until the tortillas look slightly dried out and are cooked. Dip each of the tortillas into the enchilada sauce, letting the excess sauce drip off.

3. Place the ground beef into a 1-quart microwave-safe casserole dish, using your fingers to crumble it in. Microwave on high heat for 2 minutes. Stir and cook for another 2 to 3 minutes, until the ground beef is cooked through. Remove from the heat and drain off the fat. Stir in ½ cup leftover enchilada sauce and cook for another minute.

4. Lay a tortilla flat and spoon a portion of the meat and sauce mixture in the lower half of the tortilla. Roll up the tortilla and place in a shallow, microwave-safe 9" x 13" baking dish. Continue with the remainder of the tortillas. Spoon any leftover enchilada sauce on top. Sprinkle with the cheese.

5. Microwave on high heat for 5 minutes, or until the cheese is melted and everything is cooked through. Let stand for 5 minutes before serving.

Basic Tuna Salad Sandwiches

Serves 4

Preparation time:
10 minutes

1 (7-ounce) can tuna,
   drained
3 tablespoons low-fat
   mayonnaise
1 teaspoon red wine
   vinegar
4 strips red bell pepper,
   finely chopped
1 tablespoon chopped
   fresh parsley
⅛ to ¼ teaspoon cayenne
   pepper, optional
8 slices whole-wheat
   bread
4 lettuce leaves
5 tablespoons margarine

Red wine vinegar adds a bit of bite to this easy-to-make sandwich filling. If you want, you can replace the red bell pepper with finely chopped celery, or use a combination of both.

1. In a medium bowl, stir together the canned tuna, mayonnaise, red wine vinegar, red pepper, parsley, and cayenne pepper, if using, until they are well mixed.

2. To prepare the sandwich, butter two bread slices and add 1 lettuce leaf to one slice. Spread about 2 tablespoons filling on the other slice and close up the sandwich. Repeat with the remainder of bread and sandwich filling.

Make-Ahead Sandwiches

Sandwiches can be prepared up to a day ahead of time—just wrap and refrigerate until you're ready to eat. You can also make sandwich spreads up to three days in advance; keep covered and stored in the refrigerator.

Shrimp-Filled Avocados

For a more attractive presentation, sprinkle a bit of extra lime juice on the avocados to prevent discoloration, and serve the shrimp-stuffed avocados on a bed of lettuce leaves.

1. In a large bowl, combine the shrimp, pineapple, reserved pineapple juice, lime juice, yogurt, green onions, crushed red pepper, and salt. Stir to mix well.

2. Cut the avocados in half lengthwise, removing the pit in the middle.

3. Fill the avocados with the shrimp mixture and serve.

Amazing Avocados

Its buttery flesh leads many people to mistake the avocado for a vegetable, but it is actually a type of fruit. Avocado leads all other fruits in protein content, and is a good source of vitamin E. An avocado filled with shellfish, or cottage or ricotta cheese, makes a quick and healthy midday meal. Just don't get carried away—a single avocado has more than 300 calories.

Serves 4

Preparation time:
10 minutes

2 cups cooked shrimp
1 cup drained pineapple tidbits
2 tablespoons reserved pineapple juice
1 tablespoon lime juice
2 tablespoons natural yogurt
2 green onions, finely chopped
½ teaspoon crushed red pepper, or to taste
Salt, to taste
4 avocados, peeled

Grilled Chicken Sandwich

Serves 1

Preparation time:
5 minutes
Cooking time:
15 minutes

1 boneless, skinless
   chicken breast half
¼ teaspoon salt
¼ teaspoon black or white
   pepper
2 slices crusty French or
   Italian bread
2 teaspoons margarine
1 tablespoon low-fat
   mayonnaise
½ medium tomato, thinly
   sliced

For a fancier sandwich, try replacing the margarine and mayonnaise with Italian pesto. Instead of broiling, the chicken breast can also be cooked on the grill.

1. Preheat the broiler.

2. Rinse the chicken breast under running water and pat dry. Rub the salt and pepper over the chicken to season.

3. To broil the chicken, place it on a broiling rack sprayed with nonstick cooking spray. Broil the chicken on high heat, 9 inches from the heat source, for about 7 to 8 minutes, or until cooked through.

4. Lay out the bread in front of you. Spread the margarine over the inside of one slice of bread and the mayonnaise over the inside of the other.

5. Add the sliced tomato on the slice with mayonnaise. Add the broiled chicken on the other side. Close up the sandwich.

Greek Pita Pockets with Tzatziki

A popular Greek dip, tzatziki also makes a satisfying sandwich filling. To turn this recipe into an appetizer, simply cut each pita round into eight equal wedges and bake at 250°F until crisp. Spread the dip on the pita wedges.

Serves 8

Preparation time:
10 minutes

1 English cucumber
1½ teaspoons virgin olive oil
1½ teaspoons lemon juice
1 cup plain low-fat yogurt
2 tablespoons chopped red onion
½ teaspoon garlic salt
Freshly ground black pepper, to taste
8 pita wraps

1. Peel and grate the cucumber until you have ½ cup. Thinly slice the remainder of the cucumber and set aside.

2. In a small bowl, stir the olive oil and lemon juice into the yogurt. Stir in the chopped red onion and garlic salt. Taste and season with the pepper.

3. Lay out a pita wrap in front of you. Spread up to 2 tablespoons tzatziki over the inside of the wrap. Lay a few cucumber slices on top and roll up the wrap.

4. Continue with the remainder of the pita wraps.

Choosing Olive Oil

Virgin olive oils are the best choice in recipes where the dressing isn't being heated, such as Marinated Artichoke Hearts (page 227) or Greek Pita Pockets with Tzatziki (above). Either the virgin or extra-virgin variety of olive oil can be used, although extra-virgin olive oil has less acidity and a better flavor. Pure olive oil (also simply called olive oil) has a higher smoke point than virgin oils—use it in stir-fries or whenever the oil is going to be heated.

Easy Skillet Zucchini Quiche

Removing the crust from a standard quiche recipe substantially reduces the time it takes to make. On days when you do have a bit more time, feel free to bake the quiche instead of broiling it— after combining the ingredients in the bowl, bake at 325°F for 30 minutes, or until the quiche has set.

Serves 4

Preparation time:
5 minutes
Cooking time: 15 minutes

4 eggs
½ teaspoon salt, or to taste
Black pepper, to taste
¼ teaspoon dried oregano, or to taste
1 teaspoon onion powder
2 ounces canned sliced mushrooms
1 tomato, diced
½ cup grated Swiss cheese
¼ cup grated mild Cheddar cheese
1 tablespoon margarine
1½ cups chopped zucchini, fresh or frozen

1. Preheat the broiler.

2. In a medium bowl, lightly beat the eggs with the salt, pepper, dried oregano, and onion powder. Stir in the mushrooms, tomato, and cheeses.

3. Melt the margarine in a heavy skillet over medium heat. Add the chopped zucchini and sauté for a couple of minutes, until the zucchini turns dark green.

4. Pour the egg and cheese mixture into the skillet, stirring to mix it in with the zucchini. Cook for 7 to 8 minutes, until the cheese is melted and the quiche is cooked through but still moist on top.

5. Place the skillet in the broiler. Cook until the top has set but has not yet browned.

Easy Tomato Sandwich

A simple tomato sandwich is a great way to enjoy tomatoes in season. For a heartier version, add sliced cucumbers and top with a slice of Swiss cheese.

Serves 1

Preparation time:
8 minutes

2 tablespoons
  mayonnaise
1 teaspoon lemon juice
⅛ teaspoon garlic salt, or
  to taste
⅛ teaspoon black or white
  pepper, to taste
2 slices bread, toasted
½ medium tomato, thinly
  sliced

1. In a small bowl, combine the mayonnaise, lemon juice, garlic salt, and pepper.

2. Spread the mayonnaise mixture over one side of each slice of bread.

3. Lay the sliced tomato on top of the mayonnaise mixture. Close up the sandwich.

Tomato Lore

A New World fruit, the tomato is one of the many foods Christopher Columbus introduced to Europeans following his journeys to the Americas. The tomato was slow to catch on in Europe, as it was widely believed to be poisonous. It wasn't until the 1800s that tomato consumption took off in Britain and other parts of Europe. Today, tomatoes are one of the many antioxidant-rich foods that physicians believe may help prevent cancer.

Fish Stick Tacos

Want something a little more authentic? Try a chunky red or green salsa instead of tartar sauce, such as Simple Salsa Verde (page 246).

Serves 3

Preparation time:
5–8 minutes
Cooking time:
5–7 minutes

¼ cup plain yogurt
2 tablespoons tartar
 sauce
1 teaspoon chili powder,
 or to taste
2 teaspoons chopped red
 onion
6 leftover cooked fish
 sticks
3 corn tortillas
2 cabbage leaves,
 shredded

1. In a small bowl, stir together the yogurt, tartar sauce, chili powder, and red onion.

2. Place the fish sticks on a microwave-safe plate. Use your microwave's reheat setting, or 70 percent power for 1 to 2 minutes, until the fish sticks are heated through.

3. Place the corn tortillas on a microwave-safe plate. Microwave at high heat for 30 seconds, and then for 10 seconds at a time until the tortillas look slightly dried out and are cooked.

4. Lay a tortilla in front of you. Spread a third of the yogurt mixture over the tortilla. Add a third of the shredded cabbage. Place two fish sticks inside. Fold the tortilla in half.

5. Continue filling the remainder of the tortillas.

Chapter 4
Soups

Easy Frozen Split Pea Soup

Preparation time:
10 minutes
Cooking time:
15–20 minutes

3 cups frozen peas
1 tablespoon olive oil
1 teaspoon minced garlic
¼ cup chopped red onion
3½ cups canned or
    packaged chicken
    broth
1 cup light cream
½ teaspoon salt
Juice of 1 lemon
2 tablespoons fresh
    chopped mint leaves

This refreshing soup makes a nice alternative to a plain vegetable side dish. For an extra touch, garnish with a few mint sprigs before serving.

1. Place the frozen peas in a mesh strainer. Run warm running water over them until they are defrosted.

2. Heat the olive oil in a medium saucepan over medium-high heat. Add the garlic and onion. Sauté until the onion is shiny and softened (adjust the heat, turning it down to medium if the onion is cooking too quickly).

3. Add the peas, chicken broth, and cream. Stir in the salt and lemon juice. Bring to a boil. Reduce the heat to medium-low, cover, and simmer until the peas are tender (about 5 minutes).

4. Place the soup in the blender with the mint. Purée until smooth.

5. Pour the soup into four serving bowls. Cover and chill until ready to serve.

How Much Lemon Juice?

Don't feel like squeezing lemons? While freshly squeezed lemon juice is always nice, you can also use presqueezed lemon juice. When a recipe calls for the juice of one lemon, use 2 tablespoons of presqueezed lemon juice.

Easy Coconut Soup

Toasted coconut enhances the appearance and flavor of this simple soup. Serve with Curried Chicken and Rice (page 86).

Serves 4

Preparation time:
5 minutes
Cooking time:
10–15 minutes

¼ cup unsweetened
   coconut flakes
1 cup whole milk
1 cup coconut milk
1 cup water
⅓ cup light cream
⅛ teaspoon ground
   cinnamon
3 tablespoons granulated
   sugar
¼ teaspoon salt, or to
   taste

1. Preheat oven to 325°F. Spread out the coconut flakes on a baking sheet.

2. In a medium saucepan, bring the milk, coconut milk, water, and light cream to a boil.

3. While waiting for the soup to boil, place the coconut flakes in the oven. Toast for 5 minutes, or until they turn a light brown and are fragrant.

4. When the soup comes to a boil, stir in the cinnamon, sugar, and salt. Turn the heat down to medium-low, cover, and simmer for 5 minutes.

5. To serve, garnish the soup with the toasted coconut.

Blender Beet Borscht

You can garnish this filling Russian soup with hard-boiled eggs for a complete meal. Leftover cooked beets can be used in this recipe, and the sour cream can be replaced with low fat natural yogurt.

Serves 4

Preparation time:
5–10 minutes

2 (14-ounce) cans sliced
   beets
1 cup reserved beet juice
1 cup beef broth
2 tablespoons red wine
   vinegar
5 teaspoons chopped
   fresh dill leaves
4 teaspoons Dijon
   mustard
¾ teaspoon salt
4 tablespoons sour cream

Process all the ingredients in a blender for 30 seconds, or until smooth. Serve immediately or cover and chill until ready to serve.

Easy Microwave Onion Soup

Serves 4

Preparation time:
5 minutes
Cooking time:
7–10 minutes

2½ cups low-sodium beef
    broth
1 package (¼ cup) instant
    onion soup mix
2 slices bread
½ cup shredded
    Parmesan cheese

This quick and easy version of classic French onion soup takes only minutes to make. If possible, use a good crusty bread such as French or sourdough.

1. Place the beef broth and instant onion soup mix in a microwave-safe casserole dish or bowl, stirring the soup mix into the broth.

2. Microwave the soup on high heat for 2 minutes. Stir and heat for 1 minute more, and then for 30 seconds at a time if needed until the soup is heated through.

3. While the soup is cooking, toast the bread and cut into small cubes.

4. Pour the heated onion soup into four microwave-safe bowls. Sprinkle one-quarter of the cheese over each bowl and add one-quarter of the bread cubes.

5. Place the soup bowls in the microwave. Microwave on high heat for 2 minutes. Stir and continue cooking if needed until the cheese is melted.

Warming Herbed Tomato Soup

Using canned tomatoes that are already flavored with herbs such as basil and oregano adds extra flavor. You might also add two Roasted Red Peppers (page 219), chopped into bite-size pieces.

Serves 4

Preparation time:
5 minutes
Cooking time:
10–15 minutes

1 teaspoon olive oil
1 teaspoon bottled
    minced garlic
1 (19-ounce) can
    tomatoes with herbs
2 cups beef broth
¼ teaspoon ground cumin
½ teaspoon salt
¼ teaspoon black pepper
¾ cup croutons

1. Heat the olive oil in a saucepan over medium heat.

2. Add the minced garlic and cook for about 1 minute until it begins to brown.

3. Add the canned tomatoes and beef broth. Cover and turn the heat up to medium-high to bring to a boil.

4. Stir in the ground cumin, salt, and pepper. Turn the heat down to medium-low, cover, and simmer for 2 to 3 minutes.

5. Serve the soup hot, garnished with the croutons.

Tomato Soup Toppers

Shredded cheese is a traditional garnish for tomato soup—Italian and Swiss cheeses such as Parmesan, Romano, and Gruyère are all good choices. For something different, add a dollop of your favorite Italian pesto to the cooked soup, or keep it simple with a few handfuls of chopped fresh herbs such as basil or parsley.

Frozen Garden Vegetable Soup

Serves 4

Preparation time:
5 minutes
Cooking time:
15–18 minutes

2 teaspoons olive oil
1 teaspoon minced garlic
1 onion, peeled, chopped
1 teaspoon dried parsley
2 cups frozen vegetables
2 cups low-sodium beef
    broth
1 cup water
¼ teaspoon salt
Black pepper, to taste
½ teaspoon Tabasco
    sauce

Frozen vegetables take the work out of peeling and chopping fresh vegetables in this quick and easy recipe. While the soup doesn't take long to make, if you want to speed up the cooking time even more, cook the frozen vegetables in the microwave while sautéing the onion.

1. In a medium saucepan, heat the olive oil over medium-high heat. Add the garlic and onion. Sprinkle the dried parsley over the onion. Sauté for about 4 minutes, until the onion is softened.

2. Add the frozen vegetables. Cook for about 4 to 5 minutes, until they are thawed and heated through, using a rubber spatula to break them up while cooking.

3. Add the beef broth and water. Bring to a boil (this takes about 4 minutes).

4. Stir in the salt, pepper, and Tabasco sauce.

5. Turn down the heat and simmer for 3 to 4 minutes. Serve immediately.

New England Clam Chowder

Traditionally, New England's take on clam chowder is served with hexagon-shaped oyster crackers. For a special touch, sprinkle ¼ cup of bacon bits over the soup.

Serves 4

Preparation time:
5 minutes
Cooking time: 15 minutes

1 cup frozen corn
1 tablespoon margarine
¼ cup chopped onion
½ cup clam juice
1½ cups whole milk
1 cup cream
1 teaspoon dried parsley
¼ teaspoon paprika, or to
  taste
¾ teaspoon salt
½ teaspoon black pepper
1½ cups canned chopped
  clams

1. Place the frozen corn in a microwave-safe bowl. Cover with microwave-safe plastic wrap, leaving one corner open to vent steam. Microwave on high heat for 2 minutes and then for 30 seconds at a time until cooked, stirring each time (total cooking time should be about 3 minutes).

2. Heat the margarine over medium-high heat. Add the onion. Sauté for 4 to 5 minutes, until the onion is softened.

3. Add the clam juice, milk, cream, dried parsley, paprika, salt, and pepper. Bring to a boil.

4. Stir in the cooked corn. Return to a boil.

5. Turn down the heat, cover, and simmer for 3 minutes. Add the clams and cook for 2 more minutes. Serve hot.

Soup Facts

A bisque is a creamy soup made with shellfish, while chowder is a heartier soup with fish or shellfish and vegetables in a milk-based broth. A southern U.S. specialty, gumbo is a thick soup made with meat or seafood, served over rice.

Hearty Roasted Vegetable Soup

*Here is a great way to turn leftover vegetables
into a nutritious soup.*

Serves 4

Preparation time:
5 minutes
Cooking time:
10–15 minutes

1 teaspoon olive oil
1 teaspoon bottled
    minced garlic
1 cup tomato juice
2½ cups beef broth
2 cups leftover Roasted
    Fall Harvest
    Vegetables (page 220)
1 teaspoon dried thyme
½ teaspoon salt
¼ teaspoon black pepper,
    or to taste

1. Heat the olive oil in a saucepan over medium heat.

2. Add the minced garlic and cook for about 1 minute until it begins to brown.

3. Add the tomato juice and beef broth. Cover and turn the heat up to medium-high to bring to a boil.

4. Add the roasted vegetables. Stir in the dried thyme, salt, and pepper.

5. Turn the heat down to medium-low, cover, and simmer for 2 to 3 minutes. Serve hot.

Chicken and Corn Soup

*Cayenne pepper adds a bit of spice to this nourishing chicken
and vegetable soup. You can replace the frozen corn with your
favorite type of corn in this recipe, including canned cream corn.*

Serves 4

Preparation time:
5–10 minutes
Cooking time: 15 minutes

2 teaspoons olive oil
2 shallots, peeled,
    chopped
5 cups chicken broth
2 cups frozen corn
½ teaspoon salt
⅛ teaspoon cayenne
    pepper
1 teaspoon ground cumin
1 leftover chicken breast,
    shredded
¼ cup chopped fresh
    parsley

1. Heat the olive oil in a saucepan over medium heat. Add the shallots and sauté until softened.

2. Add the chicken broth. Bring to a boil.

3. Add the frozen corn. Return to a boil.

4. Stir in the salt, cayenne pepper, and cumin.

5. Add the shredded chicken pieces. Stir in the fresh parsley. Simmer for a minute and serve hot.

Minestrone

Minestrone—literally, big soup—is one of Italy's signature dishes. Every region has its own special way of preparing this popular vegetable soup.

1. In a large saucepan over medium-high heat, bring the water to a boil. Stir in the onion soup mix.

2. Add the zucchini, carrots, white and green beans, and macaroni. Return to a boil.

3. Add the tomatoes with their juice. Return to a boil.

4. Stir in parsley, oregano, salt, and pepper.

5. Turn the heat down to medium-low, cover, and simmer for 10 minutes or until the zucchini is tender and the elbow macaroni is cooked. Pour the soup into serving bowls and garnish with the Parmesan cheese.

Serves 6

Preparation time:
5 minutes
Cooking time: 15 minutes

5 cups water
2 packages instant onion soup mix
1 zucchini, cubed
12 baby carrots
1 cup drained canned white beans
1 cup drained canned green beans
1 cup elbow macaroni
1 (28-ounce) can plum tomatoes
1 teaspoon dried parsley
1 teaspoon dried oregano
½ teaspoon salt, or to taste
¼ teaspoon black pepper, or to taste
⅓ cup grated Parmesan cheese

Easy Egg Drop Soup

Serves 4

Preparation time:
5 minutes
Cooking time:
5–8 minutes

5 cups canned or
packaged low-sodium
vegetable broth
1 cup frozen peas
10 baby carrots, cut in
half
2 green onions, finely
chopped
¼ teaspoon white pepper,
or to taste
½ teaspoon granulated
sugar
2 large eggs, lightly
beaten

The secret to this popular Chinese soup is the beaten egg, which is slowly streamed into the soup to form thin shreds. You can season the soup with salt to taste, if desired.

1. In a medium saucepan, bring the vegetable broth to a boil.

2. Add the frozen peas, baby carrots, green onion, white pepper, and sugar.

3. Cover and return to a boil. Cook for a minute.

4. Slowly stream in the eggs, stirring rapidly with a fork until it forms thin shreds.

5. Remove the soup from the heat. Serve hot.

Green Onion Safety

Like bean sprouts and other foods that are eaten raw, green onions are a frequent source of foodborne illnesses such as hepatitis A. While it's tempting to sprinkle freshly chopped green onion over soups and salads, for safety's sake it should always be cooked before serving.

Speedy Chicken Noodle Soup

Don't have leftover chicken on hand? This recipe uses canned chicken, a quick and easy alternative that is very economical.

1. Bring the water to a boil on medium-high heat. Add the ramen noodles and the contents of the flavor packet. Return to a boil, stirring.

2. Add the frozen peas. Return to a boil, reduce the heat, and simmer for 2 to 3 minutes, until the peas are cooked.

3. Add the canned chicken. Stir in the soy sauce and red pepper flakes.

4. Return to a boil, then reduce the heat and simmer for 5 more minutes.

Serves 4

Preparation time:
5 minutes
Cooking time:
12–15 minutes

*3 cups water
1 package chicken-
    flavored ramen
    noodles
1 cup frozen peas
1 cup canned chicken
1 tablespoon soy sauce
¼ teaspoon red pepper
    flakes*

Chicken Noodle Soup

Feel free to adapt this recipe according to what ingredients you have on hand. To make a quick and easy seafood version, for instance, replace the leftover chicken and vegetables with crabmeat and canned asparagus.

1. Heat the margarine over medium-high heat. Add the onion and sauté until it begins to soften. Stir in the minced gar the shallots and garlic. Sauté for 3 to 4 minutes, until the shallots are softened.

2. Stir in the celery and carrots. Cook for a minute.

3. Add the chicken broth. Cover and turn the heat up to medium-high to bring to a boil.

4. Stir in the salt, pepper, and parsley. Add the chicken and pasta.

5. Turn the heat down to medium-low, cover, and simmer for 2 to 3 minutes. Serve the soup hot.

Serves 4

Preparation time:
5–8 minutes
Cooking time: 15 minutes

*2 teaspoons margarine
1 medium onion, peeled,
    chopped
2 teaspoons bottled
    minced garlic
1 rib celery, thinly
    chopped
12 baby carrots, cut in half
5 cups reduced-sodium
    chicken broth
½ teaspoon salt
¼ teaspoon black pepper
1 teaspoon dried parsley
    leaves
1 leftover cooked chicken
    breast, chopped
1 cup leftover cooked
    pasta*

Chicken Soup with Two Types of Mushrooms

Mushrooms add a savory flavor to warming chicken soup. Instead of wine, you can use 5 cups of chicken broth or substitute 1 cup of milk or light cream.

Serves 4

Preparation time:
5 minutes

Cooking time:
12–15 minutes

1 tablespoon olive oil
2 shallots, peeled, chopped
1 tablespoon chopped garlic
1 cup sliced portobello mushroom caps
1 cup sliced oyster mushrooms
1 cup dry white wine
3 cups chicken broth
¼ teaspoon salt
¼ teaspoon freshly ground white pepper
1 tablespoon chopped fresh parsley

1. Heat the olive oil in a saucepan over medium-high heat. Add the shallots and garlic. Sauté for 3 to 4 minutes, until shallots are softened.

2. Add the mushrooms. Cook until softened. Splash the mushrooms with 1 tablespoon of the white wine.

3. Add the chicken broth and the remainder of the white wine. Bring to a boil.

4. Stir in the salt, white pepper, and parsley.

5. Turn the heat down to medium-low. Simmer, uncovered, for 5 minutes. Serve hot.

Italian Ground Beef Soup

Briefly browning the meatballs prior to adding them to the soup adds extra flavor and ensures that they are cooked through.

Serves 4

Preparation time:
10 minutes

Cooking time:
12–15 minutes

1 pound lean ground beef
½ cup crushed bread crumbs
¼ cup grated Parmesan cheese
½ teaspoon dried oregano leaves
½ teaspoon dried basil leaves
2 tablespoons minced onion
½ teaspoon bottled minced garlic
3 tablespoons milk
1 tablespoon olive oil
5 cups chicken broth
½ teaspoon salt
¼ teaspoon black pepper

1. In a medium bowl, combine the ground beef, bread crumbs, Parmesan cheese, oregano, basil, minced onion, minced garlic, and milk. Form into small meatballs about the size of golf balls.

2. Heat the olive oil in a skillet on medium-high heat. Add the meatballs. Brown the meatballs for 5 minutes, turning at least once.

3. While the meatballs are browning, bring the chicken broth to a boil in a large saucepan.

4. Add the salt, pepper, and meatballs.

5. Return to a boil. Cook for 5 to 7 minutes, until the meatballs are cooked through. Serve the soup hot.

Warming Wonton Soup

Don't have time to fill and wrap wontons to make authentic wonton soup? This recipe takes the ingredients normally used to make the wontons and combines them with Chinese vegetables in a seasoned broth.

1. Bring the chicken broth to a boil over medium-high heat.

2. Add the ground pork, breaking it up with a spatula.

3. Add the wonton wrappers, bamboo shoots, and water chestnuts. Return to a boil.

4. Stir in the salt, sugar, white pepper, and green onions. Stir in the oyster sauce.

5. Turn the heat down slightly and simmer for 5 minutes to soften the wonton wrappers and combine all the flavors. Serve hot.

Serves 4

Preparation time:
5 minutes
Cooking time: 10 minutes

5 cups chicken broth
½ pound leftover cooked
    ground pork
18 wonton wrappers
½ cup canned bamboo
    shoots
½ cup canned sliced
    water chestnuts
¼ teaspoon salt
½ teaspoon granulated
    sugar
⅛ teaspoon white pepper,
    or to taste
2 green onions, chopped
1 tablespoon oyster sauce

Leftover Meatball Soup

Add extra flavor by using canned tomatoes with herbs, or replacing the dried oregano with an equivalent amount of Italian seasoning.

1. Heat the olive oil in a saucepan over medium heat. Add the onion and garlic. Sprinkle the paprika and oregano on top of the onion. Sauté until the onion is shiny and softened (about 4 minutes).

2. Add the canned tomatoes, stirring to mix in with the onion and garlic. Add the broth and bring to a boil.

3. Add the meatballs. Stir in the pepper and turmeric. Return to a boil.

4. Turn the heat down to medium-low and simmer until the meatballs are cooked through. Serve hot.

Serves 6

Preparation time:
5 minutes
Cooking time: 15 minutes

1 tablespoon olive oil
½ cup chopped onion
1 teaspoon bottled
    minced garlic
1 teaspoon paprika, or to
    taste
½ teaspoon dried
    oregano leaves
1 cup canned tomatoes
6 cups canned or
    packaged beef broth
24 frozen meatballs,
    thawed
¼ teaspoon black pepper
1 teaspoon turmeric

Easy Oyster Bisque

Serves 4

Preparation time:
5–10 minutes
Cooking time: 15 minutes

24 canned Pacific oysters
2 teaspoons olive oil
2 teaspoons bottled
   minced garlic
2 shallots, finely chopped
2 teaspoons dried parsley
2 cups light cream
1 cup clam juice
1 teaspoon salt
¼ teaspoon black pepper,
   or to taste
2 tablespoons seafood
   cocktail sauce
8 slices sourdough bread

Seafood cocktail sauce, a spicy mixture that includes horseradish and Worcestershire, adds spice to this simple seafood bisque. It's fine to chop the shallots ahead of time and store them in a resealable plastic bag in the refrigerator until needed.

1. Drain the oysters and chop into thin pieces.

2. Heat the olive oil in a saucepan over medium-high heat. Add the garlic and shallots and sprinkle the dried parsley over them. Sauté for 2 to 3 minutes, until the shallots are softened.

3. Add the light cream and clam juice. Bring to a boil.

4. Add the oysters. Stir in the salt, pepper, and cocktail sauce.

5. Reduce the heat to medium-low. Simmer for 5 minutes. Serve hot, with the bread for dipping.

Chapter 5
Salads

Instant Mashed Potato Salad

Serves 4

Preparation time:
10 minutes

4 cups boiling water
8 ounces instant flavored
     mashed potatoes
⅔ cup mayonnaise
3 tablespoons sour cream
2 teaspoons white wine
     vinegar
1 teaspoon dried dill
4 hard-boiled eggs,
     peeled, chopped
2 ribs celery, thinly sliced

For a more tart flavor, feel free to increase the amount of white wine vinegar to 1 tablespoon.

1. Pour the boiling water into a large bowl. Add the instant flavored mashed potatoes, stirring with a fork to make sure they are completely covered. Cover and let sit for 5 minutes while preparing the mayonnaise dressing.

2. In a medium bowl, stir together the mayonnaise, sour cream, white wine vinegar, and dried dill.

3. In a large salad bowl, combine the mashed potatoes with the mayonnaise dressing, chopped eggs, and celery.

4. Chill until ready to serve.

Greek Bean Salad

Serves 4

Preparation time:
10 minutes

2 tablespoons olive oil
2 tablespoons lemon juice
2 teaspoons water
1 teaspoon granulated
     sugar
2½ cups drained canned
     chickpeas
1 medium tomato, cut into
     chunks
½ sweet onion, cut into
     rings
½ teaspoon salt
Black pepper, to taste

You can serve the bean salad with a good crusty bread that has been rubbed with a bit of leftover juice from chopping the tomato.

1. In a small bowl, whisk together the olive oil, lemon juice, water, and sugar.

2. Combine the chickpeas, tomato, and onion.

3. Toss with the lemon juice dressing.

4. Sprinkle with the salt and pepper. Serve immediately.

Classic Greek Salad

For an extra touch, cut a garlic clove in half and rub it over the salad bowl. You can use Greek oregano if it is available.

1. In a large salad bowl, combine the lettuce, red onion, tomatoes, cucumber, and bell pepper.

2. In a small bowl, whisk together the olive oil, red wine vinegar, sugar, pepper, sea salt, garlic, and oregano.

3. Drizzle the olive oil dressing over the salad.

4. Sprinkle the crumbled feta on top.

5. Add the olives. Serve immediately.

Greek Salad

A staple on Greek restaurant menus around the world, traditional Greek salad (horiatiki) is made with tomatoes, cucumbers, Greek oregano, and an olive oil dressing. Although they are popular additions, feta cheese and plump kalamata olives are optional.

Serves 4

Preparation time:
20 minutes

4 romaine lettuce leaves, washed, drained, and torn

½ red onion, peeled, cut into thin rings

12 cherry tomatoes, cut in half

1 English cucumber, thinly sliced

1 green bell pepper, seeded, cut into chunks

3 tablespoons extra-virgin olive oil

2 tablespoons red wine vinegar

1 teaspoon granulated sugar

¼ teaspoon black pepper

½ teaspoon sea salt

½ teaspoon bottled minced garlic

¼ teaspoon dried oregano, or to taste

1 cup crumbled feta cheese

12 whole olives, chopped and pitted

Five-Ingredient Taco Salad

Taco shells are found in the refrigerated section of many super-markets; look for hot chipotle salsa with the other sauces.

Serves 1

Preparation time:
7–10 minutes

1 (14-ounce) can black
   beans, drained
1 taco salad shell
1 cup packaged salad
   mix
¼ cup chipotle salsa
½ cup shredded Cheddar
   cheese
¼ cup canned, chopped
   pitted olives

1. In a small saucepan, quickly heat the black beans, stirring.

2. Line the taco shell with the salad greens.

3. Spoon the beans on top.

4. Stir in the salsa.

5. Sprinkle the shredded cheese and olives on top.

Taco Salad History

A Mexican-inspired dish, taco salads first began appearing in Mexican takeout restaurants in the 1960s. (It is possible that the idea originated at a Taco Bell restaurant.) The traditional taco salad is made with ground beef, tomatoes, chilies, and cheese, and is served with corn chips.

Cottage Cheese and Fruit Salad

*This simple salad makes an easy side dish for 4,
or a quick midday meal for 2.*

Serves 4

Preparation time:
5 minutes

2 cups cottage cheese
1 teaspoon ground
   cinnamon
½ teaspoon ground
   nutmeg
1 large green apple, thinly
   sliced
2 tablespoons apple juice
Black pepper, to taste

Combine all ingredients. Chill until ready to serve.

Tropical Fruit Salad with Pecans

A rich source of vitamin C and several B vitamins, papayas are available year round in many supermarkets. Canned litchis can be found in the canned fruit section, or at ethnic supermarkets.

Serves 4

Preparation time:
10–15 minutes

2 papayas
¼ cup tropical fruit punch
1 teaspoon granulated
   sugar
1 cup drained canned
   pineapple chunks
1 cup drained canned
   litchis
2 bananas, peeled, thinly
   sliced
½ cup pecan pieces

1. Cut the papayas in half and use a spoon to remove the seeds. Remove the peel from each half of the papaya with a paring knife. Lay the papayas flat, scooped side downward, and cut crosswise into thin strips.

2. In a small bowl, stir together the fruit punch and sugar.

3. Combine the fruit in a large salad bowl.

4. Sprinkle the juice over the top and toss gently. Garnish with the pecans.

5. Serve immediately, or cover and chill until ready to serve.

How to Pick a Papaya

When choosing a papaya, look for one that is neither too firm nor too soft, but yields to gentle pressure. The skin should be smooth and firm, and the color mainly yellow. Avoid papayas that have a wrinkled skin or a strong smell.

Basic Garden Salad

Serves 6

A simple garden salad makes a quick and easy side dish on a busy weeknight. Feel free to replace the Italian dressing with your favorite salad dressing.

4 large iceberg lettuce
  leaves
2 ribs celery, thinly sliced
¼ cup chopped green
  onion
2 carrots, peeled and
  chopped
1 tomato, thinly sliced
⅓ cup Italian salad
  dressing

1. Separate the lettuce leaves. Rinse, drain, and tear loosely.

2. In a large salad bowl, combine the lettuce, celery, green onion, carrots, and tomato.

3. Pour the dressing over the vegetables and toss gently.

Mandarin Orange Salad

Serves 4

Preparation time:
10 minutes

The sweet taste of mandarin oranges adds something extra to a plain cottage cheese salad. For a special touch, top the salad with walnuts halves or candied (sugared) walnuts.

¼ teaspoon black pepper
¼ teaspoon salt
1 cup low-fat cottage
  cheese
¼ cup reserved mandarin
  orange juice
1 teaspoon granulated
  sugar
1 head romaine lettuce
  leaves, washed,
  drained, torn
2 green onions, finely
  chopped
½ medium red onion,
  peeled and chopped
2 (10-ounce) cans
  mandarin oranges,
  drained

1. In a medium bowl, stir the pepper and salt into the cottage cheese. Stir in the mandarin orange juice and sugar.

2. Put the torn romaine lettuce leaves in a salad bowl. Toss with the onions.

3. Add the cottage cheese and the mandarin oranges on top.

4. Serve immediately, or chill until ready to serve.

Make-Ahead Salads

Many of the vegetables found in a typical salad, including lettuce, can be prepared ahead of time. Wrap the cut vegetables in paper towels and store in a resealable plastic bag in the crisper section of your refrigerator until ready to use.

Chicken and Strawberry Salad

A simple yogurt dressing jazzes up this salad made with fresh strawberries and leftover chicken.

Serves 4

Preparation time:
10–15 minutes

2 leftover cooked chicken
  breasts
1¼ teaspoons Dijon
  mustard
½ teaspoon salt
⅛ teaspoon black pepper
1 cup vanilla yogurt
1 pint strawberries,
  washed, hulled
4 cups packaged salad
  greens

1. Cut the chicken breasts into thin strips.

2. In a medium bowl, stir the mustard, salt, and pepper into the yogurt.

3. Stir in the chicken and strawberries.

4. Arrange the greens in a salad bowl. Spoon the yogurt, fruit, and chicken mixture over the greens.

5. Serve the salad immediately or cover and chill until ready to serve.

Delicious Dijon Mustard

Originating in the Dijon region in southeastern France, Dijon mustard gets its sharp taste from brown or black mustard seeds. Although mustard has been cultivated in France since ancient times, Dijon mustard was invented in the mid-1800s by Jean Naigeon, who came up with the idea of replacing the vinegar used to make mustard with verjuice, the sour juice from unripe grapes. Today, Dijon-style mustard is produced throughout the world.

Asian Chicken Noodle Salad

Serves 4

Preparation time:
10–15 minutes

1 pound cooked chicken
   breast meat
3 tablespoons red wine
   vinegar
1 tablespoon olive oil
2 tablespoons soy sauce
2 tablespoons Asian
   sesame oil
1 teaspoon granulated
   sugar
1 head romaine lettuce,
   washed, drained, torn
4 green onions, finely
   chopped
1 (11-ounce) can
   mandarin oranges,
   drained
1 cup chow mein noodles

This is a California classic—chow mein noodles, mandarin oranges, and salad vegetables, all topped with a tart vinegar and sesame oil dressing.

1. Cut the chicken into thin strips.

2. In a small bowl, whisk the red wine vinegar, olive oil, soy sauce, sesame oil, and sugar.

3. Place the salad dressing in the bottom of a large salad bowl. Stir in the romaine lettuce, green onions, and chicken strips.

4. Add the mandarin oranges and the chow mein noodles on top.

Salad Basics

Always make sure lettuce is drained thoroughly—wet, soggy lettuce can affect the salad's flavor. Shred the lettuce leaves instead of cutting them with a knife. Unless the recipe states otherwise, if preparing a salad ahead of time, add the dressing just before serving. Toss the salad gently with the dressing, taking care not to overstir.

Marinated Vegetable Salad

This simple salad requires little preparation and has a (comparatively) short marinating time. It makes a nice salad, or you could serve it as a side dish in place of cooked vegetables or over cooked pasta.

1. In a small bowl, whisk together the olive oil, apple cider vinegar, chopped basil, salt, and pepper.

2. Place the vegetables in a salad bowl and gently toss with the vinegar dressing.

3. Cover the salad and chill for one hour. Stir again gently before serving.

Serves 2

Preparation time:
15 minutes
Marinating time: 1 hour

⅓ cup olive oil
3 tablespoons apple cider vinegar
1 tablespoon chopped fresh basil
¼ teaspoon salt
⅛ teaspoon black pepper, or to taste
2 medium cucumbers, thinly sliced
2 tomatoes, chopped into chunks
½ red onion, peeled, sliced

Basic Spinach Salad

Using low-fat yogurt provides a light alternative to mayonnaise in this easy recipe. Both the salad and the dressing can be prepared ahead of time and refrigerated, but don't toss the salad with the dressing until you're ready to serve.

1. Wash the spinach leaves and drain in a colander or salad spinner.

2. In a medium bowl, stir together the yogurt, mustard, dill, salt, and pepper.

3. Combine the spinach leaves, mushrooms, chopped peppers, and bacon bits in a salad bowl.

4. Toss the vegetables with the yogurt dressing. Serve.

Serves 6

Preparation time:
10 minutes

4 cups packed fresh spinach leaves
¾ cup plain low-fat yogurt
1 teaspoon Dijon mustard
1 teaspoon dried dill
½ teaspoon salt
Black pepper, to taste
1 cup sliced fresh mushrooms
2 Roasted Red Peppers (page 219), chopped
½ cup bacon bits

Meal-Size Salad with Herbed Chicken

Instead of Italian salad dressing, you could also use the yogurt dressing in Basic Spinach Salad (page 69)—increase the yogurt to 1 cup and stir in 1¼ teaspoons Dijon mustard and dried dill, adding salt and pepper to taste.

Serves 6

Preparation time:
15 minutes

1 deli rotisserie smoked chicken
4 cups mixed salad greens
1 cup drained mandarin oranges
1 cup golden raisins
1 cup Italian salad dressing

1. Shred the chicken meat, breaking it into bite-size pieces.

2. In a salad bowl, combine the salad greens, chicken, mandarin oranges, and raisins.

3. Toss the salad with the Italian salad dressing. Serve.

Caesar Turkey Salad

Ground turkey turns a standard Caesar salad into a high-protein meal. To increase the health benefits, replace the bacon bits with chopped nuts.

Serves 3

Preparation time:
5 minutes
Cooking time: 15 minutes

2 cups ground turkey
¼ teaspoon salt
¼ teaspoon black pepper
1 teaspoon bottled minced garlic
1 head romaine lettuce, washed, drained, torn
2 cups croutons
⅓ cup bacon bits
¾ cup Caesar salad dressing
¼ cup Parmesan cheese

1. Brown the turkey in a skillet over medium-high heat.

2. Sprinkle the salt and pepper over the turkey. Stir in the minced garlic.

3. Continue cooking the turkey until it is cooked through and there is no pinkness (about 10 minutes).

4. While the turkey is cooking, in a salad bowl, combine the romaine lettuce leaves, croutons, and bacon bits.

5. Drain the turkey and add it to the salad. Toss the salad with the Caesar dressing. Sprinkle the cheese on top and serve.

Classic Three-Bean Salad

You can dress up this salad by serving it on a bed of romaine lettuce leaves.

Serves 6

Preparation time:
10 minutes

¼ cup olive oil
⅓ cup white wine vinegar
1 teaspoon Dijon mustard
½ teaspoon salt, or to taste
⅛ teaspoon black pepper, or to taste
1 teaspoon minced onion
2 cups drained, rinsed canned green beans
1 (15-ounce) can kidney beans, drained, rinsed
1 (15-ounce) can yellow beans, drained, rinsed

1. In a small bowl, whisk together the olive oil, white wine vinegar, Dijon mustard, salt, pepper, and minced onion.

2. Place all the beans in a salad bowl and toss gently with the dressing.

3. Serve the salad immediately, or cover and chill until ready to serve.

Bean Salad Basics

Beans are an excellent choice for salads, as they easily absorb the dressing. When using canned beans, always drain and rinse them to remove any "tinny" taste. Rinsing the beans also removes excess sodium.

Colorful Pasta Salad

Fusilli vegetable pasta adds color and flavor to this simple salad. To speed up the preparation time even further, use leftover cooked pasta.

Serves 4

Preparation time:
5 minutes
Cooking time: 15 minutes

Water to cook pasta, as needed
3 cups fusilli vegetable pasta
½ cup low-fat mayonnaise
½ cup plain yogurt
1 tablespoon Dijon honey mustard
1 cup green seedless grapes

1. Bring a large saucepan with the water to a boil. Cook the pasta according to the package directions, or until it is tender but still firm. Drain.

2. In a medium mixing bowl, stir together the mayonnaise, yogurt, and honey mustard.

3. Put the cooked pasta and grapes in a large salad bowl.

4. Toss gently with the yogurt and mayonnaise dressing.

Spicy Mexican Potato Salad

Serves 2

Cooking time: 10 minutes
Preparation and assembly time:
10 minutes

2 medium red potatoes
½ medium tomato,
  seeded and chopped
½ red onion, chopped
½ cup drained canned
  Mexican-style corn
1 tablespoon bottled
  chopped jalapeño
  peppers
¼ cup Orange-Cilantro
  Marinade (page 245)

This quick and easy potato salad is perfect for a romantic picnic for two. Feel free to adjust the amount of jalapeño peppers according to your own taste.

1. Wash the potatoes, peel if desired, and cut into chunks. Place the potatoes in a large, microwave-safe bowl with enough water to cover. Cover the dish with microwave-safe plastic wrap. Microwave the potatoes on high heat for 8 minutes, give the bowl a quarter turn, and then continue cooking for 1 minute at a time until the potatoes are fork-tender (total cooking time should be about 10 minutes). Drain.

2. While the potatoes are boiling, prepare the vegetables: seed and chop the tomato and chop the onion.

3. Combine the potatoes and other vegetables (including the corn and chopped peppers) in a large salad bowl.

4. Whisk the Orange-Cilantro Marinade (page 245). Add it to the salad and toss to mix thoroughly.

What Makes a Dish Microwave-Safe?

The main material that makes a dish unsuitable for microwaving is metal. During cooking, microwaves bounce off the metal instead of harmlessly passing through. This causes sparks that may damage the oven or blacken the dish. Today, most microwave-safe dishware is clearly marked.

Chapter 6
Chicken and Other Poultry

Cashew Chicken

A salty liquid made from fermented fish, fish sauce is a staple ingredient in Southeast Asian cooking. If fish sauce is unavailable, substitute one tablespoon of soy sauce.

Serves 3

Preparation time:
5 minutes
Cooking time:
8–10 minutes

¾ pound boneless,
    skinless chicken
    breast
2 tablespoons vegetable
    or peanut oil
1 tablespoon red curry
    paste
2 cloves garlic, chopped
1 yellow onion, cut into
    thin slices
¼ cup chicken broth
2 tablespoons oyster sauce
1 tablespoon fish sauce
2 scallions, chopped
1 teaspoon granulated
    sugar
½ cup roasted cashews
1 bunch cilantro sprigs,
    optional garnish

1. Cut the chicken into bite-size pieces.

2. Heat the oil in a wok or heavy skillet. Add the red curry paste and the garlic. Stir-fry until the garlic is aromatic. Add the chicken and stir-fry at high heat for 4 to 5 minutes, until the chicken is white and nearly cooked.

3. Add the onion to the pan. Stir-fry for 2 minutes, then stir in the chicken broth, oyster sauce, and fish sauce. Stir in the scallions and the sugar. Stir in the cashews.

4. Continue cooking for another minute to combine all the ingredients and make sure the chicken is cooked through. To serve, garnish with the cilantro sprigs.

Chicken with Salsa Verde

Flavorful salsa verde makes an excellent accompaniment to chicken. Serve with Mexican Fried Rice (page 146) or crusty bread.

Serves 4

Preparation time:
5 minutes
Cooking time:
15–20 minutes

Pre-made Simple Salsa
    Verde (page 246) or
    store-bought
1½ pounds chicken thighs

1. Preheat the broiler. Spray a broiling rack with nonstick cooking spray.

2. Broil the chicken thighs, 9 inches from the heat source, for 15 to 20 minutes until cooked through. Turn the chicken over every 5 minutes.

3. Serve the chicken with the Simple Salsa Verde.

Tomato Turkey Cutlets

This healthy dish is loaded with cancer-fighting foods, from turkey and tomatoes to mushrooms and garlic.

1. Heat the oil on medium-high heat. Add the garlic, onion, and turkey cutlets. Sprinkle the sage and ground cumin on top of the cutlets.

2. Add the mushrooms, splashing with the red wine vinegar. Cook for 5 to 7 minutes, until the cutlets have browned and the mushrooms are softened.

3. Add the tomatoes and the water. Stir in the salt and pepper.

4. Cook, stirring occasionally, for 5 to 7 minutes, until the turkey is cooked through.

Check the Packaging

When purchasing chicken, be sure to check the "sell by" date on the package. Poultry purchased on the "sell by" date should be used within two days.

Serves 4

Preparation time:
5–8 minutes
Cooking time: 15 minutes

2 teaspoons olive oil
2 cloves garlic, minced
1 medium onion, peeled, chopped
1 pound turkey breast cutlets
1 teaspoon sage
2 teaspoons ground cumin
1½ cups sliced fresh button mushrooms
1 tablespoon red wine vinegar
1 cup canned tomatoes
¼ cup water
¼ teaspoon salt
⅛ teaspoon black pepper

Lemon Chicken in a Rice Cooker

Steaming chicken breasts helps make them extra tender.

1. Cut any excess fat from the fillets. Cut the chicken breasts into bite-size cubes.

2. Place the chicken in the steamer and sprinkle the rosemary on top. Steam the chicken for 20 minutes, or according to the steamer directions.

3. While the chicken is steaming, bring the lemon juice, brown sugar, oyster sauce, soy sauce, and chicken broth to a boil over medium heat, stirring to dissolve the sugar.

4. Remove the chicken from the steamer. Pour the sauce over the chicken. Garnish with the chopped scallions.

Serves 2

Preparation time:
10 minutes
Cooking time:
20–30 minutes

1¼ pounds chicken breast fillets
1 tablespoon dried rosemary
2 tablespoons lemon juice
2 tablespoons brown sugar
1 tablespoon oyster sauce
1 tablespoon soy sauce
2 tablespoons chicken broth
2 scallions, chopped

Chicken with Orange-Cilantro Marinade

Serves 4

Preparation time:
15 minutes
Cooking time: 15 minutes

*2 portions Orange-
Cilantro Marinade
(page 245)*
*1½ pounds boneless,
skinless, chicken
thighs*

On weekends or evenings when you have more time, add even more flavor to this dish by increasing the marinating time to 2 hours.

1. Prepare the Orange-Cilantro Marinade (page 245). Reserve ¼ cup to use as a basting sauce.

2. Place a few diagonal cuts on the chicken so that the marinade can penetrate. Place the chicken in a large resealable plastic bag and add the marinade. Marinate the chicken for at least 5 minutes.

3. Preheat the broiler.

4. Place the chicken on a rack that has been sprayed with nonstick cooking spray. Brush some of the reserved marinade on top. Broil the chicken, 9 inches from the heat source, for about 15 minutes, until the chicken is cooked through. Every 5 minutes, turn the chicken over and brush with the reserved marinade.

The Difference Between Grilling and Broiling

What separates grilling and broiling is more than whether or not the food is cooked indoors or outside on the grill. The main difference between these two cooking methods is the location of the heat source. In broiling, heat is applied to the food from the top, whereas in grilling the heat comes from the bottom. Both methods rely upon an intense direct heat that sears the food, giving it a rich flavor.

Lemon Chicken with Broccoli Stir-Fry

Sweet brown sugar balances the tart flavor of lemon in this simple stir-fry. For extra flavor, add chicken or vegetable broth to the steaming water for the broccoli.

Serves 2

Preparation time:
5 minutes
Cooking time: 15 minutes

1 pound chicken breast
  fillets
¼ teaspoon salt, or to
  taste
¼ teaspoon black pepper,
  or to taste
1 tablespoon oyster sauce
1 tablespoon soy sauce
2 tablespoons lemon juice
2 tablespoons chicken
  broth
2 teaspoons brown sugar
2 tablespoons olive oil
1 pound broccoli florets

1. Cut the chicken fillets into thin strips. Rub the salt and pepper over them to season.

2. In a small bowl, combine the oyster sauce, soy sauce, lemon juice, chicken broth, and brown sugar. Set aside.

3. Heat the olive oil in a skillet and add the chicken. Cook the chicken, turning once, for about 10 minutes, until it is browned and nearly cooked through. Remove the chicken from the pan.

4. While the chicken is cooking, steam the broccoli: place the broccoli florets on a metal steamer tray and steam in a medium saucepan over boiling water for 6 to 8 minutes, until they are tender but still crisp. Remove and drain.

5. Add the cooked broccoli to the pan. Add the sauce and bring to a boil. Return the chicken to the pan. Stir to heat through and serve immediately.

Lemon Chicken Around the World

Nearly every cuisine has its own recipe for pairing tender chicken with a tart lemony sauce. Stir-fried lemon chicken is a popular Chinese restaurant dish, while in Greece the chicken is basted with an oil and lemon sauce during grilling. Thai lemon chicken recipes frequently include a sweet-and-sour fish sauce for dipping.

Chili Chicken with Peanuts

Serves 2

Preparation time:
5–8 minutes
Cooking time: 10 minutes

*1 pound boneless,
    skinless chicken
    thighs*
*3 tablespoons reduced-
    sodium chicken broth*
*1 tablespoon red wine
    vinegar*
1 teaspoon sugar
*4 teaspoons vegetable oil,
    divided*
¼ teaspoon salt
⅛ teaspoon black pepper
*1 tablespoon bottled,
    chopped jalapeño
    peppers*
*1 shallot, peeled and
    chopped*
1 teaspoon minced ginger
*½ cup skinless, unsalted
    peanuts*

*To make this simple stir-fry even easier, use bottled minced
ginger, available at most supermarkets.*

1. Cut the chicken into 1" cubes. In a small bowl, stir together the chicken broth, red wine vinegar, and sugar.

2. Heat 2 teaspoons vegetable oil in a heavy skillet over medium-high heat. Add the chicken cubes. Cook for about 5 minutes, stirring constantly, until they turn white and are nearly cooked. Stir in the salt and pepper while the chicken is cooking. Remove the chicken from the pan.

3. Heat 2 teaspoons oil in the pan. Add the chopped jalapeño peppers, shallot, and ginger. Cook, stirring for about 2 minutes, until the shallot is softened.

4. Stir the chicken broth mixture, pour into the pan, and bring to a boil.

5. Return the chicken to the pan. Add the peanuts. Cook for 1 to 2 more minutes to finish cooking the chicken and combine the ingredients. Serve hot.

Stir-Fried Chicken Cacciatore

Normally a slow simmered dish, this recipe transforms Italian chicken cacciatore into a quick stir-fry that is perfect for busy weeknights.

Serves 4

Preparation time:
8 minutes
Cooking time: 12 minutes

1 pound boneless,
  skinless chicken
  thighs
3½ tablespoons dry white
  wine, divided
1 teaspoon dried oregano
Black pepper, to taste
2 teaspoons cornstarch
1 shallot, peeled and
  chopped
¼ pound sliced fresh
  mushrooms
1 red bell pepper,
  seeded, cut into thin
  strips
3 tablespoons low-sodium
  chicken broth
3 tablespoons diced
  tomatoes with juice
½ teaspoon granulated
  sugar
3 tablespoons olive oil,
  divided
1 tablespoon chopped
  fresh oregano

1. Cut the chicken into thin strips about 2" to 3" long. Place the chicken strips in a bowl and add 2½ tablespoons white wine, oregano, pepper, and cornstarch, adding the cornstarch last. Let the chicken stand while preparing the other ingredients.

2. While the chicken is marinating, cut the vegetables. In a small bowl, combine the chicken broth, diced tomatoes, and sugar. Set aside.

3. Heat 1 tablespoon oil in a preheated wok or heavy skillet. When the oil is hot, add the chopped shallot. Stir-fry for a minute, until it begins to soften, then add the sliced mushrooms. Stir-fry for a minute, then add the red bell pepper. Stir-fry for another minute, adding a bit of water if the vegetables begin to dry out. Remove the vegetables from the pan.

4. Heat 2 tablespoons oil in the wok or skillet. When the oil is hot, add the chicken. Let the chicken brown for a minute, then stir-fry for about 5 minutes, until it turns white and is nearly cooked through. Splash 1 tablespoon of the white wine on the chicken while stir-frying.

5. Add the chicken broth and tomato mixture to the middle of the pan. Bring to a boil. Return the vegetables to the pan. Stir in the fresh oregano. Cook, stirring, for another couple of minutes to mix everything together. Serve immediately.

Stir-Fry Tips

When stir-frying, always make sure the oil is hot before adding the food. Stir vegetables continually, to keep them from sticking to the bottom of the pan. When stir-frying meat, allow it to brown briefly before you begin stirring.

Simple Steamed Chicken Dinner

Serves 4

Preparation time:
10 minutes
Cooking time:
20–25 minutes

Water, as needed
3 tablespoons dry white
   wine
1 teaspoon minced ginger
1 teaspoon granulated
   sugar
1 green onion, finely
   chopped
⅛ teaspoon black pepper,
   or to taste
2 pounds boneless,
   skinless chicken
   breast halves
2 zucchini, cut diagonally
   into thin slices
2 cups baby carrots

The exact amount of water needed for steaming will depend upon the size and type of equipment you are using to steam the food.

1. Prepare the equipment you are using for steaming and bring the steaming water to a boil.

2. In a small bowl, combine the white wine, ginger, sugar, green onion, and pepper. Rub the mixture over the chicken breasts.

3. Place the chicken, zucchini, and carrots in a heatproof dish or directly in the steamer tray if you are using a rice steamer/cooker.

4. Steam for 20 to 25 minutes, until the chicken is just cooked through.

5. Chop the chicken into bite-size pieces and serve with the cooked vegetables.

Three-Ingredient Drunken Chicken

This is an easy way to add extra flavor to leftover cooked chicken. Serve with cooked rice and a salad for a quick meal for one.

Serves 1

Preparation time:
10 minutes
Refrigerate: Overnight

*1 cup leftover Simple
    Steamed Chicken
    Dinner (page 80)
1 cup pale dry sherry
1 cup chicken broth*

1. Place the leftover chicken in a jar. Pour the sherry and chicken broth on top.

2. Refrigerate overnight. Serve cold.

Sherry with Extra Flavor

If you use dry sherry regularly in cooking, feel free to season it with a few slices of fresh peeled gingerroot. Store the sherry with the ginger in the refrigerator. Besides making the ginger last longer (just replace the sherry-soaked ginger with a fresh slice as needed), it imparts a nice gingery flavor to the sherry.

One-Dish Baked Chicken and Potatoes

Serves 4

Preparation time:
5 minutes
Cooking time:
15–18 minutes

2 (10-ounce) cans cream
    of celery soup
¼ cup milk
½ teaspoon paprika
⅛ teaspoon black pepper
1 pound leftover cooked
    chicken or deli
    chicken, cubed
1½ cups drained canned
    sweet potatoes
1 tablespoon curry
    powder

You can turn the heat up or down on this dish by using a milder or hotter curry powder, as desired.

1.   Preheat the oven to 250°F.

2.   Heat the soup and milk in a saucepan over medium heat until it is just boiling. Stir in the paprika and pepper.

3.   Place the chicken and sweet potatoes in a deep-sided casserole dish. Sprinkle the curry powder on top.

4.   Add the soup, stirring.

5.   Bake for 10 to 15 minutes, until the chicken is heated through.

Chicken with Havarti

Serves 4

Preparation time:
5 minutes
Cooking time: 15 minutes

4 tablespoons lemon juice
½ teaspoon garlic salt
¼ teaspoon black pepper
2 teaspoons fresh dill
    weed
4 boneless, skinless
    chicken breast halves
½ cup crumbled Havarti
    cheese

Feel free to use either plain Havarti or Havarti with dill in this recipe. Serve the chicken with steamed vegetables and cooked pasta.

1.   Preheat the broiler.

2.   In a small bowl, combine the lemon juice, garlic salt, pepper, and dill weed. Use a pastry brush to brush the chicken breasts with the lemon juice mixture.

3.   Spray a rack with nonstick cooking spray. Broil the chicken for 15 minutes or until cooked through, turning every 5 minutes. Brush any leftover lemon juice mixture on the chicken while broiling.

4.   Sprinkle the crumbled cheese over the cooked chicken.

Five-Spice Roast Chicken

Roasting chicken breasts at high heat shortens the cooking time and makes the skin turn out extra crispy. Leftovers would work very well in Leftover Coconut Chicken (page 198).

Serves 6

Preparation time:
5 minutes
Cooking time:
25–30 minutes

3 tablespoons olive oil
2 tablespoons red wine
    vinegar
2 teaspoons five-spice
    powder
½ teaspoon bottled
    minced garlic
½ teaspoon salt
¼ teaspoon black pepper
½ teaspoon brown sugar
3 pounds chicken breast
    halves, bone-in

1. Preheat the oven to 500°F. Spray a roasting rack with nonstick cooking spray.

2. In a small bowl, whisk together the olive oil, red wine vinegar, five-spice powder, garlic, salt, pepper, and brown sugar.

3. Rub the five-spice mixture over the chicken breasts.

4. Place the seasoned chicken in a large roasting pan with foil, skin side up.

5. Roast the chicken for about 25 to 30 minutes, or until it is cooked through and the juices run clear.

Freezing Poultry

Leftover cooked chicken (and turkey) freezes very well. Wrap the chicken tightly in plastic wrap or freezer paper and mark with the date (frozen poultry should be used within three months). A handy time-saving idea is to divide the leftover poultry into individual serving portions to use in sandwiches or wraps.

Skillet Chicken with Peaches

Be sure to use firm peaches that aren't overripe, or they may fall apart and become mushy during cooking.

Serves 4

Preparation time:
5–10 minutes
Cooking time:
10–15 minutes

1½ pounds chicken breast
   halves
⅓ cup orange juice
1 tablespoon white or
   cider vinegar
1 tablespoon brown sugar
2 tablespoons vegetable
   oil
½ teaspoon paprika
3 large peaches, thinly
   sliced
½ teaspoon ground
   allspice

1. Chop the chicken breasts into bite-size pieces.

2. In a small bowl, combine the orange juice, vinegar, and brown sugar.

3. In a large skillet, heat the oil on medium-high heat. Turn the heat down to medium, add the chicken, and cook, stirring frequently, until the cubes turn white and are nearly cooked through. Stir in the paprika while the chicken is cooking.

4. Add the peaches and cook, stirring, for about 2 minutes. Stir in the allspice.

5. Add the orange juice mixture. Bring to a boil. Turn down the heat and simmer for 5 more minutes. Serve hot.

Easy Tandoori Chicken

Traditionally, tandoori chicken is marinated overnight in a spicy mixture of yogurt and seasonings. In this quick and easy variation, the chicken is pan-fried with the seasonings and served with the heated yogurt dressing.

1. Combine the spices, sugar, and garlic powder in a small bowl. Rub over the chicken breasts to season.

2. In a small bowl, combine the yogurt and lemon juice. Set aside (do not refrigerate).

3. Heat the oil in a skillet on medium-high heat. Add the garlic and the chicken. Pan-fry for 3 to 4 minutes on one side until browned.

4. Add the shallot. Turn over the chicken and cook the other side until the chicken is cooked through (8 to 10 minutes total cooking time). Remove the chicken to a serving plate.

5. While the chicken is cooking, briefly heat the yogurt in a saucepan over medium heat. Remove and spoon over the chicken.

Perfectly Cooked Chicken Breasts

One way to tell if a chicken breast is cooked is to press on it. Properly cooked chicken has a "springy" texture. If the chicken is too soft it is not done, while chicken meat that is tough has been overcooked.

Serves 4

Preparation time:
5 minutes
Cooking time:
10–15 minutes

1½ teaspoons ground
  coriander
1½ teaspoons ground
  cumin
1½ teaspoons ground
  cayenne pepper
½ teaspoon ground
  ginger
¼ teaspoon sugar
½ teaspoon garlic
  powder, or to taste
4 boneless, skinless
  chicken breast halves
¾ cup natural yogurt
2 tablespoons lemon juice
2 tablespoons vegetable
  oil
1 clove garlic, peeled,
  thinly sliced
1 shallot, peeled and
  chopped

Curried Chicken and Rice

Serves 4

Preparation time:
5–10 minutes
Cooking time:
25–30 minutes

2 tablespoons lemon juice
1½ pounds boneless,
    skinless chicken
    breast halves
1 cup long-grain white
    rice
1½ cups water
2 tablespoons olive oil
½ teaspoon garlic powder
1 medium onion, chopped
1 tablespoon curry
    powder
1 tomato, thinly sliced
1 cup chicken broth
½ cup raisins
¼ teaspoon salt
⅛ teaspoon black pepper

Instead of regular cooked rice, you can, of course, use instant rice or reheat leftover cooked rice in the microwave.

1. In a medium bowl, combine the lemon juice with the chicken breasts, turning to coat them. Begin cooking the rice in the 1½ cups water (see How to Cook Long-Grain Rice, page 146).

2. Heat the olive oil in a skillet over medium-high heat. Add the chicken breasts. (Discard any excess lemon juice.) Sprinkle the garlic powder on top. Cook for 4 to 5 minutes, until the chicken is browned on both sides, turning over halfway during cooking. Remove the chicken from the pan.

3. Add the onion to the pan. Add the curry powder, stirring to mix it in with the onion. Add the tomato. Cook, stirring occasionally, until the onion is shiny and has softened (4 to 5 minutes total cooking time for the onion).

4. Add the broth to the pan. Bring to a boil.

5. Return the chicken to the pan. Stir in the raisins. Turn down the heat and simmer, covered, until the chicken is cooked through (10 to 15 minutes). Season with salt and pepper. Serve with the rice.

Using Leftover Chicken

Always store leftover cooked chicken in a sealed container in the refrigerator (if it is not being frozen). Use the chicken within three to four days.

Turkey Meat Loaf

You can add extra flavor by using Italian seasoned bread crumbs in this recipe.

1. In a large bowl, combine all the ingredients and stir, but do not overmix.

2. Spoon the mixture into a microwave-safe casserole dish and shape into a loaf.

3. Microwave on high heat for 10 minutes, and then for 5 minutes or as needed until the turkey is cooked and the juices run clear (total cooking time should be about 15 minutes).

4. Let stand for 5 minutes.

5. Pour any fat off the dish and serve.

Serves 4

Preparation time:
10 minutes
Cooking time:
10–15 minutes

1 pound lean ground
   turkey
¼ cup ketchup
¼ cup water
½ medium onion,
   chopped
2 tablespoons instant
   basil and tomato soup
   mix
1 egg, beaten
½ teaspoon black pepper
¾ cup bread crumbs

Easy Roast Turkey Breast

Roasting a turkey breast is a great alternative to cooking a whole turkey.

1. Preheat the oven to 325°F.

2. In a small bowl, stir together the vegetable oil, salt, pepper, garlic powder, and dried thyme. Use a pastry brush to brush the mixture over the turkey breast.

3. Wrap the turkey in aluminum foil and roast until the internal temperature reaches 170°F (about 2¼ to 2½ hours).

4. Baste the turkey with the drippings during the last minutes of cooking.

5. Let the turkey stand for 15 minutes, then slice and serve.

Serves 4

Preparation time:
15 minutes
Cooking time:
2½ – 2¾ hours

4 tablespoons vegetable
   oil
½ teaspoon salt
¼ teaspoon black pepper
¼ teaspoon garlic powder
2 teaspoons dried thyme
1 (6-pound) turkey breast

Pan-Fried Garlic Chicken Thighs
with Sun-Dried Tomatoes

There's almost no preparation required to make this flavorful chicken dish. Ready-to-use sun-dried tomatoes, such as Mariani's, are a great timesaver, since they don't need to be softened before using.

Serves 2

Preparation time:
2–3 minutes
Cooking time:
17–20 minutes

1 pound (6 to 8 small) boneless, skinless chicken thighs
⅛ teaspoon garlic salt
¼ teaspoon black pepper
2 teaspoons olive oil
½ medium onion, thinly sliced
2 tablespoons sun-dried tomato strips
½ cup chicken broth
2 teaspoons lemon juice
1 tablespoon chopped fresh basil leaves

1. Rinse the chicken thighs and pat dry. Rub the garlic salt and pepper over the chicken to season.

2. Heat the olive oil in a skillet over medium heat. Add the chicken. Cook for 5 to 6 minutes, until browned on both sides, turning over halfway during cooking. Stir the chicken occasionally to make sure it doesn't stick to the pan.

3. Push the chicken to the sides of the pan. Add the onion and sun-dried tomato strips. Cook in the oil for about 3 minutes, until the onion is browned.

4. Add the chicken broth. Stir in the lemon juice.

5. Simmer for 8 to 10 minutes, until the liquid is nearly absorbed and the chicken is just cooked through. Stir in the basil leaves during the last 2 minutes of cooking.

Cooking with Olive Oil

Loaded with heart-healthy monounsaturated fats, olive oil is a great choice for pan-frying, sautéing, and stir-frying. Just be sure to stick with the olive oils that don't break down at high heats (such as pure olive oil) and leave the extra-virgin olive oil for salads. Always wait until the olive oil is fully heated before adding the food.

Ground Turkey Burgers with Havarti

Using Havarti cheese instead of bread crumbs adds a sweet, buttery flavor to these healthy burgers made with ground turkey.

Serves 8

Preparation time:
10 minutes
Cooking time:
10–15 minutes

1½ pounds ground turkey
1½ tablespoon
    Worcestershire sauce
2½ tablespoons ketchup
2 green onions, minced
¼ teaspoon black pepper,
    or to taste
½ teaspoon salt, or to
    taste
¼ teaspoon dried
    oregano leaves
¼ cup crumbled Havarti
    cheese
2 teaspoons vegetable oil

1. In a large bowl, combine the ground turkey with all other ingredients except the vegetable oil, using your fingers to mix.

2. Form the ground turkey mixture into eight patties.

3. Heat the oil in a skillet over medium heat.

4. Carefully place the patties into the pan. Cook for a total of 10 to 15 minutes, turning once, until the patties are thoroughly cooked through.

How to Broil Burgers

Burgers can also be broiled or grilled. Place the burgers on a rack or grill that has been brushed with nonstick cooking spray. (If broiling, place the rack approximately 4 inches from the heat source.) Broil or grill for about 10 minutes, turning over halfway through cooking, until the burgers are heated through.

Turkey Sloppy Joes

Serves 4

Preparation time:
5–8 minutes
Cooking time: 25 minutes

1½ pounds ground turkey
1 medium onion, chopped
1 green bell pepper,
*   chopped into chunks*
½ cup water
1 cup ketchup
3 tablespoons brown sugar
3 tablespoons red wine
*   vinegar*
¾ teaspoon ground
*   cumin, or to taste*
¼ teaspoon black pepper
4 hamburger buns
⅓ cup crumbled Havarti
*   cheese*

Not a fan of hamburger buns? You can also make the sloppy joes with sandwich buns, on a loaf of French or Italian bread, or even with tortilla or nacho chips.

1. Brown the ground turkey in a skillet over medium-high heat.

2. Add the onion and bell peppers. Cook for 4 to 5 more minutes, until the onion is softened. Drain the fat out of the pan.

3. Add the water, ketchup, brown sugar, and red wine vinegar. Stir in the cumin and pepper. Turn the heat down to low and simmer, uncovered, for 15 minutes.

4. Spoon the turkey mixture over the hamburger buns. Sprinkle the crumbled cheese on top.

Chapter 7
Beef Dishes

Beef and Broccoli Stir-Fry

Apple juice provides a convenient substitute for the rice wine or dry sherry that is normally used in Chinese marinades.

Serves 3

Preparation time:
15–20 minutes
Cooking time: 8 minutes

1 pound flank steak
1½ tablespoons soy
    sauce
1 tablespoon apple juice
2 teaspoons cornstarch
2 cups broccoli florets
¼ cup water
1 tablespoon oyster sauce
1 teaspoon granulated
    sugar
1 tablespoon vegetable oil

1. Cut the beef into thin strips about 2" long. (It's easiest to do this if the beef is partially frozen.) In a medium bowl, combine the beef with the soy sauce, apple juice, and cornstarch. Let the beef marinate for 15 minutes.

2. In a large saucepan with enough water to cover, blanch the broccoli for 2 to 3 minutes, until it is tender but still crisp. Remove the broccoli and rinse under cold running water. Drain.

3. In a small bowl, combine the water, oyster sauce, and sugar. Set aside.

4. Heat the oil in a heavy skillet over medium-high heat. Add the beef. Let brown for a minute, and then stir-fry until it loses its pinkness and is nearly cooked through.

5. Add the broccoli to the pan. Stir the sauce and pour it into the pan. Cook, stirring, to mix everything together and heat through. Serve immediately.

Speedy Stir-Frying

Stir-frying is one of the quickest cooking methods—it's easy to prepare a stir-fry meal in under 30 minutes. While it may seem time-consuming to marinate the meat, marinating helps tenderize the meat and adds extra flavor. And you can prepare the vegetables and sauce while the meat is marinating.

Tex-Mex Chili

This is an excellent recipe for nights when you want a quick and easy recipe that's also quite filling. Add extra protein by sprinkling shredded cheese over the chili before serving.

Serves 4

Preparation time:
5 minutes
Cooking time: 20 minutes

1 pound ground beef
2 tablespoons chili
  powder
¼ teaspoon ground cumin
1 teaspoon salt
1 tablespoon butter or
  margarine
½ medium onion, peeled
  and chopped
½ cup drained canned
  corn
2 (15-ounce) cans red
  kidney beans, drained
1 (28-ounce) can crushed
  tomatoes
1 cup canned mild green
  chilies

1. In a large bowl, combine the ground beef with the chili powder, ground cumin, and salt, using your fingers to mix in the seasonings.

2. Place the butter or margarine and onion in a microwave-safe casserole dish. Microwave on high heat for 2 minutes, or until the onion is tender.

3. Add the ground beef. Cover the dish with microwave-safe wax paper. Microwave on high heat for 5 minutes, give the dish a quarter turn, and then microwave for 3 more minutes (the ground beef should be nearly cooked). Remove and drain off the excess fat.

4. Stir in the remaining ingredients. Microwave for 7 minutes, stir, and microwave for 7 minutes more; then microwave for 1 or 2 minutes at a time until the other ingredients are heated and the beef is cooked through.

5. Let stand for 5 minutes. Serve hot.

Chili Condiments

Preparing chili for a crowd? Make it last longer by serving it with a variety of condiments, from taco chips, shredded cheese, and sour cream to cooked spaghetti or cornbread muffins.

Kung Pao Chili con Carne

Serves 3

Preparation time:
10 minutes
Cooking time: 10 minutes

¾ pound coarsely ground
    beef
½ teaspoon salt
½ teaspoon black pepper
5 teaspoons vegetable oil,
    divided
2 cloves garlic, chopped
1 medium onion, chopped
2 teaspoons Sichuan
    peppercorn, or to
    taste
1 tablespoon chopped
    jalapeño peppers, or
    to taste
1 medium tomato, diced
1 cup drained canned
    kidney beans
¾ cup tomato sauce
¼ cup roasted cashews
1 teaspoon hot sauce,
    optional

The spices and seasonings that make Chinese cooking so popular add heat to south-of-the-border chili in this fun fusion recipe. If Sichuan peppercorn is unavailable, feel free to use freshly ground black, white, or lemon peppercorns.

1. In a medium bowl, combine the ground beef with the salt and pepper.

2. Heat 2 teaspoons oil in a heavy saucepan on medium-high heat. Add the ground beef and stir-fry until the pinkness is gone. Remove the ground beef from the pan. Drain the fat and wipe pan clean with paper towels.

3. Heat 1 tablespoon oil in the pan. Add the garlic and onion. Stir in the Sichuan peppercorn and chopped peppers. Cook, stirring, until the onion begins to soften.

4. Stir in the diced tomato. Stir in the kidney beans and tomato sauce. Bring to a boil.

5. Return the ground beef to the pan. Stir-fry for 1 to 2 more minutes to mix the flavors together. Stir in the cashews. Stir in the hot sauce. Serve hot.

Herbed Steak with Marinated Vegetables

Not a fan of artichokes? You can use the basic marinade in Marinated Artichoke Hearts (page 227) to marinade other vegetables, such as baby carrots, to serve with the herbed steak.

Serves 4

Preparation time:
5 minutes
Cooking time:
15–20 minutes

¼ cup honey mustard
1½ teaspoons fresh
    chopped oregano
1½ teaspoons fresh thyme
½ teaspoon salt
½ teaspoon cayenne
    pepper
4 boneless sirloin steaks
Marinated Artichoke
    Hearts (page 227)

1. Preheat the broiler.

2. In a small bowl, stir together the mustard, oregano, thyme, salt, and cayenne pepper.

3. Rub the spice mixture over the steaks.

4. Spray a rack with nonstick cooking spray. Place the steaks on the rack, about 4 inches from the heat source. For a medium-rare steak, broil for 12 minutes, turning over halfway during cooking

5. Let the steak stand for 5 minutes. Serve with the Marinated Artichoke Hearts (page 227).

Tender Beef

To ensure that beef remains tender during broiling, it's important not to overcook it. If the beef is not being marinated, lightly brush it with oil before placing it on the broiling pan. Turn the steak once during cooking.

Lemon Beef

Preparation time:
10 minutes
Cooking time:
10–12 minutes

1 pound skirt or flank
    steak
2½ teaspoons lemon
    pepper seasoning
2 tablespoons lemon juice
2 tablespoons soy sauce
1 teaspoon sugar
3 tablespoons vegetable
    oil, divided
1 teaspoon minced ginger
1 cup fresh sliced
    mushrooms

Feel free to replace the mushrooms with a quick-cooking green vegetable such as snow peas, or with 1 cup of packaged stir-fry vegetables.

1. Cut the beef into thin strips about 2½" long. (It's easiest to do this if the beef is still partially frozen.) Rub the lemon pepper seasoning over the beef.

2. In a small bowl, combine the lemon juice, soy sauce, and sugar.

3. Heat 2 tablespoons oil in a large skillet or wok. Add half the beef. Let sear for about 30 seconds, then stir-fry for 3 to 4 minutes, until the steak is nearly cooked. Remove the beef from the pan. Repeat with the remaining half of the beef.

4. Heat 1 tablespoon oil in the pan. Add the minced ginger and the mushrooms. Stir-fry for about 2 minutes, adding 1 tablespoon water if the mushrooms dry out.

5. Stir the lemon juice and soy sauce mixture. Pour into the pan. Add the beef to the pan. Cook for 1 to 2 minutes to finish cooking the beef and mix everything together. Serve hot.

Quick Fried Beef with Onion-Cilantro Relish

Onion-cilantro relish is an easy side dish with a bit of spice that pairs nicely with plain fried beef. You can jazz it up a bit by adding a few slices of tomato or cucumber, or to quickly heat it in 2 teaspoons of pure olive oil. Not a fan of cilantro? You can substitute chopped fresh parsley.

Serves 4

Preparation time:
10 minutes
Cooking time:
10–12 minutes

1¼ pounds flank steak
1½ tablespoons white
  wine vinegar
1½ tablespoons soy
  sauce
2 teaspoons cornstarch
1 medium sweet onion,
  minced
4 tablespoons minced
  green onion
1 cup chopped fresh
  cilantro
2 tablespoons lemon juice
½ teaspoon Asian chili
  sauce
½ teaspoon salt
2 tablespoons vegetable
  oil
1 garlic clove, thinly
  sliced

1. Cut the beef across the grain into thin strips, about 2½" to 3" long. (It's easiest to do this if the beef is still slightly frozen.) Place in a large bowl, and stir in the white wine vinegar, soy sauce, and cornstarch, mixing in the cornstarch with your fingers. Let the beef stand while preparing the relish.

2. In a medium bowl, combine the onion, green onion, and cilantro. Stir in the lemon juice, chili sauce, and salt.

3. Heat the oil in a heavy skillet. Add the garlic and half the steak. Let sear for about 30 seconds, then stir-fry, moving the beef around the pan until it loses its pinkness and is cooked through. Remove the beef from the pan and drain.

4. Repeat with the remaining half of the beef.

5. Serve the beef with the onion-cilantro relish.

Or Broil It

This Onion-Cilantro Relish would also pair very nicely with broiled steak. Instead of cutting the steak into thin strips, prepare it for broiling by rubbing with a garlic clove cut in half. Place on a rack and broil for 10 to 15 minutes, turning halfway through cooking, until the steak is cooked through and the juices run clear. Sprinkle the steak with salt and pepper during broiling.

Quick Microwave Lasagna

With flavorful marinara sauce, this dish doesn't really need any extra seasoning. But if you like, you can add a pinch of dried oregano, basil, or parsley.

Serves 2

Preparation time:
5 minutes
Cooking time: 25 minutes
(with standing time)

½ pound ground beef
1 cup crushed tomatoes
1½ cups marinara sauce
1½ cups grated
    mozzarella cheese
1½ cups ricotta cheese
12 oven-ready lasagna
    noodles

1. Crumble the ground beef into a microwave-safe bowl. Microwave the beef on high heat for 5 minutes. Give the dish a quarter turn and microwave on high heat for 4 more minutes. Make another quarter turn and microwave for 1 minute at a time until the beef is cooked through. Remove from the microwave and drain the fat.

2. Combine the ground beef with the crushed tomatoes and marinara sauce. Stir in the cheeses.

3. Lay out four of the lasagna noodles in a large bowl or a 1-quart microwave-safe casserole dish. (Break the noodles if needed to fit into the container.) Spoon one-third of the sauce mixture over the noodles, spreading evenly. Add two more layers of the noodles and sauce.

4. Cover the dish with wax paper. Microwave on high heat for 7 to 8 minutes, until the cheeses are cooked. Let the lasagna stand for 10 minutes before serving.

Sloppy Joes

Invented to cope with a meat shortage during World War II, sloppy joes are a favorite with kids, who like its soupy texture.

Serves 4

Preparation time:
5–8 minutes
Cooking time: 25 minutes

1½ pounds ground beef
½ yellow onion, chopped
½ green bell pepper, diced
1 cup water
1 cup tomato paste
2 tablespoons brown sugar
¼ teaspoon paprika, or to taste
¼ teaspoon garlic powder
¼ teaspoon black pepper, or to taste
4 hamburger buns
⅓ cup shredded Cheddar cheese

1. Place the ground beef in a large skillet and brown over medium heat. After the beef is halfway cooked, add the onion and bell pepper. Continue cooking until the beef is browned and the onion is softened.

2. Add the water. Stir in the tomato paste. Stir in the brown sugar, paprika, garlic powder, and pepper.

3. Bring to a boil. Turn down the heat, cover, and simmer for about 10 minutes, until the mixture is heated through and reaches desired thickness.

4. Spoon the beef mixture over the hamburger buns. Sprinkle with shredded cheese and serve.

Sloppy Joes with Sizzle

Feel free to jazz up this basic recipe for Sloppy Joes by replacing the tomato paste with your favorite prepared salsa, or the water with tomato soup.

Microwave Irish Stew for Two

Serves 2

2 leftover Honey Mustard
  Pork Chops (page
  117)
4 baby onions
1 tablespoon margarine
1 (8-ounce) can peas,
  with liquid
¼ teaspoon dried thyme
¼ teaspoon salt
¼ teaspoon black pepper,
  or to taste

Leftover cooked pork chops make a handy substitute for lamb in this quick and easy variation on Irish stew. For extra flavor, add a few sprigs of fresh parsley or ½ teaspoon of dried parsley.

1. Cut the pork chops into bite-size chunks. Peel the baby onions and cut in half.

2. Place the margarine and baby onions in a microwave-safe casserole dish. Microwave on high heat for 1 minute. Stir and then microwave for 1 minute at a time until the baby onions are tender (total cooking time should be 2 to 3 minutes).

3. Add the canned peas. Stir in the dried thyme, salt, and pepper. Microwave on high heat for 30 seconds.

4. Stir in the pork.

5. Use a reheat setting, or microwave at 70 percent power for 2 minutes and then for 1 minute at a time, until the pork is heated. Serve hot.

Five-Ingredient Meat Loaf

Parmesan cheese and tomato sauce are both good sources of umami, the meaty or savory flavor that is the secret ingredient in MSG (monosodium glutamate).

Serves 4

Preparation time:
5 minutes
Cooking time:
15 – 20 minutes

1½ pounds ground pork
¾ cup plus 2 tablespoons
   tomato sauce
¼ cup chopped onion
1 tablespoon balsamic
   vinegar
½ cup Parmesan cheese

1. In a large bowl, combine all the ingredients. For the tomato sauce, add ¾ cup and then add the remaining 2 tablespoons of sauce if needed.

2. Shape into a loaf and place in a microwave-safe casserole dish. Cover with microwave-safe wax paper.

3. Microwave on high heat for 15 minutes, 5 minutes at a time, rotating the dish a quarter turn between each cooking period. If the meat loaf is not cooked after 15 minutes, continue to cook for 1 minute at a time until done. (Total cooking time should be about 15 minutes.) The meat loaf is cooked when the internal temperature reaches 160°F.

4. Let stand for 5 minutes.

5. Pour any fat off the dish and serve.

Speedy Meat Loaf Muffins

Looking for an easy way to speed up cooking on nights when you're baking the meat loaf in the oven? Instead of shaping the meat loaf mixture into one big loaf, place individual portions in muffin tins. This reduces baking time and makes serving easy. Better still, leftover muffins can be frozen, making a quick and easy snack or midday meal. Bake the muffins at 350°F. for 25–30 minutes until the muffins are cooked through.

Sweet-and-Sour Meat Loaf

Be sure not to overmix the meat loaf or it can dry out during cooking. Place an instant-read kitchen thermometer in the center of the meat loaf to check for doneness.

Serves 4

Preparation time:
5–8 minutes
Cooking time:
15 – 20 minutes

1½ pounds ground beef
1 (5.5-ounce) can tomato paste
¼ cup milk
3 tablespoons brown sugar
3 tablespoons vinegar
2 teaspoons soy sauce
1 egg, beaten
½ cup crushed bread crumbs
2 tablespoons minced onion
¼ teaspoon salt, or to taste
¼ teaspoon black pepper, or to taste

1. In a large bowl, combine all the ingredients.

2. Shape into a loaf and place in a microwave-safe casserole dish. Cover with microwave-safe wax paper.

3. Microwave on high heat for 15 minutes, 5 minutes at a time, rotating the dish a quarter turn between each period. If the meat loaf is not cooked after 15 minutes, continue to cook for 1 minute at a time until done (total cooking should be about 15 minutes). The meat loaf is cooked when the internal temperature reaches 160°F.

4. Let stand for 5 minutes.

5. Pour any fat off the dish and serve.

Steak and Marinated Artichoke Hearts

This is a great choice for busy weeknights—prepare the sauce and artichoke hearts ahead of time on the weekend, and serve the steak over reheated cooked rice.

Serves 4

Preparation time:
10 minutes
Cooking time: 10 minutes

¾ *pound flank steak*
2 tablespoons vegetable oil
1 teaspoon minced fresh gingerroot
Marinated Artichoke Hearts (page 227)
Simple Stir-Fry Sauce (page 242)

1. Cut the flank steak across the grain into thin strips. (It's easiest to do this if the beef is still slightly frozen.)

2. Heat the oil in a heavy skillet or wok over medium-high heat. Add the ginger and cook for 10 seconds, then add the beef. Let the beef brown for about 30 seconds and then cook, stirring constantly, until it is no longer pink. Remove the beef from the pan. Drain on paper towels.

3. Add the artichokes to the pan. Stir-fry for 1 minute. Pour in the sauce and bring to a boil.

4. Return the beef to the pan. Cook for another minute, stirring to mix everything together. Serve hot.

Going Against the Grain

Cutting beef across or against the grain shocks the muscle fibers and relaxes them. It's a great way to tenderize leaner cuts of meat such as flank steak. To cut beef across the grain, find the muscle fibers by looking for the lines or "grains" running across the cut of beef. Cut the beef perpendicular to the grains.

Steak with Brown Sauce

Making the sauce ahead of time takes much of the work out of preparing this flavorful dish. You can also prepare the sauce while the steak is cooking.

½ teaspoon seasoned salt
½ teaspoon black pepper
4 beef tenderloin steaks
  (3 to 5 ounces each)
2 tablespoons vegetable
  oil
1 shallot, chopped
¼ cup red wine
Quick and Easy Brown
  Sauce (page 252)

1. Rub the salt and pepper over the steaks to season.

2. Heat the oil in a skillet over medium-high heat. Add the steaks. Cook for 4 to 5 minutes, until the steak is browned on the bottom.

3. Add the shallots to the pan. Turn the steak over and cook for another 4 to 5 minutes. Remove the steak and shallots from the pan. Pour off any excess fat.

4. Add the red wine to the pan and bring to a boil. Deglaze the pan by using a rubber spatula to scrape up any browned bits from the meat (do not remove the browned bits: they add extra flavor to the liquid).

5. Add the brown sauce to the pan and cook, at low-medium heat, until it is heated through. Pour the sauce over the steak.

Perfectly Done Steak

The best way to tell whether a steak is cooked the way you like it is to check the texture and appearance. Rare-cooked steak has a soft texture, and is completely pink in the center. Steak that is cooked to a medium level of doneness has a firm texture that will give a bit when you touch it. The very middle will be pink, gradually fading to a grayish-brown. Well-done steak should be quite taut and have no pinkness at all.

Easy Pepper Steak with Rice

Don't have a large skillet? Stir-fry the vegetables in a separate pan, and then combine with the beef and the broth.

Serves 4

Preparation time:
5–10 minutes
Cooking time: 10 minutes

1½ pounds beef sirloin
¼ cup beef broth
1½ tablespoons soy
   sauce
1 teaspoon Worcestershire
   sauce
½ teaspoon granulated
   sugar
1 teaspoon cornstarch
2 tablespoons olive oil
1 garlic clove, thinly
   sliced
1 onion, cut into wedges
1 red bell pepper,
   seeded, cut julienne-
   style
1 green bell pepper,
   seeded, cut julienne-
   style
1 cup sliced fresh
   mushrooms

1. Cut the beef into thin strips 2½" to 3" long. (It's easiest to do this if the steak is still slightly frozen.) In a small bowl, stir together the beef broth, soy sauce, Worcestershire sauce, and sugar. Whisk in the cornstarch.

2. In a large skillet, heat the oil over medium-high heat. Add the garlic, cook for a few seconds, then add the beef to the pan. Let sear for 30 seconds, and then stir-fry for 4 to 5 minutes, until the pinkness has gone.

3. Push the steak to the sides and add the onion, bell peppers, and mushrooms to the pan. Stir-fry for 2 to 3 minutes, until the onion and peppers are softened.

4. Stir the beef broth mixture and pour it into the middle of the pan, stirring quickly to thicken.

5. Let simmer for 5 minutes. Serve hot.

Beef Burgundy Stew

Don't have leftover beef on hand? Brown 1 pound of cubed stewing beef over medium-high heat until nearly cooked through. This will add 5 to 10 minutes to the cooking time.

Serves 2

Preparation time:
5–10 minutes
Cooking time:
12–15 minutes

1 tablespoon vegetable oil
2 baby onions, cut in half
4 ounces sliced fresh
    mushrooms
1 zucchini, thinly sliced
¼ teaspoon dried oregano
2 cups leftover cooked
    beef, cubed
¼ cup burgundy
½ cup beef broth
1 tablespoon tomato paste
1 tablespoon
    Worcestershire sauce
⅛ teaspoon black pepper

1. Heat the oil in a skillet on medium heat. Add the onions, mushrooms, and zucchini. Stir in the dried oregano. Sauté for about 5 minutes, until the vegetables are softened.

2. Add the beef. Cook for 2 to 3 minutes to heat through.

3. Add the burgundy and beef broth. Stir in the tomato paste and Worcestershire sauce. Bring to a boil.

4. Stir in the pepper. Turn down the heat and simmer for about 5 minutes. Serve hot.

Chili con Queso Dinner

Adding sausage to classic Chili con Queso ingredients turns this into a complete meal. Serve with tortilla chips, or spoon onto crusty French or Italian bread.

Serves 4

Preparation time:
5 minutes
Cooking time:
10–15 minutes

1 pound smoked pork
    sausage
1 medium onion, chopped
2 cups canned chopped
    tomatoes, with juice
1 cup canned whole
    green chilies
1 cup packaged
    shredded Monterey
    Jack cheese
¼ teaspoon black pepper
½ teaspoon salt, or to
    taste
¼ cup sour cream

1. Cook the sausage and onion in a skillet for about 5 minutes on medium heat, stirring occasionally, until the sausage is browned and the onion is softened.

2. Add the tomatoes and green chilies. Cook for a couple of minutes, until the tomato is softened.

3. Add the cheese and cook until the cheese is melted.

4. Stir in the salt and pepper. Taste and adjust seasoning if desired.

5. Stir in the sour cream. Serve hot.

Skillet Shepherd's Pie

If canned or packaged beef broth isn't available, you can use 2 beef bouillon cubes dissolved in 1 cup of boiling water.

Serves 4

Preparation time:
5–10 minutes
Cooking time:
15–20 minutes

1 pound ground beef
½ teaspoon salt
¼ teaspoon black pepper
½ medium onion, peeled
   and chopped
1 cup drained canned
   green beans
1 cup canned corn
1 portion Garlic Mashed
   Potatoes (page 232)
½ teaspoon paprika
1 cup beef broth

1. Brown the ground beef in a skillet on medium heat, using a spatula to break it up. Sprinkle the salt and pepper over the beef while it is cooking.

2. After the beef has been cooking for 5 minutes, add the onion. Cook for another 5 minutes, until the pinkness is gone from the beef and the onion is softened. Drain excess fat from the pan.

3. Add the green beans and corn to the pan.

4. Add the mashed potatoes. Stir in the paprika.

5. Add the beef broth. Simmer for 5 minutes, stirring, to heat everything through. Serve hot.

Make-Ahead Mashed Potatoes

You don't have to wait until you're preparing a dish such as Skillet Shepherd's Pie to use leftover mashed potatoes—they can also be served alone as a side dish. Reheat the potatoes by frying them in 1 or 2 teaspoons of oil, or cook in the microwave with a bit of liquid, using the microwave's reheat setting or at 70 percent power.

Skillet Beef Jerky

Frying the beef for longer than usual gives it a chewy texture similar to beef jerky, but this is much quicker to make. It would go very nicely with rice and steamed vegetables, such as Simple Steamed Mushrooms (page 229).

Serves 2

Preparation time:
5–10 minutes
Cooking time:
10–12 minutes

1 pound sirloin steak
2 tablespoons soy sauce
1 teaspoon
   Worcestershire sauce
1 teaspoon brown sugar
2 tablespoons
   vegetable oil

1. Cut the beef into thin strips 2" to 3" long. (It's easiest to do this if the beef is still slightly frozen.)

2. In a small bowl, stir together the soy sauce, Worcestershire sauce, and brown sugar.

3. In a heavy skillet, heat the oil on medium-high heat.

4. Add the beef, laying it flat in the pan. Let sear for a minute, and then stir-fry for about 10 minutes, until the beef is crisp and chewy. Keep stirring and moving the beef around the pan as it is cooking.

5. Stir the soy sauce mixture and swirl it into the pan. Stir to mix with the beef and serve.

Chapter 8
Pork and Lamb Dishes

Plum Pork Stir-Fry

Serves 4

Preparation time:
20 minutes
Cooking time: 10 minutes

1 pound pork tenderloin
2½ tablespoons soy
    sauce, divided
1 tablespoon apple cider
2 teaspoons cornstarch
¼ cup plum sauce
2 teaspoons brown sugar
3 tablespoons water
2 tablespoons vegetable
    or peanut oil
2 slices fresh gingerroot

Apple cider or apple juice takes the place of Chinese rice wine, which can be hard to find outside of Asian supermarkets, in this recipe. You can also use dry sherry if desired. (Drinking quality Chinese rice wine is not widely available in North America.)

1. Cut the pork into cubes. Place the pork in a bowl and add 1½ tablespoons soy sauce, apple cider, and cornstarch. Let the pork marinate for at least 15 minutes (if you have time, marinate the pork for 30 minutes).

2. In a small bowl, combine the plum sauce, 1 tablespoon soy sauce, brown sugar, and water.

3. Heat a wok or heavy skillet and add the oil. When the oil is hot, add the ginger slices. Let the ginger cook for 2 to 3 minutes, until browned (this is to flavor the oil).

4. Add the pork. Let sit briefly, then stir-fry, moving the pork cubes around the pan, until the pork turns white and is nearly cooked through.

5. Stir the plum sauce mixture, then pour into the pan and bring to a boil. Turn down the heat and simmer for 2 to 3 more minutes, stirring to mix the pork with the sauce. Serve hot.

Robust Rice Wine

Made from fermented sweet rice, rice wine is a staple ingredient in Chinese cooking. Besides using it in marinades, Chinese cooks frequently splash meat or poultry with rice wine during stir-frying. While dry sherry is the preferred substitute for rice wine, you can also use gin, or even apple cider, as in this recipe. For a nonalcoholic substitute, use apple juice.

Rosemary Lamb Chops

This recipe can easily be doubled to serve four people. Lamb cooked medium rare will be pink on the inside and have a slightly firm texture.

1. Pat lamb chops dry with paper towels. Rub salt and pepper over the lamb chops to season. Rub the rosemary into the lamb chops.

2. Heat 1 tablespoon olive oil in a skillet over medium-high heat. Add the lamb chops. Cook for 5 minutes, then turn over (turn the heat down if the lamb chops are cooking too quickly). Push to the sides of the skillet.

3. Heat 1 tablespoon oil in the middle of the skillet and add the shallots. Sauté the shallots while the lamb chops finish cooking (total cooking time for the lamb chops should be about 10 minutes). Drain any excess fat out of the pan while cooking.

4. Splash the lamb chops with the red wine vinegar during the last few minutes of cooking.

Serves 4

Preparation time: 5 minutes
Cooking time: 15 minutes

4 lamb loin chops, about 1" thick, 3 ounces each
¼ teaspoon salt
⅛ teaspoon black pepper
2 teaspoons dried rosemary
2 tablespoons olive oil, divided
2 shallots, chopped
1 tablespoon red wine vinegar

Ground Pork Stroganoff

Serves 4

Preparation time:
5 minutes
Cooking time: 10 minutes

2 cups ground pork
2 tablespoons margarine
1 medium onion, peeled
   and chopped
1 cup sliced fresh
   mushrooms
⅛ teaspoon nutmeg, or to
   taste
½ teaspoon dried basil
½ cup chicken broth
Salt and pepper, to taste
½ cup natural yogurt

*If you like, you can replace the chicken broth with dry white wine.
Serve the stroganoff over cooked rice or noodles.*

1. Brown the ground pork in a skillet over medium heat. Remove to a plate. Drain the excess fat from the pan.

2. While the ground pork is browning, melt the margarine in a separate skillet. Add the onion and sauté for a couple of minutes, until it begins to soften.

3. Add the mushrooms and cook for about 2 minutes, until the vegetables are softened. Stir in the nutmeg and dried basil.

4. Add the chicken broth and ground pork to the pan. Cook, stirring, for a minute to heat through. Taste and season with salt and pepper if desired.

5. Stir in the yogurt. Serve immediately over the cooked rice.

Using Chicken Bouillon for Broth

Chicken bouillon cubes are a handy substitute for store-bought or home-made chicken broth. To use, dissolve one bouillon cube in ½ cup of boiling water.

Pork with Peaches

*Be sure to use peaches that are not overripe
and won't fall apart during stir-frying.*

Serves 4

Preparation time:
5 minutes
Cooking time: 7 minutes

¾ pound pork tenderloin
1 tablespoon soy sauce
1 tablespoon apple juice
1½ teaspoons cornstarch
1 tablespoon water
2 tablespoons plus 1
    teaspoon vegetable
    oil, divided
1 teaspoon minced
    ginger, divided
2 teaspoons curry powder
2 large peaches, thinly
    sliced
½ cup chicken broth
Black pepper, to taste

1. Cut the pork into 1" cubes. Place the pork in a medium bowl and toss with the soy sauce and apple juice. Let stand for 5 minutes.

2. In a small bowl, dissolve the cornstarch in the water.

3. Heat 2 tablespoons oil in a skillet on medium-high heat. Add the pork and half the ginger. Cook, stirring constantly, until the pork is no longer pink and is nearly cooked through.

4. Push the pork to the sides of the pan. Add 1 teaspoon oil in the middle. Add the remainder of the ginger and the curry powder. Stir for a few seconds until aromatic. Add the sliced peaches. Cook for a minute, stirring continually, and add the chicken broth. Add the cornstarch and water mixture, stirring to thicken.

5. Season with the pepper. Cook for another minute, stirring to mix everything together. Serve hot.

Quick Fried Minted Lamb

Serves 4

Preparation time:
5 minutes
Cooking time: 10 minutes

8 lamb rib chops, 1" thick
½ cup mint jelly, or as
    needed

Traditionally, mint jelly is paired with roast leg of lamb, but it also goes nicely with quicker-cooking lamb cuts. You can spice up the mint jelly by adding a pinch of cayenne pepper.

1. Preheat the broiler. Spray a broiling rack with nonstick cooking spray.

2. Place the lamb chops on a rack about 4 inches from the heat source. Broil the chops for 8 to 10 minutes, turning once, until they are cooked through.

3. Serve the lamb with the mint jelly.

Make Your Own Mint Sauce

Instead of mint jelly, you can make your own mint sauce for this Quick Fried Minted Lamb. Simply process fresh mint leaves with a small amount of apple juice, white wine vinegar, and sugar to taste until you have a thick sauce. Season the sauce with salt and pepper to taste. For best results, prepare the mint sauce one hour ahead of time to give the flavors a chance to blend.

Skillet Sausage with Pasta and Marinara Sauce

Using leftover cooked pasta saves the time you'd spend waiting for the water to come to a boil and then cooking the pasta. If you don't have any leftover pasta on hand, or just prefer to cook your pasta in the traditional way, start preparing the other ingredients at about the same time as you add the dried pasta to the boiling water.

1. Heat 1 tablespoon olive oil in the skillet on medium heat. Cook the sausages in the skillet on medium heat for 3 to 5 minutes, until they are heated through. Remove the sausages from the pan and drain on paper towels. Wipe out the pan.

2. Heat the remaining olive oil in the skillet. Add the garlic cloves and the spinach. Sprinkle the salt over the spinach and cook for 2 to 3 minutes, just until spinach leaves have wilted.

3. Add the marinara sauce and bring to a boil. Return the sausage to the pan. Cook for another minute to combine all the ingredients.

4. Place the leftover pasta in a colander and quickly run hot water over it to heat. Drain.

5. Add the pasta to the skillet and combine with the other ingredients. Sprinkle with the cheese before serving.

Serves 4

Preparation time:
5 minutes
Cooking time:
12–15 minutes

2 tablespoons olive oil, divided
8 ounces precooked pork sausage, thinly sliced
2 garlic cloves, finely chopped
1 (1-pound) bag fresh spinach, washed and drained
1 teaspoon salt
1½ cups jarred tomato marinara sauce
12 ounces leftover cooked spaghetti or linguine
4 tablespoons grated Parmesan cheese

Orange-Flavored Pork Chops

Serves 4

Preparation time:
5 minutes
Cooking time: 15 minutes

¼ cup orange juice
1 tablespoon cider
    vinegar
1 tablespoon brown sugar
2 tablespoons soy sauce
½ teaspoon salt
¼ teaspoon black pepper
4 boneless pork chops,
    loin center (about 1¼
    pounds)
1 tablespoon vegetable oil
½ medium onion, peeled,
    finely chopped
1 teaspoon bottled
    minced garlic

Flavorful orange sauce is a great way to liven up plain pork chops. For extra heat, add a pinch of paprika or other hot spice to the orange juice mixture. You'll want to pair the pork chops with less strongly flavored side dishes, such as simple steamed vegetables and cooked rice.

1. In a small bowl or measuring cup, combine the orange juice, cider vinegar, brown sugar, and soy sauce. Set aside.

2. Rub salt and pepper over the pork chops to season.

3. Heat the oil over medium-high heat. Add the onion, garlic, and pork chops. Cook for about 10 minutes, until the pork chops are browned on both sides, turning the pork chops halfway through cooking. (Turn the heat down if the pork chops are cooking too quickly.) Remove the pork chops from the pan.

4. Stir the orange juice mixture and pour into the pan. Use a spatula to scrape up any browned bits and drippings from the cooked pork. Bring the orange mixture to a boil.

5. Return the pork to the skillet. Cook for 5 to 6 minutes, stirring occasionally and turning the pork chops so that they are covered with the sauce. Serve hot.

Two Meals in One

To save time during the week, use leftover pork chops and cooked rice from Orange-Flavored Pork Chops to make Pork Fried Rice (page 147). Just be sure to store the pork in a sealed bag in the refrigerator, and use within four to five days.

Honey Mustard Pork Chops

For extra flavor, stir 1 to 2 teaspoons curry powder into the heated honey mustard and margarine.

Serves 4

Preparation time:
5 minutes
Cooking time:
12–15 minutes

1 teaspoon garlic salt
¼ teaspoon black pepper,
   or to taste
4 pork loin chops,
   boneless, 1" thick
   (about 1¼ pounds)
4 tablespoons margarine
1 tablespoon Dijon honey
   mustard
1 teaspoon granulated
   sugar
2 teaspoons red wine
   vinegar
¼ teaspoon dried thyme
1 tablespoon olive oil
1 garlic clove, finely
   chopped
¼ cup Burgundy
3 tablespoons apple juice

1. Rub the garlic salt and pepper over the pork chops. Melt the margarine and honey mustard in a saucepan over low heat. Stir in the sugar, red wine vinegar, and dried thyme.

2. Heat the olive oil in a skillet on medium-high heat. Add the garlic and the pork chops. Use a pastry brush to brush half of the melted butter mixture over the pork chops. Cook for 5 minutes, or until the underside is browned.

3. Turn the pork chops over and brush with the remaining half of the mustard mixture. Cook for 5 more minutes. (Adjust the temperature to medium as needed if the chops are cooking too quickly.)

4. Add the Burgundy and apple juice to the pan and bring to a boil.

5. Cook for about 2 more minutes, until the juices in the pork run clear. Serve immediately.

One-Dish Sausage and Rice

Serves 2

Preparation time:
5 minutes
Cooking time: 15 minutes

1 cup chicken broth
1 cup long-grain instant
   rice
2 tablespoons olive oil
1 shallot, peeled and
   chopped
1 teaspoon paprika
8 ounces cooked smoked
   sausage, thinly sliced
2 sprigs fresh parsley
Salt and pepper, to taste

Using instant rice speeds up the cooking time of this simple, warming dish, while using chicken broth instead of water to cook the rice adds extra flavor.

1. Bring the chicken broth to a boil. Stir in the rice, making sure all the grains are moistened. Remove from the heat, cover, and let stand for 5 minutes.

2. While the rice is cooking, prepare the other ingredients: Heat the olive oil in a skillet over medium-high heat. Add the shallot. Sauté until softened (turn the heat down if the shallot is cooking too quickly). Stir in the paprika.

3. Stir in the sausage and parsley. Cook for a minute until the sausage is heated.

4. After the rice has been heating for 5 minutes, uncover and use a fork to fluff.

5. Stir the sausage and parsley into the cooked rice. Season with salt and pepper if desired.

Or Use Regular Rice

On evenings when you have a bit more time, try preparing One-Dish Sausage and Rice with regular long-grain rice. In a medium saucepan, bring the water and rice to a boil over medium heat. Let the rice cook until the water is nearly evaporated, add the sausage and parsley, reduce the heat, cover, and simmer until the liquid is absorbed and the rice is cooked. Let the rice sit for 5 minutes, then use a fork to fluff it up and mix in the sausage and parsley. The total cooking time will be about 25 minutes.

Personal Pizza

Chunky garden salsa is available in many local supermarkets. You can also use a homemade salsa in this recipe if desired.

Serves 1

Preparation time:
5 minutes
Cooking time:
2–4 minutes

¼ cup chunky garden
   salsa
1 pita pocket
½ cup fresh sliced
   mushrooms
¼ cup diced cooked ham
3 tablespoons shredded
   mozzarella or
   Parmesan cheese

1.   Spread the garden salsa over one side of the pita pocket.

2.   Lay the mushrooms on top of the salsa. Add the diced ham.

3.   Sprinkle the shredded cheese on top.

4.   Place the pita pocket on a microwave-safe plate. Microwave on high for 2 minutes, then for a few seconds at a time if needed until the cheese is fully melted.

Leftover Sausage and Potato Casserole

Leftover Instant Mashed Potato Salad (page 64) would work well in this dish. For a quick and easy dinner, serve the casserole with Basic Spinach Salad (page 71).

Serves 2

Preparation time:
2–3 minutes
Cooking time: 10 minutes

2 tablespoons chopped
   red onion
2 teaspoons butter or
   margarine
2 cooked sausages, thinly
   sliced
¾ cup leftover mashed
   potatoes
¾ cup canned tomato
   sauce
2 teaspoons balsamic
   vinegar
¼ teaspoon dried basil
   leaves
¼ teaspoon dried
   oregano
⅛ teaspoon black pepper,
   or to taste

1.   Place the onion and butter or margarine in a 1-quart microwave-safe casserole dish. Microwave on high heat until the onion is softened.

2.   Add the sliced sausage. Spoon the potatoes on top.

3.   In a medium bowl, stir together the tomato sauce, balsamic vinegar, basil, oregano, and pepper. Pour over the sausage and potatoes.

4.   Cover the casserole loosely with plastic wrap, leaving an opening on one end for steam to vent.

5.   Microwave on high heat for 4 minutes. Rotate the dish and microwave on medium-high heat for 3 to 4 more minutes, or until heated through.

Ham and Sausage Jambalaya

Serves 2

Preparation time:
5 minutes
Cooking time: 15 minutes

2 tablespoons olive oil
2 cloves garlic, chopped
½ medium onion,
    chopped
1 tablespoon creole
    seasoning
2 stalks celery, thinly
    chopped
½ pound smoked
    sausage, thinly sliced
½ cup cooked ham, diced
½ cup chicken broth
½ cup stewed tomatoes
1 cup cooked rice
1 green onion, finely
    chopped
Salt and pepper, to taste

Jambalaya is the southern U.S. version of the famous Spanish dish paella. A spicy blend made with paprika, dried onion, and other ingredients, creole seasoning is available in the spice section of many supermarkets. If you don't have any on hand, a simple way to season the dish is to add 1 teaspoon paprika and ¼ teaspoon dried thyme, or to taste.

1. Heat the oil in a skillet on medium heat. Add the garlic and onion. Sprinkle the creole seasoning over the onion and garlic. Cook for about 2 minutes, then add the celery. Cook for 2 to 3 more minutes, until the onion is softened.

2. Stir in the sausage. Cook for a minute until it is heated. Stir in the cooked ham.

3. Add the chicken broth and stewed tomatoes. Bring to a boil.

4. Stir in the rice and green onion.

5. Turn the heat down and simmer for 5 minutes to heat everything through. Season with salt and pepper if desired.

Mexican-Style Lamb Chops

To cook to a medium level of doneness, remove the lamb when its internal temperature reaches 155°F and let stand for 5 minutes before serving.

Serves 4

Preparation time:
5 minutes
Cooking time:
10–12 minutes

8 lamb sirloin or rib chops
2 tablespoons olive oil
1 teaspoon ground cumin
1 teaspoon chili powder,
    or to taste
Simple Salsa Verde
    (page 248)

1. Preheat the broiler on high heat. Spray the broiling rack with nonstick cooking spray.

2. Trim most of the fat from the lamb chops. In a small bowl, combine the olive oil, ground cumin, and chili powder.

3. Place the lamb chops on the broiling rack and brush with half the olive oil mixture. Place the rack 3 inches from the heat source.

4. Broil the lamb chops for 8 to 10 minutes, until they are cooked to the desired level of doneness, turning halfway through and brushing with the remainder of the olive oil mixture.

5. To serve, spoon the Salsa Verde on the lamb chops.

Make-Ahead Salsa

Salsa ingredients can be prepared up to one day ahead of time. Be sure to store the salsa in a sealed container in the refrigerator. Unfortunately, the tomato content in salsa doesn't let it freeze very well.

Lamb with Artichokes

To add extra flavor to this dish, use artichoke hearts that have been marinated in olive oil and seasonings. Be sure to squeeze any excess water from the artichoke hearts before using.

Serves 2

Preparation time:
5 minutes
Cooking time: 15 minutes

Salt and pepper, to taste
2 lamb chops
4 teaspoons olive oil
1 shallot, chopped
1 tomato, sliced
4 canned artichoke
*   hearts, halved*
½ cup low-sodium
*   chicken broth*

1. Rub salt and pepper over the lamb chops to season.

2. Heat 2 teaspoons olive oil over medium-high heat. Add the lamb chops and the shallot. Cook for 5 minutes, then turn the lamb chops over. Drain any excess fat out of the pan.

3. Heat 2 teaspoons oil in the middle of the skillet. Add the tomato and artichokes, pressing down on the tomato so that it releases its juices. Cook for about 3 minutes.

4. Add the chicken broth. Bring to a boil. Turn down the heat, cover, and simmer on low heat for 2 to 3 minutes, until the lamb chops are cooked. Serve hot.

Amazing Artichokes

A member of the thistle family, artichokes have been prized as a digestive aid since ancient times. Until the twentieth century, medical practitioners believed that a regular diet of artichokes could help improve liver function. While studies have not borne this out, it is believed that artichokes may aid in lowering cholesterol and improve blood sugar levels in diabetics, reducing the need for insulin (see www.swedish.org/110799. cfm and www.pjbs.org/pjnonline/fin419.pdf).

Easy Lamb Chops with Green Onions

Feel free to replace the chicken broth with other types of soup or stock, such as ¼ cup of Easy Microwave Onion Soup (page 52).

Serves 4

Preparation time:
5–8 minutes
Cooking time:
12–15 minutes

4 lamb chops
Salt and pepper, as
    needed
2 tablespoons olive oil,
    divided
2 garlic cloves, finely
    chopped
2 shallots, chopped
1 teaspoon paprika, or to
    taste
¼ cup chicken broth
2 teaspoons balsamic
    vinegar
¼ cup green onions

1. Season the lamb chops with the salt and pepper.

2. Heat 1 tablespoon olive oil in a skillet over medium-high heat. Add the lamb chops. Cook for 5 minutes, then turn over (turn the heat down if the lamb chops are cooking too quickly). Push to the sides of the skillet.

3. Heat 1 tablespoon oil in the middle of the skillet and add the garlic and shallots. Stir in the paprika. Sauté while the lamb chops finish cooking (total cooking time for the lamb chops should be about 10 minutes).

4. Remove the lamb chops from the pan. Add the chicken broth and balsamic vinegar to the pan and bring to a boil. Deglaze the pan, using a spatula to scrape up the browned bits of meat.

5. Return the lamb chops to the pan. Add the green onion. Cook for another minute and serve hot.

Curried Lamb with Wild Rice

This recipe can easily be adapted according to what ingredients you have on hand: you can use beef or chicken instead of lamb, or serve with scented basmati or jasmine rice instead of wild rice.

Serves 4

Preparation time:
5–8 minutes
Cooking time: 12 minutes

2 tablespoons vegetable
    oil
1 pound lean boneless
    lamb, cut into ½"
    cubes
2 garlic cloves, crushed
½ onion, peeled and
    chopped
¼ teaspoon red pepper
    flakes, or to taste
2 teaspoons curry
    powder, or to taste
1 tomato, thinly sliced
¼ cup beef broth
1 tablespoon chopped
    cilantro leaves
1 tablespoon tomato
    paste
Salt and pepper to taste
2 cups leftover cooked
    wild rice

1. Heat the oil in a skillet on medium-high heat. Add the lamb. Let the meat brown for a minute, then turn down the heat to medium and cook, stirring, for 4 to 5 minutes, until it loses its pinkness. Remove the lamb from the pan.

2. Add the garlic, onion, red pepper flakes, and curry powder. Sauté for 2 to 3 minutes, until the onion begins to soften.

3. Add the tomato slices. Cook for a minute, pressing down on the tomato so that it releases its juices.

4. Add the beef broth and cilantro. Stir in the tomato paste. Return the lamb to the pan.

5. Cook, stirring, for another minute to mix everything together. Taste; season with salt and pepper if desired. Serve hot over the cooked rice.

Long-Lasting Cilantro

It's frustrating when a large bundle of fresh cilantro wilts before you've had a chance to use it all. To make fresh cilantro last longer, place it in a cup of water, cover with a plastic bag and store in the refrigerator. Cilantro stored in this way will last up to two weeks.

Chapter 9
Fish and Seafood

Coconut Shrimp Tempura

Serves 4

Preparation time:
15 minutes
Cooking time:
15–20 minutes

1 cup unsweetened
   coconut flakes
2 eggs, refrigerated
2 cups ice cold water
2 cups rice flour
1 pound (about 24) large
   shrimp, peeled,
   deveined, tail on

Baking the battered shrimp instead of deep-frying takes much of the work out of this classic appetizer. These taste delicious on their own, or you can serve them with a spicy dipping sauce, such as Asian chili sauce.

1. Preheat the oven to 450°F. Spray a baking sheet with nonstick cooking spray. Place the coconut flakes in a bowl.

2. In a medium bowl, beat the eggs and then stir in the ice water.

3. Stir in the flour until the batter has a runny consistency similar to pancake batter. Add more flour or ice water if needed.

4. Coat each shrimp in the batter, using your fingers to do so. Dip the shrimp into the coconut, holding it by the tail, and then lay it on the baking sheet. Continue with the remainder of the shrimp.

5. Bake the shrimp until it is golden brown on the bottom. Turn over and cook the other side until done.

Terrific Tempura Batter

Few fried foods are as irresistible as Japanese tempura, consisting of seafood or vegetables coated in a light, crispy batter. It's easy to make this restaurant favorite at home—just remember to use ice water and a cold egg, and to not overbeat the batter.

Easy Oyster Stew

Serve this simple stew with oyster crackers. For a richer dish, melt 2 tablespoons of butter over low heat before adding the liquid, and replace the milk with light cream or half-and-half.

1. In a medium saucepan, bring the reserved juice and milk to a boil over medium-high heat, stirring.

2. When the liquid is just starting to bubble, stir in the salt, pepper, thyme, lemon juice, and Tabasco sauce. (Turn the heat down if needed so that the liquid is just simmering.)

3. Add the oysters and bring to a boil.

4. Add the canned corn.

5. Turn down the heat and simmer for 3 or 4 minutes to give the flavors a chance to blend. Serve hot.

Serves 4

Preparation time:
5 minutes
Cooking time: 10 minutes

½ cup reserved juice from
   canned oysters
2 cups milk
1 teaspoon salt
¼ teaspoon black pepper
1 teaspoon dried thyme
1 tablespoon lemon juice
½ teaspoon Tabasco
   sauce
24 canned Pacific oysters
1 cup drained canned
   corn

Baked Fish Fillets

Serves 4

Preparation time:
5–10 minutes
Cooking time:
15–20 minutes

1 tablespoon soy sauce
1 tablespoon lemon juice
2 teaspoons bottled
    minced ginger
Black pepper, to taste
½ teaspoon Asian chili
    sauce, or to taste
1 teaspoon salt
1 pound fish fillets, fresh
½ pound broccoli florets
10 baby carrots, cut in
    half

Cooking the vegetables with the fish means they are flavored with the natural fish juices and lemony soy sauce mixture. Cooked rice is all that's needed to turn this into a complete meal.

1. Preheat oven to 375°F.

2. In a small bowl, stir together the soy sauce, lemon juice, ginger, pepper, and chili sauce. Rub the salt over the fish fillets to season.

3. Cut four sheets of foil, each at least 12" square. Place each fish fillet in the middle of a sheet of foil and brush the fillet with a portion of the lemon juice mixture. Place one-quarter of the broccoli and carrots around the fish.

4. Fold the foil over the fish and vegetables, crimping the edges to seal. Continue with the remainder of the fish fillets.

5. Bake at 375°F for 15 to 20 minutes, until the fish is cooked through and flakes easily (be careful not to overcook the fish).

Selecting Fresh Fish

When choosing fish fillets, look for a clean smell and a firm texture, without any discoloration or brown spots. Avoid fish that have a strong fishy smell, or yield to gentle pressure. When selecting whole fish, check for bright eyes and a shiny skin.

Easy Seafood Rice Pilaf

Microwaving the rice considerably shortens the cooking time in this simple shrimp and rice dish.

Serves 4

Preparation time:
5 minutes
Cooking time: 15 minutes

1½ cups long-grain white
 rice
3 cups chicken broth
1 tablespoon olive oil
1 onion, peeled, chopped
2 cloves garlic, finely
 chopped
½ teaspoon paprika, or to
 taste
1 teaspoon salt
¾ pound large shrimp,
 shelled, deveined
1 tablespoon lemon juice

1. Place the rice and broth in a microwave-safe casserole dish. Cover with microwave-safe plastic wrap. Cook the rice on high heat for 8 minutes.

2. Check and continue microwaving until the rice is cooked (about 10 minutes). Do not stir the rice. Once the rice is finished cooking, let it stand for 5 minutes.

3. While the rice is cooking, heat the olive oil in a skillet on medium-high heat. Add the onion and garlic. Sprinkle the paprika over the onion. Sauté for 4 to 5 minutes, until the onion is softened (turn the heat down to medium if needed).

4. Sprinkle the salt over the shrimp and add to the pan. Splash the shrimp with the lemon juice and sauté until they turn pink, taking care not to overcook.

5. Fluff the rice with a fork. Stir in the shrimp mixture. Serve hot.

Four-Ingredient Baked Ginger Fish Fillets

Baking fish in foil is a great way to add extra flavor to mild fish such as red snapper and halibut.

Serves 4

Preparation time:
10 minutes
Cooking time:
15–20 minutes

2 tablespoons soy sauce
2 tablespoons lemon juice
1 tablespoon chopped
    fresh gingerroot
Freshly ground black
    pepper, to taste
1½ pounds fish fillets,
    fresh or frozen

1. Preheat the oven to 375°F.

2. In a small bowl, stir together the soy sauce, lemon juice, ginger, and pepper.

3. Cut four sheets of foil, each at least 12" square. Place a fish fillet in the middle of a sheet of foil. Brush with one-quarter of the lemon juice mixture.

4. Fold the foil over the fish, crimping the edges to seal. Continue with the remainder of the fish fillets.

5. Bake at 375°F for 15 to 20 minutes, until the fish is cooked through and flakes easily (be careful not to overcook the fish).

Cooking with Frozen Fish

In many cases, frozen fish can be taken straight from the freezer and cooked without thawing, as long as you allow for extra cooking time. If you do thaw the fish before cooking, always thaw it in the refrigerator. Frozen fish should be used within three months.

Easy Oysters Rockefeller on French Bread

Don't have any cooked bacon on hand? The microwave is perfect for cooking crisp bacon quickly: just place the bacon on a plate lined with paper towels, cover with another paper towel, and microwave on high heat for 2 to 3 minutes until the bacon is cooked.

1. Preheat the broiler. Spray the broiling rack with nonstick cooking spray.

2. Combine the spinach, bread crumbs, bacon, cream, reserved oyster juice, nutmeg, salt, garlic powder, chili sauce, and Worcestershire sauce in a blender. Process until smooth, stopping and scraping the bottom and sides if needed.

3. Add the oysters and process again until smooth.

4. Cut the French bread into 1-inch pieces. Spread a heaping tablespoon of the spinach/oyster dip on the bread. Sprinkle 1 to 1½ tablespoons of Parmesan cheese on top. Continue with the remainder of the bread.

5. Broil on high 9 inches from the heat source for about 2 minutes, until the cheese is bubbling and the bread is golden. Be careful not to burn the bread.

Serves 6

Preparation time: 5 minutes
Cooking time: 25 minutes

10 ounces frozen spinach, thawed, drained
6 tablespoons crushed bread crumbs
4 slices cooked bacon, chopped
¼ cup light cream
3 tablespoons reserved canned oyster juice
¼ teaspoon ground nutmeg
½ teaspoon salt
¼ teaspoon garlic powder
½ teaspoon chili sauce
1 tablespoon Worcestershire sauce
12 canned Pacific oysters, drained
1 loaf French bread
1 cup shredded Parmesan cheese

Shrimp Pad Thai Stir-Fry

Serves 4

Preparation time:
15 minutes
Cooking time:
7–10 minutes

8 ounces rice stick
  noodles
2 tablespoons lemon juice
2 tablespoons white
  vinegar
1½ tablespoons tomato
  sauce
2 tablespoons brown
  sugar
2 tablespoons vegetable
  oil
2 teaspoons bottled
  minced garlic
1 tablespoon bottled
  chopped red jalapeño
  peppers
20 large shrimp, peeled,
  deveined
2 eggs, beaten
1 cup mung bean sprouts
1 cup chopped fresh
  cilantro leaves
⅓ cup chopped peanuts

Boiling the soaking water for the noodles shortens the amount of time it takes for them to soften. If you purchase shrimp that is already peeled and deveined, and soften the noodles ahead of time, the pad thai will be ready in under 15 minutes.

1. In a microwave-safe bowl, bring 4 cups of water to a boil (this will take 3 to 5 minutes). Remove the bowl from the microwave. Place the noodles in the boiling water to soften. In a small bowl, stir together the lemon juice, vinegar, tomato sauce, and brown sugar.

2. Heat the vegetable oil in a wok or skillet. When the oil is hot, add the garlic and chopped jalapeños. Stir-fry for a few seconds, then add the shrimp. Cook until the shrimp turn pink (about 2 minutes).

3. Push the shrimp to the side and add the beaten egg in the middle. Scramble the egg in the pan.

4. Add the softened noodles. Stir the lemon juice and tomato sauce mixture and pour over the noodles.

5. Stir in the mung bean sprouts. Stir in the cilantro leaves. Stir-fry for a couple of minutes to combine the ingredients. Garnish with the chopped peanuts.

A Southeast Asian Specialty

Thailand's signature noodle dish, pad thai—literally meaning Thai fried dish or mixture—has a universal appeal. The distinguishing characteristic of pad thai is the intriguing mixture of sweet-and-sour and spicy flavors. For an extra touch, serve the pad thai with an assortment of lime wedges, red chilies, and extra peanuts.

Sicilian-Style Swordfish

Lemon juice tenderizes the fish while olive oil disperses the flavor of the herbs in this easy recipe. If you don't have bottled minced garlic on hand, you can substitute ¼ teaspoon garlic powder or 2 minced garlic cloves.

1. Preheat the broiler. Spray the broiling rack with nonstick spray.

2. In a bowl, whisk together the olive oil, lemon juice, garlic, oregano, parsley, and pepper.

3. Pour the marinade into a large resealable plastic bag. Add the swordfish and close up the bag. Marinate for 10 minutes, turning once or twice to make sure the steaks are coated.

4. Place the swordfish on the broiling rack approximately 4 inches from the heat source. Broil for 4 minutes, turn, and cook for 4 to 6 minutes more, until the swordfish is just done.

Serves 4

Preparation time:
15 minutes
Cooking time:
8–10 minutes

⅓ cup olive oil
⅓ cup lemon juice
2 teaspoons bottled
   minced garlic
½ teaspoon dried
   oregano
2 teaspoons dried parsley
¼ teaspoon black pepper
4 swordfish steaks

Quick Fettuccine and Tuna with Marinara Sauce

Serves 4

Preparation time:
10 minutes
Cooking time: 10 minutes

1 (28-ounce) can plum
  tomatoes with juice
1 tablespoon bottled
  minced garlic
2 tablespoons minced
  onion
1 tablespoon red wine
  vinegar
¼ cup chopped fresh
  basil leaves
¼ cup extra-virgin olive oil
1 teaspoon salt
¼ teaspoon black pepper
1 rib celery, cut diagonally
  into thin slices
2 (6-ounce) cans tuna,
  drained
1 pound leftover cooked
  fettuccine

*Using the blender takes most of the work out of making
tomato-based marinara sauce, which is then enriched with
tuna. You can, of course, cook a fresh batch of pasta
instead of reheating leftover cooked pasta if desired.*

1. Combine the tomatoes, garlic, onion, red wine vinegar, basil, olive oil, salt, and pepper in a blender or food processor. Process until it forms a thick sauce.

2. Add half the celery and process again. Add the remaining half.

3. Pour the pasta sauce into a large skillet. Add the tuna, using a spatula to break it up. Bring to a boil, turn down the heat and simmer, uncovered, for 5 minutes.

4. Reheat the cooked pasta (see Serving Leftover Pasta, page 169).

5. Place the pasta in a bowl and toss with the sauce.

Fish—Perfect For Low-Fat Diets

*Fish is an excellent choice for a low-fat diet. Lean fish such as cod and
turbot have a fat content of under 3 percent. Oily fish such as salmon
and trout are a good natural source of healthy omega-3 fatty acids.
Both types of fish should be included in any diet plan, including a
low-fat one.*

Seafood au Gratin

If using frozen fish fillets, thaw before cooking. You can spice up the dish by adding a pinch of paprika to the white sauce.

Serves 4

Preparation time:
5 minutes
Cooking time: 25 minutes

1 portion White Sauce for
   Seafood (page 245)
1 pound fish fillets
1 teaspoon salt
½ cup grated Cheddar
   cheese

1. Preheat the oven to 375°F. Spray an 8" x 8" baking dish with nonstick cooking spray.

2. In a pan or the microwave, reheat the White Sauce for Seafood (page 245).

3. Rub the salt over the fish to season. Lay the fish fillets out in the baking dish.

4. Pour the white sauce over the fish. Sprinkle the cheese on top.

5. Bake the fish for 25 minutes, or until it is cooked through.

Teriyaki Shrimp

A combination of sweet and spicy flavors, Asian sweet chili sauce is available in the ethnic or international section of most supermarkets.

1 pound large shrimp,
   shelled, deveined, tail
   on
½ teaspoon salt
3 tablespoons vegetable
   oil, divided
1 teaspoon minced garlic
1 teaspoon minced ginger
1 teaspoon Asian sweet
   chili sauce
½ pound snow peas
½ portion Teriyaki Sauce
   (page 245)
2 green onions, chopped
   into thirds

1. Place the shrimp in a bowl and toss with the salt.

2. Heat 2 tablespoons oil in a large skillet over medium-high heat. Stir for a few seconds, then add the shrimp. Stir-fry the shrimp, stirring constantly, until they turn pink (about 2 minutes). Remove the shrimp from the pan.

3. Heat 1 tablespoon oil in the pan. Add the garlic, ginger, and chili sauce. Stir for a few seconds, then add the snow peas. Stir-fry for 2 minutes, stirring constantly. (Splash the snow peas with 1 tablespoon of water if they begin to dry out.)

4. Add the teriyaki sauce to the pan and bring to a boil.

5. Return the shrimp to the pan. Stir in the green onion. Stir-fry for a minute to combine all the ingredients. Serve hot.

Quick-Cooking Seafood

Speedy cooking times make seafood the perfect choice for busy weeknights. In fact, the main concern when preparing fish and shellfish is not to overcook it. Overcooked seafood loses its natural juiciness and can be rather tough. Cook fish until the skin flakes easily with a fork. For shrimp and prawns, cook until the skin just turns pink.

Simple Seafood Ratatouille

Precooking the eggplant in water helps prevent it from soaking up too much oil when it is combined with the other ingredients.

1. Place the eggplant in a microwave-safe dish and cover with water. Cover the dish with microwave-safe plastic. Microwave on high heat for 2 minutes. Continue microwaving for 30 seconds at a time, if needed, until the eggplant is softened.

2. Heat the olive oil in a skillet on medium-high heat. Add the onion. Sauté for 2 minutes, then add the zucchini. Sauté for 2 to 3 more minutes, until the vegetables are softened.

3. Add the shrimp. Sauté for 3 to 5 minutes, or until they turn pink.

4. Add the tomatoes and bring to a boil. Stir in the red wine vinegar, salt, and pepper.

5. Add the eggplant. Simmer for 2 to 3 minutes, to combine all the flavors. Serve hot.

Serves 4

Preparation time:
10 minutes
Cooking time: 20 minutes

1 large eggplant, thinly sliced
1 tablespoon olive oil
1 medium onion, peeled, chopped
1 zucchini, thinly sliced
1 pound large shrimp, peeled, tail on
1 (28-ounce) can crushed tomatoes with herbs, drained
1 tablespoon red wine vinegar
½ teaspoon salt
¼ teaspoon black pepper

Foil-Wrapped Fish Fillets with Dill

Serves 4

Preparation time:
5–10 minutes
Cooking time:
15–20 minutes

1½ teaspoons salt
4 (5-ounce) fish fillets
¾ cup plain yogurt
1½ teaspoons granulated
    sugar
1½ teaspoons Dijon
    mustard
1 tablespoon lemon juice
2 teaspoons fresh dill
⅛ teaspoon black pepper

This sauce would go well with more strongly flavored fish, such as salmon. Serve the fish with sliced tomato and lemon wedges.

1. Preheat the oven to 375°F. Rub the salt over the fish to season.

2. In a small bowl, stir together the yogurt, sugar, mustard, lemon juice, dill, and pepper.

3. Cut four sheets of foil, each at least 12" square. Place each fish fillet in the middle of a sheet of foil. Lightly brush each fillet with a small portion of the yogurt mixture. Fold the foil over the fish, crimping the edges to seal.

4. Bake at 375°F for 15 to 20 minutes, until the fish is cooked through and flakes easily (be careful not to overcook).

5. While the fish is baking, heat the remainder of the sauce on low heat. Keep warm while the fish is cooking. Serve the fish with the heated sauce.

Storing Fresh Fish

Since fish is highly perishable, it's important to place it in cold storage as soon as you arrive home from the store. Remove the fish from its packaging and rinse under cold water. Rewrap the fish loosely in plastic wrap or wax paper. Store the fish in the coldest part of the refrigerator and use within two days.

Pan-Fried Mussels in Coconut Curry Sauce

Canned mussels take the work out of cleaning and cooking mussels in this simple curry dish. Use leftover coconut milk to make Steamed Coconut Rice (page 153) to serve with the mussels.

1. Heat the olive oil in a skillet over medium-high heat. Add the onion and garlic. Add the curry powder, stirring to mix it in with the onion.

2. Add the tomato. Cook for 1 minute, then add the canned mussels. Cook, stirring occasionally, until the onion is shiny and has softened (4 to 5 minutes total cooking time for the onion).

3. Add the coconut milk and chicken broth to the pan. Bring to a boil.

4. Stir in the raisins. Turn down the heat and simmer, covered, for 10 minutes. Season with the salt and pepper.

Serves 4

Preparation time: 5–10 minutes
Cooking time: 15 minutes

2 teaspoons olive oil
½ cup chopped onion
1 teaspoon chopped garlic
2 teaspoons curry powder
2 plum tomatoes, chopped
2 cups canned mussels
¾ cup coconut milk
¼ cup chicken broth
½ cup raisins
¼ teaspoon salt
⅛ teaspoon black pepper, or to taste

Mussels Simmered in White Wine

Be sure to discard any mussels that haven't opened after cooking. Serve the mussels with a good crusty bread for dipping into the wine and cream mixture.

Serves 3

Preparation time:
15 minutes
Cooking time: 15 minutes

30 mussels
1 tablespoon olive oil
1 clove garlic, finely
  chopped
2 shallots, chopped
2 teaspoons dried parsley
1 teaspoon dried thyme
1 tomato, chopped
¼ teaspoon red pepper
  flakes
1 cup dry white wine
⅓ cup light cream

1. Clean and debeard the mussels (don't remove the shells).

2. Heat the olive oil in a large skillet over medium-high heat. Add the garlic and shallots. Sprinkle the parsley and thyme over the shallots. Sauté for 2 to 3 minutes, until the shallots turn golden. Add the tomato and cook for a minute. Stir in the red pepper flakes.

3. Add the wine and bring to a boil. Add the mussels. Cook, covered, on high heat until the mussels start to open (4 to 6 minutes). Using a slotted spoon, remove the mussels as soon as they open.

4. Add the cream to the pan. Bring to a boil. Stir to mix everything together and serve over the mussels.

5. Place the mussels in a large bowl or individual serving bowls. Spoon the cream mixture on top.

How to Clean Mussels

Cleaning mussels is easy and only takes a few minutes. Rinse the mussels under cold running water, scrubbing with a stiff brush to remove any dirt. Grab and remove the "beard" (the fibers sticking out of the shell). Soak the mussels in cold water for 5 minutes and rinse again before using.

Fish Stick Casserole

Here's a way to put leftover pasta
and sauce to use. Simple Linguine with Tomato Sauce
(page 166) would work well in this recipe.

Serves 2

Preparation time:
5 minutes
Cooking time: 30 minutes

1 cup frozen peas
2 cups leftover pasta with
    sauce
12 fish sticks
1 (10-ounce) can cream
    of mushroom soup

1. Preheat the oven to 425°F. Grease a 8"×8" baking dish.

2. Place the frozen peas in a microwave-safe bowl. Cover with microwave plastic wrap, leaving one corner open to vent steam. Microwave the peas on high heat for 2 minutes, and then for 30 seconds at a time, until cooked (total cooking time should be 2 to 3 minutes).

3. Spread 1 cup of the leftover pasta over the bottom of the baking dish. Carefully arrange the fish sticks on top. Stir together the soup and microwaved peas. Spoon over the fish sticks.

4. Spread the remaining cup of leftover pasta on top. Bake for 30 minutes, or until the fish sticks are fully cooked. Serve hot.

Indian Seafood Curry

Serves 4

Preparation time:
5 minutes
Cooking time: 15 minutes

2 tablespoons vegetable
   oil
1 teaspoon bottled
   minced ginger
1 medium onion, chopped
1 tablespoon curry
   powder
1 medium zucchini, thinly
   sliced
¾ cup coconut milk
1½ cups chicken broth
1 tablespoon lime juice
¼ teaspoon black pepper,
   or to taste
2 cups instant rice
1 pound cooked peeled,
   deveined fresh shrimp

If fresh cooked shrimp is unavailable, you can cook the shrimp by stir-frying until they turn pink, or boil them in a large saucepan with 6 cups water for 2 minutes.

1. Heat the oil in a skillet over medium heat. Add the ginger and onion. Stir in the curry powder. Add the zucchini. Cook for 3 to 4 minutes, until the onion is softened.

2. Add the coconut milk and chicken broth and bring to a boil. Stir in the lime juice and pepper. Stir in the instant rice, making sure it is completely wet.

3. Cover the saucepan and let sit for 4 minutes.

4. Add the cooked shrimp and let sit for another minute, or until the rice has completely absorbed the liquid.

Chapter 10
Rice and Other Grains

Basic Cooked Instant Rice

Serves 2

Preparation: 2 minutes
Cooking time:
8–10 minutes

¾ cup water
¾ cup cooked instant
    long-grain rice
⅛ teaspoon salt, or to
    taste
Black pepper, to taste

Using instant rice (also called quick-cooking rice) considerably speeds up the cooking time. While these general instructions should work for most types of instant long-grain cooked rice, be sure to follow the package directions if they are different.

1. Bring the water to a boil in a medium saucepan.

2. Stir in the rice, making sure it is thoroughly wet. Stir in the salt and pepper.

3. Remove the rice from the heat. Cover the saucepan and let stand for 5 minutes, or until the water is absorbed.

4. Fluff up the rice with a fork and serve.

Easy Flavored Rice

Serves 4

Cooking time:
10–12 minutes

¾ cups chicken broth
¾ cup coconut milk
½ teaspoon curry powder
1½ cups cooked instant
    long-grain rice
2 teaspoons margarine
¼ teaspoon salt, or to
    taste
Black pepper, to taste

Cooking rice in broth, juice, or another liquid is a great way to add extra flavor. Feel free to load up the rice by stirring in ½ cup of golden Sultana raisins.

1. Bring the chicken broth, coconut milk, and curry powder to a boil in a medium saucepan.

2. Stir in the rice, making sure it is thoroughly wet. Stir in the margarine, salt, and pepper.

3. Remove the saucepan from the heat.

4. Cover the saucepan and let stand for 5 minutes. Fluff up with a fork and serve.

Pork Fried Rice

Tamari soy sauce and sweet chili sauce are available in the ethnic or international section of many supermarkets. If you're using leftover pork that was marinated (for example, leftover Orange-Flavored Pork Chops, page 118), you can leave them out altogether if desired, or simply use 1 tablespoon of regular soy sauce.

page 118

Serves 4

Preparation time: 5–10 minutes
Cooking time: 10 minutes

2 large eggs
⅛ teaspoon freshly ground black or white pepper
2 tablespoons vegetable oil
2 teaspoons chopped garlic
1 teaspoon sweet chili sauce
½ medium onion, chopped
1 cup diced leftover cooked pork or ham
3 cups cold cooked rice
1 red bell pepper, cut into thin strips
1 tablespoon tamari soy sauce, or to taste

1. In a small bowl, lightly beat the egg. Stir in the pepper.

2. Heat the oil in a skillet on medium-high heat. Add the garlic, chili sauce, and onion. Stir until the onion begins to soften. Push the onion to the sides of the pan. In the middle of the pan, add the beaten egg. Stir quickly to scramble, then mix with the onion.

3. Push the egg to the sides of the pan. Add the diced pork or ham in the middle and stir for a minute to heat through.

4. Add the rice to the pan. Cook, stirring constantly, for 2 to 3 minutes, until the rice is heated through and mixed with the other ingredients.

5. Stir in the bell pepper and the tamari soy sauce. Stir for another minute to cook the bell pepper and mix all the ingredients. Serve hot.

Perfect Rice for Fried Rice

Fried rice tastes best with cooked rice that is at least one day old. Before cooking, wet your fingers and run them through the rice to remove any clumps. This will ensure that the rice cooks more evenly.

Mexican Fried Rice

Serves 4

Preparation time:
5–8 minutes
Cooking time: 10 minutes

3 tablespoons vegetable
  oil, divided
½ medium yellow onion,
  finely chopped
1 tablespoon jarred
  chopped jalapeño
  peppers
1 tomato, diced
1 cup canned corn niblets
3 cups cold cooked rice
½ teaspoon ground cumin
2 green onions, finely
  sliced
¼ teaspoon salt, or to
  taste
⅛ teaspoon black pepper,
  or to taste

This spicy side dish would go nicely with a less highly seasoned main dish, such as Simple Steamed Chicken Dinner (page 82).

1. Heat 1½ tablespoons oil in a nonstick skillet on medium heat. Add the onion. Cook for 4 to 5 minutes, until the onion is softened.

2. Stir in the chopped jalapeño peppers. Stir in the tomato. Cook for a minute and stir in the canned corn. Remove the vegetables from the pan.

3. Heat 1½ tablespoons oil in the pan. Add the rice. Cook, stirring, for 1 to 2 minutes, until heated through. Stir in the ground cumin.

4. Return the vegetables to the pan. Stir in the green onions. Stir to mix everything together. Season with the salt and pepper. Serve hot.

How to Cook Long-Grain Rice

Cooking rice the traditional way gives you an alternative to always having to use instant rice on nights when time is limited. To cook the rice, bring the rice and water to boil in a medium saucepan, using 2 cups water for every cup of rice. When the water is boiling, turn the heat down to medium-low and partially cover. Continue cooking until "holes" start to appear in the rice. Cover fully, turn the heat down to low. Let the rice steam for at least 15 minutes more, until the water is fully absorbed.

Easy Apple Risotto

Traditionalists insist that the only way to make risotto is to stand over the pot, painstakingly stirring the liquid into the rice. However, simply letting the rice simmer in broth and apple juice does a reasonably good job, leaving you free to prepare the rest of the meal.

Serves 4

Preparation time:
5 minutes
Cooking time: 25 minutes

2 tablespoons olive oil
1 medium red apple, cored and sliced
1 teaspoon cinnamon, or to taste
1 cup arborio short-grain rice
2 tablespoons golden raisins
1½ cups chicken broth
1 cup apple juice
3 tablespoons shredded Cheddar cheese

1. Heat the olive oil in a skillet on medium-high heat. Add the apple and cinnamon. Cook, stirring, for about 2 minutes, until the apples start to become crisp.

2. Add the rice and cook for about 2 minutes, until the grains start to become shiny and translucent. Stir in the raisins.

3. Add the chicken broth and apple juice.

4. Turn the heat down to low, cover, and simmer for 20 minutes.

5. Stir in the cheese and serve.

Rustic Risotto

A classic dish from northern Italy, risotto is famous for its rich, creamy texture. The distinctive flavor and texture of risotto come from using a super-absorbent rice with grains that stick together when cooked. Arborio is the most popular rice for making risotto in North America, but other varieties of Italian rice, such as carnaroli, can also be used.

Creamy Risotto Side Dish

Serves 4

Preparation time:
5–10 minutes
Cooking time:
17–18 minutes

1 cup frozen baby peas
1 cup arborio or other
   short-grain rice
2 cups chicken broth,
   divided
½ teaspoon dried basil
   leaves
½ teaspoon dried
   oregano
½ teaspoon garlic powder
⅛ teaspoon black pepper,
   or to taste
1 teaspoon salt, divided
⅓ cup shredded
   Parmesan cheese

This won't have quite the same texture and flavor as authentic risotto, but it's a good stand-in for nights when you're in a hurry.

1. Place the frozen peas in a microwave-safe casserole dish. Cover with microwave plastic wrap, leaving one corner open to vent steam. Microwave the peas on high heat for 2 minutes, and then for 30 seconds at a time until cooked (total cooking time should be 2 to 3 minutes).

2. Add the rice and 1½ cups broth. Stir in the basil, oregano, garlic powder, pepper, and ½ teaspoon salt. Cover the dish with microwave-safe plastic wrap and microwave for 5 minutes.

3. Stir in ½ cup broth and ½ teaspoon salt. Microwave on high for 5 more minutes.

4. Stir, cover, and microwave for 5 minutes, or until the liquid is mainly absorbed and the rice grains are tender.

5. Stir in the Parmesan cheese. Serve hot.

Healthy Brown Rice

While instant brown rice is a quick and easy alternative to making regular brown rice, it can be hard to find. Another option is to make brown rice ahead of time and reheat it later.

Serves 4

Preparation time:
5 minutes
Cooking time:
50–55 minutes

1 cup brown rice
2¼ cups water

1. Bring the rice and water to boil in a medium saucepan.

2. Reduce the heat to low-medium.

3. Cook the rice, uncovered, until the water is absorbed (40 to 45 minutes).

4. Let stand for 10 minutes. Fluff and serve.

Rice Reheating Tips

For safety's sake, it's important to cool down and refrigerate the cooked rice within 2 hours after cooking. To reheat, combine the rice with 1 to 2 tablespoons water in a saucepan and cook over low heat, or heat in the microwave (follow your microwave's instructions for reheating food).

Jambalaya

This stir-fry allows you to enjoy the flavors in slow simmered jambalaya during busy weekdays. If you like, replace the spices with store-bought creole seasoning.

Serves 4

Preparation time:
5 minutes
Cooking time: 15 minutes

1½ cups Basic Cooked Instant Rice (page 146)
2 tablespoons olive oil, divided
1 garlic clove, finely chopped
½ medium onion, finely chopped
1 red bell pepper, thinly sliced
2 cups cooked shrimp
⅛ teaspoon salt, or to taste
⅛ teaspoon black pepper, or to taste
¼ teaspoon Tabasco sauce, or to taste
1 cup canned chopped tomatoes with juice
1 teaspoon chopped fresh thyme leaves

1. Prepare the Basic Cooked Instant Rice (page 146). Heat 1 tablespoon oil in a large heavy skillet or wok over medium-high heat. Add the garlic and onion. Stir-fry for about 2 minutes, until the onion begins to soften.

2. Add the red bell pepper. Stir-fry for 1 minute until it becomes tender. Add the cooked shrimp. Cook for 1 minute.

3. Heat 1 tablespoon oil in a medium saucepan. Add the cooked rice, stirring for a minute until it begins to turn light brown. Stir the salt, pepper, and Tabasco sauce into the rice.

4. Add the tomatoes and thyme leaves to the rice. Bring to a boil.

5. Add the shrimp and vegetables to the pan. Cook for another minute, stirring to mix everything together. Serve hot.

Steamed Coconut Rice

Microwave basmati rice takes less time to make and still has the rich nutty flavor of regular boiled scented rice.

Serves 6

Preparation time:
5–10 minutes
Cooking time: 22 minutes

1½ cups scented rice
1 tablespoon margarine
2 shallots
1¼ cups coconut milk
1¾ cups water
½ teaspoon salt

1. Rinse the rice in cold water and drain.

2. Place the margarine and chopped shallots in a microwave-safe 3-quart casserole dish. Microwave on high heat for 1½ minutes, stir, then microwave for 30 seconds at a time until the shallots are tender.

3. Add the coconut milk, water, rice, and salt. Microwave on high for 10 minutes.

4. Stir the rice. Cover the dish with microwave-safe wax paper. Microwave for 3 minutes and then for 1 minute at a time until the liquid is absorbed.

5. Remove the dish from the heat. Let stand for 5 minutes. Fluff and serve.

Or Cook it the Regular Way

Another way to cut down on the time it takes to prepare rice for dinner is to boil the rice in advance so that it just needs to be reheated. To cook basmati rice on the stovetop, sauté the margarine and shallots in a skillet until the shallots are softened. Add the rice, coconut milk, water, and salt and bring to a boil, uncovered. Turn down the heat to medium and boil, uncovered, until the liquid is nearly absorbed (10 to 12 minutes). Continue cooking for a few more minutes until the water is absorbed.

Spanish Rice Side Dish

This simple side dish is incredibly easy to make. To turn it into a main meal, simply add 2 cups of cooked shrimp or leftover cooked chicken.

Serves 4

Preparation time:
5 minutes
Cooking time: 10 minutes

⅔ cup tomato juice
1⅓ cups water
2 cups instant rice
½ teaspoon salt, or to taste
⅛ teaspoon black pepper
1 tablespoon olive oil, divided
2 cloves garlic, chopped
1 onion, chopped
1 teaspoon paprika, or to taste
1 green bell pepper, chopped into chunks

1. In a saucepan, bring the tomato juice and water to a boil. Stir in the rice, salt, and pepper. Remove from the heat, cover, and let stand for 5 minutes.

2. While the rice is cooking, prepare the vegetables: Heat the olive oil in a heavy skillet or wok on medium-high heat. Add the garlic and onion. Sprinkle the paprika over the onion and sauté for about 2 minutes, until the onion begins to soften.

3. Add the green pepper and continue cooking until the vegetables are softened.

4. Stir the cooked vegetables into the rice. Stir with a fork before serving.

Microwave Rice Pilaf

Feel free to dress up this easy side dish by adding a few slices of apple with the onion. On the other hand, when you're in a hurry you can leave out the onion—stir in the cinnamon and margarine after removing the rice from the microwave.

Serves 4

Preparation time:
5 minutes
Cooking time:
20–22 minutes

½ medium onion,
   chopped
1 tablespoon margarine
½ teaspoon ground
   cinnamon
1 cup long-grain white
   rice
1 cup orange juice
1 cup water
¼ cup raisins

1. Place the onion and margarine in a microwave-safe 2-quart casserole dish. Sprinkle the ground cinnamon on top. Microwave on high heat for 1½ minutes. Stir and microwave for 30 seconds at a time until the onion is tender.

2. Add the white rice, orange juice, and water. Microwave on high heat for 10 minutes. Stir the rice and microwave for short periods (first 2 minutes, then 1 minute) at a time until the water is absorbed and the rice is cooked (total cooking time for the rice should be 14 to 15 minutes).

3. Remove the rice from the microwave. Stir in the raisins.

4. Let the cooked rice stand for 5 minutes. Fluff and serve.

Know Your Rice

The main difference between long- and short-grain rice isn't the length of the grains but rather the type of starch each one contains. Long-grain rice is high in amylase, which makes it turn out light and fluffy. Short-grain rice (like the arborio rice) contains a higher ratio of amylopectin, which makes the rice grains sticky. If you like your rice light and fluffy, always use long-grain rice when making plain rice to serve as a side dish.

Easy Italian Rice Pilaf

Serves 4

Preparation time:
10 minutes
Cooking time:
13–15 minutes

1 tablespoon olive oil
2 shallots, peeled and
    chopped
1 teaspoon bottled
    minced garlic
1 tablespoon chopped
    sun-dried tomato
    strips
1 cup chopped red bell
    pepper
1 cup drained canned
    mushrooms
¼ teaspoon cayenne
    pepper
1 tablespoon balsamic
    vinegar
2¼ cups reduced-sodium
    chicken broth
2 cups instant white rice

*This comforting dish is full of flavor without being too heavy.
Reduced-sodium chicken broth is available in resealable cartons
in many supermarkets.*

1. Heat the olive oil in a skillet on medium heat. Add the shallots, garlic, and sun-dried tomato strips. Sauté for 3 to 4 minutes, until the shallots are softened.

2. Add the chopped bell pepper and the mushrooms. Sprinkle the cayenne pepper on top. Splash the vegetables with the balsamic vinegar. Cook until the vegetables are softened (total cooking time is about 5 minutes).

3. Add the chicken broth. Bring to a boil.

4. Stir in the instant rice. Cover and let stand for 5 minutes. Serve hot.

Polenta Chips

The polenta should be poured into a large baking sheet after cooking. If you're not comfortable with deep-frying, bake the chips in a 450°F oven for 20 minutes, or until they turn golden.

Serves 6

Preparation time:
10 minutes
Cooking time: 20 minutes

4 cups vegetable oil
1 cup cooked quick-
 cooking polenta,
 cooled
½ cup cornstarch
1 teaspoon cayenne
 pepper

1. In a large saucepan or deep-fat fryer, preheat the oil to 360°F.

2. Cut the polenta into thin strips, julienne-style.

3. In a small bowl, combine the cornstarch and cayenne pepper. Coat the polenta strips with this mixture.

4. When the oil is hot, carefully lower about 7 or 8 polenta chips into the hot oil (it's easiest to do this if you have a mesh basket). Deep-fry the chips until they turn golden brown (about 4 minutes).

5. Carefully remove the chips from the oil (if not using a mesh basket, lift the chips out with a slotted spoon). Drain the chips on paper towels. Continue with the remainder of the polenta chips. Serve immediately.

All about Polenta

Made from boiled cornmeal, polenta makes an interesting alternative to a side dish of rice, bread, or pasta. Although polenta is frequently boiled, it can also be baked. Taking only five minutes to make, quick-cooking polenta is available in many supermarkets. So is premade polenta, which comes packaged in tubes.

Savory Rice with Portobello Mushrooms

This simple side dish goes very nicely with chicken or other poultry. You can replace the white rice with instant brown rice or leftover Healthy Brown Rice (page 151).

Serves 4

Preparation time:
5–10 minutes
Cooking time:
10–12 minutes

2 cups instant white rice
2 cups vegetable stock
1 tablespoon margarine
1 medium onion, chopped
4 ounces portobello
  mushrooms, thinly
  sliced
2 teaspoons dried parsley
  flakes
1 teaspoon dried oregano
½ teaspoon salt

1. Cook the instant rice in the vegetable stock according to package directions or the instructions in Basic Cooked Instant Rice (page 146) (replace the water with vegetable stock).

2. Heat the margarine in a skillet on medium-high heat. Add the chopped onion.

3. Sauté the onions for 2 minutes, then add the portobello mushrooms.

4. Sauté for about 2 minutes until the onion is softened (turn down the heat to medium if the onion is cooking too quickly). Stir in the dried parsley, oregano, and salt while the onion is cooking.

5. Combine the mushrooms and onion with the cooked rice. Fluff with a fork and serve hot.

Chapter 11
Perfect Pasta

Angel Hair Pasta with Shrimp

Serves 4

Preparation time:
15 minutes
Cooking time: 15 minutes

3 quarts water
1½ teaspoons salt
¾ pound angel hair pasta
1 tablespoon olive oil
2 cloves garlic, minced
2 shallots, chopped
1 teaspoon dried basil
1 teaspoon dried oregano
1 tomato, chopped
1 pound peeled, deveined
    shrimp
2 tablespoons lemon juice
¼ cup light cream
¼ teaspoon black pepper

You can sprinkle ½ cup Parmesan cheese over the cooked shrimp and pasta. To reduce the preparation time, feel free to use leftover cooked pasta.

1. Bring a large pot with the water to a boil with the salt. Add the pasta to the boiling water. Cook until the pasta is cooked al dente. (Prepare the vegetables and shrimp while the pasta is cooking.)

2. Heat the olive oil in a skillet. Add the garlic and shallots. Sprinkle the dried basil and oregano over the shallots. Sauté for 3 to 4 minutes, until softened.

3. Add the tomato and the shrimp. Sauté the shrimp until they turn pink.

4. Add the lemon juice and cream. Cook until thickened. Stir in the pepper. Keep warm.

5. Drain the cooked pasta in a colander. Place in a large bowl. Toss the pasta with the sauce.

Pasta Cooking Tips

The key to making perfect pasta is to use plenty of water, giving the pasta room to move around, and stirring it to separate the strands. Ideally, pasta should be cooked until it reaches the al dente stage (an Italian term meaning "to the tooth"). Pasta that is cooked al dente is neither over- nor undercooked, but firm, slightly chewy, and offering a bit of resistance.

Basic Stir-Fried Noodles

Linguine and spaghetti both make handy substitutes for Chinese egg noodles. If you like, stir-fry one-half pound of fresh spinach leaves with the noodles.

Serves 4

Preparation time:
15 minutes
Cooking time: 8 minutes

2 quarts water
1 teaspoon salt
½ pound linguine
2 teaspoons soy sauce
½ teaspoon granulated
   sugar
1 tablespoon red wine
   vinegar
2 tablespoons vegetable
   oil
1 teaspoon bottled
   minced garlic

1. Bring a large pot with 2 quarts of water to a boil with the salt. Add the linguine to the boiling water. Cook for 3 to 4 minutes, until the linguine is cooked al dente. Drain in a colander.

2. In a small bowl, stir together the soy sauce, sugar, and red wine vinegar.

3. Heat the oil in a skillet over medium-high heat. Add the minced garlic. Stir for a few seconds, then add the noodles.

4. Stir for 1 minute, then pour in the sauce.

5. Stir-fry for 1 to 2 more minutes, until the noodles are heated through. Serve hot.

Marvelous Mian

They may not have the same intriguing shapes as Italian pasta, but there are many varieties of Chinese noodles, called mian. Delicate rice noodles, made from rice flour and water, are frequently added to soups and sometimes salads. Made with wheat flour, egg, and noodles, thick fresh Shanghai noodles are more than able to hold their own in stir-fries, absorbing the flavors of the sauce they are cooked with.

Colorful Pasta Primavera

Serves 4

Preparation time:
5–10 minutes
Cooking time: 10 minutes

2 tablespoons olive oil
1 white onion, peeled,
    chopped
1 zucchini, chopped
1 teaspoon dried basil
1 teaspoon dried oregano
1 cup drained canned
    asparagus tips
1 cup roasted red
    peppers
½ cup tomato sauce
½ cup light cream
½ teaspoon salt, or to
    taste
¼ teaspoon black pepper,
    or to taste
½ pound leftover cooked
    whole-wheat spaghetti
½ cup shredded
    Parmesan cheese

Traditionally, pasta primavera is loaded with fresh spring vegetables (the word primavera means "spring") but using canned vegetables helps you enjoy this Italian specialty on busy weeknights. Feel free to use homemade Roasted Red Peppers (page 221) or store-bought bottled roasted peppers.

1. Heat the olive oil in a skillet over medium-high heat. Add the onion. Sauté for a couple of minutes, then add the zucchini. Sprinkle the basil and oregano over the onion while it is cooking. Sauté until the vegetables are softened (turn the heat down to medium if needed).

2. Add the canned asparagus and the red peppers. Cook for a minute on medium heat.

3. Add the tomato sauce and cream. Cook, stirring, until it begins to bubble and thicken slightly. Stir in the salt and pepper. Turn down the heat and keep warm.

4. Reheat the cooked pasta (see Serving Leftover Pasta, page 169).

5. Place the pasta in a bowl and toss with the primavera sauce. Sprinkle with the Parmesan cheese.

Weeknight Linguine with Alfredo Sauce

Traditionally, this creamy sauce is served with fettuccine, a ribbon-shaped pasta made with egg, flour, and water. However, any dried pasta made with eggs will do.

Serves 4

Preparation time:
10 minutes
Cooking time: 20 minutes

3 quarts water
1½ teaspoons salt
¾ pound whole-wheat
    linguine
4 tablespoons margarine
3 tablespoons flour
1½ cups milk
⅔ cup grated Parmesan
    cheese
½ teaspoon dried
    oregano
½ teaspoon dried basil
½ teaspoon ground
    nutmeg, or to taste
Black pepper, to taste
1 (4.25-ounce) can
    crabmeat

1. Bring a large pot containing the water and salt to a boil. Add the pasta to the boiling water. Cook until the pasta is cooked al dente. (Prepare the Alfredo sauce while the pasta is cooking.)

2. In a small saucepan, melt the margarine on very low heat. Add the flour and stir continually to make a roux.

3. Add the milk and heat until it is nearly boiling, stirring with a whisk.

4. Add the Parmesan cheese and continue stirring with a whisk until the mixture has thickened. Stir in the oregano, basil, nutmeg, and pepper. Stir in the crabmeat and cook for another minute. Keep the sauce warm.

5. Drain the cooked pasta in a colander. Place in a large bowl. Toss the pasta with the sauce.

Pairing Pasta with Sauce

Timing is everything when it comes to combining pasta with a sauce. Ideally, the pasta should be sauced as soon as possible after it is cooked. If you are using dried pasta, start preparing the sauce after adding the pasta to the cooking water. Keep the sauce warm while cooking the pasta. Place the pasta in a warm bowl and toss thoroughly with the sauce.

Eggplant Penne

Serves 4

Preparation time:
5 minutes
Cooking time: 30 minutes

1 eggplant, about 1
   pound
5 tablespoons olive oil,
   divided
1 (28-ounce) can plum
   tomatoes, no salt
   added, with juice
1 tablespoon bottled
   minced garlic
2 tablespoons minced
   onion
1 tablespoon red wine
   vinegar
¼ cup chopped fresh
   basil leaves
1 teaspoon salt
¼ teaspoon black pepper
¾ pound penne
3 quarts water
1½ teaspoons salt

The necessary interval needed to cool the eggplant makes this dish a perfect candidate for advance prep work. Prepare the eggplant and sauce earlier in the day, and then they'll be ready when it comes time to cook the pasta.

1. Pierce the eggplant several times with a fork. Brush 1 tablespoon olive oil over the eggplant. Place in a large microwave-safe bowl and cover the dish with microwave-safe plastic wrap.

2. Microwave the eggplant for 2 minutes. Turn over, re-cover, and microwave for 2 minutes, or as needed until the eggplant has softened. Remove from the microwave and cool.

3. While the eggplant is cooling, prepare the sauce. Combine the tomatoes with juice, garlic, onion, red wine vinegar, basil, 4 tablespoons olive oil, salt, and pepper in a blender or food processor. Process until it forms a thick sauce. Chill for 15 minutes to blend the flavors.

4. When the eggplant is cool enough to handle, chop it into bite-size chunks. Pour the pasta sauce into a large skillet. Add the eggplant. Bring to a boil, turn down the heat and simmer, uncovered, for 5 minutes.

5. Bring a large pot with 3 quarts salted water to a boil. Add the penne to the boiling water. Cook until the pasta is cooked al dente. Drain in a colander. Toss the pasta with the eggplant and sauce.

Linguine with Marinated Artichoke Hearts

A combination of lemon, pepper, garlic, basil, and other season-ings, lemon pepper adds flavor to seafood and pasta dishes.

Serves 4

Preparation time:
5 minutes
Cooking time:
7–10 minutes

2 teaspoons olive oil
1 tablespoon bottled
    minced garlic
1 medium white onion,
    peeled, chopped
1 teaspoon lemon pepper,
    or to taste
Marinated Artichoke
    Hearts (page 229)
1 (28-ounce) can
    tomatoes, juice
    discarded
¾ pound leftover cooked
    linguine

1. Heat the olive oil in a skillet on medium-high heat. Add the garlic and onion. Sprinkle the lemon pepper over the onion. Sauté for 4 to 5 minutes, until the onion is softened.

2. Add the marinated artichoke hearts. Cook for 1 minute, stirring occasionally.

3. Add the canned tomatoes. Bring to a boil. Cook, stirring for a minute to heat through.

4. Reheat the pasta (see Serving Leftover Pasta, page 169). Place the pasta in a bowl and toss with the artichoke and tomato mixture.

Storing Leftover Pasta

Preparing pasta ahead of time cuts down substantially on cooking time, since you don't need to wait for the water to boil. To store cooked pasta for later use, toss the pasta with a small amount of vegetable oil (this keeps the cooled noodles from sticking together) and place in a reseal-able plastic bag in the refrigerator.

Simple Linguine with Tomato Sauce

Serves 4

Preparation time:
10 minutes
Chill time: 15 minutes

1 (28-ounce) can plum
  tomatoes, no salt
  added, with juice
1 tablespoon bottled
  minced garlic
2 tablespoons minced
  onion
1 tablespoon red wine
  vinegar
¼ cup chopped fresh
  basil leaves
¼ cup extra-virgin olive oil
1 teaspoon salt
¼ teaspoon black pepper
1 pound leftover cooked
  linguine

Here's a classic pasta dish using leftover cooked pasta. For best results, chill the sauce for at least 15 minutes to give the flavors a chance to blend before pairing with the pasta.

1. Combine the tomatoes and their juice, garlic, onion, red wine vinegar, basil, olive oil, salt, and pepper in a blender or food processor. Process until it forms a thick sauce.

2. Reheat the cooked pasta (see Serving Leftover Pasta, page 169).

3. Place the pasta in a bowl and toss with the tomato sauce.

Plum Tomatoes

A plump, oval-shaped tomato with few seeds, plum tomatoes are born to be used in a sauce. If you can't find canned plum tomatoes, look for them by their other name, Roma tomatoes.

Leftover Pasta and Burgundy Beef Casserole

This simple dish could also be cooked in the microwave: use a reheat setting or cook at 70 percent power for 1 minute, and then for 1 minute at a time until heated through.

Serves 2

Preparation time:
5 minutes
Cooking time:
15–20 minutes

2 cups leftover cooked pasta
½ portion leftover Quick and Easy Brown Sauce (page 252)
3 tablespoons Burgundy
½ pound leftover cooked steak

1. Preheat the oven to 325°F. Run the pasta under warm running water to reheat.

2. Bring the brown sauce to a boil in a medium saucepan with the Burgundy.

3. Spread 1 cup of the leftover pasta over the bottom of a baking dish. Spoon the beef over the pasta.

4. Spoon the sauce over the beef. Spread the remaining cup of pasta on top.

5. Cook for 10 to 15 minutes to heat through. Serve immediately.

Five-Ingredient Spaghetti and Meatballs

Serves 4

Preparation time:
5 minutes
Cooking time:
10–15 minutes

24 frozen meatballs
3 cups frozen vegetables
¾ pound leftover cooked
    spaghetti
3 cups pre-made tomato
    sauce
¾ cup grated Parmesan
    cheese

There are a number of good pre-made tomato sauces on the market—choose your favorite. Use your preferred frozen vegetables in this recipe—spinach, cauliflower, and a frozen stir-fry vegetable mix are all good choices.

1. Place the frozen meatballs in a microwave-safe dish. Microwave on high heat for 2 minutes, and then for 30 seconds at a time if needed until the meatballs are cooked.

2. Place the frozen vegetables in a microwave-safe dish. Cover and microwave on high heat for 3 minutes, and then for 1 minute at a time until cooked.

3. Reheat the pasta (see Serving Leftover Pasta, page 169).

4. Heat the pre-made tomato sauce in a saucepan over medium heat.

5. Toss the pasta with the tomato sauce. Stir in the meatballs and vegetables. Sprinkle the Parmesan cheese on top.

Cooking Pasta in the Microwave

Don't have leftover pasta on hand and there's no time to cook a new batch? You can quickly cook pasta in the microwave. First, heat the water in a microwave-safe dish. Add the noodles—stirring to make sure they are completely covered with the water—and cook on high heat until tender. The exact cooking time will depend on the amount of pasta to be cooked—count on at least 4 minutes for 8 ounces of dried egg noodles.

Garlic Noodles with Bacon

Here is a quick and easy way to jazz up leftover pasta. You can use other types of long pasta in the recipe, such as linguine or angel hair pasta.

Serves 4

Preparation time:
5 minutes
Cooking time: 10 minutes

8 ounces leftover cooked
   spaghetti
3 slices bacon
3 tablespoons margarine
2 tablespoons cream
   cheese
2 teaspoons bottled
   minced garlic, or to
   taste
1 cup half-and-half
⅓ cup grated Parmesan
   cheese
½ teaspoon dried basil,
   or to taste
½ teaspoon dried
   oregano, or to taste
Black pepper, to taste

1. Reheat the spaghetti (see Serving Leftover Pasta below).

2. Place the bacon on a plate covered with a paper towel. Lay two more paper towels over the bacon. Microwave on high heat for 2 minutes, and then for 1 minute at a time until the bacon is cooked. Remove and chop.

3. Melt the margarine in a saucepan over low heat. Whisk in the cream cheese. Stir in the garlic.

4. Turn the heat up and add the half-and-half. Add the Parmesan cheese and continue stirring with a whisk until the mixture has thickened. Stir in the oregano, basil, and pepper.

5. Place the cooked pasta in a large bowl. Toss with the sauce.

Serving Leftover Pasta

The easiest way to reheat leftover cooked pasta is to place it in a colander and quickly rinse under hot running water, moving your fingers through to separate the strands. To reheat pasta in the microwave, place in a microwave-safe bowl covered with wax paper or plastic wrap. Microwave on high heat for 1 minute, and then for 30 seconds at a time until the pasta is heated through.

Crab Pasta with Artichokes

Try garnishing this dish with ½ cup of sliced olives. You can use unmarinated or marinated canned artichoke hearts in this recipe.

Serves 2

Preparation time:
5 minutes
Cooking time: 20 minutes

2 quarts water
1 teaspoon salt
½ pound macaroni or
    other shell-shaped
    pasta
2 teaspoons olive oil
2 shallots, peeled,
    chopped
8 canned artichoke
    hearts, halved
1 tomato, thinly sliced
1½ cups drained canned
    crabmeat
2 tablespoons lemon juice
¼ cup chicken broth or
    light cream
¼ teaspoon black pepper,
    or to taste
½ teaspoon salt, or to
    taste

1. Bring a large pot with the water and salt to a boil. Add the pasta to the boiling water. Cook until the pasta is cooked al dente. (Prepare the remainder of the ingredients while the pasta is cooking.)

2. In a skillet, heat the olive oil. Add the shallots and sauté until softened.

3. Add the artichoke hearts. Cook for 1 minute and add the tomato, pressing down so that it releases its juice. Stir in the crabmeat and lemon juice.

4. Add the broth or light cream to the pan and bring to a boil. Season with the salt and pepper. Keep warm.

5. Drain the pasta in a colander. Place the pasta in a bowl and toss with the crabmeat and artichoke mixture. Serve hot.

Know Your Pasta!

Italian pasta comes in all sorts of shapes and sizes, from classic long pastas such as spaghetti and linguine to silky ribbons of fettuccine and tube-shaped penne and macaroni. Overall, there are over 600 types of pasta. Pasta is such an important staple worldwide that representatives of national pasta associations agreed to designate October 25th as World Pasta Day.

Shrimp Penne with Asparagus and Sun-Dried Tomatoes

Sturdy penne pasta is often paired with a thick sauce, but here it is combined with lemon-flavored shrimp and asparagus.

1. Bring a large pot with 3 quarts of water to a boil with the salt.

2. Fill a medium saucepan with enough water so that an expanding metal steamer will sit just above the water (about 1½"). Bring the water to a boil. Add the asparagus. Steam the asparagus, covered, until it is tender but still crisp (about 5 to 8 minutes). Drain.

3. In a skillet, heat the olive oil. Add the shallots and sun-dried tomato strips. Sauté the shallot until it is softened.

4. Add the shrimp. Stir in the lemon juice, pepper, and dried basil. Sauté the shrimp until it turns pink.

5. Add the noodles to the boiling water. Cook, stirring to separate the pasta, until the linguine is cooked al dente. Drain in a colander. Toss the pasta with the shrimp and asparagus. Sprinkle the Parmesan cheese over top if using.

Serves 4

Preparation time:
10 minutes
Cooking time: 15 minutes

¾ pound penne pasta
3 quarts water
1½ teaspoons salt
½ pound fresh asparagus, cut diagonally into 1" pieces
1 tablespoon olive oil
2 shallots, peeled, chopped
2 tablespoons sun-dried tomatoes
1 pound shrimp, peeled, deveined, tail on
2 tablespoons lemon juice
¼ teaspoon black pepper
1 teaspoon dried basil leaves
¼ cup grated Parmesan cheese, optional

Greek Macaroni and Cheese

Serves 3

Preparation time:
5 minutes
Cooking time: 20 minutes

½ pound leftover tubular
  pasta, cooked
4 tablespoons unsalted
  butter
3 tablespoons flour
1 teaspoon bottled
  minced garlic
1 cup whole milk
⅓ cup crumbled feta
  cheese
¼ teaspoon ground
  nutmeg, or to taste
1 teaspoon dried mint
¼ teaspoon black pepper,
  or to taste
1 teaspoon lemon juice

Here is a more adult version of the kid's favorite mac 'n' cheese, made by adding cheese and herbs traditionally used in Greek cooking to a basic white sauce and serving over pasta. You can use any small tubular shaped pasta as the macaroni, including traditional macaroni noodles.

1. Reheat the pasta (see Serving Leftover Pasta, page 169).

2. Melt the butter on very low heat. Add the flour and blend it into the melted butter, stirring continually until it thickens and forms a roux. Stir in the garlic.

3. Turn the heat up to medium low and slowly add the milk and cheese. Stir in the ground nutmeg and the dried mint. Continue stirring with a whisk until the mixture has thickened.

4. Stir in the pepper and lemon juice.

5. Toss the pasta with the sauce and serve immediately.

Pasta with Smoked Salmon

Lemon extract provides a convenient substitute for lemon zest, but if you prefer the real thing, replace the extract with 2 teaspoons of lemon zest. Be careful when adding salt, as smoked salmon and capers (even after rinsing) are both quite salty.

1. Bring a large pot containing the water and salt to a boil. Add the pasta to the boiling water. Cook until the pasta is cooked al dente. Drain in a colander.

2. Begin preparing the sauce while the pasta is cooking. Heat the olive oil over medium-high heat. Add the shallot and sauté until it begins to soften. Add the smoked salmon. Sprinkle the dried parsley over the salmon and shallot. Continue cooking for 1 to 2 more minutes, until the salmon turns a light color.

3. Stir in the whipping cream, lemon extract, and capers. Continue cooking until the cream is heated through. Do a taste test and season with the salt and pepper as needed.

4. Toss the pasta with the sauce and serve immediately.

Serves 4

Preparation time:
5–10 minutes
Cooking time:
20–25 minutes

3 quarts water
1½ teaspoons salt
¾ pound angel hair pasta
2 tablespoons olive oil
1 shallot, peeled and
    chopped
⅓ pound smoked salmon
2 teaspoons dried parsley
¾ cup whipping cream
1 teaspoon lemon extract
2 tablespoons capers,
    rinsed
¼ teaspoon salt, or to
    taste
¼ teaspoon black pepper,
    or to taste

Chapter 12
Vegetarian Entrées

Buddhist Monk's Soup

This warming soup is traditionally served on the first day of the New Year, when Buddhists believe that no living thing should be killed.

Serves 6

Preparation time:
10 minutes
Cooking time: 15 minutes

1 pound firm tofu
2 teaspoons vegetable oil
½ cup chopped sweet
  onion
1 cup sliced fresh
  mushrooms
½ teaspoon cayenne
  pepper
2 cups drained canned
  sweet potatoes
3 cups coconut milk
2 cups water
2 teaspoons lime juice
½ teaspoon salt
⅛ teaspoon black pepper,
  or to taste
¾ cup unsalted cashews

1. Drain the tofu and cut into cubes.

2. After the tofu has been draining for about 5 minutes, begin preparing the other ingredients. Heat the vegetable oil in a saucepan on medium-high heat. Add the chopped onion and mushrooms.

3. Turn the heat down to medium and sauté for about 5 minutes, until the vegetables are softened. Stir in the cayenne pepper. Add the canned sweet potatoes and cook for a minute, stirring.

4. Add the coconut milk and water. Bring to a boil. Stir in the lime juice, salt, and pepper. Add the cubed tofu.

5. Simmer for 5 minutes. Serve hot, garnished with the cashews.

Are All Buddhists Vegetarians?

Contrary to popular belief, not all Buddhists are vegetarians. While the Buddhist philosophy forbids killing animals specifically for consumption, it is permissible to eat an animal that was killed accidentally. Still, many Buddhists do follow a vegetarian diet.

Portobello Mushroom Burgers

Combining garlic and mayonnaise is a quick and easy way to make aïoli, a garlicky sauce from France that complements everything from vegetables to meat, poultry, and seafood. This recipe can easily be doubled to serve 8.

1. Wipe the mushrooms clean with a damp cloth and thinly slice.

2. In a small bowl, stir together the balsamic vinegar and vegetarian chicken-flavored broth. In a separate small bowl, stir together the garlic, mayonnaise, lemon juice, and cayenne pepper. Chill the mayonnaise mixture until needed.

3. Heat the oil in a skillet over medium-high heat. Add the shallot and cook until tender. Turn the heat down to medium and add the sliced mushrooms. Stir in the vinegar and broth mixture and the black pepper. Cook for 4 to 5 minutes until the mushrooms are tender.

4. Lay out the hamburger buns in front of you. Put a lettuce leaf on the bottom of each bun. Spread 1 tablespoon of the garlic/mayonnaise mixture inside the top of each bun and spoon one-quarter of the sautéed mushroom on top of the lettuce. Serve immediately.

Serves 4

Preparation time:
5–8 minutes
Cooking time:
10–12 minutes

4 portobello mushroom
    caps
2 tablespoons balsamic
    vinegar
1 tablespoon vegetarian
    chicken-flavored broth
2 garlic cloves, finely
    chopped
¼ cup mayonnaise
1 teaspoon lemon juice
¼ teaspoon cayenne
    pepper, or to taste
1 tablespoon olive oil
1 shallot, chopped
¼ teaspoon black pepper,
    or to taste
4 romaine lettuce leaves
4 hamburger buns

French Cassoulet

Serves 4

Preparation time: 5–10 minutes
Cooking time:
10–15 minutes

2 teaspoons olive oil
2 cloves garlic, crushed
1 white onion, peeled and
    chopped
12 ounces Gimme Lean
    Sausage style meat
    substitute, cut into
    1" pieces
1 medium tomato, chopped
1 cup tomato sauce
2½ cups drained white
    cannellini beans
1 bay leaf
1 tablespoon chopped
    fresh parsley
1½ teaspoons chopped
    fresh basil
¼ teaspoon salt, or to taste
Black pepper, to taste

Canned cannellini beans take the work out of soaking dried beans overnight. On nights when you're even more rushed than usual, replace the tomato and tomato sauce with 2 cups canned diced tomatoes.

1. Heat the oil in a skillet on medium heat. Add the crushed garlic, onion, and Gimme Lean meat substitute. Sauté for a couple of minutes.

2. Add the tomato, pressing down so that it releases its juices. Continue cooking for 2 to 3 more minutes, until the onion is softened.

3. Add the tomato sauce. Bring to a boil. Add the beans.

4. Add the bay leaf. Stir in the parsley, basil, salt, and pepper.

5. Turn the heat down and simmer, uncovered, for 5 minutes. Remove the bay leaf before serving.

Substituting Herbs

Dried herbs make a handy substitute when you don't have fresh chopped herbs on hand. When substituting dried herbs for fresh, always follow the ⅓ rule: use ⅓ the amount of dried herbs as fresh herbs that are called for in the recipe. In this recipe, for example, the fresh parsley and basil leaves could be replaced with 1 teaspoon dried parsley and ½ teaspoon dried basil.

Stuffed Red Peppers with Garlic Mashed Potatoes

It's hard to overestimate the health benefits of beans—while not completely replacing the protein found in meat, they are high in fiber, low in fat, and full of flavor.

Serves 1

Preparation time:
5 minutes
Cooking time:
10–15 minutes

½ cup leftover Garlic
    Mashed Potatoes
    (page 232)
1 tablespoon vegetarian
    chicken-flavored broth
½ teaspoon granulated
    sugar
⅛ teaspoon hot sauce, or
    to taste
½ cup drained canned
    black beans
2 medium red bell
    peppers, seeded, cut
    in half

1. Heat the garlic mashed potatoes in a small saucepan with the vegetarian chicken-flavored broth. Stir in the sugar and hot sauce. Remove from the heat.

2. In a small bowl, combine the mashed potatoes and beans. Carefully spoon one-quarter of the mixture onto each bell pepper half.

3. Place the bell pepper halves in a microwave-safe baking dish. Cover with plastic wrap, leaving an opening in one corner for steam to vent. Microwave the peppers on high heat for 5 minutes.

4. Give the dish a quarter turn and microwave on high heat for 2 minutes, and then for 1 minute at a time until everything is heated through. Let stand for 5 minutes.

Tofu Cacciatore

Serves 3

Preparation time:
5 minutes
Cooking time:
7–8 minutes

16 ounces soft tofu
1½ tablespoons olive oil
1 shallot, chopped
4 ounces vegetarian
    bacon substitute (such
    as Smart Bacon)
1 tomato, thinly sliced
½ cup canned
    mushrooms
⅓ cup vegetarian
    chicken-flavored broth
2 tablespoons tomato
    sauce
1 tablespoon chopped
    fresh basil
1 teaspoon chopped fresh
    thyme
½ teaspoon salt

*This quick and easy stir-fry allows you to enjoy the flavors
of chicken cacciatore, traditionally a slowly simmered dish,
on busy weeknights.*

1. Remove the excess water from the tofu. Cut into 1″ cubes.

2. Heat the olive oil in a skillet over medium heat. Add the shallot and bacon substitute. Cook for 2 minutes, then add the tofu. Cook, stirring the tofu cubes gently, for 1 to 2 minutes, until the tofu cubes are browned and the shallot is softened.

3. Push the tofu to the sides of the pan and add the tomato in the middle, pressing down so that it releases its juices. Stir in the canned mushrooms.

4. Add the vegetarian chicken-flavored broth and tomato sauce. Bring to a boil.

5. Stir in the fresh basil and thyme. Stir in the salt. Cook for another minute, stirring to combine the ingredients. Serve hot.

Replacing Meat with Tofu

Protein-rich and low in calories, tofu makes a great substitute for meat in vegetarian cooking. Always be sure to drain the tofu ahead of time so that it can fully absorb the spices and other flavors in a dish. Also, to make up for the lack of the soluble fat in meat that disperses flavor, consider marinating the tofu in a flavorful marinade before cooking.

Spicy Vegetable-Filled Tacos

The spicy combination of herbs and seasonings used to flavor the black beans are the same ones frequently used to marinade beef to make Tex-Mex fajitas.

Serves 6

Preparation time:
5 minutes
Cooking time:
10–15 minutes

6 taco shells
2 teaspoons vegetable oil
¼ cup chopped red onion
2 cups drained canned
    black beans
6 tablespoons vegetarian
    chicken-flavored broth
4 teaspoons lime juice
1 teaspoon Asian chili
    sauce
¼ teaspoon bottled
    minced garlic
¼ teaspoon ground cumin
¼ teaspoon salt
1 cup fresh shredded
    cabbage
¾ cup shredded Cheddar
    cheese

1. Preheat the oven to 350°F. Place the taco shells on an ungreased baking sheet. Bake for 5 to 10 minutes, until warm.

2. While the taco shells are heating, prepare the filling ingredients. Heat the vegetable oil in a saucepan over medium-high heat. Add the onion and sauté for 4 to 5 minutes, until softened.

3. Add the black beans. Stir in the broth, lime juice, chili sauce, minced garlic, cumin, and salt.

4. Remove the taco shells from the oven.

5. Fill each taco with a portion of the black bean mixture. Add the shredded cabbage. Sprinkle with 2 tablespoons of cheese.

Vegetarian Chili

Serves 4

Preparation time:
5 minutes
Cooking time:
10–15 minutes

1 tablespoon vegetable or
    olive oil
1 red bell pepper, diced
¾ cup canned corn
    niblets
1 cup canned red kidney
    beans, drained
1 cup canned black
    beans, drained
1½ cups canned whole
    tomatoes
1 (6-ounce) can tomato
    paste
2 tablespoons chili
    powder, or to taste
1 teaspoon ground cumin
1 teaspoon salt, or to
    taste
¼ teaspoon black pepper,
    or to taste
1 tablespoon brown sugar
1 tablespoon onion
    powder

Nutrient-rich beans take the place of ground beef in this chili recipe. As always, how much chili powder to use is a matter of personal taste—feel free to add more if desired.

1. Heat the oil in a large skillet. Add the bell pepper. Cook, stirring, for 3 to 4 minutes, until softened.

2. Add the canned corn, kidney beans, and black beans.

3. Stir in the whole tomatoes and the tomato paste.

4. Stir in the seasonings.

5. Bring to a boil, then turn down the heat and simmer for 5 minutes or until heated through. Serve hot.

Vegan or Vegetarian?

Although the terms vegan and vegetarian are both used to refer to people who don't eat meat, there are some significant differences between the two. While a vegetarian will not eat meat, poultry, or seafood, vegans eschew all animal products and byproducts, including eggs, milk, and sometimes honey. So, while all vegans are vegetarian, not all vegetarians are vegans.

Vegetarian Fried Rice

Although scrambled egg is frequently added to fried rice dishes, it's not necessary. If you do not have a large skillet, remove the vegetables before stir-frying the rice and add them back in at the end.

1. Heat the oil in a large skillet over medium-high heat. Add the minced ginger, chopped peppers, and onion. Cook, stirring, for about 2 to 3 minutes, until the onion begins to soften. Add the peas and stir-fry for another minute.

2. Push the vegetables to the sides and add the rice in the middle. Heat through, stirring frequently to break up any clumps in the rice.

3. Stir in the soy sauce and lemon juice.

4. Stir in the green onion and cashews.

5. Stir for another minute to heat through. Serve hot.

Serves 4

Preparation time:
5 minutes
Cooking time:
7–8 minutes

2 tablespoons vegetable oil
1 teaspoon bottled minced ginger
1 tablespoon bottled chopped red jalapeño peppers
1 medium onion, peeled and chopped
½ cup frozen peas
3 cups cold cooked brown rice
1½ tablespoons soy sauce
1½ teaspoons lemon juice
2 green onions, chopped
1 cup unsalted cashews

Meal-Size Spinach Salad with Goat Cheese

If not serving the salad immediately, cover and refrigerate. Toss with the lemon juice and vinegar dressing just before serving.

Serves 4

Preparation time:
15 minutes

2 tablespoons lemon juice
1 teaspoon balsamic vinegar
2 tablespoons olive oil
Black pepper, to taste
¼ teaspoon hot sauce
1 pound (4 cups) fresh spinach leaves
1 cup sliced fresh mushrooms
3 tablespoons sun-dried tomatoes
⅓ cup grated goat cheese

1. In a small bowl, whisk together the lemon juice, balsamic vinegar, olive oil, pepper, and hot sauce.

2. In a large bowl, combine the spinach and mushrooms.

3. Toss the vegetables with the sun-dried tomatoes and goat cheese.

4. Gently toss with the dressing.

One-Pot Beans and Rice

Feel free to use instant brown rice in this recipe. Begin cooking the instant rice just after adding the onion to the pan.

Serves 4

Preparation time:
5 minutes
Cooking time:
10–12 minutes

1 tablespoon vegetable oil
2 garlic cloves, peeled, thinly sliced
½ medium onion, chopped
¼ teaspoon ground cinnamon
¼ teaspoon ground allspice
1 tablespoon apple juice
1 (14-ounce) can black beans, undrained
1 (14-ounce) can chickpeas, undrained
½ cup chopped tomatoes
1½ cups cooked white or brown rice

1. Heat the vegetable oil in a skillet on medium-high heat. Add the garlic and onion. Cook, stirring, for 2 to 3 minutes, until the onion begins to soften. Stir in the ground cinnamon, ground allspice, and apple juice while the onion is cooking.

2. Turn the heat down to medium. Add the beans and cook for 3 to 4 minutes to heat through.

3. Add the chopped tomatoes and bring to a boil (turn the heat up if needed).

4. Stir in the cooked rice. Reduce the heat and simmer, uncovered, for 2 to 3 minutes. Serve hot.

Skillet Vegetarian Shepherd's Pie

The vegetarian version of Worcestershire sauce leaves out the anchovies. If not available, you can substitute ¾ teaspoon of soy sauce mixed with ¾ teaspoon of lemon juice.

Serves 2

Preparation time:
8–10 minutes
Cooking time:
12–15 minutes

1 tablespoon margarine
2 tablespoons chopped
 onions
1 cup baby carrots, cut
 in half
1 cup meat substitute,
 such as soy crumbles
½ cup vegetarian beef-
 flavored broth
1½ teaspoons vegetarian
 Worcestershire sauce
½ teaspoon dried
 oregano
¼ teaspoon salt, or to
 taste
¼ teaspoon black pepper,
 or to taste
1 cup leftover Garlic
 Mashed Potatoes
 (page 232)

1. Heat the margarine in a skillet. Add the onion and carrots and cook for 3 to 4 minutes, until softened.

2. Add the soy crumbles, vegetarian beef-flavored broth, and Worcestershire sauce.

3. Stir in the oregano, salt, and pepper. Cook for 5 minutes, or until the soy crumbles are heated through.

4. Stir in the mashed potato. Cook for another minute to heat through. Serve hot.

Cooking with Substitute Beef

Using beef substitutes is a quick and easy way to transform a recipe into a vegetarian dish. However, you may want to make a few adaptations. All ground beef contains a certain amount of fat, which adds extra flavor. To make up for this lack when preparing a vegetarian version of the recipe, try adding extra seasonings.

Tofu Fajitas

Serves 4

Preparation time:
10 minutes
Cooking time: 10 minutes

4 tortilla wraps
1 pound firm tofu, drained
2 tablespoons lime juice
1 teaspoon chili powder
1 teaspoon salt
¼ teaspoon ground
    cumin, or to taste
½ teaspoon freshly
    ground black pepper
¼ teaspoon garlic salt
3 tablespoons extra-virgin
    olive oil, divided
1 onion, chopped
2 tablespoons jarred
    chopped red chilies
2 red bell peppers,
    seeded, cut into
    chunks

Draining tofu earlier in the week substantially reduces the preparation time, making it easier to get a meal on the table in minutes. Store the tofu in a resealable plastic bag in the refrigerator until ready to use.

1. Heat the tortillas according to package directions.

2. Cut the tofu loosely into cubes and crumble (you should have about ½ cup crumbled).

3. In a small bowl, stir together the lime juice, chili powder, salt, cumin, pepper, and garlic salt. Whisk in 2 tablespoons olive oil. Stir the crumbled tofu into the lime juice mixture.

4. Heat 2 tablespoons olive oil in a skillet on medium heat. Add the onion, chopped red chilies, and bell pepper. Sauté for 4 to 5 minutes, then add the tofu mixture. Cook, stirring gently, for another 4 to 5 minutes, until the tofu is browned.

5. Lay a tortilla out in front of you. Spoon about ½ cup of the mixture in the center of the tortilla wrap, taking care not to come too close to the edges. Fold in the left and right sides and roll up the wrap. Repeat with the remainder of the tortillas.

How to Drain Tofu

Drained tofu acts like a super-absorbent sponge, soaking up the flavors of the foods it is cooked with. To drain the tofu, place it in a bowl and weight down with a plate or other heavy object. Let the tofu sit for 15 minutes, then drain off the excess water.

Skillet "Stuffed" Eggplant

Textured vegetable protein (TVP) makes an excellent substitute for ground beef in vegetarian dishes. This dish has the flavor and taste of traditional baked stuffed eggplant, but takes less than 30 minutes to make.

1. Trim the ends from the eggplant and cut into 1" cubes. Place the chopped eggplant in a deep-sided casserole dish and cover with water. Cover the dish with microwave-safe paper, leaving one corner uncovered. Microwave the eggplant on high heat for 5 minutes, or until softened. Remove and drain the eggplant.

2. Heat the oil in a heavy saucepan on medium-high heat. Stir in the minced onion. Add the textured vegetable protein, using a spatula to break it up. Sprinkle the salt and pepper over.

3. Add the crushed tomatoes and tomato paste to the pan. Stir in the brown sugar. Simmer for a few minutes, then stir in the bread crumbs and the cubed eggplant.

4. Cook for 2 to 3 more minutes to mix everything together and heat through. Serve hot.

Serves 4

Preparation time:
5–10 minutes
Cooking time:
15–20 minutes

2 pounds eggplant (1 large eggplant)
2 teaspoons vegetable oil
1 tablespoon minced onion
1 pound textured vegetable protein
½ teaspoon salt
¼ teaspoon black pepper
½ cup crushed tomatoes
1 (6-ounce) can tomato paste
2 teaspoons brown sugar
⅔ cup bread crumbs

Skillet Tofu Stroganoff

Serves 4

Preparation time:
5 minutes
Cooking time:
12–15 minutes

1½ pounds firm tofu,
    drained earlier
2½ cups instant brown or
    white rice
1 tablespoon vegetable oil
1 medium yellow onion,
    chopped
½ teaspoon dry tarragon
1½ cups sliced fresh
    mushrooms
1½ tablespoons red wine
    vinegar
½ cup vegetarian beef-
    flavored broth
¼ teaspoon salt, or to
    taste
¼ teaspoon black pepper,
    or to taste
½ cup natural yogurt

Using natural yogurt instead of sour cream—the traditional way of finishing off beef stroganoff—turns this into a healthy low-fat dish.

1. Cut the tofu into ¾" cubes. Cook the rice according to the instructions in Basic Cooked Instant Rice (page 146) or follow the package directions.

2. While the rice is cooking, heat the oil in a skillet over medium heat. Add the onion and sauté for 3 to 4 minutes to soften. Sprinkle the dry tarragon over the onion.

3. Add the mushrooms and sauté for about 2 minutes, stirring in the red wine vinegar.

4. Add the vegetarian beef-flavored broth, salt, and pepper. Bring to a boil. Add the tofu cubes. Turn the heat down and simmer for 5 minutes.

5. Stir in the yogurt. Serve the stroganoff over the cooked rice.

Know Your Tofu

Tofu comes in a variety of textures, from soft to extra-firm. Firm and extra-firm tofus work best for pan-fried dishes, while the creamy texture of soft tofus makes them perfect for puddings and other desserts.

Microwave Garden Vegetable Lasagna

For a vegan version of this dish, replace the cottage cheese with crumbled firm tofu that has been combined with the seasonings, and the mozzarella cheese with mozzarella-flavored soy cheese.

Serves 4

Preparation time:
10 minutes
Cooking time: 10 minutes

2 cups crushed tomatoes
1¼ cups cottage cheese
¼ cup mozzarella cheese
¼ teaspoon dried basil
¼ teaspoon dried
    oregano
⅛ teaspoon black pepper
2 zucchini, thinly sliced
1 cup frozen spinach,
    thawed and drained
3 tablespoons Parmesan
    cheese

1. In a medium bowl, stir together the crushed tomatoes and the cottage cheese. Stir in the mozzarella cheese, basil, oregano, and pepper.

2. Lay out one of the zucchini in a deep-sided casserole dish that is microwave-safe. Add half of the spinach.

3. Spoon about half of the cheese and tomato mixture over the spinach. Repeat with the remainder of the zucchini, spinach, and cheese and tomato mixture.

4. Cover the dish with microwave-safe wax paper. Microwave on high heat for 3 minutes. Give the dish a quarter turn and microwave for 2 minutes at a time until the cheese is cooked (total cooking time should be 7 to 9 minutes).

5. Sprinkle the Parmesan cheese over the top. Let stand for at least 5 minutes before serving.

Tofu and Cashew Stir-Fry

Draining the tofu earlier in the day means that this simple stir-fry can go from kitchen to table in under 15 minutes.

Serves 4

Preparation time:
5 minutes
Cooking time:
7–8 minutes

1 pound firm tofu, drained
½ cup vegetarian
   chicken-flavored broth
¼ cup soy sauce
2 tablespoons lemon juice
1 teaspoon granulated
   sugar
1 teaspoon cornstarch
2 tablespoons vegetable
   oil
1 teaspoon minced ginger
2½ cups fresh stir-fry
   vegetables
2 tablespoons water,
   optional
½ cup unsalted cashews

1. Cut the tofu into ¾" cubes.

2. In a small bowl, stir together the vegetarian chicken-flavored broth, soy sauce, lemon juice, and sugar. Whisk in the cornstarch.

3. Heat the oil in a heavy skillet or wok over medium-high heat. Add the minced ginger. Stir for a few seconds, then add the stir-fry vegetables, pushing them around the pan constantly so that they don't burn. (Add 1 or 2 tablespoons water if needed to keep the vegetables from burning.) Stir-fry for 2 to 3 minutes, until they are tender but still crisp.

4. Add the tofu cubes. Cook for 1 or 2 minutes, gently stirring the cubes, until they are browned.

5. Stir the sauce and swirl into the pan. Bring to a boil and cook for about 2 more minutes to heat through. Stir in the cashews. Serve hot.

Freezing Tofu

Freezing tofu gives it a chewy, meatier texture. For best results, use firm or extra-firm tofu. Drain the tofu before freezing (see How to Drain Tofu, page 186) and wrap tightly in plastic. Use the tofu within three months.

Sweet-and-Sour Tofu

Drained tofu acts like a sponge, absorbing the flavorful sweet-and-sour sauce. For best results, be sure to use extra-firm tofu, which can hold its shape during stir-frying.

1. In a small bowl, stir together the pineapple juice, water, vinegar, brown sugar, ketchup, and soy sauce.

2. Cut the tofu into 1" cubes. Heat the oil in a heavy skillet over medium-high heat. Add the ginger and let brown for 2 minutes. Remove the ginger.

3. Add the celery. Stir-fry for 2 minutes, stirring constantly. Add the red bell peppers. Add the straw mushrooms. Cook for another minute. (Splash the vegetables with 1 to 2 tablespoons of water if they begin to dry out during stir-frying.)

4. Add the tofu cubes. Cook, stirring, for about 1 minute to brown the tofu.

5. Stir the sauce and add it to the pan. Bring to a boil, and cook for about 2 minutes, stirring, to thicken. Serve hot.

Serves 4

Preparation time:
5–10 minutes
Cooking time:
8–10 minutes

¼ cup pineapple juice
½ cup water
¼ cup vinegar
¼ cup brown sugar
2 tablespoons ketchup
2 teaspoons soy sauce
1 pound extra-firm tofu, drained earlier
2 tablespoons vegetable oil
2 thin slices ginger
2 ribs celery, sliced on the diagonal
1 medium red bell pepper, cut into chunks
1 cup straw mushrooms

Chapter 13
When You Only Have Ten Minutes

Fast Ground Beef Stroganoff

Traditionally, this Russian dish is made with fillet of beef, but ground beef makes a quick and easy substitute.

Serves 4

Preparation time:
5 minutes
Cooking time:
5–10 minutes

2 cups leftover cooked
    noodles
1 tablespoon olive oil
½ teaspoon bottled
    minced garlic
2 cups leftover cooked
    ground beef
2 tablespoons tomato
    paste
2 tablespoons dried
    minced onion
½ teaspoon dried parsley
    flakes, or to taste
½ teaspoon dried basil
¼ teaspoon black pepper
1 cup drained canned
    mushrooms
¼ cup beef bouillon
¼ cup plain yogurt

1. Reheat the pasta (see Serving Leftover Pasta, page 169).

2. Heat the olive oil in a skillet over medium-high heat. Add the garlic and the cooked ground beef. Cook for a minute to heat through, stirring in the tomato paste, minced onion, parsley, basil, and pepper.

3. Add the mushrooms. Sauté for 1 minute and add the beef bouillon. Bring to a boil.

4. Remove the skillet from the heat and stir in the yogurt. Serve hot over the noodles.

Pan-Fried Steak with Italian Pesto

The actual cooking time for this dish will depend on how well done you like your steak.

Serves 4

Preparation time:
2–3 minutes
Cooking time: 10 minutes

2 teaspoons lemon
    pepper seasoning
½ teaspoon salt
1 pound beef tenderloin
    steaks
1 tablespoon olive oil
½ cup Italian pesto

1. Rub the lemon pepper seasoning and salt over the steaks.

2. Heat the olive oil in a skillet over medium-high heat.

3. Add the steaks to the pan. To cook the steaks to medium doneness, cook for 8 to 10 minutes, turning halfway through cooking.

4. Serve the steaks with the pesto.

Pan-Fried Seafood with Tarragon Cream Sauce

A simple white sauce adds flavor to pan-fried halibut. If you like, make the sauce ahead of time and store in a sealed container in the refrigerator until ready to use. Reheat in a saucepan over low heat, stirring continually.

Serves 4

Preparation time:
3–5 minutes
Cooking time: 10 minutes

1 tablespoon olive oil
1 teaspoon bottled
   minced ginger
1 shallot, chopped
4 (5-ounce) halibut steaks
4 tablespoons unsalted
   butter
3½ tablespoons flour
½ teaspoon dried
   tarragon
¾ cup milk
¼ cup heavy cream
½ teaspoon ground
   nutmeg, or to taste
⅛ teaspoon black or white
   pepper, or to taste
1 teaspoon lemon juice

1. Heat the olive oil in a skillet over medium-high heat. Add the ginger, shallot, and halibut.

2. Cook the halibut for 5 minutes, turn, and cook for 4 to 5 minutes more, until it is cooked through.

3. While the halibut is frying, prepare the cream sauce: In a small saucepan, melt the butter on low heat. Add the flour and blend it into the melted butter, stirring continually, until it thickens and forms a roux (3 to 5 minutes). Stir in the tarragon.

4. Increase the heat to medium. Slowly add the milk and the cream, stirring with a whisk until the mixture has thickened. Stir in the nutmeg, pepper, and lemon juice.

5. Pour the cream sauce over the halibut steaks and serve.

Fast Foil-Wrapped Fish

Another great way to quickly cook fish is to wrap it in foil and bake it in the oven. This technique, called en papillote, allows the fish to steam in its own juices, locking in the flavor. Add your favorite mixed vegetables, finish with an assortment of seasonings (fresh ginger, green onion, lemon juice, or soy sauce are all good choices), and you've got a complete meal!

Orange-Glazed Fish Fillets

Serve this flavorful seafood dish with Sautéed Asparagus (page 228) or Thai-Style Creamed Corn (page 225) and cooked rice.

Serves 4

Preparation time:
2–3 minutes
Cooking time: 8 minutes

2 tablespoons olive oil
2 tablespoons orange
  juice
1 tablespoon
  Worcestershire sauce
2 teaspoons chopped
  fresh cilantro
½ teaspoon paprika
1½ pounds red snapper
  fillets

1. Spray a rack with nonstick cooking spray.

2. In a small bowl, whisk together the olive oil, orange juice, Worcestershire sauce, cilantro, and paprika.

3. Brush the marinade over the fish fillets.

4. Broil the fish for 4 minutes. Turn over, brush with the marinade and continue for another 4 to 5 minutes, until the fish is cooked through. (Be sure not to overcook the fish.)

Spicy Scallop Ceviche

Be careful not to overcook the scallops—remove them from the heat as soon as they change color. If you don't have time to thaw the frozen scallops, you can also use cooked shrimp.

Serves 2

Preparation time:
5 minutes
Cooking time: 5 minutes

1 tablespoon olive oil
1 teaspoon bottled
  minced garlic
1 pound fresh or thawed
  frozen bay scallops
2 tablespoons lime juice
3 tablespoons lemon juice
3 tablespoons ketchup
1 teaspoon chili powder
¼ teaspoon salt
⅛ teaspoon black pepper
1 teaspoon minced onion
1 medium cucumber,
  peeled, thinly sliced

1. Heat the olive oil in a skillet over medium-high heat.

2. Add the garlic and the scallops. Cook for 4 to 5 minutes, until the scallops turn opaque.

3. In a small mixing bowl, whisk together the lime juice, lemon juice, ketchup, chili powder, salt, pepper, and minced onion.

4. Place the scallops and cucumber in a salad bowl. Toss with the dressing. Serve immediately.

Meal-Size Indonesian-Style Potato Salad

The Indonesian version of potato salad, Gado Gado salad, is a popular restaurant dish. This simplified version is perfect for busy weekdays during the summer months.

Serves 3

Preparation time:
7–8 minutes

*Spicy Peanut Sauce
(page 252)
2 leftover cooked
potatoes, cut into
chunks
3½ cups packaged salad
greens
3 leftover hard-boiled
eggs, peeled and
sliced*

1. Start preparing the Spicy Peanut Sauce (page 252).

2. While the sauce is heating, assemble the salad ingredients on a large serving platter, with the potatoes on the outside, the greens on the inside, and the hard-boiled eggs on top.

3. Pour the peanut sauce over the salad. Serve immediately.

Make-Ahead Gado Gado Salad

If you're planning to prepare a potato salad for a picnic or other outdoor gathering, you may want to do as much work as possible ahead of time. In the case of this Meal-Size Indonesian-Style Potato Salad, the hard-boiled eggs can be prepared up to five days ahead of time, while the peanut sauce can be made up to three days ahead of time. Shell the eggs, assemble the salad, and garnish with the peanut sauce just before serving (thin the sauce with a bit of water if needed).

Veggie-Loaded Salad Rolls

Feel free to use Asian rice paper wrappers instead of tortilla wrappers to make the salad rolls if desired. Thai basil leaves can be found in the produce section of many supermarkets, or you can use regular basil.

Serves 10

Preparation time:
15 minutes

⅓ cup soy sauce
1 tablespoon white
    vinegar
1 tablespoon granulated
    sugar
1 teaspoon bottled
    minced garlic
1 tablespoon bottled
    chopped jalapeño
    peppers
1½ cups packaged salad
    greens
1 cup cooked shrimp
¼ cup chopped fresh Thai
    basil leaves
8 vegetable-flavored
    tortilla wrappers

1. In a small bowl, stir together the soy sauce, vinegar, sugar, garlic, and jalapeño peppers.

2. In a bowl, stir together the salad greens, cooked shrimp, and basil leaves.

3. Lay a tortilla wrapper on a cutting board in front of you. Place about ¼ cup of the shrimp and salad mix on the bottom half of the wrapper, being careful not to come too close to the edges.

4. Roll up the wrapper like a taco, tucking in the sides. Continue filling and rolling up the remainder of the wrappers.

5. Serve the rolls cold with the soy dipping sauce.

Glazed Ham

A flavorful orange sauce, sweetened with brown sugar, is the perfect accompaniment for cooked ham. Serve the ham with Garlic Mashed Potatoes (page 232) and Quick Green Beans Amandine (page 222).

Serves 4

Preparation time:
5 minutes
Cooking time: 5 minutes

½ pound cooked ham,
    sliced
4 tablespoons orange
    juice
3 tablespoons white wine
1 teaspoon Dijon mustard
2 tablespoons brown
    sugar
½ teaspoon bottled
    minced ginger

1. Lay out the ham slices on a plate.

2. In a small saucepan, bring the orange juice, white wine, Dijon mustard, brown sugar, and ginger to a boil, stirring to dissolve the sugar.

3. Pour the sauce over the ham slices.

Simple Shrimp Pasta

Using reserved shrimp juice adds extra flavor to this simple dish with leftover shrimp and pasta. Instead of Parmesan cheese, you can use another cheese, such as a shredded Italian cheese blend, if desired.

1. Reheat the leftover pasta (see Serving Leftover Pasta).

2. Heat the olive oil with the garlic in a skillet over medium-high heat. Add the tomato, pressing down so that it releases its juices.

3. Add the shrimp. Sauté for a minute to heat through.

4. Add the Marinated Artichoke Hearts (page 229) and the reserved shrimp juice. Stir in the pepper.

5. Serve the shrimp over the cooked pasta. Sprinkle with the Parmesan cheese.

Serves 4

Preparation time:
2–3 minutes
Cooking time:
7–8 minutes

2 cups leftover cooked
  pasta
2 teaspoons olive oil
1 teaspoon bottled
  minced garlic
1 large tomato, thinly
  sliced
2 cups drained canned
  shrimp
Marinated Artichoke
  Hearts (page 229)
2 tablespoons reserved
  shrimp juice
⅛ teaspoon black pepper,
  or to taste
⅓ cup shredded
  Parmesan cheese

Leftover Coconut Chicken

Serves 4

Preparation time:
5 minutes
Cooking time:
5–7 minutes

½ cup light coconut milk
3 tablespoons peanut
butter
1 tablespoon brown sugar
1 tablespoon Asian fish
sauce
1 tablespoon lime juice
1 teaspoon Tabasco
sauce
1 tablespoon olive oil
1 teaspoon bottled
minced garlic
1 pound cooked chicken
meat
1 cup drained canned
asparagus

A Southeast Asian condiment made with fermented fish, fish sauce is found in the ethnic section of many supermarkets, or you can substitute 1½ tablespoons of soy sauce. Serve this flavorful dish with steamed jasmine or basmati rice.

1. In a medium mixing bowl, whisk together the coconut milk, peanut butter, brown sugar, fish sauce, lime juice, and Tabasco sauce.

2. Heat the olive oil in a skillet on medium-high heat. Add the garlic.

3. Add the chicken and asparagus. Cook for a minute, stirring, to heat through.

4. Whisk the coconut milk mixture one more time. Add it to the pan and bring to a boil.

5. Cook for another minute, stirring to blend all the flavors. Serve hot.

Storing Leftover Food

Always store leftover food within two hours after cooking, in shallow, sealed containers. With a few exceptions, most leftover food can be used safely for up to three days. Throw away any stored food that looks unusual or has a strange odor.

Pan-Fried Steak with Fresh Fruit

*If ripe peaches aren't in season, you can substitute 1 cup
of drained canned peaches. Serve the stir-fried steak
over cooked rice.*

Serves 4

Preparation time:
5 minutes
Cooking time: 5 minutes

¾ pound beef stir-fry
    strips
1 tablespoon soy sauce
1 tablespoon red wine
    vinegar
Black pepper, to taste
2 teaspoons cornstarch
2 tablespoons orange
    juice
2 tablespoons water
1 teaspoon liquid honey
1 tablespoon vegetable oil
1 teaspoon bottled,
    minced gingerroot
2 large peaches, not
    overripe, sliced

1. In a medium bowl, combine the beef with the soy sauce, red wine vinegar, pepper, and cornstarch.

2. In a small bowl, stir together the orange juice, water, and honey.

3. Heat the oil in a skillet over medium-high heat. Add the minced ginger. Stir-fry for 10 seconds. Add the beef strips. Let brown for 30 seconds, then stir-fry, moving the strips around the pan. Stir-fry the beef for 3 to 5 minutes, until it loses its pinkness and is nearly cooked through.

4. Push the beef to the sides of the pan. Add the peaches to the middle of the pan. Stir-fry the peaches for a minute.

5. Stir the orange juice mixture and pour into the pan. Bring to a boil. Cook for another minute to blend all the flavors. Serve hot.

Easy Cajun Shrimp

Serves 4

Preparation time:
5 minutes
Cooking time: 5 minutes

*1 tablespoon
    Worcestershire sauce*
1 tablespoon lemon juice
2 tablespoons ketchup
1 tablespoon water
*1 pound shelled,
    deveined medium
    shrimp*
*3 tablespoons Cajun
    Spice seasoning*
1 tablespoon margarine

A salt-based mixture with chili powder and other spices, Cajun Spice seasoning can be found in the spice section of most supermarkets. To turn this into a one-dish meal, add two thinly sliced ribs of celery, prepare a double portion of sauce, and serve over cooked rice.

1. In a small bowl, stir together the Worcestershire sauce, lemon juice, ketchup, and water.

2. Rinse the shrimp and pat dry with paper towels. Place the shrimp in a bowl and toss with the Cajun Spice seasoning.

3. Melt the margarine in a skillet over medium-high heat, tilting the skillet so that the margarine covers the bottom of the pan.

4. Add the shrimp to the pan. Cook for about 3 minutes, until they turn pink.

5. Add the sauce and bring to a boil. Stir to mix everything together. Serve hot.

Reheating Leftovers

Instead of simply warming the food, reheat leftovers to an internal temperature of 165°F before serving This kills any bacteria that may have formed. Be sure to bring soups, sauces, and gravies to a rolling boil before reusing.

Stir-Fried Ground Turkey Paprikash

Sweet Hungarian paprika works best in this recipe, but if it is unavailable you can use hotter Spanish paprika.

Serves 4

Preparation time:
3–4 minutes
Cooking time:
5–6 minutes

*2 cups leftover cooked
  pasta
1 tablespoon vegetable oil
1 teaspoon bottled
  minced garlic
½ sweet onion, peeled
  and chopped
1 tablespoon paprika
½ teaspoon ground cumin
1 cup packaged stir-fry
  vegetables
½ cup canned or
  packaged beef broth
2 cups leftover cooked
  ground turkey
½ cup low-fat yogurt*

1. Reheat the pasta (see Serving Leftover Pasta, page 169).

2. Heat the oil in a skillet over medium-high heat. Add the garlic and onion. Stir-fry for 2 minutes, sprinkling the paprika and ground cumin over the onion.

3. Add the stir-fry vegetables. Stir-fry for 2 minutes or until the vegetables begin to soften. Splash with 1 tablespoon of the beef broth if they begin to dry out.

4. Add the ground turkey and stir-fry for a minute to heat through. Add the beef broth and bring to a boil.

5. Stir in the yogurt. Serve over the reheated noodles.

Got Leftover Leftovers?

Although it may be tempting, discard any reheated leftovers that aren't consumed the second time around. There is some evidence that reheating food more than once increases the risk of foodborne illness.

Easy Cooked Shrimp Scampi with Leftover Pasta

Serves 4

Preparation time:
5 minutes
Cooking time: 5 minutes

2 cups leftover cooked
    pasta
1 tablespoon olive oil
1 teaspoon lemon juice
½ stick unsalted butter
1 tablespoon bottled
    minced garlic
2 cups cooked shrimp
¼ teaspoon paprika
1 tablespoon chopped
    fresh parsley

Did you know: scampi is the Italian word for shrimp.

1.   Reheat the pasta (see Serving Leftover Pasta, page 169).

2.   Heat the olive oil, lemon juice, butter, and garlic in a skillet over medium heat, stirring to melt the butter. (Turn down the heat if the butter begins sizzling.)

3.   Add the shrimp. Cook for a minute, stirring to heat through and mix it in with the melted butter.

4.   Stir in the paprika and fresh parsley.

5.   Serve the shrimp over the reheated pasta.

Chapter 14
Grilling

Basic Grilled Steak with Barbecue Sauce

Serves 4

Preparation time:
10 minutes
Cooking time:
10 minutes

1½ pounds flank steak
½ cup store-bought
    barbecue sauce

Instead of store-bought barbecue sauce, you can also use Spicy Barbecue Sauce (page 250) in this recipe. Just prepare the sauce ahead of time and refrigerate until ready to use. How much barbecue sauce to use is a matter of personal preference; feel free to add more if desired.

1   Preheat the grill.

2.   Trim the steak of excess fat.

3.   Arrange the beef on the hottest part of the grill.

4.   Grill, turning occasionally, until the beef is cooked (about 8 minutes). Brush the steak with the barbecue sauce during the last few minutes of cooking.

5.   Let the steak rest for 2 to 3 minutes before serving.

Barbecue Sauce

Tomato-based, with brown sugar and vinegar, the classic barbecue sauce is an intriguing combination of sweet and tart flavors. Spices in the sauce frequently include cayenne pepper and garlic.

Grilled Steak and Onion Salad

This marinade tenderizes lean flank steak,
making it perfect for grilling.

1. Preheat the grill.

2. In a medium bowl, combine the balsamic vinegar, olive oil, Worcester-shire sauce, shallots, salt, parsley, and basil.

3. Arrange the beef on the hottest part of the grill. Brush with the balsamic vinegar dressing.

4. Grill the beef, turning occasionally and basting with the dressing, until it is cooked (about 8 minutes).

5. Let the steak rest for 2 to 3 minutes. Cut into thin strips and serve with the salad greens.

Serves 4

Preparation time:
10 minutes
Cooking time:
10–12 minutes

¼ cup balsamic vinegar
¼ cup olive oil
2 tablespoons
   Worcestershire sauce
2 shallots, chopped
½ teaspoon salt
1 tablespoon fresh
   chopped parsley
1 teaspoon chopped fresh
   basil leaves
1½ pounds flank steak
3 cups packaged salad
   greens

Grilled Corn on the Cob

Serves 6

Preparation time:
25 minutes
Cooking time:
30–40 minutes

6 ears sweet corn, husks
    on
4 tablespoons olive oil, or
    as needed
¼ cup melted butter, or
    as needed

Grilling corn on the cob takes more time than many other types of vegetables but the results are worth it. Corn on the cob is a natural for the grill, as the husks help protect the sweet corn from drying out. For extra flavor, use a flavored herb butter to brush on the corn.

1. Remove the thin strands of silk from the corn. Fill a large saucepan with enough cold water to cover the corn. Add the corn and let it soak for 20 minutes.

2. While the corn is soaking, preheat the grill.

3. Drain the corn thoroughly. Carefully pull back the husks as far as possible without removing them. Pull off any excess silk. Brush the olive oil over the ears of corn with a pastry brush, using about 1 tablespoon per ear of corn. Smooth the husks back over the corn and tie at the ends with an extra piece of husk or with a piece of twine.

4. Grill the corn on medium heat for 30 to 40 minutes, turning occasionally, until it is tender when pierced with a fork. Remove the corn from the grill and pull off the husks. (Be sure to wear oven mitts, as the corn and husks are hot.) Serve the corn with the melted butter.

Preparing Vegetables for Grilling

As with meat, poultry, and seafood, the high heat needed for grilling can dry out vegetables. A simple way to prevent this is to soak the vegetables in cold water for 30 minutes prior to cooking. Pat the soaked vegetables dry with paper towels and brush with a bit of olive oil before placing them on the grill.

Teriyaki Chicken

Lemon juice tenderizes the meat in this acid-based marinade, while olive oil disperses the sweet teriyaki flavor through the chicken. Instead of a bowl, you can marinate the chicken in a large zip-top bag, turning occasionally to make sure the chicken is coated.

Serves 4

Preparation time:
10 minutes
Marinating time: 2 hours
Cooking time:
15–20 minutes

*4 boneless, skinless
    chicken breast halves
    (about 1½ pounds)
½ cup teriyaki sauce
⅓ cup olive oil
⅓ cup lemon juice
1 teaspoon bottled
    minced ginger
Salt and pepper, to taste*

1. Rinse the chicken breasts and pat dry. Cut a few diagonal slits in the chicken to allow the marinade to penetrate.

2. In a large bowl, whisk together the teriyaki sauce, olive oil, lemon juice, minced ginger, salt, and pepper. Reserve ¼ cup to use as a basting sauce.

3. Add the chicken. Marinate in the refrigerator for 2 hours, turning once to ensure the chicken is completely coated in the marinade.

4. Preheat the grill.

5. Grill the chicken until it is cooked through (10 to 15 minutes), turning every 5 minutes and basting with the reserved marinade.

Using Marinades for Basting

A flavorful marinade makes a great basting sauce. However, there are potential health risks if the marinade has sat holding raw food. Be sure to stop basting at least 5 minutes before removing the food from the grill. The safest solution is to double up the marinade recipe, reserving half to use as a basting sauce.

Thai-Style Lime Chicken

Made from tamarind fruit—a tropical fruit that is rich in antioxidants—tamarind paste can be found in many Asian or ethnic supermarkets.

Serves 4

Preparation time:
10 minutes
Cooking time: 15 minutes

⅓ cup lime juice
⅓ cup olive oil
2 tablespoons fish sauce
1 tablespoon soy sauce
2 tablespoons tamarind
   paste
1 teaspoon bottled
   minced garlic
¼ cup chopped fresh
   cilantro leaves
4 boneless, skinless
   chicken breast halves

1. Preheat the grill.

2. In a blender, process the lime juice, olive oil, fish sauce, soy sauce, tamarind paste, garlic, and cilantro until smooth.

3. Place the marinade and the chicken breasts in a large, resealable plastic bag. Marinate the chicken in the refrigerator for at least 15 minutes. Remove and drain off excess marinade.

4. Place the chicken on the grill. Grill for 15 minutes or until the chicken is cooked through, turning over halfway through cooking.

Easy Korean Bulgogi

In this quick and easy version of the popular Korean dish, a soy sauce and sesame oil dressing is brushed on the steak while it is cooking. On evenings when you have more time, you can double the amount of dressing and use it to marinate the beef for at least 15 minutes before grilling.

Serves 4

Preparation time:
10 minutes
Cooking time: 10 minutes

4 tablespoons Kikkoman
    soy sauce
2 tablespoons apple cider
    vinegar
2 tablespoons Asian dark
    sesame oil
1 teaspoon bottled
    minced garlic
2 tablespoons granulated
    sugar
2 pounds beef sirloin
    steak, thinly sliced
2 tablespoons toasted
    white sesame seeds

1. Preheat the grill. In a small bowl, stir together the soy sauce, apple cider vinegar, sesame oil, garlic, and sugar.

2. Arrange the beef on the hottest part of the grill. Brush with the dressing.

3. Grill the beef, turning occasionally and basting with the dressing, until it is cooked, about 8 minutes.

4. While the steak is grilling, toast the sesame seeds in a frying pan over medium-low heat, shaking the pan continually, until the seeds turn golden and have a nutty flavor (about 5 minutes). Pour the seeds over the steak.

5. Let the steak rest for 2 to 3 minutes. Cut into thin strips. Serve with salad greens.

Bulgogi Trimmings

Traditionally, bulgogi is served with a number of side dishes, including sticky rice, green onions, and lettuce for wrapping up the cooked meat. Condiments include a dipping sauce made with Asian sesame oil and salt, soybean paste, and spicy Korean pepper paste.

Japanese Sukiyaki

Serves 6

Preparation time:
15 minutes
Cooking time: 15 minutes

1½ pounds sirloin steak
1 cup Kikkoman soy
    sauce
½ cup Japanese sake
6 tablespoons granulated
    sugar
2 green onions, thinly
    chopped
8 ounces fresh shiitake
    mushrooms, cleaned,
    stems removed

*Sake, the Japanese version of rice wine, has a sweeter |
flavor than Chinese rice wine. Sake can commonly be
found in liquor stores.*

1. Preheat the grill. Cut the beef into thin strips about 3" long.

2. In a medium bowl, combine the soy sauce, sake, sugar, and chopped
    green onions. Pour half the mixture into a separate bowl. Add the thinly
    sliced beef and marinate for 10 minutes.

3. Heat the reserved half of the mixture in a saucepan over medium-low
    heat. Keep warm on low heat while the steak is cooking.

4. Thread the marinated beef and the mushrooms onto skewers. Cook for
    5 minutes, turn, and grill for 5 more minutes.

5. Serve the beef with the reserved heated marinade to use as a dipping
    sauce.

Buffalo Wings

Grilling the wings and using store-bought blue cheese dressing takes most of the work out of this spicy appetizer from Buffalo, New York. Use your favorite brand of hot sauce.

1. Preheat the grill. Rub the salt and pepper over the chicken wings.

2. In a medium bowl, stir the vinegar into the blue cheese dressing.

3. In a saucepan on low heat, melt the butter with the hot sauce, stirring.

4. Place the chicken wings on the grill and brush with the butter and hot sauce mixture.

5. Grill the wings for 10 minutes or until they are cooked, turning halfway and brushing frequently with the hot butter. Serve the wings with the blue cheese dressing for dipping.

Grill Your Potato Salad

Potato salad is a popular side dish for Buffalo wings, but preparing it ahead of time can lead to food safety issues. An easy way to avoid the problem is to prepare your potato salad on the grill. Partially cook the potatoes by boiling them until they can be pierced with a knife, but are not tender. Grill the potatoes on high heat for approximately 20 minutes, until tender, then combine them in a large bowl with cooked bacon, celery, onion, or whatever else you prefer. Toss the salad with your favorite mustard or red wine vinaigrette.

Serves 5

Preparation time:
10 minutes
Cooking time: 10 minutes

1 teaspoon salt
1 teaspoon black pepper
15 chicken wings
1½ tablespoons apple
  cider vinegar
1¼ cups blue cheese
  dressing
1 stick unsalted butter
½ cup hot sauce

Grilled Tuna Steaks

Serves 4

Preparation time:
5 minutes
Cooking time: 10 minutes

½ cup olive oil
3 tablespoons lemon juice
¼ teaspoon black pepper
4 tuna steaks, 8 ounces each
Simple Salsa Verde (page 248)

Not sure how long to cook tuna? For well-done tuna, grill for 9 to 10 minutes, until it is opaque right through. For medium doneness, cook the tuna for 6 to 7 minutes.

1. Preheat the grill.

2. In a small bowl, stir together the olive oil, lemon juice, and pepper. Brush over the tuna steaks.

3. Place the tuna on the hottest part of the grill. Cook for 10 minutes or to the desired level of doneness, using tongs to turn the tuna over halfway through cooking and taking care not to overcook.

4. Serve the grilled tuna with the Simple Salsa Verde (page 248).

Pork Satay with Spicy Peanut Sauce

Serves 6

Preparation time:
10 minutes
Marinating time:
30 minutes
Cooking time: 10 minutes

1½ pounds boneless pork loin
Spicy Peanut Sauce (page 252)

Using bamboo skewers to grill the pork? Be sure to soak them in water for 30 minutes to keep them from burning.

1. Cut the pork into 1" cubes.

2. Arrange the pork in a shallow glass dish. Stir in the peanut sauce.

3. Marinate the pork in the refrigerator for 30 minutes.

4. Heat the grill. Thread the pork onto bamboo skewers.

5. Grill the pork for about 10 minutes, until it is cooked through, turning occasionally.

Grilled Salmon

Serve this simple dish with Grilled Harvest Vegetables (page 217) or Instant Mashed Potato Salad (page 64) for a quick and easy meal.

Serves 4

Preparation time:
10 minutes
Cooking time: 15 minutes

1 cup peach yogurt
¼ cup olive oil
2 teaspoons dried dill
   leaves
½ teaspoon salt
4 salmon fillets, 8 ounces
   each

1. Preheat the grill.

2. In a small bowl, stir together the yogurt, olive oil, dill leaves, and salt.

3. Take a piece of aluminum foil and cut it into four rectangular pieces, each large enough to wrap around one salmon fillet.

4. Place the fillets in the foil squares and brush liberally with the yogurt mixture. Close up the foil packet.

5. Place the packets on the grill. Grill the salmon for 15 minutes or until it is cooked through.

Choosing Fish for the Grill

It's best to use a firm-fleshed, thickly cut fish that won't fall apart on the grill. Trout, swordfish, salmon, halibut, and red snapper are all good choices. Some delicate fishes like flounder may take on the taste of the charcoal and so aren't ideal candidates for grilling. You'll also want to avoid any fish that flakes easily, such as haddock or pollack.

Grilled Portobello Mushrooms

Serves 4

Preparation time:
5 minutes
Cooking time: 15 minutes

1 pound portobello
   mushrooms
½ stick unsalted butter
¼ cup olive oil
2 tablespoons balsamic
   vinegar
1 shallot, chopped
½ teaspoon salt
½ teaspoon dried parsley
½ teaspoon dried basil
   leaves

Flavorful portobello mushrooms are a great choice for grilling—cooking enhances their meaty flavor, and their high water content and thick texture means they won't dry out during cooking or fall apart on the grill.

1. Preheat the grill.

2. Wash the mushrooms and remove the stems.

3. In a small saucepan over low heat, melt the butter with the olive oil, balsamic vinegar, shallot, salt, parsley, and basil.

4. Place the mushroom caps on the grill with the gills facing upward. Brush the mushrooms with some of the melted butter mixture.

5. Grill the mushrooms for up to 10 minutes or until they are tender, turning halfway and brushing frequently with the melted butter mixture.

Grilled Harvest Vegetables

Soaking the vegetables before grilling helps prevent them from drying out. Serve the grilled vegetables with garlic aioli—a French garlic and oil sauce that is available at most supermarkets.

1. Preheat the grill.

2. Soak all the vegetables in water for 30 minutes. Drain.

3. Use a pastry brush to brush the olive oil over the vegetables.

4. Lay the bell pepper halves, onions, and zucchini slices directly on the grill. Place the mushrooms in a grilling basket and lower onto the grill.

5. Grill the vegetables for 5 to 6 minutes or until they are cooked through, turning over halfway during cooking. (Cooking times for individual vegetables may vary slightly.)

Grill Baskets

Grill baskets are ideal for cooking smaller pieces of food such as shrimp or mushrooms that can fall through the grilling rack, or for fragile foods such as fish fillets. To ensure the food doesn't stick to the basket, spray it with a nonstick cooking spray, or brush with oil before adding the food. Depending on the design, the grill basket may have a long heat-proof handle to make it easier to manipulate the food. If yours does not, be sure to wear oven mitts.

Serves 6

Preparation time:
30 minutes
Cooking time: 6 minutes

⅔ cup olive oil
3 red bell peppers, cut in
   half, seeds removed
2 sweet onions, peeled,
   cut into quarters
3 zucchini, thinly sliced
10 button mushrooms,
   cleaned, stems
   removed

Grilled Chicken Salad

Preparation time:
10 minutes
Cooking time: 15 minutes

⅓ cup olive oil
⅓ cup red wine vinegar
2 tablespoons soy sauce
1 teaspoon Dijon mustard
½ teaspoon salt, or to
taste
⅛ teaspoon black pepper,
or to taste
1 tablespoon minced
onion
1 pound boneless,
skinless chicken
breast halves
1 head lettuce
1 pint cherry tomatoes
1 English cucumber, thinly
sliced
½ cup crumbled feta
cheese
12 whole pitted olives,
chopped

A simple mixture of olive oil, red wine vinegar, soy sauce, and spices doubles as marinade and salad dressing in this easy recipe that is perfect for summer entertaining.

1. Preheat the grill. In a medium bowl, whisk together the olive oil, red wine vinegar, soy sauce, mustard, salt, pepper, and minced onion. Reserve ¼ cup to baste the chicken.

2. Place the chicken breasts on the grill and brush with the reserved marinade. Grill the chicken until it is cooked through, turning every 5 minutes and brushing with the marinade (total cooking time will be about 10–15 minutes).

3. While the chicken is grilling, combine the lettuce, tomatoes, and cucumber in a large salad bowl.

4. Let the chicken cool for a few minutes, and then shred, tearing it into small strips with your hands.

5. Mix the chicken into the salad. Whisk the remaining dressing one more time and then pour it into the salad and gently toss. Sprinkle the crumbled feta cheese and olives on top.

Chapter 15
Vegetable Sides

Microwave French Fries

Serves 2

Preparation time:
5–7 minutes
Cooking time:
15–20 minutes

½ pound (2 medium)
   russet or red potatoes,
   peeled
¼ cup white vinegar
¼ teaspoon garlic salt
¼ teaspoon cayenne
   pepper

Preparing French fries in the microwave is quicker and healthier than deep-frying them in hot oil. Be sure not to overcook the potatoes or they will deflate and become soft.

1. Scrub the potatoes under cold running water and use a paring knife to cut out any bruises or green spots. Cut into thin strips the size and shape of French fries.

2. Toss the cut potatoes in a bowl with the vinegar, stirring so that all the potato strips are coated.

3. Take approximately half the potato strips and arrange on a microwave-safe plate. Sprinkle the cut potatoes with the garlic salt.

4. Microwave the cut potatoes on high heat for 7 minutes, and then for 1 minute at a time until they are cooked through. (The potatoes will not brown like regular French fries, but will be fork-tender.)

5. Repeat with the remainder of the cut potatoes, sprinkling with the cayenne pepper instead of garlic salt.

Quick-Cooking with Potatoes

One way to speed up the preparation time when you're cooking potatoes is to leave on the peel. Potato peels add a crunchy texture, and carry fiber and vitamin B2 (riboflavin). Just be sure to scrub the potato skin under cold running water to remove any pesticide residue or other toxins.

Roasted Red Peppers

Roasting is a great way to bring out the sweet flavor of red bell peppers. To add extra color, try using a combination of red and yellow bell peppers. Green peppers can also be roasted; however, the flavor will not be as sweet.

Serves 4

Preparation time:
5 minutes
Cooking time: 15 minutes

4 red bell peppers
2 tablespoons olive oil

1. Preheat the broiler and line it with aluminum foil. Cut the stems off the red peppers; cut the peppers in half and remove the seeds.

2. Place the peppers on the broiling pan with the skin side facing up. Use a pastry brush to brush the peppers with the olive oil.

3. Broil the peppers for 15 minutes, or until most of the skin is blackened.

4. Use tongs to remove the peppers from the broiler and cover in aluminum foil or plastic wrap. Let the wrapped peppers stand for at least 10 minutes before removing the covering. Peel off the skins and cut into thin slices or squares as desired.

Versatile Peppers

Roasted red peppers add flavor to pasta dishes, heartier soups, and dips. You'll often find them used in combination with aromatic basil, pungent garlic, or cheese. Their sweet flavor pairs particularly well with goat cheese—for a quick snack, serve the roasted peppers and goat cheese on crusty bread.

Quick Green Beans Amandine

Feel free to use your favorite brand of soy sauce in this recipe, and to substitute toasted sesame seeds or walnuts for the almonds if desired.

Serves 4

Cooking time:
7–10 minutes

2 cups canned
    French-cut green
    beans
2 teaspoons butter or
    margarine
2 teaspoons soy sauce
2 tablespoons slivered
    almonds

1. Heat the green beans to a boil in a small saucepan on medium heat.

2. Use a strainer to drain the juice from the beans.

3. Place the beans in a bowl or return them to the saucepan.

4. Immediately stir in the butter or margarine and the soy sauce.

5. Garnish with the slivered almonds. Serve immediately.

Roasted Fall Harvest Vegetables

Roasting is a great way to bring out the natural sweetness of vegetables. You can combine leftovers with chicken broth to make roasted vegetable soup.

Serves 4

Preparation time:
10 minutes
Cooking time:
35–40 minutes

1 butternut squash,
    peeled, cut into 1"
    cubes
2 shallots, peeled and cut
    in half
4 carrots, peeled and cut
    julienne
2 zucchini, cut into 1"
    pieces
2 tablespoons olive oil
1½ teaspoons dried
    oregano
1½ teaspoons dried basil
Salt and pepper, to taste

1. Preheat oven to 400°F.

2. In a large bowl, toss the prepared vegetables (the squash, shallots, carrots, and zucchini) with the olive oil, oregano, basil, salt, and pepper.

3. Spray a large baking sheet with cooking spray. Lay the butternut squash and carrots out on the baking sheet, cut-side down, and add the shallots. Roast for 20 minutes, stirring occasionally, then add the zucchini. Roast the vegetables for another 15 to 20 minutes, stirring a few times, until the vegetables are tender and browning at the edges.

Stir-Fried Broccoli in Oyster-Flavored Sauce

If your kitchen cupboard includes a selection of Asian sauces and seasonings, you can enhance the sauce by adding light and dark soy sauce and a few drops of toasted Asian sesame oil.

1. Combine the chicken broth, oyster sauce, and sugar in a small bowl or measuring cup. Set aside.

2. Heat a large skillet over medium-high heat. Add the oil. When the oil is heated, add the ginger slices. Stir for a few seconds, then add the onion. Stir-fry the onion for about 2 minutes, until it begins to soften, and add in the garlic salt.

3. Add the florets, stir-frying for about 3 minutes until they are tender but crisp. Add 1 or 2 tablespoons water to the florets if they begin to dry out.

4. Stir the sauce and pour it over the broccoli. Bring to a boil and stir-fry for another minute to mix the sauce with the broccoli. Add salt and pepper as desired. Serve hot.

Oyster Sauce

Made from an extract of boiled oysters and seasonings, oyster sauce is available in the ethnic or international section of many supermarkets. Use it whenever you want to add a savory flavor to marinades and sauces. There are also several vegetarian brands available, made from either oyster or shiitake mushrooms.

Serves 4

Preparation time: 5 minutes
Cooking time: 7 minutes

¼ cup canned or packaged chicken broth
2 tablespoons oyster sauce
1 teaspoon granulated sugar
2 tablespoons vegetable oil
2 slices ginger
½ onion, chopped
¼ teaspoon garlic salt, or to taste
1 pound broccoli florets
Salt and black pepper, to taste

Sesame Spinach

Serves 4

Preparation time:
5 minutes
Cooking time:
7–8 minutes

1 cup water
2 cups frozen spinach
2 teaspoons butter
2 teaspoons
    Worcestershire sauce
4 tablespoons toasted
    sesame seeds

Toasted sesame seeds add a fragrant, nutty flavor to this simple vegetable dish. Use margarine instead of butter if desired.

1. In a medium saucepan, bring the water to a boil. Add the frozen spinach and return to a boil.

2. Turn the heat down to medium, cover, and simmer until the spinach is heated through (about 5 minutes).

3. Drain the cooked spinach in a colander.

4. Place in a bowl and stir in the butter and Worcestershire sauce.

5. Garnish with the toasted sesame seeds.

How to Toast Sesame Seeds

Spread the seeds out in a frying pan and cook on low-medium heat, shaking the pan occasionally, until the seeds are fragrant and turn a light golden brown. If not using immediately, store the sesame seeds in a sealed container in the cupboard.

Thai-Style Creamed Corn

Homemade creamed corn takes only minutes to make and has much more flavor than store-bought. Thai basil adds a distinctive licorice flavor, but if it is unavailable you can substitute regular basil leaves.

1. In a small bowl, stir together the cornstarch and 1 tablespoon of the coconut milk.

2. In a small saucepan, heat the oil on medium-low heat. Stir in the garlic and shallot and sauté for 2 to 3 minutes until softened. Stir in the chopped jalapeño peppers. Add the corn and chicken broth and bring to a boil, stirring.

3. Stir in the brown sugar, salt, and pepper. Add the remaining coconut milk and bring to a boil. Turn the heat down and simmer for 5 minutes.

4. Stir the cornstarch slurry and add in the middle of the saucepan, stirring quickly to thicken. Stir in the chopped basil. Serve hot.

Serves 4

Preparation time:
5–10 minutes
Cooking time: 10 minutes

1 teaspoon cornstarch
¼ cup coconut milk, divided
1 tablespoon vegetable oil
1 teaspoon chopped garlic
1 shallot, chopped
1 teaspoon canned jalapeño peppers, chopped
2 cups frozen or canned corn
¼ cup chicken broth
1 tablespoon brown sugar
Salt and pepper, to taste
¼ cup chopped Thai basil leaves

Sautéed Cabbage with Apple

To turn this cabbage side dish into a lunch or light dinner, add leftover cooked ham, sausage, or ground beef.

Serves 4

Preparation time:
10 minutes
Cooking time: 12 minutes

2 tablespoons olive oil
2 apples, peeled, cored, and chopped
4 cups shredded green cabbage
¼ teaspoon paprika, or to taste
⅛ teaspoon garlic salt, or to taste
2 tablespoons red wine vinegar

1. Heat the olive oil in a skillet over medium heat. Add the apples and cabbage.

2. Turn the heat to low and cook for about 10 minutes, until the cabbage is wilted and the apple has softened.

3. Stir in the paprika, garlic salt, and red wine vinegar. Serve immediately.

Three Mushroom Stir-Fry

Stir-frying is a great way to bring out the flavor of fresh mushrooms. For extra color, try replacing the oyster mushroom with half of a red bell pepper, cut into chunks.

Serves 4

Preparation time:
5 minutes
Cooking time:
3–4 minutes

¼ pound fresh shiitake mushrooms
¼ pound fresh button mushrooms
1 oyster mushroom
1 tablespoon vegetable oil
1 shallot, chopped
1 tablespoon lemon juice
1 tablespoon red wine vinegar
Black pepper to taste, optional

1. Wipe the mushrooms clean with a damp cloth or brush with a mushroom brush. Thinly slice the shiitake and button mushrooms. Cut the oyster mushroom into thin pieces. (If you like, remove the leathery "gill" underneath the cap of the oyster mushroom.)

2. Add the oil to a heavy skillet preheated on medium-high heat. Add the shallot and the mushrooms. Stir-fry for a minute.

3. Stir in the lemon juice and red wine vinegar. Cook the vegetables for another minute, stirring continually to keep them from burning. Season with pepper if desired. Serve hot.

Stir-Fried Broccoli with Garlic

Stir-frying has the advantage of being both quick and healthy—the short cooking time means that vegetables retain more of their nutrients.

Serves 3

Preparation time:
5 minutes
Cooking time: 8 minutes

2 tablespoons olive oil
2 garlic cloves, peeled
　　and finely chopped
½ teaspoon red pepper
　　flakes, or to taste
½ pound broccoli florets
⅛ teaspoon salt, or to
　　taste
2 tablespoons water
1 red bell pepper,
　　seeded, cut into
　　chunks
2 teaspoons lemon juice
2 teaspoons soy sauce

1. Heat the olive oil in a skillet on medium-high heat. Add the garlic cloves and red pepper flakes.

2. Add the broccoli. Stir briefly, sprinkling the salt over the broccoli while cooking, until the florets turn bright green.

3. Add the water and let the broccoli cook for 2 or 3 more minutes.

4. Add the red bell pepper. Stir in the lemon juice and soy sauce. Cook, stirring, for another minute. Serve immediately.

Preparing Vegetables Ahead of Time

One way to speed up meal-preparation time is to chop several days' worth of vegetables ahead of time. Store the vegetables for each meal in a sealed bag in the refrigerator until ready to use.

Simple Glazed Baby Carrots

Using tender baby carrots saves you from the work of having to peel and chop regular-size carrots.

Serves 4

Cooking time:
15–20 minutes

1 tablespoon olive oil
1 pound baby carrots
1 cup orange juice
1 cup water
2 tablespoons butter
2 tablespoons brown
    sugar
Fresh parsley, for garnish,
    optional

1. Heat the olive oil in a skillet over medium heat.

2. Add the carrots, orange juice, and water. Turn down the heat, cover, and simmer until the carrots are tender (about 12 minutes).

3. While the carrots are cooking, melt the butter and brown sugar in a saucepan, stirring to dissolve the sugar.

4. Add the brown sugar mixture to the carrots. Cook for another 5 minutes, or until the liquid is reduced and the carrots are nicely glazed. Garnish with the fresh parsley before serving.

Sautéed Asparagus

Blanching asparagus shortens the cooking time, making it easier to combine with other, quicker-cooking vegetables in sautéed or stir-fry dishes.

Serves 4

Preparation time:
10 minutes
Cooking time: 5 minutes

1 pound asparagus, cut
    diagonally into 2"
    pieces
2 tablespoons olive oil
1 garlic clove, finely
    chopped
2 teaspoons finely
    chopped fresh
    gingerroot
1 red bell pepper,
    seeded, cut into thin
    strips
2 tablespoons soy sauce
¼ teaspoon red pepper
    flakes

1. Fill a large saucepan with enough water to cover the asparagus and bring to a boil. Briefly blanch the asparagus, cooking in the boiling water for 1 minute. Remove the asparagus with a slotted spoon and rinse with cold water. Drain.

2. Heat the olive oil in a skillet on medium-high heat. Add the garlic, ginger, and asparagus.

3. Cook for 1 minute, then add the red bell pepper. Stir in the soy sauce and red pepper flakes. Cook until the asparagus is tender but still crisp. Serve hot.

Marinated Artichoke Hearts

Using frozen artichokes takes the work out of cleaning and boiling fresh artichokes. Serve them as a simple side dish or over cooked pasta.

Serves 2

Thawing time: 5 minutes
Preparation time:
5–10 minutes

8 frozen artichoke hearts,
   halved
¼ cup olive oil
¼ cup red wine vinegar
2 tablespoons lemon juice
¼ teaspoon garlic powder
Seasoned salt, to taste

1. Thaw the artichokes in the microwave according to the package directions.

2. In a small bowl, combine the olive oil, red wine vinegar, lemon juice, garlic powder, and seasoned salt.

3. Place the artichokes in a resealable bag. Pour in the dressing. Store in the refrigerator until ready to use.

Simple Steamed Mushrooms

While mushrooms are commonly grilled or sautéed, they can also be steamed. Serve this simple side dish with Lemon Beef (page 98) and a green salad for a complete meal.

Serves 2

Preparation time:
5 minutes
Cooking time: 5 minutes

4 large portobello
   mushrooms
1 cup chicken broth, or as
   needed
1 tablespoon balsamic
   vinegar
Black pepper, to taste

1. Wipe the mushrooms clean with a damp cloth. Separate the stems from the caps.

2. Bring the chicken broth to boil in a medium saucepan. (The pan should have about 1½" of liquid.) Place a metal steamer in the saucepan.

3. Place the mushroom pieces in the steamer.

4. Steam the mushrooms for 3 to 4 minutes. Use a pastry brush to brush on the balsamic vinegar. Season with the pepper.

5. Steam the mushrooms for 2 to 3 more minutes, until they are tender.

Speedy Stir-Fried Ratatouille

This quick and easy dish makes a light lunch for two people or a side dish for four. Blanching the eggplant in the microwave takes only a couple of minutes, and helps prevent it from soaking up too much oil when it is stir-fried.

Serves 2

Preparation time:
10 minutes
Cooking time: 10 minutes

1 pound eggplant (one-
    half large eggplant),
    cut in ½" cubes
2 tablespoons vegetable
    or peanut oil
½ teaspoon salt, or to
    taste
1 zucchini, thinly sliced on
    the diagonal
1 onion, peeled and
    sliced
¼ teaspoon dried
    oregano, or to taste
1 red bell pepper, cut in
    ½" cubes
1 tablespoon chicken
    broth, or as needed
½ cup canned tomatoes
⅛ teaspoon black pepper,
    or to taste

1. Place the eggplant in a microwave-safe dish and cover with water. Microwave the eggplant on high heat for 2 minutes, then continue microwaving for 30 seconds at a time as needed, until it is tender but still crisp.

2. Heat the oil and the salt in a heavy skillet on medium-high heat, tilting the skillet so that it covers the bottom of the pan and halfway up the sides.

3. Add the zucchini and the onion to the pan. Stir in the dried oregano. Cook the vegetables for 2 minutes, stirring constantly to keep them from burning.

4. Add the eggplant to the pan. Stir for a few seconds, then add the bell pepper. Cook, stirring for a few more seconds. (Total stir-frying time at this point should be about 3 minutes.) Stir in the chicken broth as needed, if the vegetables begin to dry out.

5. Turn the heat down to low-medium. Stir in the canned tomatoes. Simmer for 2 to 3 minutes, stirring occasionally to mix everything together. Stir in the pepper. Serve immediately.

Chinese Five-Spice Potatoes

Did you know: There are two basic types of potatoes—floury potatoes (such as fingerling potatoes) break down more easily, making them perfect for mashing and baking, while waxy potatoes (such as red potatoes) hold their shape better for roasting.

1. Preheat the oven to 375°F.

2. Wash the potatoes. Cut in half lengthwise, then crosswise into quarters. Cut each quarter in half.

3. Combine the melted butter or margarine, five-spice powder, salt, and pepper in a small bowl.

4. Lay the potatoes on a baking sheet. Use a pastry brush to brush the potatoes with the seasoned butter mixture. Bake the potatoes until golden brown and tender, about 50 minutes.

Fabulous Five-Spice Powder

An intriguing mix of sweet, sour, pungent, salty, and bitter, five-spice powder is an indispensable ingredient in Chinese cuisine. But that doesn't mean it needs to sit in the cupboard when you're not cooking Chinese food! Use this aromatic spice blend whenever you want to lend extra flavor to dry rubs and marinades for meat and poultry.

Serves 4

Preparation time:
10 minutes
Roasting time:
50 minutes

3 baking potatoes
2 tablespoons melted
    butter or margarine
2 teaspoons five-spice
    powder
½ teaspoon salt
Freshly ground black
    pepper, to taste

Garlic Mashed Potatoes

Serves 6

Preparation time:
5–10 minutes
Cooking time: 20 minutes

4 medium red potatoes
4 tablespoons butter or
    margarine
¼ cup milk
2 teaspoons garlic
    powder, or to taste
½ teaspoon salt, or to
    taste

Cooking the potatoes in the microwave speeds up the preparation time, since you don't have to wait for the water to boil. Serve these flavorful potatoes with Honey Mustard Pork Chops (page 119.)

1. Wash and peel the potatoes. Cut them roughly into bite-size chunks.

2. Place the potatoes in a deep microwave-safe dish and cover with water.

3. Microwave the potatoes at high heat for 10 minutes. Give the dish a quarter turn and continue microwaving for 1 or 2 minutes at a time until the potatoes are cooked through and can easily be pierced with a fork. (Total cooking time should be about 15 minutes.) Drain.

4. Place the potatoes in a large bowl. Add the butter or margarine and use a fork or a potato masher to whip the potatoes, while gradually adding the milk until the potatoes have reached the desired consistency (do not add more milk than is needed). Stir in the garlic powder and salt.

Chapter 16
Party Time

No-Cook Spring Rolls

Serves 8

Preparation time:
15 minutes

8 rice paper wrappers
2 cups packaged
    coleslaw mix
¼ cup hoisin sauce
1 teaspoon lime juice
1½ tablespoons water
⅛ teaspoon garlic
    powder, or to taste
¼ teaspoon red pepper
    flakes, or to taste
1 tablespoon chopped
    peanuts

These rolls are incredibly easy to make—the secret is rice paper wrappers, which only need to be briefly dipped in warm water before using. You'll find them in the refrigerated section of many local supermarkets.

1. Carefully dip each rice paper wrapper in a small bowl filled with warm water to moisten (about 20 seconds).

2. Lay the wrapper on a cutting board in front of you. Place about ¼ cup of the packaged coleslaw mix on the bottom half of the wrapper, being careful not to come too close to the edges.

3. Roll up the wrapper like a taco, tucking in the sides. Continue filling and rolling up the remainder of the rice paper wrappers.

4. In a small bowl, stir together the hoisin sauce, lime juice, water, garlic powder, and red pepper flakes. Garnish the dip with the chopped peanuts.

5. Serve the rolls cold with the hoisin dip.

No-Cook Substitutes for Rice Paper Wrappers

The beauty of rice paper wrappers is that once the wrapper is softened in water, it can be filled and served without any further cooking. While spring roll wrappers or even phyllo dough can be used as a substitute for rice paper wrappers, the rolls will then need to be fried after they are filled. If you're looking for a quick and easy no-cook substitute for rice paper wrappers, one option is to use a tortilla wrapper—try using one of the flavored wraps, such as spinach or roasted red pepper.

Italian-Inspired Bruschetta

Using canned diced tomatoes with seasonings means there is no need to chop and seed tomatoes in this take on the popular Italian appetizer.

Serves 8

Preparation time:
5 minutes
Cooking time: 2 minutes

2 cloves garlic
8 slices crusty French or
   Italian bread
¾ cup diced tomatoes
   with basil and garlic
1½ tablespoons extra-
   virgin olive oil
Salt and pepper, to taste
½ cup grated Parmesan
   cheese

1. Preheat the broiler on high heat. Spray a broiling rack with nonstick cooking spray.

2. Cut the garlic cloves in half. Rub both sides of each slice of bread with a garlic clove half.

3. In a medium bowl, stir together the diced tomatoes and olive oil. Season with salt and pepper to taste.

4. Spread the tomato mixture over each slice of bread. Sprinkle the Parmesan cheese on top.

5. Lay the bread slices out on the rack. Broil the toast on high heat for up to 2 minutes, until the cheese has melted and the bread is toasted.

Deviled Eggs

For a fancier presentation, use a pastry tube to fill the hollowed cooked egg white with the spicy egg yolk mixture.

Serves 6

Preparation time:
10 minutes

6 hard-boiled eggs,
   peeled
3 tablespoons
   mayonnaise
1 green onion, finely
   chopped
1 tablespoon
   Worcestershire sauce
1½ teaspoons ketchup
½ teaspoon curry powder
Black pepper, to taste

1. Cut the eggs in half lengthwise. Use a spoon to carefully remove the yolks. Do not discard the cooked egg white.

2. Place the yolks in a small bowl. Use a fork to mash the yolks until they are fluffy. Stir in the mayonnaise, green onion, Worcestershire sauce, ketchup, curry powder, and pepper.

3. Carefully spoon a small amount of the mashed egg yolk mixture into each egg half. Chill until ready to serve.

Microwave Tex-Mex Nachos

A processed cheese with a creamy texture, Velveeta's quick-melting properties make it an excellent choice for microwave recipes.

Serves 4

Preparation time:
5–8 minutes
Cooking time:
3–5 minutes

5 cups nacho chips
6 ounces Velveeta
   cheese, sliced
2 cups red kidney beans
1 tablespoon chili powder,
   or to taste
½ teaspoon ground cumin
3 tablespoons sour cream
½ cup sliced olives,
   optional

1. Lay out the nacho chips on a plate.

2. Place the Velveeta cheese in a 2-quart microwave-safe casserole dish. Microwave on high until the cheese is nearly melted, stopping and stirring every 30 seconds (total time will be about 1½ minutes).

3. Stir in the kidney beans, chili powder, ground cumin, and sour cream. Microwave on high heat for 1 minute, and then as needed until the cheese is melted and everything is heated through.

4. Spoon the cheese and bean mixture over the nacho chips. Garnish with the olives.

Simple Cheese and Fruit Platter

You can vary this basic arrangement by making use of fresh fruit in season.

Serves 8

Preparation time:
10 minutes

1 cup green seedless
   grapes
1 pint fresh blueberries
½ pint strawberries
2 cups sliced pineapple
½ pound cheddar cheese,
   cubed
½ pound Danish Havarti,
   sliced
2 packages water
   crackers

1. Rinse the grapes and blueberries in cold water. Drain and pat dry.

2. Rinse the strawberries, hull, and cut in half.

3. Arrange the fruit, cheese, and crackers on two large serving trays. Serve immediately.

Beef Ciabatta

Italian for "slipper," ciabatta is a fat, oval-shaped bread with a distinctive flavor that is reminiscent of sourdough bread.

1. Cut the ciabatta loaf in half lengthwise.

2. Heat the vegetable oil in a heavy skillet over medium-high heat. Add the sausage and the onion. Sauté the onion for 4 to 5 minutes, until it is softened.

3. Add the tomato, pressing down so that it releases its juices. Add the mushrooms and bell pepper. Cook for about another 4 to 5 minutes, stirring, until the vegetables are tender but still crisp and heated through.

4. Spread the mixture on one half of the ciabatta loaf. Top with the mozzarella cheese. Add the other half and close up the sandwich. Cut into four equal slices.

Freezing Shredded Cheese

The easiest solution for what to do with leftover shredded cheese is to freeze it. You can freeze shredded cheese for up to two months. Thaw the cheese in the refrigerator and use as soon as possible.

Serves 6

Preparation time:
10 minutes
Cooking time:
10–12 minutes

1 loaf ciabatta bread
2 tablespoons vegetable oil
½ pound chorizo or andouille sausage, sliced
½ red onion, sliced
1 tomato, thinly sliced
½ cup sliced fresh mushrooms
½ red bell pepper, cut julienne-style
½ cup shredded mozzarella cheese

Basic Guacamole

Salsa takes the work out of dicing tomatoes, while bottled jalapeño peppers replace fresh chili peppers in this simple guacamole recipe. If you wish, you can increase the heat by mixing in 1 teaspoon of chili powder.

Serves 4

Preparation time:
10 minutes

3 avocados
⅔ cup salsa
1 tablespoon bottled
    chopped jalapeño
    peppers
2 tablespoons finely
    chopped cilantro, or
    to taste
1 tablespoon lemon juice
1 (6-ounce) bag tortilla
    chips

1. Peel the avocados. With a knife, cut the avocados in half and remove the round pit in the middle. Place the pitted avocados in a medium bowl and mash with a fork or potato masher.

2. In a medium bowl, stir together the remaining ingredients except for the chips. Add the mashed avocado, stirring to mix it in. If the guacamole is too chunky, mash a bit more.

3. Serve the guacamole with tortilla chips.

Baked Pita Chips

These make a lighter alternative to taco or potato chips as a dip accompaniment. They go very nicely with an Italian salsa or with Roasted Red Pepper Dip (page 240).

Serves 6

Preparation time:
10 minutes
Cooking time:
10–15 minutes

3 pita wheels
2 tablespoons olive oil
1½ teaspoons lemon juice
½ teaspoon garlic salt, or
    to taste
½ teaspoon dried basil
½ teaspoon dried
    oregano
Black pepper, to taste

1. Preheat the oven to 350°F.

2. Cut each pita wheel into six even wedges.

3. In a small saucepan, heat the olive oil and lemon juice over low heat. Stir in the garlic salt, basil, oregano, and pepper.

4. Place the pita wedges on two baking sheets sprayed with nonstick cooking spray. Use a pastry brush to brush the olive oil and spice mixture on top.

5. Cook for 10 minutes, or until the pita wedges are crisp. Cool and serve.

Microwave Cheese Fondue

Be sure to stir the cheese frequently during the second half of cooking to keep it from curdling. For a nonalcoholic fondue, substitute 1 cup of apple juice for the white wine.

Serves 6

Preparation time:
5 minutes
Cooking time:
5–7 minutes

1 garlic clove, peeled and
  cut in half
4 cups shredded Swiss
  cheese
4 teaspoons cornstarch
¼ teaspoon nutmeg
⅛ teaspoon paprika, or to
  taste
1 cup dry white wine
2 teaspoons lemon juice
1 loaf French or garlic
  bread, sliced

1. Rub the garlic clove over the insides of a 2-quart casserole dish that is microwave-safe.

2. Combine the cheese, cornstarch, nutmeg, and paprika in the dish. Stir in the white wine and lemon juice.

3. Microwave the fondue on high heat for 3 minutes. Open the door and stir the fondue.

4. Continue microwaving the cheese fondue for 1 minute at a time, stirring each time, until the cheese is completely melted (total cooking time is about 5 minutes).

5. Serve the fondue in the casserole dish, with the bread for dipping.

Fondue Facts

The secret to making fondue is to use hard, aged cheeses such as Swiss Emmental and Gruyère—the high fat content means they melt easily. The high acid content in dry white wine also helps melt the cheese.

Easy Garlic Toast

Serves 12

Preparation time:
10 minutes
Cooking time:
1–2 minutes

12 (1") slices crusty
    French bread (one-
    half loaf)
¾ cup butter, softened
¾ teaspoon garlic powder
⅛ teaspoon salt, or to
    taste
⅛ teaspoon black pepper,
    or to taste
½ teaspoon dried basil
    leaves
1 teaspoon lemon juice
1 teaspoon balsamic
    vinegar

*Balsamic vinegar gives a sharp kick to the garlic butter spread.
Bread cooks quickly in the broiler—start checking the garlic toast
after one minute to make sure it doesn't burn.*

1. Preheat the broiler on high heat. Spray a broiling rack with nonstick cooking spray.

2. In a small bowl, beat together the softened butter, garlic powder, salt, pepper, basil, lemon juice, and balsamic vinegar.

3. Spread the garlic butter over one side of the bread slices (about 1½ tablespoons per bread slice). Store any leftover garlic butter in a sealed container in the refrigerator to use on bread or toast as desired.

4. Lay the bread slices out on the rack.

5. Broil the toast on high heat for up to 2 minutes, until the butter has melted and the bread is toasted.

Roasted Red Pepper Dip

Serves 4

Preparation time:
10 minutes

Roasted Red Peppers
    (page 221)
½ cup Italian basil pesto
    sauce
½ cup low-fat plain yogurt
1 tablespoon olive oil

*Serve this flavorful red-pepper dip with Baked Pita Chips
(page 238) and an assortment of cut vegetables such as
carrots, cauliflower, and broccoli.*

1. Cut the roasted peppers into small squares if needed.

2. In a large bowl, stir together the pesto sauce and low-fat yogurt. Stir in the roasted peppers and olive oil.

3. Use immediately, or store in a sealed container within the refrigerator until ready to use.

Greek Hummus Dip

Can't find chickpeas at the local supermarket? Look for them under their other name, garbanzo beans.

1. Process all the ingredients in a blender or food processor until smooth.
2. Place the dip in a sealed container in the refrigerator for 1 hour, to give the flavors a chance to blend.

Make-Ahead Hummus

Hummus is one of the few party dips that freezes well. Store the hummus in a resealable plastic bag or a small container before freezing. Thaw the hummus in the refrigerator. If the dip is a bit dry, stir in one or two teaspoons of olive oil before serving.

Crab and Cream Cheese Dip

Rich mascarpone cheese—the key ingredient in Italian tiramisu—adds a touch of decadence to this tasty dip. You can substitute canned crabmeat for fresh lump crabmeat in this recipe—be sure to drain the meat before using.

1. Combine the ingredients in a medium bowl.
2. Cover and chill for 1 hour to give the ingredients a chance to blend.

Yields 1½ cups

Preparation time:
15 minutes

1½ cups canned chickpeas, rinsed and drained
2 tablespoons reserved juice from the chickpeas
3 tablespoons lemon juice
2 tablespoons creamy peanut butter
¼ teaspoon garlic powder
¼ teaspoon paprika, or to taste
¼ teaspoon ground cumin
⅛ teaspoon salt, or to taste
Black pepper, to taste

Yields 2 cups

Preparation time:
10 minutes

½ pound cream cheese, softened
¼ cup mascarpone, softened
8 ounces fresh lump crabmeat
1 tablespoon lemon juice
2 teaspoons Worcestershire sauce
1½ green onions, finely chopped
½ teaspoon garlic powder, or to taste
¼ teaspoon paprika, or to taste

Chili con Queso Dip

Yields 1¾ cups

Preparation time:
5 minutes
Cooking time:
7–10 minutes

½ cup Monterey jack
cheese
½ cup cream cheese
½ cup canned diced
tomatoes
½ teaspoon onion powder
2 tablespoons jarred red
chili peppers

Traditionally, this spicy Tex-Mex dip is meant to be served with square queso chips, but tortilla chips or Baked Pita Chips (page 238) work just as well.

1. Combine all the ingredients in a medium microwave-safe bowl, stirring to mix everything together.

2. Microwave on high heat for 3 minutes. Stir and microwave for 1 minute at a time until the cheese is melted. Stir again before serving.

Skillet con Queso

Don't have a microwave? This tasty dip can also be prepared on the stovetop. Replace the onion powder with ¼ cup chopped onion and sauté with the chili peppers in one tablespoon of olive oil, until the onion is softened. Add the tomatoes, heat to boiling, and let simmer for 2 minutes. Top with the cheeses and cook over low heat until the cheese is melted. You can also load up the dish with one diced green bell pepper.

Chapter 17
Make-Ahead Marinades and Sauces

Simple Stir-Fry Sauce

Yields ½ cup

Preparation time:
5 minutes

1 tablespoon soy sauce
1 tablespoon red wine
    vinegar
1 tablespoon brown sugar
2 tablespoons hoisin
    sauce
¼ cup water
1 teaspoon Asian sesame
    oil
Black pepper, to taste

This sauce is a great way to finish off a simple meat and vegetable stir-fry. You can prepare the sauce ahead of time and store it in a sealed container in the refrigerator until ready to use.

1. In a medium bowl, combine all the ingredients.

2. If not using the sauce immediately, refrigerate in a sealed container and use within 3 to 4 days.

Easy White Sauce for Vegetables

Serves 4

Cooking time:
10 minutes

4 tablespoons unsalted
    butter
3 tablespoons flour
1 cup milk
½ teaspoon ground
    nutmeg, or to taste
Salt and black pepper, to
    taste

One of the simplest sauces to make, white sauce is an excellent way to liven up fish, vegetables, or cooked pasta. Use this white sauce recipe with about 2½ cups of cooked vegetables.

1. In a small saucepan, melt the butter on low heat. Add the flour and blend it into the melted butter, stirring continually until it thickens and forms a roux.

2. Slowly add the milk and continue stirring with a whisk until the mixture has thickened. Stir in the nutmeg, salt, and pepper. Serve immediately.

Beautiful Béchamel Sauce

Believed to have been created by a chef working in the court of French King Louis XIV, the official name of white sauce is béchamel sauce, after Louis de Bechameil, a chief steward in the King's Court. In addition to standing on its own, white sauce forms the base of many other famous French sauces. Rich Mornay sauce is made by adding eggs, cream, and shredded cheese to the basic sauce, while velouté sauce is made with stock instead of milk.

White Sauce for Seafood

This simple sauce goes nicely with poached whitefish, such as sole. You can dress it up by combining the milk with a good stock or white wine, and adding fresh chopped parsley or chives at the end of cooking.

1. In a small saucepan, melt the butter on low heat. Add the flour and blend it into the melted butter, stirring continually until it thickens and forms a roux (3 to 5 minutes). Stir in the dill weed.

2. Increase the heat to medium. Slowly add the milk and the cream, stirring with a whisk until the mixture has thickened.

3. Stir in the nutmeg and pepper.

4. Stir in the lemon juice. Serve immediately.

Serves 4

Cooking time: 10 minutes

4 tablespoons unsalted butter
3 tablespoons flour
½ teaspoon dried dill weed
¾ cup milk
¼ cup heavy cream or whipping cream
½ teaspoon ground nutmeg, or to taste
⅛ teaspoon black or white pepper, or to taste
1 teaspoon lemon juice

Teriyaki Sauce

This recipe replaces the mirin found in classic Japanese teriyaki sauce with white grape juice and lemon juice. If you like, you can increase the amount of brown sugar to 4 teaspoons.

In a small saucepan, combine all the ingredients and bring to a boil, stirring to dissolve the brown sugar. Serve the sauce immediately.

Yields ⅔ cup

Preparation time: 2 minutes
Cooking time: 5 minutes

1 green onion, finely chopped
⅓ cup Japanese soy sauce
¼ cup white grape juice
1 teaspoon lemon juice
2 teaspoons bottled chopped fresh ginger
3 teaspoons brown sugar

Marinade for Beef or Pork

Yields about 1¼ cup

Preparation time:
5 minutes

½ cup soy sauce (such as
    Kikkoman)
4 tablespoons red wine
    vinegar
4 tablespoons vegetable
    oil
2 tablespoons brown
    sugar
2 tablespoons liquid
    honey
3 garlic cloves, crushed
½ teaspoon crushed red
    pepper

This marinade would go nicely with up to two pounds of beef steak that is going to be grilled or broiled. The recipe is very adaptable, and can easily be doubled if you're planning to barbecue for a crowd.

1. In a medium bowl, whisk together the soy sauce, red wine vinegar, and vegetable oil. Whisk in the remaining ingredients.

2. Pour the marinade over the meat. Cover and marinate in the refrigerator for at least 4 hours. Discard the excess marinade before cooking, or boil for 5 minutes if planning to use as a basting sauce for the meat.

What Makes a Marinade?

A good marinade tenderizes and enhances the flavor of meat, poultry, and seafood. All marinades contain an acid—such as flat beer, lemon juice, vinegar, or soy sauce—that flavors and tenderizes food by breaking down its proteins. A combination of herbs and spices is usually added for extra flavor. Finally, vegetable oil may be added to disperse the flavor more quickly, and help prevent the food from drying out.

Orange-Cilantro Marinade

This marinade pairs nicely with a firm-fleshed fish such as whitefish, or with shrimp. Serve the fish with Healthy Brown Rice (page 151) and a plain salad for a complete meal.

1. In a small bowl, whisk together the orange juice and olive oil.

2. Whisk in the remaining ingredients.

3. Store in a sealed container in the refrigerator. Use the marinade within three days.

Marinating Times

Deciding how long to marinate food can be a little tricky. Food that has been left too long in a marinade can develop a "mushy" texture. A general rule is to marinate meat and poultry for at least one hour. On the other hand, delicate fish should not be marinated for more than 30 minutes. However, total marinating time will depend on the amount of acid in the marinade—the more acid a marinade contains, the less marinating time is required.

Yields ⅔ cup

Preparation time:
10 minutes

¼ cup orange juice
¼ cup extra-virgin olive oil
2 teaspoons lime juice
Zest of 1 orange
3 tablespoons freshly
    chopped cilantro
3 teaspoons minced
    garlic
½ teaspoon salt
¼ teaspoon freshly
    ground black pepper
1 teaspoon Tabasco
    sauce

Simple Salsa Verde

Yields 1 cup

Preparation time:
10 minutes

6 canned tomatillos,
sliced
½ sweet onion, peeled
and chopped
2 tablespoons jarred
chopped jalapeño
peppers
½ bunch chopped fresh
cilantro leaves (about
3 tablespoons)
1 tablespoon lime juice
1 tablespoon reserved
tomatillo juice, or to
taste
¼ teaspoon garlic powder
or 2 cloves garlic,
minced
½ teaspoon salt
1 teaspoon chili powder,
or to taste
⅛ teaspoon freshly
ground black pepper,
or to taste

Although most people think of salsa as a dip for tortilla chips, the word salsa is simply the Spanish word for sauce. You can use this flavorful dip with chips, grilled meat, or seafood, or even pair it with ¾ pound of cooked pasta.

1. Briefly process the tomatillos, sweet onion, chopped jalapeños, and cilantro in a food processor.

2. Add lime juice, reserved tomatillo juice, garlic powder or minced garlic, salt, chili powder, and pepper. Process until the salsa has a chunky consistency. Store in a sealed container in the refrigerator until ready to use.

Types of Salsa

While many people are familiar with the classic Mexican salsa that combines tomatoes and herbs with hot chili peppers and tart lime juice, there are many variations. In Mexican salsa verde, green tomatillos take the place of tomatoes (verde is Spanish for "green"). A spicy fruit salsa that is often served as a salad, pico de gallo means "beak of the rooster," and refers to the spicy chili peppers used in the seasoning. And salsa ranchera or ranch sauce is a peppery sauce meant to be served with heuvos rancheros, the Mexican version of fried eggs.

Teriyaki Marinade

*Use this simple marinade to make Teriyaki Chicken (page 209).
It would also go very nicely with beef.*

Yields ⅔ cup

Preparation time:
5 minutes

2 teaspoons grated fresh
    gingerroot
¼ cup soy sauce
2 tablespoons brown
    sugar
¼ cup pineapple juice
1 shallot, peeled and
    chopped
¼ cup pineapple tidbits

1. Combine all the ingredients in a large bowl. Pour into a large resealable plastic bag.

2. Add the chicken or beef that is to be marinated. Reseal the bag and marinate in the refrigerator for about 1 hour, turning occasionally so that all the food is coated in the marinade.

Quick and Easy Teriyaki Marinade for Stir-Fries

With a little adjusting, this simple marinade can be used to make a quick and easy stir-fry. Place ¾ to 1 pound sliced beef in a bowl, and add 2 tablespoons pineapple juice, 2 tablespoons soy sauce, 1 teaspoon fresh gingerroot, and 1 teaspoon brown sugar. Marinate the beef for 20 minutes. Before you begin stir-frying, remove the beef with a slotted spoon, discarding any excess marinade.

Spicy Barbecue Sauce

This thick tomato-based sauce goes very nicely with grilled pork.

1. Heat the oil in a medium saucepan over medium heat.

2. Add the onion and garlic. Cook, stirring, until the onion begins to soften.

3. Stir in the tomato paste, Worcestershire sauce, vinegar, sugar, mustard, and cayenne pepper.

4. Turn the heat down and simmer for 10 minutes, stirring occasionally.

Alfredo Sauce

This classic butter and cream sauce was invented by an Italian restaurateur in the 1920s. Whether or not to add flour as a thickener is a matter of personal preference—you can leave it out if desired.

1. In a small saucepan, melt the butter on low heat. Add the flour and blend it into the melted butter, stirring continually until it thickens and forms a roux (3 to 5 minutes).

2. Increase the heat to medium. Slowly add the cream, stirring with a whisk until the mixture has thickened.

3. Add the Parmesan cheese and continue stirring with a whisk until the mixture has thickened.

4. Remove from the heat. Stir in the nutmeg, red pepper flakes, pepper, and basil.

5. Keep warm until the pasta is ready.

No-Cook Pasta Sauce

This is a quick and easy version of Italian tonnato sauce, without the anchovies. Serve the sauce with 8 ounces of cooked pasta. Sprinkle the cooked pasta with ¼ cup of Parmesan cheese if desired.

Serves 4

Preparation time:
5 minutes

2 tablespoons capers
1 (6-ounce) can tuna in
    oil, undrained
1 cup low-fat mayonnaise
2 tablespoons lemon juice
¼ teaspoon garlic
    powder, or to taste
½ teaspoon salt
Black pepper, to taste

1. Rinse the capers to remove excess salt.

2. Process the tuna and mayonnaise in a blender or food processor.

3. Add the other ingredients and continue processing until smooth.

4. Store the sauce in a sealed container in the refrigerator until ready to serve.

Storing Sauce

Leftover sauce can be stored in a sealed container in the refrigerator for up to three days. Reheat the sauce before serving, thinning with a small amount of water if necessary. For longer storage, freeze the sauce in ice cube trays for up to three months.

Spicy Peanut Sauce

This easy dipping sauce takes only five minutes to make, and goes nicely with spring rolls or other Asian dumplings. If you don't have fish sauce, you can substitute 2 tablespoons of soy sauce.

Yields 1 cup

Preparation time:
5 minutes
Cooking time: 5 minutes

½ cup coconut milk
½ cup peanut butter
2 tablespoons lime juice
1 tablespoon soy sauce
1 tablespoon fish sauce
1 garlic clove, minced
½ teaspoon red pepper
   flakes, or to taste

1. In a small saucepan, heat the coconut milk.

2. Stir in the peanut butter, lime juice, soy sauce, fish sauce, garlic, and red pepper flakes.

3. Heat, stirring occasionally, until the peanut butter is melted and the ingredients combined.

4. Store in a sealed container in the refrigerator until ready to use.

Quick and Easy Brown Sauce

This flavorful sauce pairs nicely with beef and green vegetables. In Chinese cuisine, brown sauce (made with oyster sauce and soy sauce and minus the butter) is often featured in beef and broccoli stir-fries.

Serves 2

Preparation time:
5 minutes
Cooking time: 5 minutes

1½ tablespoons butter
1 tablespoon flour
½ cup beef broth
1 tablespoon
   Worcestershire sauce
½ teaspoon honey
   mustard
½ teaspoon granulated
   sugar
⅛ teaspoon red pepper
   flakes, optional

1. In a small saucepan, melt the butter on low heat. Add the flour and blend it into the melted butter, stirring continually until it thickens and forms a roux.

2. Add the beef broth. Stir in the Worcestershire sauce, mustard, sugar, and red pepper flakes if using. Bring to a boil, stirring continually.

3. Use the sauce immediately or store in a sealed container in the refrigerator until ready to use.

Chapter 18
Beverages

Easy No-Boil Apple-Flavored Iced Tea

This recipe is so simple, you don't even need to brew the tea! For extra flavor, add 1 cup orange or cranberry juice to the chilled tea before serving.

Serves 4

Preparation time:
5 minutes
Chill: Overnight

2 bags Earl Grey black
tea
2 cups apple juice
2 cups water
2 tablespoons honey
Ice cubes, as desired

1. Combine the tea bags, apple juice, and water in a large glass pitcher. Leave in the refrigerator overnight.

2. Stir in the honey. Serve the iced tea over ice cubes.

Sun-Brewed Tea

As its name implies, sun tea is tea that is brewed outdoors in the sun. Fans of sun tea claim that it has a more delicate flavor than tea prepared with boiling water. However, health professionals warn that heating water without bringing it to a full boil means that harmful bacteria in the water or on the teabags may not be destroyed.

Homemade Café Mocha

Café mocha is the perfect pick-me-up on a cold winter's day. You can jazz up this drink for guests by replacing the low-fat milk with whole milk, and garnishing with chocolate syrup, whipped cream, and grated chocolate.

Serves 1

Heating time: 5 minutes

1 cup low-fat milk
2 teaspoons instant coffee
2 tablespoons sweetened
hot chocolate
¼ teaspoon ground
cinnamon

Bring the ingredients to boil in a medium saucepan, stirring frequently to dissolve the chocolate. Serve warm.

Gingery Tea

This simple drink is believed to aid digestion. Make the tea stronger or weaker by increasing or reducing the amount of ginger as desired.

1. Bring the water to a boil.

2. Place the ginger in a cup and pour ¾ cup of the water over.

3. Let the tea steep for 15 minutes (longer if you want a stronger tea).

4. Stir in the honey. Garnish with lemon slices.

Serves 2

Preparation time:
5 minutes
Steeping time:
15 minutes

1 cup water
1 tablespoon freshly grated gingerroot
2 teaspoons honey, or to taste
Lemon slices, for garnish

Selecting Fresh Ginger

Look for ginger that has a fresh unwrinkled skin, firm body, and a nice tan color. Store the ginger in a cool, dark place until ready to use.

Masala Chai

This spiced milk drink from India is traditionally made with strong black tea.

1. Crush the cardamom and cloves with a mortar and pestle, or by rolling over them with a rolling pin.

2. In a medium saucepan, bring the water and cream to a boil. Add the sugar, stirring to dissolve.

3. Add the crushed spices, ginger, and cinnamon. Bring back to a boil.

4. Add the teabags, then remove the pan from the heat and let stand for 5 minutes. Strain and serve.

Serves 3

Preparation time:
5 minutes
Cooking time: 10 minutes

2 cardamom pods
3 whole cloves
1½ cups water
1½ cups light cream
1 tablespoon granulated sugar
¼ teaspoon ground ginger
1 cinnamon stick, broken into pieces
2 bags Earl Grey black tea

Indian Spiced Chai

Serves 1

Cooking time:
8–10 minutes

1 cup water
2 black tea bags
1 cup light cream
1½ teaspoons granulated
   sugar
¼ teaspoon ground
   cardamom
⅛ teaspoon ground
   ginger
¼ teaspoon ground
   cinnamon

This is a quick and easy version of Masala chai, made with ground spices and tea bags instead of tea leaves.

1. Bring the water to a boil. Add the tea and let steep for 3 minutes.

2. While the tea is steeping, in a small saucepan, bring the cream, sugar, ground cardamom, ground ginger, and ground cinnamon to a boil, stirring to dissolve the sugar.

3. Add the brewed tea to the milk and spices.

4. Simmer for a minute and serve.

Thirst-Quenching Chai

This popular Asian beverage is made with brewed black tea, milk, and spices. There are numerous recipes for chai; the most popular, Masala chai, is a spicy beverage containing many of the same spices found in Indian curries.

Easy Iced Coffee

Of course, nothing beats the taste of brewed coffee, but this easy drink made with instant coffee is great when you want a cold drink in a hurry.

Serves 2

Preparation:
5 minutes

2½ teaspoons instant
    coffee
1½ cups water
½ cup heavy cream or
    whipping cream
4 teaspoons liquid honey
¼ teaspoon ground
    cinnamon
4 ice cubes

Combine all the ingredients in a blender. Process for about 15 to 30 seconds, until smooth.

Flavorful Ice Cubes

The next time you're making Classic Lemonade (page 259), Easy Iced Coffee, or other flavorful drinks, prepare more than you need and freeze the extra in ice cube trays. Use the ice cubes to add extra flavor to fruit or alcoholic drinks.

Mexican-Inspired Hot Chocolate

This is a quick and easy version of champurrado, a hot spiced drink made with Mexican chocolate.

Serves 1

Preparation time:
5 minutes
Cooking time:
5–10 minutes

1 cup warm water
3 tablespoons
    unsweetened cocoa
3 tablespoons brown
    sugar, or to taste
⅛ teaspoon ground
    aniseed
⅛ teaspoon cayenne
    pepper
1 cup milk
½ teaspoon vanilla extract

1. In a small saucepan, bring the water and unsweetened cocoa to a boil over low heat.

2. Stir in the brown sugar, ground aniseed, and cayenne pepper.

3. In a separate small saucepan, bring the milk to a boil. Add the milk to the chocolate mixture and heat to boiling.

4. Stir in the vanilla extract. Serve hot.

Two-Step Asian Bubble Tea

Serves 4

Chill: Overnight
Cooking time: 30 minutes

2 Earl Gray black tea
    bags
12 cups water, divided
1 cup tapioca pearls
4 cups milk
Ice cubes, as desired

*This is the Southeast Asian version of a comforting warm milk
and tea drink, made with chewy tapioca pearls.*

1. The night before, prepare the iced tea, following the instructions in Easy No-Boil Apple-Flavored Iced Tea (page 254), but replacing the 2 cups of apple juice and 2 cups of water with 4 cups water.

2. In a large saucepan, bring 8 cups of water to a boil. Cook the tapioca pearls in the boiling water according to the package directions. Cool and rinse under cold water.

3. Combine the iced tea, milk, and ice cubes in a cocktail shaker. Shake thoroughly to mix together.

4. Divide the cooked tapioca pearls between four glasses, laying out one-quarter of the pearls at the bottom of each glass. Pour 1 cup of the tea/milk mixture into each glass. Do not stir. Serve with a thick straw.

Bubble Tea Accompaniments

Bubble tea just tastes better when it's served in a see-through plastic cup, with a thick straw for sipping. Feel free to top the bubble tea with a sugary syrup, using brown or white sugar (or both!) and whatever ratio of sugar to water that you prefer.

Classic Lemonade

The secret to good lemonade lies in using boiling water, so that the sugar fully dissolves. While freshly squeezed lemons will give a more intense flavor, you can use bottled lemon juice if desired.

Serves 4

Preparation time:
10 minutes
Chill time: 20 minutes

2 cups water
1 cup sugar
½ cup lemon juice

1. In a medium saucepan, bring the water and sugar to a boil, stirring to dissolve the sugar.

2. Stir in the lemon juice.

3. Chill until ready to serve.

Extra Special Lemonade

There are many variations on classic lemonade. To make pink lemonade, replace half of the lemon juice with cranberry juice. Raspberry lemonade is made by adding fresh or thawed frozen raspberries to the lemon juice, sugar, and water mixture. And for a quick and easy version of a Gin Fizz, spike this Classic Lemonade with ¼ cup gin.

Red and Blue Berry Smoothie

Chilling the banana firms it up, adding more texture to the smoothie. If available, use a frozen mixed-berry blend.

Serves 1

Chill time: 15 minutes
Assemble time:
5 minutes

1 banana
½ cup frozen raspberries
½ cup frozen blueberries
1 cup milk
⅛ teaspoon ground
   cinnamon, or to taste
4 ice cubes
1 tablespoon granola,
   optional

1. Peel the banana and chill for 15 minutes. Chop into a few pieces.

2. Put the banana, berries, milk, and cinnamon into a blender. Process until liquefied.

3. Add the ice cubes and process again.

4. Pour the smoothie into a large drinking glass and sprinkle the granola on top.

Green Tea Smoothie

Serves 2

Chill time: 15 minutes
Preparation time:
5 minutes

1 medium banana
1 cup water
1 green tea bag
4 crushed ice cubes
½ cup low-fat peach
    yogurt
½ cup orange juice
1 tablespoon granulated
    sugar

Peach yogurt provides a handy substitute for fresh fruit in this quick and easy smoothie that includes healthy green tea. On days when you have more time, you can replace the peach yogurt with one chopped fresh peach, pitted and sliced, and ½ cup of milk.

1. Peel the banana and chill for 15 minutes. Chop into a few pieces.

2. Bring the cup of water to a boil. Add the tea bag and let steep for 3 minutes.

3. Remove the tea bag and add the ice cubes to chill.

4. Pour the tea into the blender. Add the yogurt, orange juice, and sugar.

5. Process until smooth.

Smoothie or Milkshake?

While you can't make a milkshake without milk and ice cream, in a smoothie the dairy products are optional. The main ingredients that make up a smoothie are fruit, fruit juice, and ice. While the fruit provides flavor, ice cubes or crushed ice give the smoothie a thick texture that is similar to a milkshake.

Chocolate Espresso

This rich drink is perfect for days when you want to treat yourself to something special. You can adjust the ratio of hot chocolate to coffee as desired.

Serves 1

⅓ cup instant coffee
   crystals
3 tablespoons sweetened
   hot chocolate
½ cup water
¼ cup milk
¼ cup light cream
¼ teaspoon ground
   nutmeg
¼ teaspoon ground
   cinnamon

Bring all the ingredients to a boil in a medium saucepan, stirring. Serve hot.

Dark Chocolate

There is evidence that chocolate may be good for you! Dark chocolate contains compounds called flavonoids that may help prevent cancer and heart disease. And the saturated fat in chocolate is stearic acid, a fatty acid that does not raise blood cholesterol levels. Chocolate contains a monounsaturated fat, oleic acid, which actually helps lower blood cholesterol levels.

Chapter 19
Desserts

Chocolate Chow Mein Clusters

Serves 4

Preparation time:
5 minutes
Cooking time:
5–10 minutes

2 cups dry crispy chow
    mein noodles
2 cups coconut chocolate
    macaroon candy
⅓ cup light cream

Kids love this sweet treat, but for a more adult version, you can add 2 or 3 teaspoons of liqueur. Grand Marnier, amaretto, or kirsch brandy are all good choices. If chocolate macaroon candy is unavailable, feel free to use chocolate rosebuds.

1. Place the chow mein noodles in a large bowl.

2. To melt the coconut chocolate macaroon candy on the stovetop, place the macaroons and cream in a bowl over a saucepan half-filled with water, making sure the water doesn't touch the bottom of the bowl. Bring the water to a near boil over medium-low heat, stirring the chocolate macaroon candy constantly so that the chocolate doesn't burn.

3. To melt the chocolate in a microwave, place the chocolate macaroon candy and cream in a microwave-safe bowl. Melt on high heat for 1 minute, stir, and continue microwaving for 30 seconds at a time until the chocolate is melted.

4. Stir the chocolate into the noodles. Chill for 10 to 15 minutes.

Chocolate Melting Tips

Unfortunately for cooks with a sweet tooth, chocolate scorches easily when heated. When melting chocolate in the microwave, always be sure to stir the chocolate between cooking periods. For stovetop melting, make sure the bottom of the bowl containing the chocolate does not come in contact with the heated water.

Skillet Bars

The secret to this recipe is to use quick-cooking oats, which are thinner than regular cooking oatmeal and have been steamed.

1. Place the quick-cooking oats in a large mixing bowl. Set aside.

2. In a skillet, melt the butter on medium-low heat. Add the sugars and cook until they are dissolved and bubbling.

3. Stir in the dried fruit, stirring to mix it in with the dissolved sugar. Push to one side of the skillet.

4. Turn the heat up to medium and add the evaporated milk in the other half of the skillet. When the milk is just starting to boil, stir to mix it in with the dried fruit and sugar mixture.

5. Pour the mixture into the bowl with the quick-cooking oats and mix thoroughly. Press onto a greased 8" × 8" or 9" × 9" baking pan. Chill.

Serves 6

Preparation time:
5 minutes
Cooking time:
10–15 minutes

3 cups quick-cooking oats
3 tablespoons butter
¾ cup brown sugar
¾ cup granulated sugar
1½ cups dried fruit and nut mix
¾ cup unsweetened evaporated milk

Preparation time:
5–10 minutes
Cooking time:
2–4 minutes

*1 pint fresh strawberries
2 (3.5-ounce) Toblerone
    bars
⅓ cup half-and-half
    cream
½ teaspoon almond
    extract
25 vanilla wafers*

Fast Chocolate Fondue

A microwave is perfect for melting chocolate—no more standing over a stove and constantly stirring and adjusting the temperature to make sure the chocolate doesn't burn!

1. Wash the strawberries, drain, and remove the hulls on top.

2. Break the chocolate bars into several pieces.

3. Place the chocolate and cream in a microwave-safe bowl. Microwave at high heat for 1 minute, stir, and then microwave for another minute. Stir in the almond extract.

4. Continue microwaving for 15 seconds at a time, stirring each time, until the chocolate is melted. (Be sure not to burn the chocolate.)

5. Serve the fondue with the strawberries and vanilla wafers for dipping.

Decadent Chocolate Fondue

Chocolate fondue is the perfect choice when you need to make a delicious dessert in a hurry. Many dessert pots are microwave-safe, meaning you can cook and serve the fondue in the same dish. Instead of strawberries, you can use other firm fresh fruit in season, or canned fruit such as pineapple.

Easy Blueberry Ice Cream Parfait

Parfaits are the perfect quick dessert—elegant, easy to make, and full of flavor. To transform this into a low-calorie dessert, simply use sugar-free strawberry preserves and replace the ice cream with your favorite flavor of yogurt.

1. Line the bottom of each parfait glass with ¼ cup of blueberries.

2. Spoon ¼ cup of the ice cream on top of the blueberries.

3. Spoon ¼ cup of the strawberry preserves on top of the ice cream.

4. Garnish with the mint leaves.

Serves 6

Preparation time:
10 minutes

1½ cups fresh or frozen (thawed) blueberries
1½ cups chocolate chip ice cream
1½ cups strawberry preserves
Mint leaves, for garnish

Microwave S'mores

The classic campfire treat, invented in the early twentieth century, s'mores are easy to make at home in a microwave oven.

Serves 6

Preparation time:
5 minutes
Cooking time:
3–5 minutes

12 whole graham crackers
  (2-part square)
1 cup semisweet
  chocolate chips
½ cup mini marshmallows

1. Lay 6 graham crackers in a microwave-safe shallow baking dish.

2. In a small bowl, stir together the chocolate chips and marshmallows.

3. Arrange the chocolate and marshmallows over the graham crackers.

4. Microwave on high heat for 1½ minutes, and then for 15 or 30 seconds at a time until the chocolate and marshmallows are melted.

5. Remove and top each s'more with a graham cracker to make a sandwich.

Stovetop S'mores

Don't have a microwave? Don't worry, you don't need to start up a campfire in the backyard—s'mores can also be made on the stovetop. Just melt the marshmallows and chocolate over low heat, according to the instructions for melting chocolate in Chocolate Chow Mein Clusters (page 264). Spread a portion of the chocolate over half the graham crackers and lay the remaining crackers on top, pressing down to make a sandwich.

Steamed Pears

Brushing the peeled pears with lemon juice helps prevent them from browning. Be sure to use a firm pear (such as Bartlett) that is not overripe.

Serves 4

Preparation time:
7–10 minutes
Cooking time:
5–10 minutes

4 Bartlett pears
4 tablespoons liquid
    honey
3 tablespoons golden
    raisins
¼ teaspoon ground
    cinnamon
2 tablespoons lemon juice

1. Peel and core the pears.

2. In a small bowl, stir together the honey, raisins, and ground cinnamon.

3. Stand the pears in a deep-sided, microwave-safe casserole dish. Brush the pears with the lemon juice. Carefully spoon the honey mixture into the core of each pear.

4. Cover the dish with microwave-safe plastic wrap.

5. Microwave the pears on high heat for 5 minutes. Give the dish a quarter turn and then microwave for 1 minute at a time until the pears are cooked through (they should be tender and easy to pierce with a fork).

How Does a Microwave Work?

Microwaves are electromagnetic waves that operate within the same frequency as radio waves. When the microwaves hit the food, they cause water molecules in the food to jiggle and vibrate. This molecular movement creates the heat that cooks the food. The need for water molecules to create heat means that it's best to stick with foods with a high liquid content.

Microwave Fudge

Serves 6

Preparation time:
5 minutes
Cooking time:
4–5 minutes

1½ cups semisweet
   chocolate chips
½ cup margarine
1½ cups sweetened
   condensed milk
2 teaspoons vanilla
   extract
2 cups chopped pecans

Sweetened condensed milk gives a rich, caramel-like flavor to this easy fudge recipe. The recipe calls for margarine, but you can, of course, use butter if desired.

1. Grease an 8" × 8" baking pan.

2. Combine the chocolate chips, margarine, condensed milk, and vanilla extract in a microwave-safe dish.

3. Microwave on high heat for 2 minutes. Stir and microwave for 1 minute. Stir and microwave for another minute. Continue microwaving for short periods as needed, stirring each time, until the chocolate is thoroughly melted. (Take care not to burn the chocolate.)

4. Pour the mixture into the baking pan. Stir in the pecans.

5. Cover and refrigerate or freeze until set.

Five-Minute Chocolate "Mousse"

Serve this simple dessert in tall parfait glasses, topped with chocolate sprinkles or maraschino cherries.

Serves 6

Preparation time:
5 minutes
Chill time: 1 hour

2 teaspoons instant coffee granules
2½ cups whipping cream
2 cups semisweet chocolate chips
4 tablespoons granulated sugar
1 teaspoon vanilla extract

1. In a medium heavy saucepan, heat the coffee granules and whipping cream until hot but not boiling (this will help melt the chocolate chips). Stir frequently to dissolve the coffee granules.

2. Place the chocolate chips and sugar in a blender. Add the vanilla extract and the heated cream.

3. Process for a minute, or until smooth and the chocolate chips are melted.

4. Pour into serving dishes, cover, and chill for about 1 hour.

Basic Peanut Butter Cookies

Preparation time:
10 minutes
Cooking time: 12 minutes

1 cup chunky peanut
   butter
1 cup margarine, room
   temperature
½ cup granulated sugar
½ cup brown sugar
1 teaspoon vanilla extract
1 large egg
¾ cup chocolate chips
1 teaspoon baking soda
½ teaspoon salt
1½ cups all-purpose flour

While rolling the cookies, keep the remainder of the cookie dough covered in plastic wrap so that it doesn't dry out. Feel free to replace the chocolate chips with raisins if desired.

1. Preheat the oven to 375° F. Grease 2 9" × 13" baking sheet.

2. In a large mixing bowl, stir together the peanut butter, margarine, sugars, vanilla extract, and the egg, mixing well. Stir in the chocolate chips.

3. In a separate medium mixing bowl, stir the baking soda and salt with the flour. Gradually stir the flour into the creamed peanut butter mixture with a wooden spoon.

4. Roll the dough into balls about 1–1½" in diameter. Place on the baking sheets, approximately 2" apart. (You will have more cookies than can fit on the 2 sheets and will need to use one of them again.) Press down in the middle of each cookie with a wet fork.

5. Bake for 12 minutes, or until the cookies are browned around the edges and a toothpick placed in the middle comes out clean. Cool and store in a sealed container.

Freezing Cookies

Fresh-baked cookies can be frozen and enjoyed later. To freeze, place the cookies in individual resealable plastic bags, or between layers of wax paper in a sealed container. For best results, do not freeze the cookies for longer than three months.

Low-Cal Raspberry Parfait

*This light, healthy dessert is perfect for weeknights.
You can replace the raspberries with blueberries
or other seasonal fruit as desired.*

Serves 8

Preparation time:
7–10 minutes

2 cups plain fat-free
    yogurt
1 teaspoon vanilla extract
2 cups fresh or frozen
    thawed raspberries
2 cups Instant Granola
    (page 19) or store-
    bought granola

1. In a medium mixing bowl, stir together the yogurt and vanilla extract.

2. Line the bottom of a parfait or dessert glass with ¼ cup of raspberries.

3. Spoon ¼ cup of the yogurt mixture on top of the raspberries.

4. Sprinkle ¼ cup of the granola on top of the yogurt.

5. Continue with the remainder of the parfaits.

No-Bake Cookies

Serves 6

Preparation time:
5 minutes
Cooking time:
15–20 minutes

2½ cups Rice Krispies
  cereal
1½ cups dried fruit and
  nut mixture
2 tablespoons butter
1 cup granulated sugar
½ cup sweetened
  condensed milk
1 teaspoon vanilla extract

Light, crunchy Rice Krispies cereal is perfect for making these easy no-bake cookies. You can replace ½ cup of the dried fruit and nuts with ½ cup of dried cranberries if desired.

1. Combine the Rice Krispies cereal and the fruit and nut mixture in a large mixing bowl. Set aside.

2. In a skillet, melt the butter and sugar on medium-low heat. Cook, stirring constantly, until the sugar is dissolved and bubbling (5 to 6 minutes).

3. Add the sweetened condensed milk and bring to a boil, stirring constantly, until it is just bubbling and is thickened (5 to 6 minutes).

4. Pour into the bowl with the Rice Krispies and dried fruit and nut mixture. Stir in the vanilla extract. Chill in the coldest part of the refrigerator for 5 minutes.

5. Roll into small balls and place on two greased 9" × 13" baking sheets. Cool until ready to serve.

Evaporated or Condensed Milk?

Both evaporated and condensed milk have approximately 60 percent of the water removed through an evaporation process. However, in the case of condensed milk, the evaporated milk is sweetened with sugar. This makes it perfect for desserts and cookies such as the ones in this recipe.

Pan-Fried Pineapple Rings with Brown Sugar

This simple dessert features the classic combination of tart pineapple and brown sugar. Use sweetened or unsweetened coconut flakes as desired.

Serves 4

Preparation time:
5 minutes
Cooking time:
6–7 minutes

¼ cup brown sugar
¼ cup reserved, canned
    pineapple juice
1 teaspoon vanilla extract
2 tablespoons coconut
    flakes
2 teaspoons margarine
1 (20-ounce) can
    pineapple rings,
    drained

1. In a medium saucepan, heat the brown sugar, pineapple juice, and vanilla extract over medium to medium-low heat, stirring to dissolve the sugar. Turn the heat down to low and keep warm.

2. Place the coconut flakes in a frying pan over medium heat. Cook for a minute, stirring or shaking the pan.

3. Melt the margarine in the pan. Add the pineapple and cook, continuing to shake the pan. Continue cooking until the coconut is browned and the pineapple is heated through (total cooking time for the coconut is 2 to 3 minutes). Remove the pan from the heat.

4. Pour the brown sugar and pineapple mixture on top. Serve immediately.

Easy Rice Pudding

Serves 4

Preparation time:
5 minutes
Cooking time: 10 minutes

1 cup instant rice
1 cup boiling water
6 tablespoons orange
   juice
1½ cups plain yogurt
2 tablespoons granulated
   sugar
1½ teaspoons ground
   cinnamon
¾ cup golden raisins

The cinnamon and sugar blend in this recipe also goes nicely on toast. Simply spread the cinnamon and sugar on two slices of buttered toast and enjoy!

1. Prepare the instant rice in the boiling water (see Basic Cooked Instant Rice, page 146, for instructions). Set aside.

2. Stir the orange juice into the yogurt.

3. Stir in the sugar and ground cinnamon and raisins.

4. Stir in the cooked rice.

Raisin Softening Tip

Place the raisins in a microwave-safe bowl and drizzle with water (2 teaspoons per ½ cup of raisins). Cover with plastic wrap and microwave on high heat for 30 seconds, and then for 15 seconds at a time until the raisins are softened and fragrant. The total cooking time for ½ cup of raisins should be about 45 seconds.

Make-Ahead Freezer Cookie Dough

The higher than usual proportion of butter to flour in this make-ahead recipe helps keep the dough from drying out.

Yields about 48 cookies

Preparation time:
20 minutes
Chill time: at least 2 hours

*2 sticks unsalted butter,
    softened
1 cup granulated sugar
1 tablespoon lemon juice
2 cups all-purpose flour
¼ teaspoon salt
½ cup dried cranberries
½ cup dried fruit and
    nut mix*

1. In a large mixing bowl, cream together the butter and sugar. Blend in the lemon juice.

2. Using an electric mixer set at low speed, gradually add the flour and salt until you have a soft dough.

3. Gradually add the cranberries and dried fruit and nut mixture.

4. Roll the dough into two separate logs. Wrap each log firmly in plastic wrap and chill until ready to bake.

Marshmallow Gelatin Dessert

Serves 4

Preparation time:
5 minutes
Cooking time: 5 minutes
Chill time: about 1 hour

*1 envelope unflavored
    gelatin
4 tablespoons sugar
1 cup boiling water
½ cup cranberry juice
½ cup reserved pineapple
    juice
1 cup drained pineapple
    tidbits
1 cup mini marshmallows*

For best results, make sure the cranberry juice is cold. To speed up the setting time, use a metal mold (gelatin sets more quickly in a metal container).

1. In a medium mixing bowl, stir together the gelatin and sugar. Add the boiling water, stirring until the gelatin is fully dissolved.

2. Stir in the cranberry juice and reserved pineapple juice.

3. Pour into a bowl or serving mold. Chill until mixture has thickened but not completely set.

4. Stir in the pineapple and marshmallows.

5. Continue chilling until fully set.

Pineapple Facts

Did you know: Fresh pineapple is never used in gelatin desserts because it contains an enzyme, bromelain, that prevents gelatin from setting. However, canned pineapple is safe to use, since the enzyme is destroyed during the canning process.

Cranberry Chews

Dried cranberries and lemon juice add a tart flavor to these chewy cookies. This recipe yields about 40 cookies.

Serves 8

Preparation time:
15 minutes
Cooking time: 10 minutes

1½ cups all-purpose flour
½ teaspoon baking soda
¾ teaspoon ground cinnamon
½ teaspoon salt
1½ sticks unsalted butter, softened
¾ cup granulated sugar
1 large egg
1 tablespoon lemon juice
¾ cup dried cranberries

1. Preheat the oven to 350°F. Grease two 9" × 13" baking sheets.

2. In a bowl, stir together the flour, baking soda, ground cinnamon, and salt.

3. In a separate large mixing bowl, use an electric mixer to mix together the butter and sugar. Gradually beat in the egg and lemon juice. Blend in the flour mixture. Stir in the dried cranberries.

4. Drop a heaping teaspoon of dough onto the baking sheet. Space the cookies on the cookie sheets about 2" apart. Press down gently with a fork.

5. Bake the cookies for 10 minutes, or until the edges are golden brown and crisp. Remove and let cool.

Rice Krispies Squares

Vanilla extract and cashews add extra flavor to this easy-to-make treat. You can replace the cashews with peanuts if desired.

Serves 8

Preparation time:
5 minutes
Cooking time: 5 minutes

½ stick unsalted butter
4 cups regular-size
  marshmallows
1 teaspoon vanilla extract
6 cups Kellogg's Rice
  Krispies cereal
1 cup salted cashews

1. Place the butter in a microwave-safe bowl. Microwave on high heat for 45 seconds, and then for 15 seconds at a time or as needed until the butter is melted.

2. Stir in the marshmallows and the vanilla extract. Microwave on high heat for 45 seconds. Continue microwaving and stirring until the marshmallows are melted.

3. Stir in the Rice Krispies and the cashews.

4. Spread out the mixture in a greased 9" × 13" pan.

5. Serve immediately or chill until ready to serve.

Easy Chocolate Chip "Ice Cream"

Chocolate chip and peppermint make a classic combination.

Serves 6

Preparation time:
5 minutes
Cooking time:
5–10 minutes

⅓ cup water
⅔ cup sugar
2 cups milk
1½ teaspoons peppermint
  extract
1 egg, beaten
1⅓ cups semisweet
  chocolate chips

1. In a heavy saucepan, bring the water and sugar to a boil, stirring to dissolve the sugar.

2. Place the milk in a large bowl. Stir in the peppermint extract.

3. Stir in the sugar and water mixture. Stir in the egg.

4. Place in the freezer.

5. When the milk is partially frozen, stir in the chocolate chips. Continue freezing. Let thaw briefly before serving.

Chapter 20
Quick Baked Breads, Cakes, and Pies

Coffee Cake

Serves 6

Preparation time:
10 minutes
Cooking time:
30–35 minutes

2 cups flour
1½ teaspoons baking
  powder
1 teaspoon baking soda
½ teaspoon salt
1 teaspoon ground
  cinnamon
½ teaspoon ground
  nutmeg
¼ teaspoon ground
  ginger
½ banana
½ cup vegetable oil
1 teaspoon vanilla extract
1½ cups French vanilla
  yogurt

There's no beating and mixing required in this quick and easy cake recipe. For an added touch, top the cake with a mixture of ¾ cup vanilla yogurt, 3 tablespoons granulated sugar, and 1½ tablespoons pineapple juice. Brush over the cake during the last 10 minutes of baking.

1. Preheat the oven to 350°F. Grease an 8" × 8" cake pan.

2. In a medium mixing bowl, combine the flour, baking powder, baking soda, salt, cinnamon, nutmeg, and ginger. In a large mixing bowl, mash the banana with a potato masher. Whisk in the vegetable oil and vanilla extract.

3. Add the dry ingredients and the vanilla yogurt alternately to the wet ingredients. Stir until well combined.

4. Pour the batter into the prepared cake pan.

5. Bake at 350°F for 30 to 35 minutes, or until a toothpick inserted in the middle comes out clean.

Do You Need to Sift?

Sifting dry ingredients in a baking recipe serves several purposes, from lightening flour to thoroughly blending all the dry ingredients and removing any clumps. Now that most commercially produced flour is pre-sifted, many recipes skip this step. If a recipe does call for sifted flour, be sure to sift before measuring so as not to affect the recipe proportions. If a recipe doesn't call for sifting, be sure to thoroughly combine the dry ingredients with a fork.

Quick Banana Bread

As the name implies, quick breads are quicker and easier to make than yeast-based bread. You can add ½ cup of cranberries to the bread batter just before baking.

Serves 8

Preparation time:
15 minutes
Baking time: 60 minutes, or as needed

1½ cups mashed bananas
   (3 large bananas)
¼ cup milk
¼ cup reserved pineapple
   juice
1 large egg
1 teaspoon vanilla extract
2 cups all-purpose flour
1 teaspoon baking
   powder
½ teaspoon baking soda
1 cup granulated sugar
½ teaspoon salt
½ teaspoon ground
   cinnamon
1 cup drained crushed
   pineapple

1. Preheat the oven to 350°F. Grease a 9" × 5" bread pan.

2. In a large mixing bowl, mash the bananas. Whisk in the milk, reserved pineapple juice, egg, and vanilla extract.

3. In a separate mixing bowl, combine the flour, baking powder, baking soda, sugar, salt, and ground cinnamon.

4. Gradually stir the dry ingredients into the wet ingredients. Stir in the crushed pineapple.

5. Pour the batter into the prepared bread pan, spreading it out evenly. Bake at 350°F for 60 minutes, or until a toothpick placed in the middle of the bread comes out clean.

Quick Breads

If you've ever whipped up a batch of muffins, you have experienced cooking quick breads. Instead of yeast, quick breads rely on baking powder and baking soda for lift. Quick breads are less labor-intensive (no need for rolling and punching out bread dough), and take less time to make than standard yeast-based bread doughs.

Quick Zucchini Bread

This recipe is a great way to introduce children to zucchini. You will need two zucchini for this recipe—be sure to drain any excess liquid from the grated zucchini before stirring it into the batter.

Serves 8

Preparation time:
15 minutes
Baking time: 60 minutes

1½ cups mashed bananas
   (3 large bananas)
⅓ cup milk
½ cup vanilla-flavored
   yogurt
1 large egg
1 teaspoon vanilla extract
2 cups all-purpose flour
2 teaspoons baking
   powder
½ teaspoon baking soda
1 cup granulated sugar
½ teaspoon salt
½ teaspoon ground
   cinnamon
2 cups grated zucchini

1. Preheat the oven to 350°F. Grease a 9" × 5" bread pan.

2. In a large mixing bowl, mash the bananas. Whisk in the milk, yogurt, egg, and vanilla extract.

3. In a separate mixing bowl, combine the flour, baking powder, baking soda, sugar, salt, and cinnamon.

4. Gradually stir the dry ingredients into the wet ingredients. Stir in the grated zucchini.

5. Pour the batter into the prepared pan, spreading it out evenly. Bake at 350°F for 60 minutes, or until a toothpick stuck in the middle of the bread comes out clean.

Adjusting for Altitude

Reduced air pressure means that baking at an altitude above 3,000 feet can wreak havoc with recipes—cakes fall and quick breads lack flavor. If baking at a high altitude is affecting how your quick breads turn out, one solution is to reduce the amount of baking powder. Experts recommended using ¼ less teaspoon for every teaspoon called for in the recipe.

Easy Chocolate Cake

Souring the milk with lemon juice adds extra flavor to this simple cake that doesn't require any mixing or beating.

1. Preheat the oven to 350°F. Grease an 8" × 8" baking pan.

2. In a small bowl, sour the milk by stirring in the lemon juice.

3. In a large bowl, combine the flour, salt, baking soda, and sugar. Stir in the chocolate.

4. Stir in the vegetable oil, soured milk, vanilla extract, and vinegar. Do not beat but make sure the mixture is well blended.

5. Pour the batter into the prepared cake pan. Bake the cake for 30 to 35 minutes, until cooked through (begin checking the cake after 30 minutes). Cool. Carefully remove the cake from the pan.

Serves 8

Preparation time:
10–15 minutes
Cooking time:
30–35 minutes

1 cup milk
1 tablespoon lemon juice
1½ cups all-purpose flour
½ teaspoon salt
1 teaspoon baking soda
1 cup granulated sugar
1 package sweetened
   hot chocolate (3
   tablespoons)
⅓ cup vegetable oil
1 teaspoon vanilla extract
1 tablespoon white
   vinegar

Sour Cream Cake

Serves 8

Preparation time:
15 minutes
Cooking time:
40–45 minutes

1 banana, mashed
2 tablespoons vegetable
    oil
¼ cup pineapple juice
1 teaspoon vanilla extract
1 cup all-purpose flour
1 teaspoon baking soda
½ teaspoon salt
½ cup granulated sugar
¾ cup sour cream
¾ cup crushed pineapple

This cake tastes even better the next day. Feel free to increase the amount of sugar to ¾ cup if desired.

1. Preheat the oven to 350°F. Grease an 8" × 8" cake pan.

2. In a large mixing bowl, mash the banana with a potato masher. Whisk in the vegetable oil, pineapple juice, and vanilla extract. In a medium mixing bowl, combine the flour, baking soda, salt, and sugar.

3. Stir about half the dry ingredients into the wet ingredients. Stir in ½ cup sour cream, then the remaining half of the dry ingredients. Stir in the remaining ¼ cup sour cream and the crushed pineapple.

4. Pour the batter into the prepared cake pan.

5. Bake at 350°F for 40 minutes, or until a toothpick inserted in the middle comes out clean.

How to Measure Flour

While many types of recipes are fairly forgiving, accurate measurements are critical in baking. When measuring flour, always spoon the flour loosely into a measuring cup, and then pull the edge of a knife across the top to level it off. Never pack the flour into the cup, or use a measuring cup with a pouring lip that can't be leveled off at the top.

Easy Cake Mix Cherry Cobbler

Blending the cake mix and butter gives this cobbler a nice crisp topping. However, you can also cut the butter into several small pieces and lay them on top of the cake mix before baking.

Serves 8

Preparation time:
10 minutes
Cooking time: 60 minutes

1 (19-ounce) can crushed
   pineapple with juice
1 (20-ounce) can cherry
   pie filling
1 package yellow cake
   mix
1½ sticks butter, softened
⅓ cup frozen lime juice,
   thawed
1½ cups Cool Whip Lite
   whipped topping,
   thawed

1. Preheat oven to 350°F. Grease two 8" × 8" cake pans.

2. In a large mixing bowl, stir together the pineapple and cherry pie filling. Pour the cake mix into a large mixing bowl. Cut the butter into the cake mix with a knife, and then use your fingers to combine the cake mix and butter until it has a crumb-like texture.

3. Spread half of the pineapple and cherry pie mixture into each pan. Sprinkle half the cake mix on top of the fruit mixture in each pan.

4. Bake the cakes for 60 minutes, or until the topping is crisp and browned.

5. While the cakes are baking, in a large bowl stir the lime juice into the Cool Whip topping, blending thoroughly. Spread over the baked cakes.

Delicious Dump Cake

Another name for Easy Cake Mix Cherry Cobbler is Dump Cake. One of the easiest cakes to make, dump cake gets its name from the fact that the ingredients are dumped into the pan, with no beating or mixing. Feel free to vary the basic recipe by experimenting with different cake mix flavors, and replacing the cherry pie with apple pie filling or canned fruit.

Cherry and Apple Crumble

Serves 6

Preparation time:
15 minutes
Cooking time:
30–40 minutes

1 cup all-purpose flour
1 teaspoon ground
    cinnamon
½ stick butter, softened
¼ cup brown sugar
1 cup cherry pie filling
1 cup apple pie filling

Using pie filling instead of fresh fruit takes most of the work out of this popular dessert. If you don't want to combine the two flavors, you can substitute one (20-ounce) can of cherry, apple, or your own favorite fruit pie filling.

1. Preheat the oven to 350°F. Grease a 9" × 9" pan.

2. Place the flour in a medium mixing bowl. Stir in the ground cinnamon. Cut the butter into the bowl, then use your fingers to combine the flour and butter until it has a crumb-like texture. Stir in the brown sugar, again using your fingers to mix it in.

3. Put the two pie fillings into the bottom of the pan, stirring to combine.

4. Sprinkle the crumb mixture over the pie filling.

5. Bake the crumble at 350°F for 30 minutes, or until the top is browned and crisp and the filling is bubbling. Place on a wire rack to cool for about 20 minutes before serving.

Crisp or Crumble?

Both of these desserts consist of fruit that is topped with a crumb coating and baked. However, while flour is the main ingredient in a crumble topping, crisp toppings usually include oats.

Cream Cheese Apple Pie

Sweetened condensed milk adds a decadent touch to this simple frozen dessert. Sift the sugar if needed to prevent any clumps from forming in the dessert.

1. In a large mixing bowl, combine the cream cheese, vanilla extract, and ground cinnamon.

2. Stir in the sweetened condensed milk. Do not beat, but stir until the cream cheese has a smooth texture and all the ingredients are well combined.

3. Spoon the mixture into the pie crust.

4. Freeze until it has set.

5. Spoon the applesauce on top and serve.

Serves 6

Preparation time:
10 minutes

1 (8-ounce) package
   cream cheese
½ teaspoon vanilla extract
½ teaspoon ground
   cinnamon
⅓ cup sweetened
   condensed milk
1 pre-made 9" graham
   cracker pie crust
1 cup applesauce

Preparation time:
5–8 minutes

1 cup Cool Whip Lite
   whipped topping,
   thawed
½ cup sweetened
   condensed milk
½ cup lemon juice
1½ tablespoons
   sweetened coconut
   flakes
1 pre-made 9" graham
   cracker pie crust

Five-Ingredient Frozen Lemon Pie

Sweetened condensed milk lends texture and flavor, while Cool Whip adds a sweet decadence to this easy recipe that kids will love. Be sure to use a quality lemon juice from concentrate, such as ReaLemon.

1. In a medium mixing bowl, combine the Cool Whip topping, sweetened condensed milk, lemon juice, and coconut flakes.

2. Spoon the mixture into the pie crust.

3. Cover and freeze until set. Let thaw for 5 minutes before serving.

Fun with Cool Whip

Cool Whip is a nondairy imitation whipped cream that is used to make frozen pies and as a dessert topping. The beauty of Cool Whip is that there's no whipping involved—it's ready to use straight from the container. However, if you're one of those people who think that it tastes a little bland, you can stir in some fruit juice for extra flavor.

Frozen Lime Pie

Flavorful French vanilla yogurt takes the place of sweetened condensed milk in this recipe, reducing the total calorie count. Minute Maid frozen limeade works well in this recipe.

1. In a medium mixing bowl, stir the lime juice and salt into the yogurt.

2. Add the Cool Whip topping. Stir until thoroughly blended.

3. Spoon the mixture into the pie crusts, using a knife to spread out evenly.

4. Cover and freeze until set. Let thaw for 5 minutes before cutting and serving.

Serves 8

Preparation time:
5–8 minutes

½ cup frozen lime juice, thawed
½ teaspoon salt
1 cup French vanilla-flavored yogurt
1 cup Cool Whip Lite whipped topping, thawed
2 pre-made 6" graham cracker pie crusts

Yogurt Pecan Pie

Pecans and mango-flavored yogurt give this simple dessert a tropical flavor. To enhance the effect, you can stir 1 to 2 tablespoons of sweetened coconut flakes into the whipped topping mixture before spreading it over the pie crust.

Serves 6

Preparation time:
5–10 minutes

¾ cup mango-flavored
   yogurt
¾ cup Cool Whip Lite
   whipped topping,
   thawed
2 tablespoons sweetened
   condensed milk
1 pre-made 9" graham
   cracker pie crust
½ cup pecans

1. In a medium mixing bowl, combine the yogurt, Cool Whip, and sweetened condensed milk, blending thoroughly.

2. Spread the mixture into the pie crust, using a knife to spread it out evenly.

3. Cover and freeze until set.

4. Let thaw for 5 minutes before serving. Garnish with the pecans.

Cinnamon Crumb Cake

A simple crumb coating made with flour, butter, and brown sugar is a great way to finish off a coffee cake. To quickly soften butter, place it on a microwave-safe plate and microwave for 10 to 15 seconds, 5 seconds at a time, as needed.

Serves 6

Preparation time:
5–10 minutes
Cooking time:
30–35 minutes

1 cup flour
½ stick butter, softened
¼ cup brown sugar,
   packed
1 Coffee Cake (page 284)

1. Preheat the oven to 350°F. Grease an 8" × 8" cake pan.

2. Place 1 cup flour in a medium mixing bowl. Cut the butter into the bowl, then use your fingers to combine the flour and butter until it has a crumb-like texture. Add the brown sugar, again using your fingers to mix it in.

3. Follow the directions for Coffee Cake (page 284).

4. When you are ready to bake the cake, sprinkle the crumb coating over the top of the cake before placing it in the oven.

5. Bake the cake at 350°F for 30 to 35 minutes, or until a toothpick inserted in the middle comes out clean.

Quick and Easy 30-Minute, 5-Ingredient Recipes

With our busy lifestyles today, cooking often gets relegated to the bottom of the list. But your life doesn't have to be filled with takeout, frozen TV dinners, expensive restaurant meals, and junk food. With some planning and organization, plus a few new cooking skills, you can make meals using recipes that take 30 minutes or less, using 5 ingredients or fewer.

Cooking and baking your own food means that you will spend less money, offer more nutritious meals to your family, and you'll certainly spend less time in the kitchen than ever before. With the judicious use of convenience and value-added foods, making delicious recipes is easier than ever.

New recipes that start with deli ingredients means you can make complicated recipes in just minutes. For instance, use a deli fruit salad as an ingredient in creamy fruit parfaits, or buy a rotisserie chicken to use for grilled cheese and chicken sandwiches. Planning what I call "overlapping meals," where leftovers from one day are used as ingredients in meals later in the week, also expands your recipe repertoire exponentially while staying within the five-ingredient limit. Have Spicy Vegetarian Chili and Corn Bread on the menu Monday, and Tuesday toast the corn bread and use it to make Southern Corn Bread Salad. Thursday, Taco Salad is on the menu, using the leftover chili.

Preparing recipes in 30 minutes or less means you'll need to learn some special skills. Efficient shopping, organizing your kitchen and your cooking habits, and planning meals for the week are at the top of the list. You'll learn streamlined preparation techniques and how to follow simple rules like starting the longest-cooking ingredients first to create a pocket of time while you work on others. And you'll find an extensive ingredient substitution list, for those times when you run out of a key ingredient in the middle of a recipe. I'll also include a primer on different cooking techniques so you will become an expert in grilling, microwaving, broiling, and stir-frying.

Of course, staying within that 30-minute time limit will depend on your kitchen expertise, the number of distractions (kids, pets, ringing telephones and doorbells) in your home, and any help you may have. With a little bit of concentration, you should be able to prepare these recipes in 30 minutes or less.

You'll also learn how to enjoy food preparation. I'll remind you to listen to the sounds of foods, enjoy the aromas, and relish the feeling of coziness as you revive the family table.

Once you build a repertoire of quick and easy 30-minute, 5-ingredient dishes, you'll learn how to stock your pantry, fridge, and freezer with enough ingredients so you'll never again be caught without the means of preparing an excellent meal for your friends and family. So join me and learn how you can feed your family delicious, nutritious, and super-easy quick meals ready in 30 minutes or less, using 5 ingredients. And enjoy imagining what you'll do with all your extra time!

Chapter 21

Starting Out with Quick and Easy 30-Minute, 5-Ingredient Recipes

Learning how to prepare food as a chef does, organizing your techniques and your kitchen, instinctive measuring, and planning a cooking schedule as you read a recipe are all key to preparing food in under 30 minutes. With some practice, these techniques and methods will become second nature. All of your kitchen work will be streamlined, and you will be able to prepare every recipe more quickly and efficiently.

The Game Plan

Let's start by learning how to read a recipe. The ingredient list is organized in order of use, stating amounts in package sizes, cups, tablespoons, and weights. Be sure you have all of the ingredients on hand. Read through the recipe twice so you understand all of the preparation steps. Make sure you have all of the necessary utensils and equipment. Use a food glossary to look up terms you may not understand. The directions are written with time saving in mind, starting with the preparation that takes the longest. It may help you to add notes to the recipe to mark the jobs you can "multitask" and those that require constant attention.

When you start learning new methods of cooking, measuring, and preparing food, go slow. It will take some experience before you can peel and chop an onion in less than a minute. Learn how to prepare foods properly and your speed will increase as you become more comfortable with new techniques.

The Basics

These recipes all require five ingredients or less, not counting flour, sugar, cornstarch, oil, water, baking powder and soda, and seasonings like salt, pepper, vanilla, and dried herbs and spices. Those are basic, inexpensive ingredients everyone should have on hand. Fresh herbs are counted as an ingredient. Many recipes use different parts of the same food to decrease the ingredient list. For instance, Ambrosia uses canned mandarin oranges in the salad and the juice from the oranges in the dressing.

Since these recipes use so few ingredients, the ingredients must be top quality. You won't be able to disguise limp broccoli or soft apples in these recipes. And the short cooking time, too, requires that the ingredients be premium. Fruits and vegetables should be heavy for their size and bright colored, with no discoloration, wrinkling, or soft spots. Fish should smell sweet and the flesh should be firm. Meats should be bright red, with even marbling and little juice in the package. And chicken should be firm and pink, again with little juice in the package.

Cook Once, Eat Twice

Leftovers are not only desirable when quick cooking, they will save you time tomorrow. When you're making rice, cook twice as much as you need. Then tomorrow night you can make a rice-based dish in about 10 minutes since the rice is already cooked and chilled. And it doesn't take any more time to cook more food, unless you are microwaving. Use the leftover foods within two to three days for food-safety reasons.

Organizing

Every kitchen is planned and arranged differently, but there are key principles to follow when organizing your work area. Kitchen organizers focus on the "work triangle." This is the shape formed when you walk from the sink to the fridge to the stove. For best efficiency, the length of each leg should be no more than nine feet and no less than four feet. If your kitchen isn't laid out this way, you can create your own triangle, or triangles, for different tasks. Many kitchen designers now think that having two or three smaller work triangles is more efficient than one large one. Put a cutting board between the stove and sink and you've created a small work triangle. Place a rolling butcher-block counter near the refrigerator and you can create a small work triangle with the pantry.

Be sure your equipment and measuring utensils are kept in an accessible place. Keep pots and pans near the stove, towels and dishwashing materials near the sink, flour and sugar near your baking center, and can openers and spoons near the pantry and work surfaces.

Professional organizers recommend that you literally plot out the steps you take and the movements you make when working in your kitchen. This takes only about an hour to do while you're making a recipe. It may help to have someone watch you cook to make suggestions about streamlining your methods. If you find, for instance, that you walk between the pantry and the drawer containing your measuring spoons many times, it will help to move those spoons closer to the pantry.

Paper management can be just as important as equipment management in a kitchen. Keep all your loose recipes together, keep similar cookbooks together on your bookshelves, and have a place specifically set aside for bill filing and paying.

Shopping

Grocery shopping is one of the most time-consuming aspects of cooking. To streamline your shopping trips and use the time most efficiently, there are several things you can do.

Try to plan meals at least a week in advance. By doing this, not only will you be able to better balance your family's nutritional intake, but you can take advantage of sales and specials at the grocery store. You can include some of your family's favorite recipes and try a new recipe or two each week.

Always keep a running list of staples along with another list of foods specific to recipes you will be making each week. The staples list keeps track of foods that are currently in your pantry that you use regularly. For instance, olive oil, flour, sugar, baking powder, eggs, milk, butter, and bread may be on your staples list. Whenever you use up a staple food, add it to your list so you won't run out of these items when you're cooking.

Use the menus you have planned for the week along with grocery fliers and your coupons to plan out your weekly list. Try to arrange it according to the layout of your favorite supermarket. Go shopping at less crowded times of the day. Clean out your pantry, fridge, and freezer before your weekly shopping trip. Discard products past their use-by dates, wipe down the shelves, and organize food items so they're easy to find. After your shopping trip, think about prepping some foods after you unpack.

Shopping Do's

- Use a cooler to store frozen foods if you live some distance from the store.
- Divide hamburger into patties, wrap, and freeze.
- Cut larger pieces of meat into serving-size pieces, rewrap, and label.
- Wash herbs, shake dry, wrap in paper towels, and place in plastic bags.
- Wash, peel, and chop hard vegetables like carrots, cauliflower, and broccoli.
- Wash salad greens, dry thoroughly, and store in plastic bags.

Shopping Don'ts

- Go shopping with kids in tow, if at all possible.
- Shop when you are tired, hungry, or ill.

- Take the long way home. Perishable food should be refrigerated promptly.
- Rinse delicate fruits like strawberries and raspberries.
- Prepare fresh mushrooms or any fruit that can turn brown after cutting.
- Let perishable food sit on your counter for more than an hour; refrigerate or freeze these products immediately.

Convenience Foods

One of the best ways to limit the total number of ingredients used in a recipe is to use convenience foods that combine several ingredients in one product. For instance, frozen bell peppers and onions are packaged together and sold as a stir-fry ingredient. And cooked ground beef in a spicy tomato sauce is available in the meat department of your supermarket; this one product substitutes for eight or nine ingredients needed if it was made from scratch.

Make sure that your family likes the convenience food before you stock up. When you find a winner, buy multiples and fill your freezer and pantry. With these foods and the recipes in this book, you'll be prepared for any occasion.

Equipment

Have multiple sets of utensils that you use frequently. Every kitchen should have at least two sets of nested measuring cups and spoons. Glass measuring cups that are angled so you can accurately measure by looking straight down into the cup will help shave minutes off prep time. Have more than one whisk, several heat-resistant spatulas, wooden and metal spoons, forks, knives, slotted spoons, and hot pads.

You may want to invest in a food processor, a convection oven, or a stand mixer with attachments, depending on the food you cook most often. A rice cooker needs no attention and cooks rice to perfection very quickly. Steaming food is faster than simmering or boiling it, so a few bamboo or stainless steel steamers may be a good addition to your kitchen. Immersion blenders and countertop rotisserie cookers are other appliances that may be put to good use in your kitchen. Egg slicers and apple corers make quick work of preparation chores, and mini food processors are great for quickly chopping and mincing ingredients.

Then there are garlic presses, bottle and jar openers, grill pans, dual-contact grills, strawberry stemmers, and shrimp deveiners. Think carefully before purchasing new equipment. If you really think you'll use it often, buy it. But if it isn't used several times in a month, have a garage sale and use the money to go out to dinner!

Cooking Methods

These quick-cooking methods are simple and they don't require special equipment, pots, or pans. When you learn how to use all of these cooking techniques, you'll be able to make any recipe in this book in 30 minutes or less.

Grilling

Grilling is cooking food quickly over high heat. This method adds flavor and, when using an outdoor grill, helps keep your kitchen cool on hot days. Make sure the grill is ready to use before you begin cooking: charcoal should be gray, with no apparent flames. Gas grills usually have a readiness indicator.

Whether you use a gas grill, charcoal grill, or an indoor dual-contact grill, keep it clean! Indoor grills will wipe clean with a damp paper towel. Outdoor grills can be cleaned using a wire brush or special compounds that will dissolve hardened grease.

Watch food carefully when it's on the grill. Follow the instructions. Many recipes call for cooking the food covered to create an ovenlike environment. Be sure to use a set of tongs, not a fork, to turn food. And keep kids and pets away from the hot grill until it's completely cool.

Microwaving

Microwave ovens cook by generating electromagnetic waves that react with water and sugar molecules in foods. The molecules begin to vibrate and twist, creating friction that heats up the food and cooks it.

Read your microwave user manual carefully. Many new microwave ovens come complete with preprogrammed cooking times for commonly used foods. You simply choose the food you want to cook, put it in the oven in a microwave-safe container, and then select the cooking code for that food.

Be sure to use only microwave-safe bowls, cups, plates, plastic wrap, and waxed paper in the oven. Arrange food with the thickest parts toward the outside of the bowl or plate. Carefully observe stirring and rearranging instructions and standing times. And follow the safety recommendations in the manual to the letter!

Stir-Frying

Stir-frying quickly cooks small pieces of foods over high heat in a small amount of oil. For best results, the food should be about the same size, shape, and thickness. This increases the time you'll spend preparing the foods, but the cooking time will be only a few minutes. And you really do have to stir constantly while the food is cooking.

Heat the pan before you add the oil for best results. And if you have a wok, use it! The rounded shape helps you toss the food as it cooks and provides higher heat on the bottom of the pan and less intense heat on the sides, letting you control cooking temps and speed.

Steaming

Steaming is a moist-heat method of cooking food that's quick and very healthy, too. Once the water underneath the steamer comes to a simmer, you're ready to cook. You can buy stainless steel steamers, collapsible basket steamers, or stackable bamboo steamers; all work equally well. Make sure the simmering water in the bottom pan doesn't touch the steamer for best results.

Fish and more delicate vegetables are the best choices for steaming because they cook quickly. If you have stackable steamers, pay careful attention to rotating and layering the steamers so all the food cooks evenly.

Cooking in paper, or *en papillote*, is also a steaming method. Parchment paper or foil is used to enclose the food and holds in the steam the food produces as it cooks. Chicken, fish, vegetables, and fruit are great choices for cooking *en papillote*.

Pan Frying or Sautéing

Preheat your pans for pan frying and sautéing before you add the oil or butter and the food won't stick. When pan-frying meats, season the meat well, place it in the pan, then leave it alone for a few minutes. If you move the meat before it has formed a crust and has seared, it will tear and be less juicy and tender.

Don't crowd the pan when cooking with this method or the temperature will lower and the food will boil or steam rather than sear and cook through. The recipe will let you know when to stir or turn the food.

Once you remove the cooked meat, deglaze the pan by adding a small amount of liquid—broth, water, or juice. Scrape up the browned bits and the drippings left in the pan to add lots of flavor to your gravy. And this step cleans the pan, too!

Deep-Frying

This is a dry-heat method because no liquid is used. Special deep fryers can be purchased to make the job easier if you use this cooking method often. Again, don't overcrowd the pan when deep-frying or the food will steam, absorb oil, and turn out soggy.

Be sure to leave at least one to two inches of headspace at the top of the pan to allow space for the oil to bubble up when the food is added. Use tongs to slide the food into the fryer, stand back to avoid splattering, and drain foods well on paper towels before serving.

Broiling

This dry-heat method is similar to grilling. Preheat the broiler before you begin prepping the foods. Most broilers work best when the oven door is ajar. Spray the broiling pan with nonstick cooking spray for easy cleanup. Arrange the racks so the food is the correct distance from the heat source, and be sure to watch the foods carefully and turn when the recipe directs.

Broiling is used for tender or marinated meats and vegetables. This is also a good way to roast chilies and tomatoes for Southwest-style cooking. This cooking method is controlled by timing and by rearranging the oven racks to move the food closer to or farther away from the heat source.

Pressure Cooking

There are new pressure cookers on the market that are totally self-contained, with digital controls and excellent safety features. Most of these cookers have a quick-release feature that makes it possible for you to cook using this appliance in less than 30 minutes.

Pressure cookers work by increasing pressure in a closed and locked container, which allows the food to boil at a higher temperature than 212°F. Be sure to carefully read the instructions of your pressure cooker. The type that sit on the stovetop are still available; you must watch them carefully to regulate the heat and cooking times.

Quick Chilling

There are several methods you can use to quickly chill foods. Spread the food in a shallow pan and place in the freezer for 20 minutes. You can also place the pan or bowl into a larger pan or bowl that you have filled with ice cubes and cold water; stir occasionally so the food cools evenly. Fill a glass or plastic bottle with ice and water, seal it, and use to stir soups or sauces that you want to cool down quickly.

Or you can combine these methods. Place the pan or bowl of food into the pan full of ice water and use a bottle filled with ice to stir. Some freezers have a "quick freeze" shelf, usually located at the top of the freezer, that will cool and freeze foods more quickly. Read the manual to see if your freezer has this capability.

Shortcuts and Techniques

There's a reason that chefs all prepare food in the same way; they save energy and make the most of every second when they can consistently peel and chop an onion in under a minute or julienne a green pepper in two. Other shortcuts include learning to estimate quantities when cooking, preheating appliances and pans, and cleaning as you go.

Prep Once

As you read through the recipe, note ingredients that are used more than once and prepare the entire amount needed at one time. For instance, if salad recipes use 2 tablespoons of grated Parmesan cheese in the dressing and 2 tablespoons sprinkled on top of the completed salad, grate ¼ cup of cheese while preparing ingredients.

For easiest cleanup, store ingredients used more than once on waxed paper or parchment paper rather than in little dishes or plates. A very large cutting board can also be very efficient for storing ingredients before you are ready to use them.

Since these ingredients will be used so quickly, there's no need to cover them or return them to the fridge or freezer while they are waiting to be used. If there is a delay of more than an hour in your cooking schedule, cover and chill all prepared foods to keep them at the peak of freshness and wholesomeness.

Chop Like a Pro

Use a well-sharpened, balanced chef's knife. Hold the knife in your dominant hand and keep the tip of the knife on the work surface or cutting board. Move the handle up and down to slice through the food. Hold the food, with the flat- or cut-side down, in your nondominant hand, and curl your fingers under to protect them as the knife blade cuts next to the knuckle. Start slow; as you gain experience, you'll be able to chop and slice faster.

When mincing foods like herbs and garlic, rock the knife back and forth on the food, using your dominant hand to hold the handle and the other on top of the knife to guide the blade. Occasionally, stop and scrape the material together into a small pile, then continue mincing.

You can use a scissors for many of the ingredients that need to be trimmed, sliced, or chopped: top and tail green beans; mince herbs; and chop tomatoes, pears, and peaches still in the can. Be sure to label the scissors (or hide them) so they're only used on food.

Instinctive Measuring

Cooking recipes (soups, salads, most meats) do not require the precise measurements that baking recipes do. So take a few minutes and train your eye to recognize common measurements. Measure out 1 teaspoon, 1 tablespoon, ¼ cup, ⅓ cup, ½ cup, and 1 cup of flour or cornstarch and line them up on a piece of waxed paper. Scoop them into your hand, one at a time, and notice how high the flour is piled up and how it looks on your palm. Now practice pouring out the different amounts onto your hand and measure your guesses. If you go through this two or three times, you'll be able to cut minutes off your cooking time and still measure accurately.

For liquid ingredients, generally one "turn" around a bowl or pot will measure 2 to 3 tablespoons of that liquid, whether it's oil or buttermilk. Meat stocks and broths are usually 1¾ cups per can or 4 cups per shelf-stable box.

Baking recipes require that you always measure ingredients because they are precise chemical formulas developed for narrowly defined results. If you add more flour than the recipe calls for, your baked product will be heavy and dry. If you add too much liquid, a cake or bread will fall. So take the time when baking to measure precisely. Using mixes is a great baking shortcut, because mixes are just a mixture of the premeasured dry ingredients.

Clean as You Work

Keep a dishpan or one sink full of hot, soapy water. As you work, drop utensils, bowls, pots, and pans into the water to soak. Cleaning as you go is more efficient than trying to tackle a big mess at the end. Have a bag or bowl on hand to hold vegetable trimmings if you have a compost pile. Prepare ingredients near the sink so it's easy to rinse vegetables and fruits before chopping or slicing them. And keep a garbage bag nearby so you can quickly discard packages and wrappings.

Wipe up spills on cooking surfaces as soon as the appliance cools down. This will save many minutes of scrubbing and is easier on you and the appliance. And wipe spills from your counters and floors when they occur. Keep a damp sponge or kitchen towel on hand in a designated place so it is readily available to clean and mop.

If you have a dishwasher, rinse and load dishes as you work. This is far easier to do as you go along, rather than waiting and facing a big job when you're done cooking. Read your dishwasher manual and follow instructions about prerinsing dishes and how to stack dishes for maximum efficiency.

Timing and Cooking

Remember this term: *mise en place*. This French phrase means that before you start cooking, you have all of the ingredients and equipment you will need on hand so you don't have to stop in the middle of the process and search for something. Before you begin, get all of your ingredients out of the fridge, freezer, pantry, and garden. It may help to remove the lids of the ingredients, then as you add them to the pot or bowl, put the lid or cover back on the bottle or can.

Timing is critical when cooking foods quickly. You must usually do two tasks at once (the word *meanwhile* in recipes is a clue to multitasking). This isn't difficult; you can chop vegetables while pasta cooks, stir together a sauce while meatballs cook in the microwave oven, or prepare greens for a salad while the chicken cooks on the grill.

Organize a plan for every recipe you make. Note the tasks that will take the longest, and start them first. For instance, in a baking recipe, the oven must be preheated; this can take from 5 to 10 minutes, so the first thing you'll do is turn on the oven. When cooking pasta, a large pot of water has to come to a rolling boil; put this on the stove first, and cover the pot so the water boils faster. Preheat heavy-duty pans so they are waiting for you. A hot pan will cook foods better, searing the outside immediately and developing great flavors.

Once your pots and oven are preheating, start prepping the ingredients. Begin with the foods that take longest to cook. Prepare those ingredients and get them cooking while you prep other foods.

Don't forget to watch the foods that are cooking while you're prepping others. Every 2 to 3 minutes, you should stir sautéing vegetables, check on foods that are thawing or cooking in the microwave oven, stir pasta boiling in the pot, and check on anything under the broiler or on the grill.

Keep distractions to a minimum. Pets and kids underfoot in the kitchen will not only slow you down, they can present a safety hazard.

When baking, think about measuring out all of your ingredients, in order, on a large sheet of waxed paper or parchment paper. And when the batter or dough is complete, read over the recipe again to make sure that you have added all of the ingredients. For instance, it's very easy to omit the baking powder or soda from a cake recipe; then you'll have a flop on your hands.

When you start cooking, keep the overall plan of recipe preparation in mind. Pay careful attention to each step and follow the schedule you created carefully.

Chapter 22

Appetizers and Beverages

Serves 6–8

½ cup apricot preserves
⅓ cup finely chopped dried
　apricots
2 tablespoons water
1 tablespoon honey
½ teaspoon chopped fresh
　thyme leaves
2 cups grated Parmigiano-
　Reggiano cheese

Parmesan Wafers with Apricots

Your guests will never believe that this recipe uses just five ingredients and is ready in less than 30 minutes. The crisp and savory wafers are the perfect accompaniment to the sweet and tart apricot topping.

1. Preheat oven to 350°F. Line a cookie sheet with parchment paper.

2. In a heavy saucepan, combine preserves, apricots, water, honey, and thyme leaves and bring to a simmer. Simmer for 5 to 8 minutes, stirring frequently, until dried apricots are softened and mixture is thickened. Remove from heat and let cool slightly.

3. Meanwhile, using a tablespoon, place mounds of cheese 4 inches apart on prepared cookie sheet and gently pat to form 2-inch rounds. Bake at 350°F for 4 to 6 minutes or until cheese is melted and turns light golden brown.

4. Let crisps cool for 5 minutes on baking sheet, then remove to a paper towel to cool. Serve with warm apricot mixture as a dip.

Why Parmigiano-Reggiano Cheese?

You must use the expensive authentic Italian Parmigiano-Reggiano cheese because it is of such high quality and, as such, has the most density and a lower fat content. When the wafers bake in the oven, there will be little fat rendered, and the wafers will become crisp and delicate as they cool.

Pesto Dip

This easy dip has wonderful crunch from the toasted pine nuts. Pine nuts are usually used when making pesto; they are ground along with the basil leaves and olive oil.

Serves 8–10

⅓ cup pine nuts
1⅓ cups sour cream
¼ cup plain yogurt
½ cup prepared pesto
¼ cup grated Parmesan cheese

1. To toast nuts, spread on small cookie sheet and bake in preheated 350°F oven for 5 to 8 minutes; watch carefully, shaking pan once during baking. Let nuts cool completely.

2. Combine all ingredients in medium bowl and mix well. Serve immediately with dippers like carrot sticks, celery sticks, breadsticks, crackers, and tortilla chips.

Dill Dip

If you can find fresh dill, by all means use it in this easy and savory dip. Good choices for dippers include baby carrots, bell pepper strips, small sticks of celery hearts, and cauliflower florets.

Serves 8

1 8-ounce package cream cheese, softened
½ cup mayonnaise
½ cup plain yogurt
2 teaspoons dried dill weed
2 cloves garlic, finely minced
½ teaspoon salt

In medium bowl, beat cream cheese until soft and fluffy. Add mayonnaise and yogurt and mix well. Stir in dill weed, garlic, and salt until combined. Serve immediately, or cover and refrigerate for 20 minutes to 2 hours before serving.

Fresh Herbs, Dried Herbs

When substituting fresh herbs for dried herbs, multiply the amount by three. So, if a recipe calls for ½ teaspoon of dried thyme, you would use 1½ teaspoons of fresh thyme. The same proportion applies if you are substituting dried herbs for fresh. When a recipe calls for 1 tablespoon of fresh dill, use 1 teaspoon dried dill weed.

Serves 6–8

¼ cup olive oil

3 tablespoons raspberry
    vinegar, divided

1 tablespoon honey

¼ teaspoon ground ginger

¼ teaspoon salt

2 avocados, peeled

1 cantaloupe, peeled and
    seeded

Melon and Avocado Cocktail

This elegant recipe is the perfect starter for a fancy dinner party. If the event is formal, use a melon baller to create balls from the avocado flesh for a fancier presentation. Serve it in parfait or sherbet glasses with small silver spoons.

1. In medium bowl, combine olive oil, 2 tablespoons vinegar, honey, ginger, and salt, and mix well with wire whisk. Cut avocados into chunks, or make balls using a melon baller. Sprinkle remaining tablespoon vinegar over prepared avocado.

2. Use a melon baller on cantaloupe to make small balls. Place cantaloupe and avocado in serving bowl and drizzle raspberry vinegar dressing over all. Serve immediately.

How to Ripen Avocados

The avocados you buy in the store are almost always rock hard, so purchase them a few days in advance. To ripen, store them together in a closed paper bag on the kitchen counter, checking every day to see if the flesh gives when gently pressed.

Cheese Puffs

These little puffs will melt in your mouth. The dough you are making is a cream puff dough, or choux pastry, flavored with thyme and two kinds of cheese.

～

Makes 24 puffs

½ cup milk
¼ cup butter
⅛ teaspoon salt
¼ teaspoon dried thyme
    leaves
½ cup plus 1 tablespoon flour
1 egg
⅓ cup mascarpone cheese
¼ cup cold-pack processed
    cheese food

1. Preheat oven to 425°F. In medium saucepan, combine milk and butter and bring to a rolling boil over high heat. Add salt, thyme leaves, and flour and cook over high heat, stirring constantly, until mixture forms a ball and cleans the sides of the pan.

2. Remove from heat and stir in egg, beating well to incorporate. Add mascarpone cheese along with the cheese food and beat until mixture is well blended.

3. Drop by teaspoonfuls onto parchment paper- or Silpat-lined baking sheets and bake at 425°F for 12 to 18 minutes or until puffed and golden brown. Serve immediately.

Mascarpone Cheese
Mascarpone cheese is a soft Italian cheese that's known as a triple crème cheese. This means it has a very high fat content, about 50 percent, and a rich and smooth texture. Substitutions include ricotta cheese and cottage cheese that has been blended to smoothness in a food processor.

3 tablespoons lemon juice
½ teaspoon salt
2 ripe avocados
¼ cup finely chopped red onion
1 tomato, chopped
¼ cup sour cream
⅛ teaspoon pepper

Guacamole

Avocados turn brown, or oxidize, rapidly when the flesh is exposed to air. To prevent this, drizzle lemon juice or lime juice over the avocados as soon as you cut them open.

1. In medium bowl, combine lemon juice and salt and stir to dissolve salt. Cut avocados in half, remove pit, then peel and place in bowl with lemon-juice mixture; toss to coat. Mash avocados using a fork; make the mixture as smooth or chunky as you like.

2. Stir in red onion, tomato, sour cream, and pepper and mix well. Serve immediately or cover by placing plastic wrap directly on the surface of the guacamole and refrigerate for 20 to 25 minutes.

Burying the Pit?

Burying the pit in a bowl of guacamole does nothing to stop the mixture from browning. The browning occurs when cells of certain fruits and vegetables are exposed to air. The only way to stop it is to add an acid ingredient, like lime juice, or limit the exposure to air by placing plastic wrap directly on the surface of the guacamole.

Spicy Meatballs

Peach jam and chili sauce sound like an unlikely combination, but the flavors blend perfectly. This sweet and sour recipe is very delicious and so easy to make.

~

Serves 8–10

1 16-ounce package frozen
    mini meatballs
1 tablespoon olive oil
1 onion, chopped
¼ teaspoon salt
Dash white pepper
¾ cup chili sauce
½ cup peach jam
¼ cup water

Bake meatballs as directed on package. Meanwhile, heat olive oil in a heavy saucepan and add onion, salt, and pepper. Cook and stir until onion is starting to turn brown and caramelize. Add chili sauce, peach jam, and water; stir; and bring to a boil. Add the cooked meatballs and stir to coat. Serve in a chafing dish or Crock-Pot.

Holding Appetizer Dips

Most hot appetizer dips like Spicy Meatballs can be held in a Crock-Pot during a party. Place the hot food into the Crock-Pot and turn it to low. Stir the food every 10 to 15 minutes so it doesn't scorch. The Crock-Pot will keep the dip warm for up to 2 hours.

Yields 24

24 frozen mini filo shells
8 ounces Brie cheese
12 strawberries
½ cup blueberries
2 tablespoons apple jelly
½ teaspoon dried thyme
   leaves
¼ teaspoon salt

Berry Filo Shells

*These beautiful little shells are filled with melted Brie cheese, then topped
with a mixture of fresh cool berries and thyme. This unusual appetizer
has a wonderful combination of textures, temperature, and flavors.*

1. Preheat oven to 350°F. Unwrap the mini filo shells and place on a baking sheet. Let stand at room temperature for 10 minutes until thawed. Meanwhile, cut Brie into 24 pieces. Fill each filo shell with a piece of Brie. Bake at 350°F for 4 to 5 minutes or until Brie melts.

2. While shells are baking, chop strawberries and combine with blueberries, apple jelly, thyme leaves, and salt in small bowl. When shells are deep golden brown and Brie is melted and bubbly, remove from oven and top each with a spoonful of the berry mixture. Serve immediately.

Mini Filo Shells
*If you can't find mini filo shells, make your own. Layer four sheets of filo
dough with butter and cut into 3" × 3" squares. Place in a buttered mini
muffin tin, press down, and bake at 375°F for 4 to 6 minutes until lightly
browned and crisp. They can be stored at room temperature for a
couple of days.*

Coconut Fruit Dip

This sweet and rich fruit dip is the perfect accent for strawberries, slices of kiwi fruit, apples, mandarin oranges, peach or mango slices, and pear slices. For a dessert, offer fruit plus some slices of pound and angel food cake.

Makes 2 cups

1 cup mascarpone cheese
1 cup marshmallow crème
3 tablespoons frozen orange juice concentrate
¼ teaspoon salt
2 tablespoons honey
½ cup toasted flaked coconut

In medium bowl, beat mascarpone cheese until light and fluffy. Add marshmallow crème, orange juice concentrate, salt, and honey and beat well. Fold in coconut and serve with fruit dippers.

Toasting Coconut

To toast coconut, spread into a thin, even layer on a cookie sheet and bake in a preheated 325°F oven for 4 to 6 minutes, stirring once during cooking time, until coconut is lightly browned and fragrant. Cool on paper towels; store at room temperature for up to 3 days.

4 cloves garlic
*2 tablespoons extra-virgin
    olive oil*
*1 15-ounce can garbanzo
    beans, drained*
¼ cup tahini
2 tablespoons lemon juice
¼ cup sour cream
½ teaspoon salt
*⅛ teaspoon crushed red
    pepper flakes*

Hummus

*Roasting garlic usually takes about 35–40 minutes in a hot oven.
But you can sauté the cloves in oil on the stovetop for just about
10 minutes. The cloves will become sweet and nutty tasting.*

1. Peel garlic cloves but leave whole. Place in a small heavy saucepan along with olive oil over medium heat. Cook the garlic until it turns light brown, stirring frequently, for about 5 to 8 minutes; watch carefully. Remove from heat and let cool for 10 minutes.

2. Combine the garlic and oil with all remaining ingredients in blender or food processor and blend or process until smooth. Spread on serving plate, drizzle with a bit more olive oil, and serve immediately with pita chips.

About Tahini
True hummus is made with tahini, which is a peanut-butter-like paste made of ground sesame seeds. It adds a rich flavor and smooth, creamy texture to any recipe. You can make hummus without it, but do try it with tahini at least once.

Crab Cakes

Crab cakes are a wonderful appetizer to start a dinner party on the porch. These little cakes are light, creamy, and crunchy. Serve them with more of the Dijon mustard/mayonnaise combo, with a few lemon wedges on the side.

~

Serves 8

1 egg
3 tablespoons Dijon mustard
    and mayonnaise
    combination
½ teaspoon salt
½ teaspoon Old Bay
    seasoning
⅛ teaspoon white pepper
8 round buttery crackers,
    crushed
1 pound lump crabmeat,
    picked over
4 tablespoons olive oil

1. In medium bowl, combine egg, mustard/mayonnaise combo, salt, Old Bay seasoning, pepper, and cracker crumbs; mix well. Let stand for 5 minutes. Meanwhile, carefully pick over the crabmeat, removing any cartilage or bits of shell. Add crabmeat to cracker-crumb mixture and mix gently but thoroughly.

2. Using a ¼-cup measure, scoop out some crab mixture and press into a small cake on waxed paper. When crab cakes are all formed, place in freezer for 5 minutes. Heat olive oil in nonstick skillet and sauté crab cakes, turning once, until they are golden brown, about 3 to 4 minutes per side. Serve immediately.

Using Canned Crabmeat

You can substitute canned crabmeat for the lump crabmeat. Two 8-ounce cans, well drained, will equal about a pound of lump crabmeat. Taste a bit of the crabmeat; if it tastes salty, rinse it briefly under cold water and drain well again before using in the recipe.

12 Parmesan Crescents (page
    331)
⅓ cup mayonnaise
⅓ cup grated Parmesan
    cheese
¼ cup chopped grape
    tomatoes
¼ cup chopped green onion

Parmesan Cups with Cheesy Filling

*Form the Parmesan Crescents into mini muffin cups when hot, then fill
with a savory cheese and tomato filling for a fabulous appetizer.*

1. Bake Parmesan Crescents as directed in recipe; except when just out
   of oven, wait for 1 minute, then remove the still-pliable crisps from the
   cookie sheet and press each into a greased mini muffin cup. Let cool.

2. Meanwhile, in small bowl, combine remaining ingredients. When cups
   are cool, fill each with a spoonful of the mayonnaise mixture. Serve
   immediately or cover and chill for 1 to 2 hours before serving.

Layered Reuben Dip

Mixing the cream cheese with the Thousand Island dressing in the base of this dip ensures the flavor of the dressing will be in every bite. Serve it warm with pretzel sticks, toasted rye crackers, and pita chips.

Serves 8

1 8-ounce package cream cheese, softened
½ cup Thousand Island dressing, divided
2 cups shredded Swiss cheese, divided
¼ pound thinly sliced corned beef, chopped
1 cup sauerkraut, drained

1. In medium bowl, beat cream cheese until fluffy. Stir in ¼ cup Thousand Island dressing and 1 cup Swiss cheese and mix well to combine. Spread in bottom of 9" microwave-safe glass pie plate.

2. Top cream cheese mixture with corned beef and sauerkraut, spreading evenly to cover. Drizzle with remaining ¼ cup Thousand Island dressing, and top with remaining 1 cup Swiss cheese.

3. Microwave dip on high for 3 to 5 minutes, turning once during cooking time, until cheese melts and mixture is hot. Let stand on a flat surface for 3 to 4 minutes and serve.

Sauerkraut
You can buy sauerkraut packaged in cans, in jars, fresh in the produce section of the supermarket, and frozen. Fresh sauerkraut usually has less sodium. Taste the sauerkraut before using it to check the salt content. If it tastes especially salty, rinse it briefly under cold running water and press between paper towels to drain.

30 cherry tomatoes
3 ounces cream cheese, softened
¼ cup whipped salad dressing
2 tablespoons roasted garlic paste
⅓ cup grated Parmesan cheese

Garlic Stuffed Cherry Tomatoes

These little appetizers are a bit fussy to make, but they are so delicious. Serve with some chilled white wine to begin your dinner party.

1. Cut off the tops of the cherry tomatoes and, using a small teaspoon, scoop out the flesh, leaving the shell intact. Drain upside down on paper towels.

2. In small bowl, beat cream cheese until soft and fluffy. Add salad dressing, roasted garlic paste, and Parmesan cheese and beat well. Stuff a teaspoon of this mixture into each cherry tomato. Serve immediately or cover and refrigerate up to 4 hours.

Roasted Garlic Paste
You can buy roasted garlic paste in gourmet shops and often in the produce or baking aisle of your supermarket. If you can't find it, roast a head of garlic at 350°F for 1 hour, then cool and press out the flesh; mix well and store in refrigerator for up to 1 week or in the freezer up to 1 month.

Spicy Mixed Nuts

This simple sweet and hot glaze brings plain mixed nuts to life. You can increase the amount of cayenne and white pepper if you like your food really spicy.

Yields 2 cups

¼ cup butter
2 tablespoons brown sugar
1 teaspoon salt
¼ teaspoon cayenne pepper
⅛ teaspoon white pepper
2 tablespoons Worcestershire sauce
2 cups mixed nuts

1. In heavy saucepan, melt butter with brown sugar, salt, peppers, and Worcestershire sauce. Cook mixture over low heat until blended, stirring frequently. Place nuts in single layer on microwave-safe baking sheet and drizzle the butter mixture over them. Toss gently but thoroughly.

2. Microwave the mixture on high power for 5 to 9 minutes, stirring three times during cooking, until nuts are darkened and crisp and butter is absorbed. Cool on paper towels, then store in airtight container.

Mixed Nuts

Be sure to carefully read the labels of the mixed nuts you purchase for baking and cooking. The best buys are usually generic brands of cashews, almonds, and pecans, without peanuts. You can purchase them in bulk or buy the nuts separately and mix your own blend.

Yields 2 cups

2 cups large pitted green
  olives
¼ cup olive oil
3 cloves garlic, minced
3 tablespoons lemon juice
½ teaspoon paprika
⅛ teaspoon pepper
1 teaspoon dried oregano
  leaves

Marinated Olives

*Heating the marinade and the olives helps the olives absorb the
flavors very quickly, so they can be served almost immediately.*

Drain olives well and discard brine. In small saucepan, heat olive
oil and garlic over medium heat until garlic sizzles, about 3 minutes.
Remove from heat and add lemon juice and seasonings and stir well.
Add olives and stir well. Cook over medium heat, stirring frequently,
until olives are hot, about 2 to 4 minutes. Remove to serving bowl and
let cool for 10 to 15 minutes, tossing gently from time to time. Serve
warm. Refrigerate leftovers.

Olive Sizes

*Olive sizes have some funny names. From smallest to largest, they are:
bullets, fine, brilliant, superior, large, extra large, jumbo, extra jumbo,
giants, colossal, super colossal, mammoth, and super mammoth. For
comparison, super mammoth contain about 42 per pound, giants are 70
per pound, large are 110 per pound, and bullets are 160 per pound.*

Sparkling Punch

You can make this easy punch using lots of different combinations of frozen juice concentrates. Browse through your supermarket's frozen juice section and try several flavors.

Serves 24
___

1 12-ounce can frozen tangerine juice concentrate

1 6-ounce can frozen orange juice concentrate

2 cups water

¼ cup lime juice

2 28-ounce bottles ginger ale, chilled if desired

2 sprigs fresh mint

In large pitcher or punch bowl, combine tangerine juice concentrate and orange juice concentrate with water and lime juice; mix well until concentrates dissolve. Add ginger ale and mint; mix gently and serve.

Be Party-Ready

Keep a couple of bottles of ginger ale, plain or flavored sparkling water, or juice chilled in the refrigerator and you'll be ready to whip up a punch, smoothie, or frosty at a moment's notice. Having crushed ice ready to use in your freezer is also a good idea.

Pineapple Orange Frosty

Whipped topping mix can be found in the baking aisle of the supermarket, near the gelatin and pudding mixes. It's the secret ingredient in this easy drink recipe.

Serves 6
___

2 6-ounce cans pineapple-orange juice

1 6-ounce can frozen orange juice concentrate

2 envelopes whipped topping mix

2 cups crushed ice

6 sprigs fresh mint

In a blender or food processor, combine the pineapple-orange juice, the orange juice concentrate, the whipped topping mix, and the crushed ice. Cover and blend or process at medium speed until mixture is thick, blended, and smooth. Serve immediately, garnished with mint sprigs.

1 cantaloupe

1 12-ounce can frozen
    lemonade concentrate

½ cup water

½ cup orange juice

⅛ teaspoon ground ginger

1 28-ounce bottle ginger ale,
    chilled

Melon Ginger Punch

*Cantaloupes are ripe when they give slightly to gentle pressure.
You can ripen cantaloupes by placing them in a paper bag
with a banana or apple; check once a day.*

1. Peel cantaloupe, remove seeds, and cut into 1" chunks. Place in blender or food processor along with lemonade concentrate, water, orange juice, and ginger. Cover and blend or process until mixture is smooth.

2. Place mixture in large pitcher or punch bowl and stir in ginger ale. Serve immediately.

Specialty Melons

Most melons can easily be substituted for each other. The newer varieties of specialty melons include Santa Claus, Crenshaw, Persian, and orange-fleshed honeydew. These melons are ripe when they smell sweet and the skin gives gently when pushed with a finger.

Hot Cocoa

Preparing hot chocolate mix with milk instead of water makes a wonderfully creamy, rich drink, perfect to sip after an afternoon of ice skating.

Serves 4

½ cup whipping cream
1 tablespoon powdered sugar
¼ cup marshmallow crème
4 1-ounce envelopes hot
  chocolate mix
4 cups milk

1. In small bowl, combine cream, powdered sugar, and marshmallow crème. Beat on high speed until stiff peaks form; set aside.

2. Divide hot chocolate mix among 4 mugs. In medium saucepan, heat milk until bubbles form around edge and steam rises. Pour a bit of milk into each mug and stir briskly until hot chocolate mix dissolves. Add remaining milk to mugs, stirring as the milk is added. Top each serving with a spoonful of the whipped-cream mixture.

Make Your Own Hot Chocolate Mix

To make your own hot chocolate mix, in medium bowl, combine 4 cups dry milk powder, 1 cup chocolate-flavored nondairy creamer powder, 1 cup powdered sugar, ¼ cup cocoa, and 2 cups instant chocolate drink mix. Blend well, then store in airtight container. Substitute ¼ cup of this mix for a 1-ounce envelope.

1½ cups water
1 cup superfine sugar
2 cups crushed ice
⅛ teaspoon salt
2 6-ounce cans pineapple-
    orange juice
½ cup freshly squeezed
    lemon juice

Lemonade

Pineapple-orange juice adds a more complex flavor to plain lemonade.
Keep a batch in the fridge during the hot summer months.

1. In medium saucepan, combine water and superfine sugar. Bring to a boil; cook and stir until sugar is dissolved, about 2 minutes.

2. Place crushed ice in large bowl and pour sugar water over ice. Stir until most of the ice is dissolved and mixture is cold. Pour into a pitcher and add salt, pineapple-orange juice, and lemon juice. Mix thoroughly and serve over ice.

Chapter 23

Bread and Breakfast

1 cup flour
¼ cup whole wheat flour
¾ cup sugar
½ teaspoon ground
   cinnamon
1 3-ounce package instant
   butterscotch pudding
   mix
½ teaspoon baking soda
½ teaspoon baking powder
½ cup butter, melted
2 eggs
1 cup canned pumpkin pie
   filling

Pumpkin Bread

It's important to use pumpkin pie filling, not canned pumpkin puree, in this easy recipe, because it contains spices and emulsifiers that flavor the bread and add to its texture.

1. Spray a glass 9" × 5" loaf pan with baking spray and set aside.

2. In a large bowl, combine flour, whole wheat flour, sugar, cinnamon, pudding mix, baking soda, and baking powder, and stir to blend. Add melted butter, eggs, and pumpkin pie filling and stir just until blended. Pour into prepared pan.

3. Microwave the pan on 75 percent power for 8 minutes, then rotate the pan one-half turn and continue microwaving for 8 to 10 minutes on 75 percent power or until a toothpick inserted in the center comes out clean. Let stand on a flat surface for 5 minutes, then remove from pan and cool completely on wire rack.

Quick Breads

Quick breads use baking soda or baking powder for leavening; they are quick to stir up and quick to bake. For best results, measure all ingredients carefully and be sure to mix the wet and dry ingredients just until combined. Overmixing will make the bread tough, with large tunnels running through it.

Corn Bread

Corn bread is best served hot, with some softened or whipped butter and honey or butter and salsa, depending on whether you want it sweet or spicy!

———

Serves 9

1¼ cups pancake mix
¾ cup yellow cornmeal
½ teaspoon paprika
1 cup buttermilk
$\frac{1}{3}$ cup frozen corn kernels, thawed
¼ cup vegetable oil
1 egg

1. Preheat oven to 400°F. Grease a 9" square baking pan and set aside.

2. In medium bowl, combine pancake mix, cornmeal, and paprika and mix well. In another medium bowl, combine buttermilk, corn kernels, oil, and egg and beat with wire whisk. Stir into dry ingredients just until combined. Pour into prepared pan.

3. Bake for 17 to 23 minutes or until edges are golden brown and top springs back when touched with finger. Serve warm.

Make Your Own Pancake Mix

You can make your own mix: combine 1 cup dry buttermilk powder, 3 cups flour, 1 cup whole wheat flour, ¾ cup sugar, 2 tablespoons baking powder, 1 tablespoon baking soda, and 1 teaspoon salt. To make pancakes, combine 1½ cups mix, 1 egg, 2 tablespoons melted butter, and 1 cup water and mix well; cook on greased griddle.

½ cup butter, softened
1½ cups shredded Swiss
    cheese
½ cup grated Parmesan
    cheese
1½ cups flour
½ teaspoon cayenne pepper
2 tablespoons water, if
    needed
½ cup ground pine nuts

Cheese Crackers

The two kinds of cheese and the pine nuts give these wonderful little crackers perfect flavor and crunch. You can change the amount of cayenne pepper if you'd like; more or less, it's up to you!

1. Preheat oven to 375°F. In large bowl, combine butter and cheeses and mix well. Add flour along with cayenne pepper and mix until a crumbly dough forms. You may need to add a bit of water to make the dough workable.

2. Add pine nuts to the dough and mix well. Form 1-inch balls, place on ungreased cookie sheets, and flatten with the bottom of a glass until the crackers are ¼ inch thick. Bake for 15 to 18 minutes until crisp and golden. Cool on wire rack.

Freezing Dough
Most doughs can be frozen and thawed and baked later. To freeze cookie or cracker dough, divide into balls as recipe directs and freeze in single layer on a baking sheet. When frozen solid, remove from sheet and package in freezer bags. Bake as directed, adding one-third to one-half of the baking time to allow dough to thaw.

Pineapple Puff Pastries

This recipe sounds a lot harder to make than it is. Follow the directions carefully and you should be able to shape all of the pastries in about 5 minutes.

Yields 8 rolls

1 sheet frozen puff pastry
    dough, thawed
5 tablespoons plus 1
    teaspoon pineapple-
    flavored cream cheese,
    softened
3 tablespoons pineapple
    preserves
2 tablespoons butter, melted
2 tablespoons sugar
½ teaspoon cinnamon

1. Preheat oven to 375°F. Roll out puff pastry dough on lightly floured surface to 12" × 12" rectangle. Cut into four 6" × 6" squares. Cut each square in half diagonally to make 8 triangles.

2. Arrange triangles on work surface so the long edge is away from you and the right angle is toward you. Spread each with 2 teaspoons of the cream cheese to within ½" of edges, and top with about 1 teaspoon pineapple preserves.

3. Bring the upper left-hand corner of each triangle down to the bottom right-angle point and press to seal. Then bring the upper right hand corner of each triangle down to the bottom point and press to seal, forming a square. Press outer edges to seal, leaving the center line open. Brush each with butter. Combine sugar and cinnamon in a small bowl and sprinkle over dough.

4. Bake for 9 to 14 minutes or until rolls are golden brown. Serve warm.

12 eggs, beaten
¼ cup light cream
¼ cup mascarpone cheese
½ teaspoon salt
⅛ teaspoon white pepper
¼ teaspoon dried marjoram
*   leaves*
3 tablespoons butter
1 cup shredded Havarti or
*   Swiss cheese*

Scrambled Eggs with Cheese

Scrambled eggs are best served hot, right from the saucepan,
so have your family waiting for the eggs rather than holding the eggs
for them. Serve along with hot, crisp bacon and buttered toast.

1. In a large bowl, combine eggs with cream, mascarpone cheese, salt, pepper, and marjoram. Beat with egg beater or hand mixer until smooth.

2. Heat butter in large skillet over medium heat. Add egg mixture. Cook eggs, stirring occasionally, until they are set, about 10 to 12 minutes. Add Havarti cheese, cover pan, and remove from heat. Let stand for 2 to 3 minutes, then remove lid, stir cheese gently into eggs, and serve.

Cheese Substitutions

Most cheeses can be substituted for each other in recipes. Ricotta cheese is a good substitute for mascarpone, as is softened or whipped cream cheese. Gruyère and Swiss are good substitutes for Havarti, and Colby cheese works well in place of Cheddar. Cotija, a Mexican hard cheese, is a great substitute for Parmesan cheese.

Mini Popovers

Popovers "pop" without any leavening in the batter because it contains lots of gluten and liquid. When the popovers are placed in the hot oven, the batter almost explodes with steam, and the gluten keeps the shell together.

Yields 24 popovers

2 eggs
⅔ cup milk
⅔ cup flour
1 tablespoon oil
¼ teaspoon salt

1. Preheat oven to 425°F. Spray mini muffin pans with baking spray and set aside.

2. Combine all ingredients in medium bowl and beat well with wire whisk until batter is blended and smooth. Pour 1 tablespoon of batter into each prepared muffin cup. Bake for 15 to 22 minutes or until popovers are deep golden brown and are puffed. Serve immediately.

Parmesan Crescents

Thaw puff pastry as directed on the package. These little rolls are crisp and tender, nicely flavored with cheese. They are delicious served with hot soup or stew, or alongside a grilled steak.

Yields 8 rolls

½ cup grated Parmesan cheese
1 sheet puff pastry, thawed
1 egg, beaten
½ teaspoon dried basil leaves

1. Preheat oven to 375°F. Sprinkle half of cheese on work surface and place pastry on cheese. Roll out puff pastry to a 12" × 12" sheet. Brush surface with egg and sprinkle evenly with remaining Parmesan cheese and the basil leaves.

2. Cut pastry into four 6" × 6" squares, then cut each square in half diagonally to form 8 triangles. Loosely roll up triangles to form a crescent and place on parchment paper-lined cookie sheets; curve ends to form a crescent shape. Bake at 375°F for 10 to 14 minutes or until rolls are puffed and golden brown.

Yields 44 muffins

1 9-ounce package blueberry
    quick-bread mix
5 tablespoons orange juice,
    divided
¾ cup milk
¼ cup oil
1 egg
½ cup powdered sugar

Orange-Glazed Blueberry Muffins

These mini muffins are the perfect quick breakfast for families on the run.
They are tender and sweet and very delicate; kids love them.
Serve warm for best flavor.

1. Preheat oven to 375°F. Line 44 mini muffin cups with paper liners and set aside.

2. In large bowl combine quick-bread mix, 4 tablespoons orange juice, milk, oil, and egg and stir just until dry ingredients disappear. Fill prepared muffin cups two-thirds full of batter. Bake for 10 to 15 minutes or until muffins spring back when gently touched with finger. Cool for 3 minutes, then remove to wire rack.

3. In small bowl combine powdered sugar and 1 tablespoon orange juice; drizzle this mixture over the warm muffins and serve.

Reheating Muffins
You can make muffins ahead of time and store in airtight containers, then reheat for best taste and texture. To reheat, place a few muffins on a microwave-safe plate, cover with microwave-safe paper towels, and heat for 10 seconds per muffin, until warm.

Peach Pancakes

Serve these wonderful pancakes on warmed plates with warmed maple syrup, peach jam, and some powdered sugar sprinkled on top, along with Canadian bacon and orange juice.

Serves 4

2 ripe peaches, peeled and diced
4 tablespoons sugar, divided
¼ teaspoon cinnamon
¾ cup flour
1 teaspoon baking powder
1 egg, separated
¾ cup milk
1 teaspoon vanilla
2 tablespoons butter

1. In small bowl, toss peaches with 2 tablespoons sugar and cinnamon. In medium bowl, combine flour, remaining 2 tablespoons sugar, baking powder, egg yolk, milk, and vanilla and stir just until combined.

2. Beat egg white until stiff; fold into flour mixture, then fold in peach mixture. Grease a skillet heated to medium with butter and cook pancakes, flipping once, until done.

Cooking Pancakes
Use a ¼-cup measure to scoop out the batter, and pour onto a hot, greased skillet. Cook pancakes until the edges start to look dry and cooked and bubbles form on the surface, about 2 to 4 minutes. Carefully flip the pancakes and cook until the second side is light brown, 1 to 2 minutes longer.

Yields 6 scones

2 cups flour
⅔ cup oatmeal
⅓ cup brown sugar
1½ teaspoons baking powder
¼ teaspoon cinnamon
6 tablespoons butter
2 eggs
6 tablespoons heavy cream,
    divided
1 tablespoon sugar
⅛ teaspoon cinnamon

Oat Scones

*You could add chopped nuts, raisins, dried cranberries, or currants
to these wonderfully tender, crumbly scones. Serve them hot just out
of the oven with butter, honey, and a selection of jams and jellies.*

1. Preheat oven to 400°F. Line a cookie sheet with parchment paper and set aside. In a large bowl combine flour, oatmeal, brown sugar, baking powder, and ¼ teaspoon cinnamon. Cut in butter until particles are fine.

2. In a small bowl combine eggs and 5 tablespoons cream and beat until smooth. Add to oatmeal mixture and mix until a dough forms. Shape into a ball, then press into a 9" circle on prepared cookie sheet. Cut dough into 8 wedges and separate slightly. Brush with remaining 1 tablespoon cream and sprinkle with 1 tablespoon sugar mixed with ⅛ teaspoon cinnamon. Bake for 12 to 15 minutes until edges are golden brown. Serve hot with butter.

Cherry Oat Muffins

*Use quick cooking oatmeal for best results in these tender
and flavorful muffins. You can use either bing cherries or sour
cherries, or use dried cherries to save some more time.*

1. Preheat oven to 375°F. Line 24 muffin cups with paper liners and set aside. In a large bowl, combine oatmeal, flour, baking powder, baking soda, and brown sugar. In small bowl, combine buttermilk, oil, and eggs and beat well. Add to oatmeal mixture and stir just until combined. Stir in cherries.

2. Fill prepared muffin cups two-thirds full with batter. Bake for 17 to 22 minutes or until muffins are rounded and tops are golden brown.

Pitting Cherries
There are several ways to pit cherries. You can cut the cherry in half and pry the pit out with your fingers. Cherry pitters work well; be sure that you see the pit come out each time. Or you can push a straw through the center of the cherry, removing the pit and stem at the same time.

Yields 24 muffins

1½ cups oatmeal
1½ cups flour
1 teaspoon baking powder
½ teaspoon baking soda
⅔ cup brown sugar
1 cup buttermilk
½ cup oil
2 eggs
1½ cups halved, pitted
 cherries or frozen cherries,
 unthawed

1 cup half-and-half or low-fat
 evaporated milk
1 egg, beaten
½ teaspoon vanilla
2 tablespoons powdered
 sugar
3 tablespoons butter
8 slices whole wheat bread

French Toast

Serve this crisp and creamy toast with maple syrup, powdered sugar, and some crisp bacon, cold orange juice, strong hot coffee, and a melon wedge or two.

1. Preheat griddle over medium heat. In a shallow casserole dish, combine half-and-half, egg, vanilla, and powdered sugar and beat until combined.

2. Melt butter on preheated griddle, then dip bread into egg mixture, coating both sides. Let the bread sit in the egg mixture for 1 minute. Immediately place onto sizzling butter on griddle. Cook over medium heat for 6 to 9 minutes, turning once, until golden brown.

French Toast Toppings
You can top French Toast with any pancake or waffle topping. Offer heated maple syrup, several kinds of jam, heated fruit syrups, powdered sugar, cinnamon sugar, and even peanut butter or Nutella spread. Or combine some fresh fruits with apple jelly and heat until warm.

Caramel Rolls

You could add chopped pecans or dark raisins to this easy recipe if you'd like. Place them on the topping before adding the rolls.

Yields 12 rolls

¼ cup caramel fudge ice cream topping
2 tablespoons brown sugar
2 tablespoons heavy cream
¼ cup butter, softened
¼ cup brown sugar
½ teaspoon cinnamon
1 8-ounce can refrigerated crescent roll dough

1. Preheat oven to 375°F. Spray a 9" round cake pan with nonstick baking spray. In a small bowl combine ice cream topping, 2 tablespoons brown sugar, and heavy cream and mix well. Spread mixture evenly in the prepared cake pan.

2. In another small bowl, combine butter, ¼ cup brown sugar, and cinnamon and mix well. Unroll dough and separate into 4 rectangles. Press seams to seal. Spread butter mixture over rectangles. Roll up dough, starting at short edge, and pinch edges of dough to seal. Cut each roll into 3 slices and arrange the twelve rolls on the topping in cake pan.

3. Bake for 15 to 20 minutes, until dough is deep golden brown. Invert pan onto serving plate and remove pan. If any caramel remains in pan, spread onto rolls. Serve warm.

Yields 16 breadsticks

3 tablespoons butter
2 cloves garlic, minced
½ cup grated Parmesan
cheese
¼ cup grated Romano cheese
½ teaspoon dried Italian
seasoning
1 11-ounce can refrigerated
breadstick dough

Cheese Breadsticks

These delicious breadsticks taste like the famous ones from a national restaurant chain that serves soup and breadsticks to go! Serve with Savory Minestrone (page 527) on a cold winter day.

1. Preheat oven to 375°F. Line cookie sheets with parchment paper and set aside. In a microwave-safe dish, place butter and garlic. Cook on 100 percent power for 1 to 2 minutes, until garlic is fragrant. Pour butter mixture onto a shallow plate and let stand for 5 minutes.

2. Meanwhile, on another shallow plate, combine cheeses and Italian seasoning and mix. Open dough and separate into 8 breadsticks; cut each in half crosswise to make 16 breadsticks. Dip each breadstick into butter mixture, then roll in cheese mixture to coat. Place on prepared cookie sheets, about 2 inches apart.

3. Bake breadsticks for 12 to 16 minutes or until they are puffed and light golden brown. Let cool for a few minutes and serve.

Parmesan or Romano?
Parmesan and Romano are often listed as substitutes for each other, but they are different cheeses. Parmesan cheese is made from cow's milk and has a milder flavor and less salty taste than Romano, which is made from sheep's milk (Pecorino Romano) or goat's milk (Caprino Romano).

Sausage Rolls

Cheese, sausage, thyme, and some puff pastry make delicious little rolls that are perfect for breakfast on the run. Bake them ahead of time, freeze them, then microwave each on high for 1–2 minutes until hot.

Yields 24 rolls

24 pork sausage links
1 17-ounce package frozen puff pastry, thawed
1 cup grated Cheddar cheese
½ cup grated Parmesan cheese
1 teaspoon dried thyme leaves
1 egg, beaten
¼ teaspoon salt

1. Preheat oven to 400°F. Line cookie sheets with parchment paper and set aside. In a heavy skillet, cook pork sausage links over medium heat until golden brown and cooked, about 5 to 7 minutes. Remove to paper towels to drain.

2. Unfold puff pastry sheet and place on a lightly floured surface. In a small bowl, combine cheeses and thyme leaves and toss to combine. Sprinkle this mixture over the puff pastry and gently press cheese mixture into pastry; roll to a 12" × 18" rectangle. Cut into three 12" × 6" rectangles, then cut each rectangle in half to make 6 squares. Cut each square into four 3" × 3" squares. Place a cooked and drained sausage on the edge of each square and roll up to enclose sausage; press pastry to seal.

3. In small bowl, beat egg with salt and brush over sausage rolls. Place on prepared cookie sheets and bake for 12 to 18 minutes until puffed and golden brown. Serve hot.

Puff Pastry
Puff pastry is found frozen near the pie shells and cakes in your supermarket. Follow the directions for thawing and using the pastry. Many brands require thawing overnight in the refrigerator so the butter that is encased in the layers of pastry doesn't melt. Keep a couple of boxes on hand to make easy snacks.

Stuffed French Toast

Broiling French Toast helps significantly cut the cooking time and ensures that the bread will be crisp.

1. Preheat broiler. Spread 3 tablespoons melted butter in a 15" × 10" jelly-roll pan and set aside. In a small bowl, combine ¼ cup mascarpone cheese and preserves and mix.

2. Spread preserves mixture on 4 bread slices and top with remaining slices. Cut these sandwiches in half to make triangles.

3. On a shallow plate, beat remaining ¼ cup mascarpone cheese until fluffy, then add eggs, remaining 1 tablespoon melted butter, vanilla, and cinnamon, and beat until smooth. Dip sandwiches in egg mixture, turning to coat. Place coated sandwich triangles in butter on jelly-roll pan. Broil 6 inches from heat source for 4 to 5 minutes, then carefully turn the sandwiches and broil for 3 to 5 minutes longer on second side until golden brown and crunchy. Serve immediately.

Broiling

When broiling foods, be sure to watch the food carefully as it burns easily. Most foods should be placed about 4 to 6 inches away from the heated coils, and most ovens require that the oven door be slightly open when broiling. Use the broiler pan that came with your oven, or a heavy-duty stainless steel pan that won't buckle under the high heat.

Toasted Garlic Bread

This crisp bread is perfect to serve alongside spaghetti and meatballs and a tender baby spinach salad. Make extra pieces and refrigerate; use the leftovers to make Bread-Crumb Frittata (page 343).

⟶

1. Slice bread about ¼ inch thick. In a heavy skillet, heat olive oil over medium heat and sauté garlic until soft and fragrant, about 2 to 3 minutes. Pour oil and garlic into medium bowl and let stand for 10 minutes. Add butter, lemon pepper, and Cotija cheese and mix well.

2. Preheat broiler. Spread butter mixture onto both sides of each piece of bread. Place on cookie sheet and broil 6 inches from heat source for 3 to 5 minutes, until light brown. Turn and broil for 2 to 3 minutes on second side, until light brown and crisp. Watch carefully, as these can burn easily. Serve hot.

Serves 6

1 loaf French bread
1 tablespoon olive oil
4 cloves garlic, minced
½ cup butter
1 teaspoon lemon pepper
½ cup grated Cotija cheese

1 tablespoon olive oil
3 cloves garlic, minced
½ cup butter, softened
2 cups shredded provolone
  cheese
1 teaspoon dried Italian
  seasoning
1 1-pound loaf unsliced
  Italian or French bread

Melty Cheese Bread

This bread is a perfect choice to serve alongside any Italian pasta dish.
You can make it ahead of time, then bake it just before serving.

1. Preheat oven to 350°F. In a small saucepan, heat olive oil over medium heat. Add garlic; cook and stir for 2 to 3 minutes, until garlic is fragrant. Remove from heat and pour into a heatproof bowl.

2. Meanwhile, in a medium bowl, combine butter, cheese, and Italian seasoning and mix well until blended. Stir in garlic mixture. Slice bread into 1-inch slices. Spread cheese mixture onto one side of each bread slice. Reassemble loaf, placing coated sides against uncoated sides.

3. Wrap loaf in heavy-duty foil. Bake for 15–22 minutes or until bread is hot and cheese has melted.

Garlic Bread Options
To make crisp garlic bread, slice the bread thinly, spread sparingly with coating, and bake it uncovered on the oven rack or cookie sheets. For soft and chewy garlic bread, slice the bread 1-inch thick, use more cheese, and wrap the bread in foil, then bake it. You can unwrap the bread for the last 3 to 5 minutes to help crisp the crust if you'd like.

Bread-Crumb Frittata

*This excellent and easy recipe is a wonderful way to use up any
leftover bread; simply toast it and crush it by placing in
a plastic food bag and rolling it with a rolling pin.*

Serves 4

5 slices Toasted Garlic Bread
   (page 341)
3 tablespoons butter
1 onion, finely chopped
8 eggs, beaten
½ teaspoon salt
Dash black pepper
1 cup grated Italian-blend
   cheese

1. Preheat broiler. Crush Toasted Garlic Bread into fine crumbs and set
   aside. In a heavy ovenproof skillet, melt butter over medium heat. Add
   onion and cook until tender, about 4 to 5 minutes. Season eggs with
   salt and pepper and add to skillet and stir.

2. Cook eggs for 2 minutes, lifting edges to let uncooked mixture flow
   underneath, until eggs begin to set. Add bread crumbs. Continue cooking, shaking pan occasionally, until eggs are almost set but still moist.
   Top with cheese and place under broiler for 2 to 3 minutes, until cheese
   melts and eggs are set. Cut into wedges and serve immediately.

Baked Eggs

*Dry mustard and Muenster cheese add a bit of a kick to baked eggs. Serve this
easy casserole with cantaloupe wedges and some Caramel Rolls (page 337).*

Serves 4

3 tablespoons butter, melted
8 eggs
½ teaspoon salt
⅛ teaspoon white pepper
½ teaspoon dry mustard
¼ cup heavy cream or
   evaporated milk
1 cup shredded Muenster
   cheese
¼ cup grated Parmesan
   cheese

1. Preheat oven to 350°F. Pour melted butter into a 9" square glass baking
   pan. In a large bowl, beat eggs with salt, pepper, mustard, and cream
   until blended. Pour into butter in pan and sprinkle with cheeses.

2. Bake for 15 to 20 minutes, until eggs are set, puffed, and golden brown
   around the edges. Cut into squares and serve immediately.

4 (3" × 3") squares Corn Bread
     (page 327)
1 15-ounce can black beans,
     rinsed and drained
1 pint grape tomatoes
1½ cups cubed Pepper Jack
     cheese
1 cup spicy ranch salad
     dressing

Southern Corn Bread Salad

The toasted Corn Bread is crisp on the outside and tender on the inside, providing wonderful texture to this beautiful salad.

1. Preheat oven to 400°F. Cut Corn Bread into 1-inch squares and place on a cookie sheet. Bake for 5 to 8 minutes, until toasted, watching carefully. Remove to wire rack and let stand for 5 minutes to cool slightly. Place bread in serving bowl.

2. Add black beans, tomatoes, and 1 cup of the cheese to the Corn Bread and toss gently. Drizzle with salad dressing, toss again, then top with remaining cheese. Serve immediately, or cover and chill for 2 hours before serving.

Bread Salads

Many cultures use leftover or stale bread in salads. In America, Southern Corn Bread Salad is probably the most well known. Italians make a bread salad called panzanella *with stale bread, and Greeks make* fattoush *with crisp pieces of flatbread or pita bread.*

Cornmeal Pancakes

*Crunchy cornmeal adds great taste and flavor to these easy pancakes.
Serve them with warmed maple syrup and fruit preserves.*

Serves 6–8

2 cups flour
1 cup yellow cornmeal
3 tablespoons sugar
½ teaspoon salt
1 teaspoon baking powder
1 teaspoon baking soda
2 cups buttermilk
½ cup sour cream
2 eggs
3 tablespoons butter

1. In a large bowl, combine flour, cornmeal, sugar, salt, baking powder, and soda and mix with wire whisk to blend. In a medium bowl, combine buttermilk, sour cream, and eggs and beat with an eggbeater until smooth.

2. Add buttermilk mixture to flour mixture and stir with a wire whisk until combined. Let batter stand while preparing griddle.

3. Heat griddle until a drop of water sizzles as soon as it touches the hot surface. Lightly grease griddle with butter. Pour batter by ¼ cupfuls onto griddle and cook for 3 to 4 minutes until edges look dry and bubbles form. Carefully turn pancakes and cook on second side for 2 to 4 minutes, until golden. Serve immediately.

Serves 6
_____

12 eggs
½ cup cream
½ teaspoon salt
⅛ teaspoon white pepper
3 tablespoons butter
1 cup shredded Monterey
    Jack cheese
½ cup prepared basil pesto

Scrambled Eggs with Pesto

Pesto adds great flavor and color to simple scrambled eggs.
You could call these Green Eggs, especially if you serve them with ham!
Orange juice and pork sausages make a nice accompaniment too.

1. In a large bowl, beat eggs with cream. Season with salt and pepper. In a heavy skillet, melt butter and add eggs. Cook over medium heat, stirring occasionally, until eggs are almost set.

2. Sprinkle eggs with cheese, cover, and remove from heat. Let stand for 2 to 3 minutes, then remove cover, add pesto, and stir gently to mix. Serve immediately.

Flavors of Pesto

Pesto can be made from almost any green herb or edible leaf. Spinach pesto is made by blending thawed frozen spinach with cheese, olive oil, and garlic. Mint pesto can be made with fresh mint leaves, oil, and walnuts. And pesto can include any type of nut, most cheeses, and any combination of herbs and spices.

Chapter 24

Beef Entrées

6 4-ounce beef tenderloin
   steaks
½ cup balsamic and oil
   vinaigrette
1 sweet red onion, chopped
2 cloves garlic, minced
1 tablespoon olive oil
¾ cup crumbled feta cheese
   with herbs

Greek Tenderloin Steak

*Beef tenderloins are also called filet mignon. This method
of preparing steak can be varied with different cheeses.
Serve with a green salad and corn on the cob.*

1. Prepare and preheat grill. Place steaks in baking pan and pour vinaigrette over. Let stand at room temperature for 10 minutes.

2. Meanwhile, in heavy saucepan, cook onion and garlic in olive oil over medium heat until tender and just beginning to brown around the edges, about 6 to 8 minutes. Remove from heat and set aside.

3. Drain steaks and place on grill; cook, covered, 4 to 6 inches from medium heat for 7 minutes. Turn, cover, and cook for 4 to 8 minutes, until desired doneness. Uncover grill and top each steak with some of the feta cheese. Cover grill and cook for 1 minute, until cheese melts. Place steaks on serving plate and top with onion mixture.

Easy Steak Doneness Tests
Put your hand palm up, and touch your thumb and index finger together. Feel the pad at the base of your thumb; that's what rare steaks feel like. Touch your thumb and middle finger together; the pad will feel like a medium-rare steak. Ring finger and thumb is medium, and thumb and pinky feels like a well-done steak.

Beef Stir-Fry

Serve this delicious stir-fry with some hot cooked rice, Grape and Melon Salad (page 488), and Sherbet Roll (page 575) for dessert.

Serves 4

1 pound sirloin steak
2 tablespoons stir-fry sauce
2 tablespoons oil
1 onion, chopped
1½ cups sugar snap peas
1 red bell pepper, thinly sliced
½ cup stir-fry sauce

1. Thinly slice the steak across the grain. Place in medium bowl and toss with 2 tablespoons stir-fry sauce. Set aside.

2. Heat oil in large skillet or wok over medium-high heat. Add onion; stir-fry for 3 to 4 minutes until crisp-tender. Add peas and bell pepper; stir-fry for 2 to 3 minutes. Add beef; stir-fry for 3 to 4 minutes, until browned. Add stir-fry sauce and bring to a simmer; simmer for 3 to 4 minutes, until blended. Serve over hot cooked rice.

Stir-Fry Variations

Once you've learned a stir-fry recipe, you can vary it with many different cuts of meat and lots of vegetables. Just be sure that the veggies are cut to about the same size so they cook in the same amount of time. And experiment with different bottled stir-fry sauces you'll find in the Asian aisle of your supermarket.

Serves 4

4 cube steaks
3 tablespoons flour
1 tablespoon chili powder
1 teaspoon salt
2 tablespoons olive oil
1 14-ounce can diced
 tomatoes with green
 chilies
1 10-ounce can condensed
 nacho cheese soup
1 cup sliced mushrooms

Spicy Cube Steaks

This comforting, old-fashioned recipe is delicious served with refrigerated mashed potatoes, heated with some sour cream and Parmesan cheese.

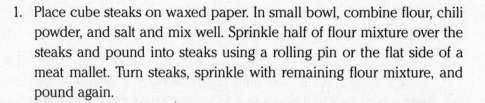

1. Place cube steaks on waxed paper. In small bowl, combine flour, chili powder, and salt and mix well. Sprinkle half of flour mixture over the steaks and pound into steaks using a rolling pin or the flat side of a meat mallet. Turn steaks, sprinkle with remaining flour mixture, and pound again.

2. Heat olive oil in large saucepan over medium-high heat. Add steaks; sauté for 4 minutes on first side, then turn and sauté for 2 minutes. Remove steaks from saucepan. Pour tomatoes and soup into pan; cook and stir until simmering, scraping up browned bits. Add steaks back to pan along with mushrooms; simmer for 15 to 20 minutes, until tender.

Cube Steaks

Cube steaks are typically round steaks that have been run through a machine that pierces the steak all over to break up connective tissue so the meat is more tender. You can pound your own round steaks using the pointed side of a meat mallet.

Grilled Steak Kabobs

The combination of barbecue sauce and cola beverage adds nice spice and flavor to these easy grilled kabobs. Serve with hot cooked rice, a green salad, and some breadsticks.

Serves 4

1 pound sirloin steak
¾ cup barbecue sauce
2 tablespoons cola beverage
¼ teaspoon garlic pepper
8 ounces cremini mushrooms
2 red bell peppers, cut into
  strips

1. Cut steak into 1-inch cubes and combine with barbecue sauce, cola beverage, and garlic pepper in a medium bowl. Massage the marinade into the meat with your hands; let stand for 10 minutes.

2. Meanwhile, prepare vegetables and prepare and preheat grill. Thread steak cubes, mushrooms, and bell peppers onto metal skewers and place on grill over medium coals. Grill, covered, brushing frequently with remaining marinade, for 7 to 10 minutes, turning frequently, until steak is desired doneness. Discard any remaining marinade.

Grill Temperatures
Check the temperature of them by carefully holding your hand about 6 inches above the coals and counting how many seconds you can hold your hand steady before it gets too hot. If you can hold your hand for 5 seconds, the coals are low; 4 seconds, medium; 3 seconds, medium-high; and 2 seconds, high.

2 tablespoons vegetable oil
1 onion, chopped
2 cloves garlic, minced
1 16-ounce package cooked
   sirloin tips in gravy
1 10-ounce can beef broth
1½ cups water
1 16-ounce package frozen
   mixed vegetables
½ teaspoon dried marjoram
   leaves
⅛ teaspoon pepper

Quick Beef and Vegetable Stew

*Precooked meats in gravy are a fabulous new product you
can find in the meat aisle of your supermarket. You get
the rich taste of a slow-cooked dinner with almost no work!*

In large saucepan, heat vegetable oil over medium heat. Add onion and garlic; cook and stir for 3 to 4 minutes, until crisp-tender. Stir in sirloin tips and gravy along with beef broth and water. Bring to a simmer over medium heat. Add frozen vegetables, marjoram, and pepper and bring back to a simmer. Simmer for 5 to 7 minutes, until vegetables are hot and stew is slightly thickened. Serve immediately.

Serves 4

1 cup leftover beef mixture
   from Beef Tacos (page
   358)
1 cup leftover refried bean
   mixture from Beef Tacos
   (page 358)
1 10-ounce bag mixed salad
   greens
2 cups blue corn tortilla chips
2 cups shredded Colby cheese

Taco Salad

*You can use Spicy Vegetarian Chili (page 432) in place of the beef
mixture and refried bean mixture. Top the salad with chopped
tomato and chunky salsa, sour cream, or more tortilla chips.*

In large saucepan, combine beef mixture and refried bean mixture and stir over medium heat until hot. Meanwhile, place salad greens on plates and top with tortilla chips. When beef mixture is hot, spoon over tortilla chips and top with shredded cheese. Serve immediately.

Tortilla Chips
You can make your own tortilla chips. Choose flavored or plain corn or flour tortillas and cut them into wedges using a pizza cutter. Heat 2 cups oil in large pan over medium-high heat and fry tortilla wedges until crisp. Drain on paper towels, sprinkle with salt and seasonings, and serve.

Pesto Steaks

This elegant dish deserves some superb accompaniments.
Make Grilled Asparagus (page 511) and Pasta Pilaf (page 512).
For dessert, Chocolate Toffee Torte (page 566) is perfect.

Serves 4

4 tenderloin steaks
1 teaspoon salt
⅛ teaspoon white pepper
1 cup basil pesto, divided
⅓ cup blue cheese
½ cup fresh basil leaves

1. Prepare and heat grill. Place steaks on a platter; sprinkle both sides with salt and pepper. Using a very sharp knife, cut into the side of each steak, creating a pocket. Be careful not to cut through to the other side. Fill each pocket with about 2 tablespoons pesto.

2. Grill steaks, covered, over medium coals for 5 minutes. Turn steaks, cover again, and cook for 4 minutes. Top each steak with 2 tablespoons of pesto and sprinkle blue cheese on top of the pesto. Cover and grill for 2 to 5 minutes, until desired doneness is reached. Meanwhile, roll basil leaves into a round shape and cut into thin strips, creating a chiffonade. Place steaks on serving platter and sprinkle with basil chiffonade. Let stand 5 minutes, then serve.

Tenderloin Steaks

The tenderloin of beef, or filet mignon, is the most expensive cut of beef available, but it is also economical because there is no waste. The steaks do not need to be trimmed; most of the fat is intramuscular and not visible, but it creates great flavor.

1 16-ounce package frozen
    meatballs
3 tablespoons oil
1 onion, chopped
2 cloves garlic, minced
2 9-ounce boxes frozen Asian
    vegetables in sesame-
    ginger sauce
½ cup beef broth

Ginger Meatball Stir-Fry

*Serve this excellent quick stir-fry over hot cooked rice, with a
deli fruit salad on the side. The only work you have to perform is
chopping onions and garlic, then cook for a few minutes.*

1. Place meatballs in a 12" × 8" microwave-safe dish and heat on high
   power for 4 minutes. Rearrange meatballs and heat on high power for
   2 minutes longer. Set aside.

2. In heavy skillet or wok, heat oil over high heat. Add onion and garlic;
   stir-fry for 4 to 5 minutes, until onion is crisp-tender. Add frozen vegetables in sauce and beef broth and bring to a boil over high heat. Cover,
   reduce heat, and simmer for 5 minutes.

3. Uncover pan and add meatballs. Stir-fry for 3 to 5 minutes longer, until
   vegetables and meatballs are hot and sauce is slightly thickened. Serve
   immediately.

Cooking Rice
*To cook rice, combine 1 cup long-grain, converted, or Texmati rice in a
heavy saucepan with 2 cups water or broth and a pinch of salt. Bring
to a boil, reduce heat to low, cover, and simmer for 15 to 20 minutes,
until liquid is absorbed. Remove from heat and let stand for a few minutes, then fluff with fork and serve.*

Almost-Instant Shepherd's Pie

Shepherd's Pie is an old-fashioned recipe that's a great way to use up leftover mashed potatoes. The premade refrigerated type also works very well.

Serves 6

1 20-ounce package cooked
   ground beef in taco sauce
1 16-ounce package frozen
   broccoli, cauliflower, and
   carrots
¼ cup water
2 9-ounce packages
   refrigerated garlic
   mashed potatoes
1 cup sour cream
½ cup grated Parmesan
   cheese

1. Preheat oven to 400°F. Place ground beef and sauce in a heavy saucepan and heat over medium heat for 5 to 7 minutes, until hot, stirring occasionally.

2. Meanwhile, place frozen vegetables in 2-quart casserole and sprinkle with ¼ cup water. Cover and microwave on high for 5 minutes, stirring once during cooking time; drain well. Then place potatoes in microwave-safe bowl and heat on high for 5 minutes. Remove from microwave, stir, and add ½ cup sour cream; let stand. Add drained vegetables to beef mixture and simmer for 2 to 4 minutes longer.

3. Place hot beef mixture in 2-quart casserole dish. Stir potatoes, add Parmesan cheese, and spread over ground-beef mixture. Bake for 12 to 15 minutes, until casserole is hot and potatoes begin to brown.

2 cups sliced cooked Spicy
   Grilled Flank Steak (page
   362)
½ cup salsa
1 4-ounce can diced green
   chilies, drained
2 cups shredded Pepper Jack
   cheese
12 10-inch flour tortillas

Steak Quesadillas

Serve these spicy little Tex-Mex sandwiches with more salsa, chopped tomato, sour cream, and guacamole, along with some fresh fruit.

1. Slice steak across the grain and combine in medium bowl with salsa and green chilies. Place six tortillas on work surface and divide steak mixture among them. Top with cheese and remaining tortillas.

2. Heat griddle or skillet over medium-high heat. Cook quesadillas, pressing down with spatula and turning once, until tortillas begin to brown and cheese melts, about 4 to 7 minutes. Cut into quarters and serve immediately.

Guacamole
To make your own guacamole, combine 2 mashed avocados with ¼ cup mayonnaise, 2 tablespoons fresh lemon or lime juice, ½ teaspoon salt, dash cayenne pepper, a dash of hot sauce, and 1 chopped tomato. Blend well and put into small bowl. Press plastic wrap onto the surface and refrigerate for 2 to 4 hours before serving.

Steak and Bean Enchiladas

These hearty enchiladas are wonderful served with Spanish rice made from a mix and a crisp butter lettuce salad with a garlic ranch dressing.

Serves 4

1 16-ounce flat iron steak
1 teaspoon salt
⅛ teaspoon cayenne pepper
1 tablespoon chili powder
1 teaspoon ground cumin
3 tablespoons oil
2 16-ounce cans pinto beans,
  drained
1 16-ounce can enchilada
  sauce
8 10-inch flour tortillas
2 cups shredded Pepper Jack
  cheese, divided

1. Preheat oven to 400°F. Cut the steak, against the grain, into thin strips. Sprinkle steak with salt, pepper, chili powder, and cumin. Heat a large skillet over medium-high heat and add oil; heat until the oil ripples. Add steak; stir-fry for 2 to 4 minutes, until steak is desired doneness. Remove steak from pan using slotted spoon and place in large mixing bowl.

2. Add drained beans and half of enchilada sauce to steak and stir to mix. Divide mixture among the flour tortillas and top with half of the cheese. Roll up tortillas to enclose filling. Place in 3-quart casserole dish. Drizzle with remaining enchilada sauce and sprinkle with rest of the cheese. Bake for 15 to 18 minutes, until heated through.

About Flat Iron Steak
This cut of meat is actually a brand-new cut! It's the top blade steak that has been cut in half to remove some very tough connective tissue that runs through the center of the meat. This steak is inexpensive, tender, and well flavored, especially when quickly grilled or sautéed.

1 16-ounce package cooked
    ground beef in taco sauce
2 tablespoons olive oil
1 onion, chopped
1 15-ounce can seasoned
    refried beans
12 crisp taco shells
2 cups shredded Co-Jack
    cheese

Beef Tacos

Tacos are a kid-friendly supper that's very easy, especially when you start with fully cooked ground beef in taco sauce. Serve with all the traditional toppings: guacamole, sour cream, chopped tomatoes, and more taco sauce.

1. Preheat oven to 400°F. Heat beef and sauce according to package directions. Meanwhile, heat olive oil in large skillet over medium heat. Cook onion, stirring frequently, until tender, about 5 to 6 minutes. Stir in refried beans and cook for 3 to 4 minutes longer, until hot.

2. Place taco shells on a baking sheet and heat at 400°F for 4 to 7 minutes, until crisp. Serve the ground-beef mixture along with the refried-beans mixture, the taco shells, and shredded cheese and let diners make their own tacos.

Tacos: Crisp or Soft?
You can make crisp tacos, usually with preformed shells heated in the oven, or soft tacos, made by heating tortillas until softened, then filling and folding to enclose the filling. Soft tacos are essentially the same as burritos, but they aren't fried or baked after filling. Don't worry too much about the nomenclature—just enjoy the food!

Meaty Spaghetti

*Starting with fully cooked meatloaf means this spaghetti is
ready in about 20 minutes; it's also perfectly seasoned.*

Serves 6

1 16-ounce package cooked
    meatloaf in tomato
    sauce
2 tablespoons olive oil
1 onion, chopped
1 28-ounce jar pasta sauce
1 pound spaghetti pasta
1 cup grated Parmesan
    cheese

1. Bring a large pot of water to a boil over high heat. Remove meatloaf from package and crumble. In heavy saucepan, heat olive oil over medium heat. Cook onion for 4 to 5 minutes, stirring frequently, until crisp-tender. Add crumbled meatloaf, tomato sauce from package, and pasta sauce. Bring to a simmer; cook for 7 to 9 minutes, until sauce is slightly thickened.

2. Meanwhile, add spaghetti to boiling water and cook according to package directions, until al dente. Drain well and place on serving platter. Top with meat mixture and sprinkle with Parmesan cheese. Serve immediately.

Recipe Substitutions
You could use leftover meatloaf in this easy spaghetti recipe, or use frozen precooked meatballs, heated according to the package directions, along with one 8-ounce can of tomato sauce. For more nutrition, add some preshredded carrots to the pan when adding the meatloaf and let simmer in the sauce.

Serves 4–6

1½ pounds ground beef
1 onion, chopped
2 tablespoons flour
1 4-ounce can chopped
    jalapeños, undrained
2 8-ounce cans tomato sauce
    with seasonings
2 14-ounce cans diced
    tomatoes with garlic,
    undrained
1 cup water

Five-Ingredient Chili

*Using tomato products seasoned with spices and
garlic cuts down on the ingredient list. Serve the chili with
sour cream, shredded cheese, and chopped tomato.*

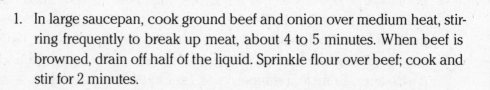

1. In large saucepan, cook ground beef and onion over medium heat, stirring frequently to break up meat, about 4 to 5 minutes. When beef is browned, drain off half of the liquid. Sprinkle flour over beef; cook and stir for 2 minutes.

2. Add remaining ingredients, bring to a simmer, and simmer for 10 to 15 minutes, until flavors are blended and liquid is thickened. Serve immediately.

Five-Way Chili
In Cincinnati, "five-way chili" means chili served with spaghetti, cheddar cheese, beans, and chopped raw onions. If you vary the additions, you'll be serving "two-way" (with spaghetti), "three-way" (spaghetti and cheese), and "four-way" (three-way plus raw onions). "One-way," of course, is plain chili.

Beef and Tortellini

This simple dish is packed full of flavor. Serve it with some grated Parmesan cheese, a green salad with lots of tomatoes, and some sautéed broccoli.

﹏

1. Bring a large pot of water to boil over high heat. Meanwhile, in large saucepan, cook ground beef and onion over medium heat, stirring to break up meat, for 4 to 6 minutes, until beef is browned. Drain well. Cook tortellini in boiling water according to package directions, until tender; drain well.

2. Combine beef mixture, cooked and drained tortellini, and Alfredo sauce in large saucepan and cook over medium heat for 5 minutes, stirring occasionally, until mixture is combined and sauce bubbles. Stir in pesto, cover, remove from heat, let stand for 5 minutes, and serve.

Serves 4

1 pound ground beef
1 onion, chopped
1 16-ounce package frozen
   beef-filled tortellini
1 10-ounce jar four-cheese
   Alfredo sauce
1 9-ounce container
   refrigerated pesto

Pressure-Cooker Beef Goulash

The pressure cooker makes beef tender and delicious in minutes. Serve this hearty dish over hot cooked buttered noodles with a spinach salad.

﹏

1. Cut steak into 1-inch pieces. In small bowl, combine flour, salt, pepper, and paprika. Sprinkle over beef cubes and rub into meat. Heat olive oil in pressure cooker; add beef and brown on all sides, stirring frequently, about 3 to 5 minutes. Meanwhile, prepare the onion and potatoes.

2. Add onion and potatoes to pressure cooker along with water and tomato sauce. Lock the lid and bring up to high pressure. Cook for 12 minutes, then release pressure using quick-release method. Test to be sure potatoes are tender; if not, lock lid and cook for 2 to 3 minutes longer. Then release pressure, stir in sour cream, and serve over hot cooked noodles or mashed potatoes.

Serves 6

2 pounds beef round steak
3 tablespoons flour
1 teaspoon salt
⅛ teaspoon pepper
1 tablespoon sweet paprika
2 tablespoons olive oil
1 onion, chopped
3 russet potatoes, chopped
½ cup water
2 8-ounce cans tomato sauce
   with roasted garlic
1 cup sour cream

Serves 4–6

3 garlic cloves
1 teaspoon salt
1 tablespoon grill seasoning
¼ teaspoon dry mustard
¼ teaspoon cayenne pepper
2 tablespoons balsamic vinegar
1½ pounds flank steak

Spicy Grilled Flank Steak

Grill seasoning contains lots of spices, usually including cumin, oregano, pepper, garlic, and sugar. Use it for hamburgers as well as grilled steaks.

1. Prepare and heat grill. On cutting board, mince garlic cloves, then sprinkle with salt. Using the side of the knife, mash garlic and salt together to create a paste. Place in a small bowl and add remaining ingredients except flank steak; mix well. Prick both sides of the steak with a fork and rub the marinade mixture into the steak. Let stand for 10 minutes.

2. Place steak on grill over medium coals and cover. Grill for 5 minutes, then turn steak, cover, and grill for 3 to 5 minutes longer, until medium-rare or medium. Let steak stand for 5 minutes, then slice across the grain to serve.

It's All in the Slicing
Flank steak is a lean, flavorful cut that is tender only if sliced correctly. Look at the steak: you'll see parallel lines running through it. That's called the grain of the steak. When you cut the steak, cut against, or perpendicular to, those lines and the steak will be tender and juicy.

Herbed Steak

The combination of balsamic vinegar and mustard with fresh thyme seasons these tender steaks to perfection. Cook a few more and you can make Asian Beef Rolls (page 463) or Grilled Steak Sandwiches (page 482) tomorrow.

(page 463) or Grilled Steak Sandwiches (page 482) tomorrow.

~

Serves 6

6 6-ounce strip steaks
1 teaspoon salt
⅛ teaspoon white pepper
2 tablespoons olive oil
2 tablespoons Worcestershire
   sauce
2 tablespoons fresh thyme
   leaves
½ teaspoon dried oregano
   leaves
¼ cup balsamic vinegar
2 tablespoons mustard

1. Prepare and preheat grill. Place steaks in a glass baking dish; pierce all over with a fork. Sprinkle on both sides with salt and pepper. In small bowl, combine remaining ingredients and mix well. Pour over steaks, turning to coat, rubbing marinade into steaks with hands. Let stand for 10 minutes.

2. Place steaks on grill over medium coals and drizzle with any remaining marinade. Cover grill and cook for 5 minutes. Turn steaks and cook for 4 to 6 minutes longer, until desired doneness. Let stand 5 minutes, then serve.

Steak Grilling Temps

An instant-read meat thermometer is always a good utensil to have on hand. When grilling steaks, 140°F is rare, 145°F is medium-rare, 160°F is medium, and 170°F is well done. Be sure to let the steak stand for a few minutes before carving and serving to let the juices redistribute.

2 eggs
½ teaspoon dried Italian
seasoning
½ teaspoon onion salt
⅛ teaspoon garlic pepper
¾ cup soft bread crumbs
¾ cup ketchup, divided
1½ pounds meatloaf mix
1 cup shredded Co-Jack
cheese, divided

Mini Meatloaf

Meatloaves made in muffin tins are cute, fun to make, and fun to eat. Serve with some ketchup and frozen French fries to give your kids a treat.

1. Preheat oven to 350°F. In large bowl, combine eggs, Italian seasoning, onion salt, garlic pepper, bread crumbs, and ½ cup ketchup and mix well. Add meatloaf mix and ½ cup cheese and mix gently but thoroughly to combine.

2. Press meat mixture, ⅓ cup at a time, into 12 muffin cups. Top each with a bit of ketchup and remaining cheese. Bake at 350°F for 15 to 18 minutes, until meat is thoroughly cooked. Remove from muffin tins, drain if necessary, place on serving platter, cover with foil, and let stand 5 minutes before serving.

About Meatloaf Mix
Meatloaf mix is found in the meat aisle of the supermarket. It usually consists of one-third beef, one-third pork, and one-third veal, but read the label to find out what the blend is in your area. The veal lightens the mixture, and the pork adds a slightly different flavor and texture, because meatloaf made with all beef tends to be heavy.

Quick Beef Stroganoff

Beef Stroganoff is an elegant dish that usually takes a while to make, but using precooked meat products means the dish is ready in about 20 minutes.

⌒

1. Bring a large pot of water to a boil. Meanwhile, heat olive oil in large saucepan over medium heat. Add onion; cook and stir for 3 to 4 minutes, until crisp-tender. Add contents of beef package along with green beans. Bring to a simmer; cook for 6 to 7 minutes, until beef and green beans are heated.

2. When water is boiling, add egg noodles. Cook according to package directions, until al dente, about 4 to 5 minutes. Meanwhile, stir sour cream into beef mixture, cover, and remove from heat. When noodles are done, drain well, place on serving platter, and spoon beef mixture over.

Serves 4

2 tablespoons olive oil
1 onion, chopped
1 16-ounce package fully cooked beef tips with gravy
1 16-ounce package frozen cut green beans, thawed and drained
4 cups egg noodles
1 cup sour cream

1 pound strip steak
2 tablespoons oil
1 onion, sliced
3 tablespoons flour
½ teaspoon salt
1 tablespoon curry powder
⅛ teaspoon white pepper
1 12-ounce jar baby corn on
   the cob, drained
½ cup frozen orange juice
   concentrate
1 15-ounce can evaporated
   milk

Curried Beef Stir-Fry

Serve this richly seasoned curry on hot cooked rice, with mango chutney and chopped cashews, toasted coconut, and raisins or currants for condiments.

1. Cut steak into ½-inch pieces across the grain and set aside. Heat oil in a large skillet over medium-high heat. Add onion; stir-fry for 3 to 4 minutes, until crisp-tender. Add steak; stir-fry for 3 to 4 minutes, until steak is browned. Sprinkle with flour, salt, curry powder, and pepper. Stir-fry for 2 to 3 minutes longer.

2. Stir in remaining ingredients; stir-fry over medium heat for 5 to 6 minutes, until liquid is thickened and corn is hot. Serve over hot cooked rice.

Recipe Substitutions
If you can't find baby corn on the cob, you can substitute frozen asparagus cuts, frozen stir-fry vegetables, frozen green beans, frozen sweet corn, or sliced mushrooms in this easy stir-fry. If your family likes spicy foods, increase the curry powder as much as you'd like.

Chapter 25

Seafood

4 halibut fillets

3 tablespoons olive oil, divided

Salt and pepper to taste

2 cups chopped, seeded tomatoes

⅔ cup pesto sauce

½ cup grated Parmesan cheese

Halibut Bruschetta

Bruschetta is an Italian appetizer of toasted bread slices topped with a fragrant tomato salad. In this recipe, halibut replaces the bread for an easy and elegant main dish.

1. Preheat broiler. Place fillets on broiler pan and brush with half of the olive oil; sprinkle with salt and pepper. In small bowl, combine tomatoes, remaining olive oil, pesto, and Parmesan cheese; season with salt and pepper to taste.

2. Broil halibut fillets for 8 to 12 minutes or until fish flakes easily when tested with a fork. Top with tomato mixture and broil for 1 to 2 minutes longer. Serve immediately.

Other Fish Choices

You can use other mild fish fillets in this easy, nutritious, and beautiful recipe. Think about using orange roughy, tilapia, or cod. This topping would also be wonderful on salmon or swordfish fillets or steaks. Cook all of these fish just until the fish flakes when you insert a fork and twist it.

Shrimp Scampi Kabobs

Lemon and garlic are the main seasonings in Shrimp Scampi. This is an easy way to make scampi on your grill. Serve with hot cooked rice.

Serves 6

3 lemons
¼ cup olive oil
4 cloves garlic, minced
1 teaspoon dried thyme leaves
½ teaspoon salt
⅛ teaspoon white pepper
1½ pounds large raw shrimp, cleaned
18 large mushrooms
2 yellow squash, cut into 1-inch pieces

1. Prepare and preheat grill. Using lemon zester, remove peel from 1 of the lemons. Place in medium bowl. Squeeze juice from the peeled lemon and add to peel in bowl. Cut remaining lemons into 6 wedges each and set aside. Add oil, garlic, thyme, salt, and pepper to lemon mixture in bowl and mix well. Add shrimp and let stand for 10 minutes.

2. Drain shrimp, reserving marinade. Place shrimp, mushrooms, squash pieces, and lemon wedges alternately on twelve 8"-long metal skewers. Brush skewers with marinade, then grill 4 to 6 inches from medium-hot coals for 8 to 14 minutes, turning once, until shrimp are curled and pink and vegetables are tender. Brush skewers often with marinade. Discard any remaining marinade.

Cleaning Shrimp
If the shrimp you buy still have the shell and tail on them, you must clean them before use. Cut a shallow slit along the back; remove the shell, tail, and legs; then rinse out the dark vein running along the shrimp, using your fingers to remove it if necessary.

2 6-ounce cans crabmeat, drained

1 cup frozen pepper and onion stir-fry mix

1 10-ounce container refrigerated four-cheese Alfredo sauce

1½ cups shredded Monterey Jack cheese

12 6-inch spinach-flavored flour tortillas

Crab Burritos

You can make these excellent burritos with two pouches of boneless skinless salmon, 12 ounces of cooked small or medium shrimp, or 2 cups of flaked and cooked fish.

1. Preheat oven to 350°F. Drain crabmeat well, pressing with paper towel to absorb excess moisture. Place in medium bowl. Thaw pepper and onion mix in microwave on 30 percent power for 2 to 3 minutes; drain well and add to crabmeat. Stir in half of the Alfredo sauce and ½ cup Monterey Jack cheese.

2. Fill tortillas with 2 tablespoons crabmeat mixture and roll up. Place in 13" × 9" glass baking dish. Top each filled burrito with some Alfredo sauce and sprinkle with remaining Monterey Jack cheese. Bake for 10 to 16 minutes until burritos are hot and cheese is melted. Serve immediately.

Broiled Cod Montauk

Mayonnaise helps keep the fish moist while it cooks. Serve this simple dish with a lettuce and vegetable salad and some soft breadsticks.

Serves 6

½ cup mayonnaise
1 teaspoon Dijon mustard
1 tablespoon lemon juice
2 tablespoons grated
 Parmesan cheese
½ teaspoon dried tarragon
 leaves
6 6-ounce cod fillets

1. Preheat broiler. In small bowl, combine mayonnaise, mustard, lemon juice, cheese, and tarragon, and mix well.

2. Place cod on broiler rack. Broil 4 to 6 inches from heat source for about 4 minutes. Remove from oven, turn fillets, and spread mayonnaise mixture over each fillet. Return pan to oven and broil for 3 to 5 minutes longer, until fish flakes when tested with fork and mayonnaise mixture begins to bubble and brown. Serve immediately.

Mayo: Low-Fat or Regular?

You can find mayonnaise in low-fat, no-fat, and regular versions; they all taste pretty much the same. You can use any type in most cooking recipes, salad dressings, and sandwich spreads. In baking, however, you should use full-fat mayonnaise unless the recipe says otherwise.

4 6-ounce salmon fillets
½ cup water
½ cup white wine or fish stock
1 tablespoon olive oil
1 onion, finely chopped
1 10-ounce container
  refrigerated Alfredo
  sauce
½ teaspoon dried basil leaves
½ cup grated Parmesan
  cheese

Poached Salmon with Alfredo Sauce

You can find jarred Alfredo and other cheese sauces by the pasta sauces in the supermarket; they are a good substitute for the refrigerated sauces.

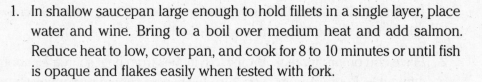

1. In shallow saucepan large enough to hold fillets in a single layer, place water and wine. Bring to a boil over medium heat and add salmon. Reduce heat to low, cover pan, and cook for 8 to 10 minutes or until fish is opaque and flakes easily when tested with fork.

2. Meanwhile, in heavy saucepan, heat olive oil over medium heat. Add onion and cook until tender, about 4 to 5 minutes. Add Alfredo sauce and basil; cook and stir over low heat until sauce bubbles.

3. Place salmon on serving plates; cover with sauce and sprinkle with Parmesan cheese. Serve immediately.

Poaching
Poaching is cooking meat or fruit in a liquid that is just below the boiling point. This method retains and concentrates the flavor of the food, and the results are juicy and tender. Fish is usually poached because the delicate flesh cooks gently with this method and does not dry out.

Shrimp and Rice

Serve this spicy shrimp dish with Lemon Cucumber Salad (page 492), Mini Popovers (page 43) and Oatmeal Cookie Parfaits (page 562).

1. In large saucepan, heat olive oil over medium heat. Add onion; cook and stir until crisp-tender, about 3 to 4 minutes. Add rice and stir to coat. Add chicken broth, bring to a boil, then cover, reduce heat, and simmer for 15 minutes.

2. Add tomatoes to rice mixture and bring to a simmer. Add shrimp, oregano, and pepper, and simmer for 4 to 6 minutes, until rice is tender and shrimp are pink and curled. Serve immediately.

Serves 4

2 tablespoons olive oil
1 onion, finely chopped
1 cup Texmati rice
1½ cups chicken broth
1 14-ounce can diced tomatoes with green chilies, undrained
1½ pounds medium raw shrimp, cleaned
½ teaspoon dried oregano leaves
⅛ teaspoon cayenne pepper

Easy Jambalaya

Jambalaya is a festive Southern dish that usually takes hours to make. Serve this easy version with some melon wedges, croissants, and ice cream sundaes for dessert.

Prepare rice mix as directed on package. Meanwhile, in large saucepan, heat olive oil over medium heat. Add onion; cook and stir for 4 to 5 minutes, until tender. Add tomatoes, shrimp, and sliced sausages; bring to a simmer, and cook for 2 to 3 minutes. When rice is cooked, add to saucepan; cook and stir for 3 to 4 minutes, until blended. Serve immediately.

Serves 4

1 8-ounce package yellow rice mix
2 tablespoons olive oil
1 onion, chopped
1 14-ounce can diced tomatoes with green chilies
1 8-ounce package frozen cooked shrimp, thawed
2 Grilled Polish Sausages (page 429), sliced

Frozen Shrimp
You can buy frozen shrimp that has been shelled, deveined, and cooked. To thaw it, place in a colander under cold running water for 4 to 5 minutes, tossing shrimp occasionally with hands, until thawed. Use the shrimp immediately after thawing.

3 cloves garlic, minced
½ teaspoon salt
½ cup butter, softened
1½ cups fine bread crumbs
*¼ teaspoon dried marjoram
   leaves*
*¼ teaspoon dried tarragon
   leaves*
⅛ teaspoon white pepper
*2 pounds cooked, shelled
   shrimp, thawed if frozen*
¼ cup lemon juice

Shrimps de Jonghe

*The bread-crumb mixture for this elegant dish can be prepared ahead of time.
Purchase cooked, shelled, and deveined shrimp from your butcher.*

1. Preheat oven to 425°F. In medium bowl, mash garlic with salt to form a paste. Add butter and beat until combined. Add bread crumbs, marjoram, tarragon, and white pepper and mix well.

2. Butter a 2-quart casserole dish. In large bowl, combine shrimp and lemon juice; toss to coat, then drain shrimp. Layer shrimp and bread crumb mixture in prepared casserole dish. Bake for 15 to 20 minutes, until hot and bread crumbs begin to brown.

Purchasing Shrimp
You can find cooked, shelled, and deveined shrimp in the meat aisle of the regular grocery store. This product is also stocked in the freezer section of the meat aisle; thaw according to package directions. Fresh cooked shrimp should be used within two days. It should smell sweet and slightly briny; if there is any off odor, do not buy it.

Salmon Steaks with Spinach Pesto

This elegant dish is perfect for company. Serve it with Pasta Pilaf (page 512), Melty Cheese Bread (page 342), and Roasted Sugar Snap Peas (page 515), with a bakery cake for dessert.

Serves 6

¼ cup lemon juice, divided
2 tablespoons oil
½ teaspoon dried basil leaves
6 salmon steaks
1 10-ounce container refrigerated pesto
½ cup frozen chopped spinach, thawed and drained
¼ cup chopped salted cashews

1. In glass baking dish, combine 2 tablespoons lemon juice, oil, and basil leaves. Add salmon steaks, turn to coat, and let stand for 10 minutes at room temperature.

2. While steaks marinate, combine pesto, spinach, and remaining 2 tablespoons lemon juice in a blender or food processor. Process or blend until mixture is smooth. Place in small bowl and stir in cashews.

3. Remove steaks from marinade and place on broiler pan. Broil 4 to 6 inches from heat source for 5 minutes, turn steaks, and broil for 5 to 8 minutes longer, until fish flakes when tested with fork. Top each with a spoonful of the pesto mixture and serve.

Spark Up Pesto

Adding spinach and lemon juice to prepared pesto makes the sauce a bright green color and perks up the flavor. And adding more nuts, whether pine nuts, cashews, or walnuts, makes the sauce a bit crunchy. Spinach also adds more nutrition and helps cut the fat, and it doesn't alter the flavor.

Serves 4

1 tablespoon olive oil
1 red bell pepper, chopped
1 pound shelled, deveined
   large raw shrimp, thawed
   if frozen
1 9-ounce package
   refrigerated cheese
   ravioli
1½ cups water
¾ cup pesto sauce
½ cup grated Parmesan
   cheese

Shrimp Pesto Ravioli

You can use fish fillets, cut into cubes, in place of the shrimp, or substitute bay scallops. Serve this easy dish with some breadsticks and a fruit salad.

1. In heavy skillet, heat oil over medium heat. Add red bell pepper and stir-fry for 3 to 4 minutes, until crisp-tender. Add shrimp; cook and stir for 4 to 6 minutes, until shrimp curl and turn pink. Remove shrimp and peppers from skillet.

2. Add ravioli and water to skillet and bring to a boil over high heat. Reduce heat to medium-high, cover, and simmer for 4 to 6 minutes, until ravioli are hot, stirring occasionally. Drain off excess liquid and return shrimp and pepper to skillet. Cook and stir over medium-high heat, stirring occasionally, until shrimp are cooked and mixture is hot. Stir in pesto, place in serving dish, sprinkle with cheese, and serve.

Honey Mustard Salmon

Honey and mustard make an irresistible flavor combination with rich and savory salmon fillets. You can multiply this recipe for a larger crowd; marinating and cooking times remain the same.

Serves 4

⅓ cup honey mustard salad dressing
2 tablespoons honey
½ teaspoon dill seed
2 tablespoons butter, melted
4 6-ounce salmon fillets

1. In shallow casserole dish, combine salad dressing, honey, dill seed, and butter and mix well. Add salmon fillets and turn to coat. Cover and let stand at room temperature for 10 minutes.

2. Prepare and preheat grill or broiler. Remove salmon from marinade and place, skin-side down, on grill or broiler pan. Cover and grill, or broil, 6 inches from heat for 8 to 12 minutes, until salmon is cooked and flakes when tested with a fork, brushing with remaining marinade halfway through cooking time. Discard remaining marinade. Serve immediately.

Menu Ideas
Any fish dish is delicious served with a salad made from baby spinach. Toss together spinach, sliced water chestnuts, sliced mushrooms, and red bell pepper, and drizzle with some creamy garlic salad dressing. Top it with croutons or Parmesan shavings. Add some ready-to-bake breadsticks and your meal is complete.

½ pound spaghetti pasta
4 pounds cleaned mussels
¼ cup olive oil
6 cloves garlic, minced
1 red bell pepper, cut into
    strips
½ teaspoon dried oregano
    leaves
1½ cups dry white wine
Salt and pepper to taste

Garlic Mussels

This is such a beautiful dish; the shiny black mussel shells contrast with the red pepper and the creamy beige flesh. Serve it with fresh fruit and crusty bread.

1. Bring a large pot of water to a boil; cook spaghetti pasta according to package directions. Meanwhile, place mussels in a colander; pick over them to remove any opened mussels; rinse well and set aside.

2. In large stockpot big enough to hold the mussels, heat olive oil over medium high heat. Add garlic; cook and stir until fragrant, 1 to 2 minutes. Add red bell pepper; cook and stir for 3 to 4 minutes, until crisp-tender. Sprinkle with oregano and pour wine into pot; bring to a boil. Add salt and pepper, then add mussels.

3. Cover pot and turn heat to medium-low. Cook, shaking pan frequently, for 4 to 7 minutes or until all mussels open. (Discard any mussels that do not open.) Remove mussels and bell peppers from pot and place in serving bowl. Strain liquid and pour half over mussels. Combine remaining liquid with cooked and drained spaghetti; serve immediately with the mussels.

About Mussels

Mussels used to be difficult to prepare because they needed to be cleaned, debearded, and scrubbed. Now you can buy them precleaned, with the beards off; just rinse and use. Be sure to discard open mussels and those with broken shells before cooking, and discard mussels that aren't open after cooking.

Fruity Tuna Steaks

Curry powder, orange juice, and apricot jam add great flavor to tender tuna steaks. Because the steaks are simmered in the sauce, they pick up more flavor.

Serves 4

2 tablespoons olive oil
1 onion, chopped
2 teaspoons curry powder
⅓ cup frozen orange juice
    concentrate
2 tablespoons water
¼ cup apricot jam
Salt and pepper to taste
4 6-ounce tuna steaks

1. In heavy skillet, heat olive oil over medium heat. Add onion; cook and stir for 2 minutes. Sprinkle curry powder over onions; cook and stir for 2 to 3 minutes longer, until onions are crisp-tender.

2. Add orange juice concentrate and water to skillet along with apricot jam and salt and pepper. Bring to a boil, then reduce heat to a simmer and add tuna. Cook for 8 to 10 minutes per inch of thickness, turning tuna once during cooking time, until fish flakes when tested with fork. You can serve tuna medium-rare if you'd like.

3. Place tuna on serving plate. If necessary, reduce sauce by turning heat to high and simmering until thickened, 3 to 4 minutes. Pour sauce over tuna and serve.

Serves 4–6

2 tablespoons olive oil
4 cloves garlic, minced
1 serrano pepper, minced
1 cup dry white wine
2 pounds sea scallops
1 teaspoon salt
⅛ teaspoon cayenne pepper
2 tablespoons butter

Steamed Spicy Scallops

A peppery wine sauce finished with butter coats these
tender scallops that are steamed to perfection.

———

1. In large saucepan, heat olive oil over medium heat. Add garlic and serrano pepper; cook and stir for 2 to 3 minutes, until fragrant. Add wine,
reduce heat to low, and simmer while cooking scallops.

2. Meanwhile, place water in the bottom of a steamer and bring to a boil
over high heat. Sprinkle scallops with salt and cayenne pepper and
place in steamer top. Place over boiling water, cover, and steam scallops for 2 minutes. Gently stir scallops, cover again, and steam for 2 to
5 minutes, until scallops are opaque.

3. Remove serrano pepper sauce from heat and swirl in butter until melted.
Place scallops on serving plate and top with sauce. Serve immediately.

Scallops

There are three kinds of scallops available. Sea scallops are the largest,
about 30 to the pound, and are white, sometimes with an orange tint.
Bay scallops are smaller, about 50 to the pound, are sweet and white
with a hint of pink. And calico scallops, the smallest of all, are darker in
color and not as tender.

Scallop Tacos

These pretty tacos are sweet, spicy, and crunchy. Serve them with a pineapple and melon salad for a cooling contrast.

Serves 4

2 tablespoons olive oil
1 onion, chopped
1 pound scallops
½ teaspoon salt
2 teaspoons chili powder
½ teaspoon cumin
¼ teaspoon red pepper flakes
8 taco shells
1 cup mango salsa
2 cups finely shredded
    cabbage

1. Preheat oven to 375°F. In a heavy skillet, heat olive oil over medium-high heat. Add onion; cook and stir until tender, about 4 to 5 minutes. Meanwhile, sprinkle scallops with a mixture of salt, chili powder, cumin, and red pepper flakes. Add to skillet; cook for 2 minutes, then turn scallops and cook until opaque, about 2 to 4 minutes.

2. While scallops are cooking, put taco shells on a baking sheet and heat in the oven until crisp, about 5 to 7 minutes. Combine mango salsa and cabbage in medium bowl.

3. Make tacos with cabbage mixture, heated taco shells, and scallop mixture and serve immediately.

Salsa

There are so many types of salsa available today. You can find mango salsa, black bean salsa, vegetable salsa, and plain old tomato salsa in any supermarket. They range in spiciness from mild to extra hot. Be sure to read labels carefully to make sure you're buying the flavor and heat intensity you want.

CHAPTER 5: SEAFOOD

381

Serves 3–4

3 tablespoons butter
1 red bell pepper, finely
    chopped
8 eggs
2 tablespoons water
½ teaspoon salt
⅛ teaspoon white pepper
1 pound cooked shrimp
1½ cups grated Havarti
    cheese

Shrimp Omelet

*This fluffy omelet filled with shrimp, bell pepper, and cheese is perfect
for a lazy Sunday brunch served with caramel rolls and a citrus salad.*

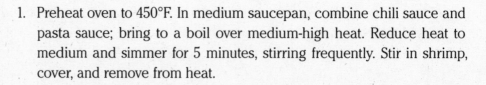

1. In large nonstick skillet, melt butter over medium heat. Add bell pepper; cook and stir for 3 to 4 minutes, until crisp-tender. Meanwhile, in large bowl, beat eggs with water, salt, and pepper.

2. Add egg mixture to pan. Cook for 2 minutes. Continue cooking, lifting egg mixture to allow uncooked portion to flow underneath. When eggs are almost set but still glossy after about 4 minutes longer, top with shrimp and cheese. Cover and cook for 2 more minutes, until cheese melts. Fold omelet and serve immediately.

Serves 6

½ cup chili sauce
1½ cups pasta sauce
2 cups medium cooked
    shrimp
2 tablespoons olive oil
6 4- to 6-ounce mild white
    fish fillets
½ teaspoon salt
⅛ teaspoon red pepper flakes
2 tablespoons lemon juice

Fish Creole

*You can use any mild white fish fillets in this flavorful recipe;
halibut, orange roughy, grouper, or cod would be good choices.*

1. Preheat oven to 450°F. In medium saucepan, combine chili sauce and pasta sauce; bring to a boil over medium-high heat. Reduce heat to medium and simmer for 5 minutes, stirring frequently. Stir in shrimp, cover, and remove from heat.

2. Meanwhile, place oil in glass baking dish. Arrange fish in dish and sprinkle with salt, pepper flakes, and lemon juice. Bake for 8 to 10 minutes or until fish flakes easily when tested with a fork. Place on serving dish and top with shrimp sauce. Serve immediately.

Salmon Florentine

Jarred four-cheese Alfredo sauce is a great timesaver. Find it near the pasta in the regular grocery store; stock up, because you can make many recipes with it.

Serves 4

4 6-ounce salmon fillets
1 teaspoon salt
⅛ teaspoon white pepper
½ teaspoon dried Italian
    seasoning
2 tablespoons olive oil
1 10-ounce jar four-cheese
    Alfredo sauce
1 cup frozen chopped spinach,
    thawed and well drained
½ cup grated Parmesan
    cheese

1. Preheat broiler. Sprinkle salmon with salt, pepper, and Italian seasoning and drizzle with olive oil. Place on broiler pan and let stand for 5 minutes.

2. In large skillet, heat Alfredo sauce over medium-low heat until bubbly. Place salmon fillets under broiler 4 to 6 inches from heat source for 5 minutes. Stir spinach into Alfredo sauce and let simmer over low heat. Turn salmon fillets and broil for 3 to 4 minutes longer, until salmon is almost done.

3. Place salmon on ovenproof serving platter and top with Alfredo-sauce mixture. Sprinkle with Parmesan cheese. Broil for 2 to 4 minutes, until cheese melts and begins to brown. Serve immediately.

4 6-ounce red snapper fillets
½ teaspoon salt
⅛ teaspoon white pepper
½ teaspoon dried thyme
   leaves
1 lemon
2 cups sliced mushrooms
2 cups sliced yellow summer
   squash
⅓ cup dry white wine

Red Snapper en Papillote

Parchment paper not only holds in the steam to cook this delicate fish to perfection, it makes for a beautiful presentation too.

1. Preheat oven to 400°F. Cut four 12" × 18" rectangles from parchment paper and trim each into a large heart shape. Fold in half, then unfold and place one fillet in the center of each heart half. Sprinkle with salt, pepper, and thyme leaves. Thinly slice lemon and place on fillets.

2. Arrange vegetables around the fish and sprinkle everything with the wine. Fold the other half of the parchment paper over the food and crimp the edges together to seal. Place on cookie sheets and bake for 12 to 16 minutes or until fish flakes when tested with a fork. Place parchment packages on plates to serve.

Parchment or Foil?

You can use parchment paper or foil to cook food en papillote. The parchment paper makes a prettier presentation at the table, but the foil is a better choice when the recipe cooks longer than 15 minutes, because the paper can burn. Let your guests open their packages at the table; warn them to be careful of the steam.

Mussels in Spicy Broth

Serve the broth on the side after straining for another course;
top with some minced parsley, cilantro, or chopped green onions.

Serves 3–4

4 pounds fresh mussels,
*   cleaned*
2 oranges
2 tablespoons olive oil
1 cup sliced mushrooms
1 jalapeño pepper, minced
2 cups fish stock
½ teaspoon salt
⅛ teaspoon red pepper flakes

1. Pick over mussels, discarding any that stay open when tapped and those with broken or cracked shells. Rinse and set aside. Remove 1 teaspoon orange zest from oranges and squeeze juice; set aside.

2. In a large stockpot, heat olive oil over medium heat and add mushrooms and jalapeño pepper. Cook and stir for 4 to 5 minutes, until mushrooms begin to brown. Remove mushrooms with slotted spoon and set aside. Add fish stock, orange juice and zest, salt, and red pepper flakes; bring to a boil.

3. Add mussels, cover pot, and cook until the mussels open, about 4 to

7 minutes, shaking pot frequently and rearranging mussels once during cooking time. Transfer mussels to serving bowl. Serve broth with mushrooms as a separate course.

Fish Stock

If you can't find fish stock in cans or boxes, you can make your own. In a large pot, combine 1 pound fish trimmings (not salmon) with 1½ quarts water; a bay leaf; a quartered onion; 3 garlic cloves; 2 stalks celery, chopped, including leaves; and 1 teaspoon salt. Simmer for 20 to 30 minutes, strain broth, and freeze.

1 cup jasmine rice
2 cups chicken broth
2 lemons
½ cup butter
1½ pounds medium raw
    shrimp, cleaned
¼ teaspoon garlic powder
⅛ teaspoon garlic pepper
½ teaspoon garlic salt

Microwave Shrimp Scampi

This dish can be multiplied to serve more people.
You must proportionally increase the microwave cooking
time: if you double the shrimp, double the cooking time.

1. Combine rice and chicken broth in medium saucepan and bring to a boil over high heat. Cover pan, lower heat to medium low, and simmer for 15 minutes.

2. Meanwhile, grate lemon zest from lemons and squeeze juice. Combine the zest, juice, and butter in microwave-safe dish. Microwave on high for 2 minutes. Sprinkle shrimp with garlic powder, garlic pepper, and garlic salt and add to butter mixture; toss to coat shrimp. Cover and microwave on high for 2 minutes. Uncover dish, stir shrimp, cover, and microwave on high for 1 to 3 minutes longer, until shrimp curl and turn pink.

3. Let shrimp stand, covered, for 2 to 3 minutes. Fluff rice with a fork. Serve shrimp and sauce over rice.

Quick-Cooking Rice
You don't have to use instant rice when you want some in a hurry. Read labels at the grocery store. There are some kinds of rice, including Texmati and jasmine, that cook in only 15 minutes. As a bonus, those rice varieties are fragrant and full of flavor.

Chapter 26

Chicken and Turkey

Serves 4

1 pound boneless, skinless
   chicken breasts
Salt and pepper to taste
2 tablespoons olive oil
2 cloves garlic, minced
2 cups frozen bell pepper and
   onion stir-fry
2 tablespoons lemon juice
½ cup crumbled feta cheese

Greek Chicken Stir-Fry

*Stir-fry with a twist! These ingredients add spark and great
flavor to a typical chicken stir-fry. Serve over steamed rice,
prepared instant couscous, or hot cooked noodles.*

1. Cut chicken breasts into 1-inch pieces and sprinkle with salt and pepper. Heat olive oil in a wok or large skillet over medium-high heat. Add
   chicken and garlic and stir-fry until chicken is cooked, about 4 to 5
   minutes. Remove chicken and garlic to plate with slotted spoon and set
   aside.

2. Add frozen vegetables to skillet and stir-fry for 5 to 7 minutes until hot
   and crisp-tender. Add chicken to skillet and sprinkle with lemon juice.
   Stir-fry for 1 minute longer. Sprinkle with feta cheese, remove pan from
   heat, cover, and let stand for 2 to 3 minutes longer to melt cheese. Serve
   immediately.

Greek Food

*Seasonings and ingredients that add a Greek flavor include feta cheese,
oregano, olives, spinach, filo dough, pita bread, rice, fresh seafood,
grape leaves, lamb, and yogurt. The food is fairly spicy, with some
unusual food combinations that include spinach and raisins, and beef
and olives.*

Herbed Chicken Breasts

*Serve these well-flavored, tender chicken breasts with a rice pilaf,
a spinach salad, and some oatmeal cookies for dessert.*

Serves 8

2 tablespoons olive oil
2 tablespoons butter
2 cloves garlic, cut in half
¼ cup lemon juice
2 tablespoons chopped flat-
    leaf parsley
½ teaspoon dried thyme
    leaves
½ teaspoon salt
⅛ teaspoon white pepper
8 chicken breasts

1. In a small saucepan, combine olive oil, butter, and garlic over medium heat. Cook and stir until garlic sizzles; then remove garlic and discard. Add lemon juice, herbs, and salt and pepper to oil and butter in pan; stir; and remove from heat. Let cool for 5 to 10 minutes. Loosen chicken skin from the flesh and pour a tablespoon of the lemon herb mixture between the skin and flesh. Smooth skin back over flesh.

2. Place chicken pieces, skin-side down, on broiler pan. Brush with lemon mixture. Broil chicken, 4 to 6 inches from heat source, for 7 to 8 minutes, brushing often with the lemon mixture. Turn chicken and broil 6 to 9 minutes longer, brushing frequently with lemon mixture, until chicken is thoroughly cooked. Discard any remaining lemon mixture.

Chicken Breasts: Boned or Not?

Chicken breasts are sold boneless and skinless, and with bone in and skin on. The one you choose depends on what you're cooking. The skin and bone do add more flavor, so in simple broiled recipes, bone-in chicken is a good choice. When you want cubed chicken for stir-fries and sandwiches, boneless, skinless breasts are better.

Serves 4

¼ cup flour
½ teaspoon salt
⅛ teaspoon pepper
½ teaspoon dried marjoram
  leaves
4 boneless, skinless chicken
  breasts
¼ cup butter
1 cup chicken stock
½ cup white grape juice
1 cup red grapes, cut in half

Chicken Veronique

*Sweet and tart grapes complement juicy and tender chicken
in this wonderful recipe perfect for entertaining. Make sure to
serve it over hot cooked rice to soak up the delicious sauce.*

1. On a shallow plate, combine flour, salt, pepper, and marjoram. Coat chicken breasts in this mixture. In a heavy skillet over medium heat, melt butter. Add chicken breasts and cook for 4 minutes. Turn chicken over and cook 3 to 6 minutes longer, until chicken is just done. Remove chicken from pan and cover with foil to keep warm.

2. Add stock and grape juice to pan and bring to a boil, scraping up pan drippings. Boil over high heat for 6 to 8 minutes, until sauce is reduced and thickened. Return chicken to pan along with red grapes, and cook over low heat for 2 to 3 minutes, until grapes are hot and chicken is tender.

Serves 6

6 boneless, skinless chicken
  breasts
¼ cup lemon juice
1 teaspoon salt
⅛ teaspoon pepper
½ teaspoon dried thyme
  leaves
¼ cup unsalted butter
½ cup grated Parmesan
  cheese

Parmesan Chicken

*This simple recipe demands the highest quality ingredients. Serve it
with some hot cooked couscous, bakery rolls, and melon wedges.*

1. Cut chicken breasts into 1-inch pieces. Sprinkle with lemon juice, salt, pepper, and thyme leaves. Let stand at room temperature for 10 minutes.

2. Melt butter in a heavy saucepan over medium heat. Sauté chicken until thoroughly cooked, about 5 to 6 minutes, stirring frequently. Sprinkle cheese over chicken, turn off heat, cover pan, and let stand for 2 to 3 minutes to melt cheese. Serve over hot cooked couscous.

Basil Spinach Risotto

This recipe does not contain chicken, but it does use chicken broth to add fabulous flavor. Be sure to save some to make Basil Spinach Risotto Cakes (page 392).

Serves 4

3 tablespoons olive oil
1 onion, finely chopped
1½ cups Arborio rice
½ teaspoon dried basil leaves
4 cups chicken broth
2 cups chopped fresh spinach
1 cup grated Parmesan
  cheese

1. In a heavy saucepan, heat olive oil over medium heat. Add onion; cook and stir for 4 to 5 minutes, until tender. Add rice; cook and stir until rice is opaque and coated. Sprinkle in basil leaves.

2. Meanwhile, in a medium saucepan, heat chicken broth over low heat. Add ½ cup of the chicken broth to the rice mixture; cook and stir until liquid is absorbed. Continue to add broth, ½ to 1 cup at a time, stirring frequently, until rice is tender and mixture is creamy.

3. Stir in spinach, cover pan, and let stand for 3 to 4 minutes, until spinach is wilted. Remove cover, stir in cheese, and serve.

About Risotto
Risotto is an Italian dish made from short-grain rice; Arborio is the most popular type. This rice has a lot of starch, which is released during the cooking and stirring process to thicken the broth. When finished, the rice should be tender but with a tiny bite still left in the middle, and the broth thick and smooth.

Serves 3–4

2 cups Basil Spinach Risotto
(page 391)
1½ cups soft bread crumbs,
divided
3 eggs, divided
½ cup shredded Gouda
cheese
3 tablespoons olive oil
½ cup basil pesto

Basil Spinach Risotto Cakes

These little cakes are full of flavor. Serve them with a mixed fruit salad and Braised Carrots (page 516), with Layered Brownies (page 540) for dessert.

1. In medium bowl, combine risotto, ½ cup bread crumbs, 1 egg, and Gouda cheese and mix well. Form into 8 small patties. In shallow bowl, beat remaining 2 eggs until combined. Place 1 cup bread crumbs on shallow plate. Dip each cake into the eggs, then into bread crumbs.

2. Heat olive oil in heavy skillet over medium-high heat. Sauté patties, 4 at a time, until golden brown on both sides and heated through, about 3 to 5 minutes per side. Place on serving platter and drizzle with the pesto. Serve immediately.

Pesto
You can find refrigerated pesto in the supermarket's dairy aisle, or make your own by combining 2 cups fresh basil leaves, 2 cloves garlic, ½ cup grated Parmesan cheese, and ½ cup olive oil in a blender; blend until puréed. Freeze in ice cube trays to store.

Herb-Crusted Chicken Breasts

Soaking chicken in buttermilk, even if just for a few minutes, makes it tender and juicy. You can use white or whole wheat bread in this easy and delicious recipe.

~

1. Heat oven to 375°F. In large bowl, combine buttermilk with salt and cayenne pepper and mix well. Add chicken breasts, turn to coat, and set aside.

2. Place bread on cookie sheet and bake at 375°F until crisp, about 5 to 7 minutes. Remove from oven and break into pieces. Place in blender or food processor; blend or process until crumbs are fine. Pour crumbs onto large plate and add herbs and cheese; mix well.

3. Remove chicken from buttermilk mixture and roll in crumb mixture to coat. Set on wire rack. In a heavy skillet, heat olive oil over medium heat. Add chicken, two pieces at a time, and cook for 2 to 3 minutes on each side until browned. Remove to cookie sheet. Repeat to brown remaining chicken. Bake chicken at 375°F for 12 to 14 minutes or until thoroughly cooked. Serve immediately.

Serves 6

1 cup buttermilk
1 teaspoon salt
⅛ teaspoon cayenne pepper
6 boneless, skinless chicken breasts
3 slices bread
½ teaspoon dried thyme leaves
½ teaspoon dried basil leaves
½ teaspoon dried tarragon
½ cup grated Parmesan cheese
⅓ cup olive oil

1½ pounds chicken tenders
1 teaspoon cayenne pepper
1 tablespoon hot pepper
   sauce
1 egg, beaten
½ teaspoon salt
1 cup dry bread crumbs
1 cup creamy blue cheese
   salad dressing
½ cup chopped celery
¼ cup olive oil

Spicy Chicken Tenders with Creamy Dip

*This recipe is reminiscent of Buffalo Chicken Wings, a spicy appetizer
that combines chicken with a creamy blue cheese dip.*

1. Spread chicken tenders onto waxed paper. On shallow plate, combine
   cayenne pepper, hot pepper sauce, egg, and salt and mix well. Place
   bread crumbs on another plate. Dip chicken tenders, two at a time, into
   egg mixture then into bread crumbs to coat. Place on wire rack while
   coating remaining tenders.

2. In small bowl, combine salad dressing and celery; cover and chill until
   ready to serve. Heat olive oil in heavy skillet over medium heat. Fry
   chicken tenders, 4 or 5 at a time, for 6 to 9 minutes, turning once, until
   brown and crisp on the outside and fully cooked. Drain on paper towels as they are finished. Serve hot with the celery dip.

Chicken Tenders
*Chicken tenderloin is part of the breast; it is a small thin muscle under-
neath, next to the bone. Chicken tenders can be made from the tenderloin or just cut from any part of the breast. They cook very quickly and
are great for children, because their shape makes them easy to pick up,
dunk, and eat.*

Green Chili Chicken Burritos

Serve these easy burritos with salsa and guacamole. A mixed fruit salad would be a nice addition to the meal, with a bakery apple pie for dessert.

Serves 6

2 9-ounce packages grilled
    chicken strips
1 4-ounce can chopped green
    chilies, drained
1 cup sour cream
¼ teaspoon cayenne pepper
6 flour tortillas
1½ cups shredded Pepper
    Jack cheese, divided

1. Preheat oven to 400°F. In microwave-safe bowl, combine chicken strips and green chilies. Microwave on medium power for 2 to 3 minutes, stirring once during cooking time, until ingredients are hot. Stir in sour cream and cayenne pepper.

2. Divide mixture among the tortillas. Sprinkle with 1 cup of the cheese. Roll up to enclose filling. Place in 2-quart casserole dish and top with remaining cheese. Bake for 7 to 11 minutes, until cheese melts and burritos are hot.

Spice It Up
There are lots of ingredients you can use to add spice to your food. Canned chopped green chilies, jalapeño peppers, salsas, taco sauce, and chili powder are all good choices. You can also use cayenne pepper, Tabasco sauce, fresh chilies like habañeros and Anaheim peppers, and ground dried chilies.

Serves 4–6

1 pound boneless, skinless
    turkey thighs
3 tablespoons flour
1 teaspoon garlic salt
⅛ teaspoon white pepper
2 tablespoons olive oil
2 cups frozen green beans,
    thawed and drained
1 cup frozen soybeans,
    thawed and drained
1 cup chicken stock
2 tablespoons cornstarch

Turkey and Bean Stir-Fry

*Serve this quick and easy stir-fry over hot cooked rice,
along with a green salad and brownies for dessert.*

1. Cut turkey into 1-inch pieces. On shallow plate, combine flour, garlic salt, and pepper and mix well. Add turkey pieces and toss to coat.

2. In large skillet or wok, heat olive oil over medium-high heat. Add turkey; stir-fry for 4 to 5 minutes, until browned. Add beans and soybeans; stir-fry for 3 to 6 minutes longer, until hot. In small bowl, combine chicken stock with cornstarch and mix with wire whisk. Add stock mixture to turkey mixture; cook and stir over medium-high heat, until liquid bubbles and thickens. Serve immediately.

Thawing Frozen Vegetables
You can thaw frozen vegetables by placing them in a colander and running warm water over until thawed. Or you can use the defrost setting on your microwave oven. You can also let the vegetables stand at room temperature for 1 to 2 hours, until thawed. Be sure to drain well after thawing so you don't add too much liquid to the recipe.

Lemon Chicken en Papillote

Lemon and chicken are perfect partners. The tart lemon tenderizes the chicken and adds great flavor. Serve these "packages" at the table and let your guests open them.

Serves 4

4 boneless, skinless chicken breasts
½ teaspoon salt
⅛ teaspoon lemon pepper
1 lemon, cut into thin slices, seeds removed
1 yellow summer squash, thinly sliced
1 zucchini, thinly sliced
¼ cup pine nuts

1. Preheat oven to 425°F. Cut four 12" × 18" pieces of cooking parchment paper. Fold in half, cut into a half-heart shape, then unfold. Place chicken breasts on one side of the fold and sprinkle with salt and lemon pepper. Top with lemon slices.

2. Arrange summer squash and zucchini around chicken and sprinkle pine nuts over all. Fold hearts in half and seal the edges by tightly folding them together twice. Place on cookie sheets and bake for 10 to 15 minutes, until chicken registers 170°F on a meat thermometer. Serve immediately.

Chicken Fried Rice

If you don't have leftover cooked chicken and rice, you can get some cooked chicken from your local deli and purchase cooked rice from any Chinese take-out place.

Serves 4

2 cooked Herbed Chicken Breasts (page 398)
2 tablespoons olive oil
2 cups cooked rice (from Grilled Ham Steak, page 418, or Creamy Chicken over Rice, page 403)
1 cup frozen sugar snap peas, thawed and drained
⅓ cup apricot jam
2 tablespoons soy sauce
¼ cup water

Remove cooked meat from chicken; discard skin and bones. Cut chicken into 1-inch pieces. Heat olive oil in wok or heavy skillet. Add chicken and rice; stir-fry for 4 to 5 minutes, until heated, stirring gently to separate rice grains. Add peas, jam, soy sauce, and water and stir-fry for 4 to 5 minutes longer, until peas are hot and flavors are blended. Serve immediately.

1 12- or 14-inch Boboli pizza
    crust
1 cup pizza sauce
4 cooked turkey cutlets (from
    Turkey Cutlets with
    Pineapple Glaze, page
    401)
1 8-ounce can pineapple
    tidbits, drained
1½ cups shredded Swiss
    cheese

Turkey Pizza

*Pizza is fun to make at home. Use your family's favorite
foods and flavors to create your own specialty. This one
is a variation of the classic ham and pineapple pizza.*

1. Preheat oven to 400°F. Place pizza crust on a large cookie sheet and
    spread with pizza sauce. Cut turkey cutlets into thin strips and arrange
    on pizza sauce along with well-drained pineapple tidbits. Sprinkle with
    cheese.

2. Bake pizza for 15 to 20 minutes or until pizza is hot and cheese is
    melted and beginning to brown. Let stand for 5 minutes, then serve.

Pizza Crusts
*There are lots of places to buy pizza crust. The deli department at your
local grocery store has Boboli pizza crusts, focaccia, thin prebaked
pizza crusts, and refrigerated pizza dough. You can even buy pizza
dough from your local pizza parlor; roll it out, bake for a few minutes
at 400°F, then freeze for later use.*

Spicy Chicken Paillards

Paillards (pronounced pie-YARDS) are thinly pounded pieces of meat, usually chicken or veal, which are coated in flour and spices and quickly sautéed.

1. Place chicken breasts between two sheets of plastic wrap. Pound gently, starting at the middle and working out, until the breasts are about ⅓-inch thick. Sprinkle with salt and pepper.

2. In shallow bowl, combine egg, Tabasco sauce, and water and mix well to blend. On shallow plate, combine flour, chili powder, cayenne pepper, and cornmeal. Dip paillards, one at a time, into egg mixture, then into flour mixture to coat.

3. Heat a large skillet over medium-high heat. Add butter and heat until sizzling. Add chicken pieces, two at a time, and cook for 2 minutes. Turn and cook for 2 to 4 minutes longer, until chicken is just done: 165°F on an instant-read thermometer. Remove to serving platter and cover with foil to keep warm while you cook the other two paillards. Serve immediately.

Serves 4

4 boneless, skinless chicken breasts
½ teaspoon salt
Dash white pepper
1 egg, beaten
½ teaspoon Tabasco sauce
2 tablespoons water
⅓ cup flour
1 tablespoon chili powder
⅛ teaspoon cayenne pepper
2 tablespoons cornmeal
3 tablespoons butter

Serves 4

1 pound turkey tenderloin
½ cup orange juice
2 tablespoons Dijon mustard
¼ cup honey
2 garlic cloves, minced
½ teaspoon salt
⅛ teaspoon pepper

Grilled Turkey Tenderloin

The marinade for this simple recipe is a nice blend of sweet and spicy. Serve the tenderloin with a mixed fruit salad and some toasted garlic bread.

1. Prepare and preheat grill. Butterfly the tenderloin by cutting it in half lengthwise, being careful not to cut all the way through. Stop about one inch from the other side. Spread the tenderloin open, cover it with plastic wrap, and pound gently with a meat mallet or rolling pin to flatten.

2. For marinade, combine remaining ingredients in a large resealable plastic bag. Add the turkey, close the bag, and knead the bag, pressing the marinade into the turkey. Let stand at room temperature for 10 minutes.

3. Cook turkey about 6 inches above medium-hot coals for 5 minutes; brush with any leftover marinade. Turn turkey and cook for 4 to 6 minutes on second side, until thoroughly cooked. Discard any remaining marinade.

The Tenderloin

Whether you are cooking beef tenderloin, pork tenderloin, or turkey tenderloin, remember that this popular cut is low in fat and should be cooked quickly. This cut comes from a part of the animal that isn't used much, so it is tender, with little connective tissue.

Turkey Amandine

*This recipe is a great way to use up leftover Thanksgiving turkey;
and if you have gravy left after the feast, use that!
Serve over hot cooked couscous, mashed potatoes, or rice.*

~

In heavy saucepan, heat olive oil over medium heat. Add carrots; cook and stir until crisp-tender, about 4 to 5 minutes. Add chopped turkey and stir. Add gravy and whipping cream and bring to a simmer. Cook for 3 to 5 minutes, until turkey and carrots are hot and tender. Sprinkle with almonds and serve.

Serves 4

2 tablespoons olive oil
1 cup sliced carrots
2 cups chopped Grilled Turkey
    Tenderloin (page 400)
1 14-ounce jar turkey gravy
½ cup whipping cream
½ cup toasted sliced almonds

Turkey Cutlets with Pineapple Glaze

*Turkey cutlets cook very quickly and are a great choice for a fast meal.
Cook them just until done so they stay tender and juicy.*

~

1. In small saucepan, heat 2 tablespoons olive oil over medium-high heat. Add onion; cook and stir for 5 to 6 minutes, until onion begins to brown around the edges. Stir in pineapple, pineapple preserves, and gingerroot; bring to a boil. Lower heat to medium-low and simmer while preparing turkey.

2. Meanwhile, combine flour, salt, and pepper on shallow plate. Dip cutlets, one at a time, into flour mixture. Heat 3 tablespoons olive oil in large skillet over medium-high heat. Sauté cutlets, three or four at a time, for 2 to 3 minutes on each side, until browned and thoroughly cooked. Place on serving platter and top with pineapple mixture; serve immediately.

Serves 4

5 tablespoons olive oil,
    divided
1 onion, minced
1 8-ounce can crushed
    pineapple, drained
⅓ cup pineapple preserves
1 tablespoon finely minced
    gingerroot
8 turkey cutlets
¼ cup flour
1 teaspoon salt
⅛ teaspoon white pepper

1½ cups chicken broth
2 tablespoons chili powder
½ teaspoon salt
⅛ teaspoon cayenne pepper
4 boneless, skinless chicken breasts
1 cup chunky salsa
2 tablespoons tomato paste
2 tomatoes, chopped

Microwave Salsa Chicken

Serve this delicious dish over couscous, topped with some sour cream, chopped tomatoes, and diced avocado.

1. Place chicken broth into a microwave-safe dish. Microwave on high for 3 to 5 minutes, until boiling. Meanwhile, sprinkle chili powder, salt, and cayenne pepper on the chicken and rub into both sides. Pierce chicken on the smooth side with a fork. Carefully place, smooth side down, in hot liquid in dish.

2. Microwave the chicken on high power for 8 minutes, then remove dish from oven and carefully drain off chicken broth. Meanwhile, in small bowl, combine salsa, tomato paste, and tomatoes and mix well. Turn chicken over, rearrange chicken in dish, and pour salsa mixture over. Return to microwave and cook for 2 to 6 minutes, checking every 2 minutes, until chicken is thoroughly cooked. Let stand for 5 minutes and serve.

Tomato Paste
Tomato paste is a concentrate of fresh tomatoes, sometimes made with seasonings like basil, garlic, and oregano. You can find it in cans or in tubes. Purchase it in tubes and you can add a small amount to particular dishes without having to store leftover paste.

Creamy Chicken over Rice

*Serve this easy dish with some steamed asparagus,
a spinach salad, and ice cream sundaes for dessert.*

Serves 4–6

1½ cups Jasmati rice
2½ cups water
4 boneless, skinless chicken
    breasts
1 teaspoon salt
⅛ teaspoon pepper
3 tablespoons olive oil
1 onion, finely chopped
1 10-ounce container
    refrigerated four-cheese
    Alfredo sauce
1 3-ounce package cream
    cheese, softened

1. In heavy saucepan, combine rice and water; bring to a boil over high heat. Cover, reduce heat to low, and simmer for 15 to 20 minutes, until rice is tender. Meanwhile, cut chicken into 1-inch pieces and sprinkle with salt and pepper. Heat olive oil in a large saucepan over medium heat. Add onion; cook and stir until crisp-tender, about 3 to 4 minutes. Add chicken; cook and stir until chicken is thoroughly cooked, about 5 to 6 minutes.

2. Add Alfredo sauce and cream cheese to chicken mixture; cook and stir over low heat until sauce bubbles. When rice is tender, fluff with fork. Serve chicken over rice.

Aromatic Rice Varieties

There are lots of different rice varieties available in the supermarket. Jasmati rice is the American version of jasmine rice, a fragrant long-grain rice that cooks quickly and is always fluffy. You can find basmati, Texmati, Wehani, Louisiana pecan, Della, and jasmine. These rices smell like nuts or popcorn while they cook.

Serves 4

4 boneless, skinless chicken
  breasts
½ teaspoon salt
⅛ teaspoon pepper
2 cups sliced mushrooms
3 garlic cloves, minced
1 cup pasta sauce
1½ cups shredded Gouda
  cheese

Grilled Chicken Packets

*This one-dish meal is so simple to make. You can make the packets ahead
of time and keep them in the fridge until it's time to grill and eat.*

1. Prepare and heat grill. Tear off four 18" × 12" sheets of heavy-duty aluminum foil. Place chicken breasts in center of each sheet and sprinkle with salt and pepper. Divide mushrooms and minced garlic among foil sheets and top each with pasta sauce. Sprinkle with cheese.

2. Fold foil over ingredients and seal the edges of the foil packets, making double folds on all of the seams. Place over medium coals and cover grill. Cook for 20 to 25 minutes, rearranging once during cooking time, until chicken is thoroughly cooked. Serve immediately.

Sautéed Chicken Patties

Caramelized onions add great flavor to these tender chicken patties.
Serve them over mashed potatoes to soak up all the sauce.

———✦———

Serves 4–6

4 tablespoons olive oil,
*   divided*
1 onion, finely chopped
1 teaspoon sugar
1 egg
2 cups panko, divided
½ teaspoon salt
⅛ teaspoon white pepper
1½ pounds ground chicken
1½ cups chicken broth
½ teaspoon dried marjoram
*   leaves*

1. Heat 2 tablespoons olive oil in heavy pan over medium heat. Add onion; cook and stir for 3 minutes, then sprinkle with sugar; cook, stirring occasionally, until onion begins to turn light brown, 8 to 10 minutes.

2. Meanwhile, in large bowl, combine egg, ½ cup panko, salt, and pepper and mix well. Add caramelized onions; do not rinse pan. Add ground chicken to egg mixture and mix gently but thoroughly. Form into 6 patties and coat in remaining panko.

3. Add remaining olive oil to pan used to cook onions; heat over medium heat. Add chicken patties, 3 at a time, and sauté for 4 minutes. Carefully turn patties and sauté for 3 to 6 minutes longer, until thoroughly cooked. Repeat with remaining chicken patties. Remove all chicken patties to serving platter. Add chicken broth and marjoram to saucepan and bring to boil over high heat. Boil for 2 to 3 minutes to reduce liquid; pour over chicken patties and serve.

Panko

Panko, or Japanese bread crumbs, are very light crumbs that make a coating exceptionally crisp and crunchy. You can substitute regular dry bread crumbs if you can't find them, but the coating won't be as crisp. Don't substitute soft, or fresh, bread crumbs, as the texture will be entirely different.

1½ cups chicken broth
½ teaspoon salt
⅛ teaspoon pepper
½ teaspoon dried thyme
  leaves
4 boneless, skinless chicken
  breasts
1 10-ounce package frozen
  broccoli, thawed
1 10-ounce container
  refrigerated four-cheese
  Alfredo sauce
1 cup crushed round buttery
  crackers

Microwave Chicken Divan

This method of cooking chicken breasts in the microwave yields tender, moist chicken. Serve with a spinach salad and some fresh fruit.

1. Place chicken broth into a microwave-safe dish. Microwave on high for 3 to 5 minutes, until boiling. Meanwhile, sprinkle salt, pepper, and thyme on the chicken and rub into both sides. Pierce chicken on the smooth side with a fork. Carefully place, smooth side down, in hot liquid in dish.

2. Microwave the chicken on high power for 8 minutes, then remove dish from oven and carefully drain off chicken broth. Meanwhile, drain thawed broccoli and combine in medium bowl with Alfredo sauce. Rearrange chicken in dish, turn over, and pour broccoli mixture over; sprinkle with cracker crumbs. Return to microwave and cook for 3 to 6 minutes, checking every 2 minutes, until chicken is thoroughly cooked. Let stand for 5 minutes and serve.

Quick Chicken Cordon Bleu

Pancetta is Italian bacon that is cured with spices, but not smoked. The deli department in your supermarket sells it thinly sliced.

⟨divider⟩

Serves 4

1 cup grated Parmesan
   cheese, divided
4 boneless, skinless chicken
   breasts
8 slices pancetta
1 14-ounce jar Alfredo sauce
4 slices baby Swiss cheese

1. Preheat oven to 400°F. Place ½ cup Parmesan cheese on a plate and dip chicken breasts into cheese to coat. Wrap pancetta around chicken breasts and place in a 2-quart casserole dish. Bake for 10 minutes. In medium bowl, combine Alfredo sauce with remaining ½ cup Parmesan cheese.

2. Remove casserole from oven and pour Alfredo sauce mixture over chicken. Return to oven and bake for 10 minutes longer. Top each chicken breast with a slice of cheese and return to the oven. Bake for 5 minutes longer or until chicken is thoroughly cooked and cheese is melted.

Deconstructing Recipes

One way to make recipes simpler to make is to deconstruct them. Chicken cordon bleu is typically made by stuffing ham and cheese into chicken breasts and then baking. Wrapping the chicken in pancetta and topping with cheese results in the same taste but is much quicker to make.

4 chicken breasts
½ teaspoon salt
⅛ teaspoon white pepper
¼ cup Dijon mustard, divided
2 tablespoons honey
2 tablespoons mayonnaise
½ teaspoon dried thyme
    leaves
4 slices Muenster cheese

Mustard-Glazed Chicken Breasts

When broiling, be sure that you place the food the specified distance from the heat source. This recipe is excellent served with Braised Carrots (page 516) and a lettuce salad.

1. Preheat broiler. Sprinkle chicken with salt and pepper and brush with 2 tablespoons Dijon mustard. Place on broiler pan, skin-side down, and broil 6 inches from heat source for 4 minutes.

2. Meanwhile, combine honey, mayonnaise, thyme leaves, and remaining 2 tablespoons Dijon mustard in small bowl. Turn chicken skin-side up and spoon on half of honey mixture. Return to oven and broil 6 inches from heat source for 4 minutes. Top with remaining honey mixture and place cheese slices on chicken. Return to oven and broil for 2 to 4 minutes, until chicken is thoroughly cooked and cheese is melted and begins to brown. Serve immediately.

Chicken Doneness
Chicken has to be cooked well done. Using a meat thermometer inserted in the thigh, not touching bone, whole chickens should be cooked to 180°F, chicken breasts to 165°F, ground chicken to 165°F, and chicken thighs to 170°F. Another test is to slice into the chicken; the juice should run clear with no tinge of pink.

Corn-Bread-Crusted Chicken Breasts

Serve this wonderful entrée with Herbed Couscous (page 510) and Honey-Orange Carrots (page 505). For dessert, serve Lemon Angel Cake (page 578).

~

1. Crumble Corn Bread finely and place in shallow bowl along with oregano; mix well. In another shallow bowl, beat eggs with salt and cayenne pepper. Dip chicken breasts into egg mixture, then place in Corn Bread crumbs to coat, pressing crumbs firmly onto chicken.

2. In heavy saucepan, heat butter and olive oil over medium heat until foamy. Add chicken and cook for 4 minutes, then carefully turn and cook for 4 to 8 minutes longer, until chicken is thoroughly cooked. Top chicken with salsa and serve.

Serves 6

2 3-inch squares Corn Bread (page 327)
½ teaspoon dried oregano
2 eggs, beaten
½ teaspoon salt
⅛ teaspoon cayenne pepper
6 boneless, skinless chicken breasts
2 tablespoons butter
2 tablespoons olive oil
1½ cups chunky salsa

Pesto Turkey Cutlets

The sauce for these cutlets is so delicious you must serve this over hot cooked rice or couscous, with steamed broccoli or green beans on the side.

~

1. In small bowl, combine flour, salt, basil, pepper, and ¼ cup Parmesan cheese and mix well. Break eggs into shallow bowl and beat well. Dip cutlets into egg, then into flour mixture to coat. Place on wire rack.

2. Heat olive oil in heavy skillet over medium heat. Sauté cutlets, 4 at a time, for 3 minutes, then turn and cook for 2 to 3 minutes on other side. As cutlets are cooked, remove to a platter. When all cutlets are cooked, add Alfredo sauce to skillet; bring to a simmer.

3. Add pesto to skillet and stir to mix. Return cutlets to the pan with the sauce and heat for 1 to 2 minutes. Sprinkle with remaining ½ cup Parmesan cheese and serve immediately.

Serves 6

12 turkey cutlets
⅓ cup flour
1 teaspoon salt
1 teaspoon dried basil leaves
⅛ teaspoon white pepper
¾ cup grated Parmesan cheese, divided
2 eggs, beaten
3 tablespoons olive oil
1 16-ounce jar four-cheese Alfredo sauce
1 10-ounce container refrigerated pesto

Serves 4

½ pound linguine pasta
2 cooked Herbed Chicken
  Breasts (page 389)
1½ cups heavy cream
1 10-ounce container
  refrigerated pesto
1 cup grated Parmesan
  cheese

Chicken Pesto Linguine

*This simple recipe is divine. Serve it with Lemon Pesto Pilaf (page 503)
and Roasted Sugar Snap Peas (page 515). For dessert,
Flaky Peach Tarts (page 577) are sublime.*

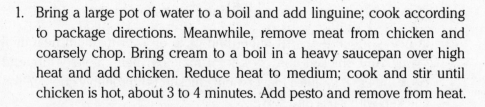

1. Bring a large pot of water to a boil and add linguine; cook according
   to package directions. Meanwhile, remove meat from chicken and
   coarsely chop. Bring cream to a boil in a heavy saucepan over high
   heat and add chicken. Reduce heat to medium; cook and stir until
   chicken is hot, about 3 to 4 minutes. Add pesto and remove from heat.

2. Drain linguine when cooked al dente and add to chicken mixture.
   Return to medium heat and toss using tongs until linguine is coated.
   Sprinkle with Parmesan cheese and serve immediately.

Boiling Cream
*Whenever you are instructed to bring milk or cream to a boil, watch it
carefully and don't leave the stove. Because of the proteins and fat in
dairy products, they boil over very easily. When the milk or cream just
begins to bubble, reduce the heat and stir or, if necessary, remove it
from the heat until the foam subsides.*

Chapter 27

Pork and Ham

Serves 4

4 boneless pork loin chops
4 garlic cloves, finely chopped
2 teaspoons cumin seed
½ teaspoon dried oregano
    leaves
½ teaspoon salt
⅛ teaspoon cayenne pepper
2 tablespoons olive oil
¼ cup orange juice
2 tablespoons lime juice

Cuban Pork Chops

*Evoke a taste of the tropics with this simple, well-flavored recipe. Serve it with
a rice pilaf, spinach salad and some cantaloupe slices drizzled with honey.*

1. Trim excess fat from pork chops. In small bowl, combine garlic, cumin,
   oregano, salt, and cayenne pepper and mix well. Sprinkle this mixture
   on both sides of chops and rub into meat. Let stand at room temperature for 10 minutes.

2. Heat olive oil in heavy saucepan over medium heat. Add pork chops
   and cook for 5 minutes. Carefully turn and cook for 5 minutes on second side. Add orange juice and lime juice and bring to a simmer.

3. Cover pan and simmer chops for 5 to 10 minutes or until pork chops are
   tender and just slightly pink in the center, and sauce is reduced. Serve
   immediately.

Ham Asparagus Wraps

The asparagus has to be cooked in this recipe because it doesn't bake long enough to soften. Use any flavor of cream cheese and bottled Alfredo sauce you'd like.

Serves 4
_____

4 ¼-inch-thick slices deli ham
½ cup soft cream cheese with
   garlic
12 spears Grilled Asparagus
   (page 511)
1 10-ounce jar garlic Alfredo
   sauce
½ cup grated Parmesan
   cheese

Preheat oven to 375°F. Place ham on work surface and spread each piece with some of the cream cheese. Top each with three spears of asparagus and roll up. Place in 12" × 8" glass baking dish and pour Alfredo sauce over all. Sprinkle with Parmesan cheese. Bake at 375°F for 15 to 20 minutes, until ham rolls are hot and sauce is bubbling. Serve immediately.

Ham Slices

For recipes that require you to enclose other ingredients in ham slices, do not use the thin slices of boiled ham meant for making sandwiches. You can use slices from spiral sliced hams or go to the deli and ask for ham to be sliced from the whole ham.

Serves 4

½ cup golden raisins
1¼ cups orange juice, divided
¼ cup olive oil, divided
1 red onion, chopped
1 teaspoon sugar
4 center cut boneless pork
    chops
1 teaspoon salt
⅛ teaspoon pepper
1 teaspoon dried thyme

Pork Chops with Onion Conserve

You'll have three pans cooking on the stove while making this recipe, but it still takes only 30 minutes!

1. In small heavy saucepan, combine raisins and 1 cup orange juice; bring to a simmer over medium heat. Meanwhile, in another heavy saucepan, heat 2 tablespoons olive oil over medium heat. Add red onion; cook over medium heat for 10 minutes, stirring frequently, until onion begins to turn brown. Add sugar to onion; cook for 2 minutes. Add raisin mixture; bring to a boil over high heat, then reduce heat to low and simmer while cooking pork chops.

2. Meanwhile, sprinkle pork chops with salt, pepper, and thyme. Heat remaining 2 tablespoons olive oil in large skillet and add pork chops. Cook over medium heat, turning once, until pork is done, about 10 minutes. Remove pork from pan; cover to keep warm.

3. Add ¼ cup orange juice to drippings remaining in pan; turn heat to high and bring to a boil; reduce heat and simmer for 2 to 3 minutes, until juice is reduced. Return pork chops to pan along with onion/raisin mixture. Cover and cook for 2 minutes, then serve.

About Raisins
Raisins are dried grapes, but the way they are dried determines the color. Both golden and dark raisins are made from Thompson variety grapes, but the dark raisins are dried in the sun, while golden raisins are oven-dried. The sunlight causes the raisins to darken. Golden raisins may also be treated with sulfur dioxide; read labels carefully!

Ham and Asparagus Casserole

Ham and asparagus are natural partners; the sweet saltiness of the ham compliments the slight bitterness of the asparagus.

Serves 4

1 pound asparagus
1½ cups cubed fully cooked
    ham
1 10-ounce container
    refrigerated Alfredo sauce
1 cup shredded Gruyère
    cheese
½ teaspoon dried thyme
    leaves
1 cup bread crumbs
2 tablespoons olive oil

1. Snap tough ends off asparagus and discard. Place in saucepan and cover with water. Bring to a boil; boil for 3 to 4 minutes, until asparagus is just tender. Drain thoroughly. Place in 2-quart baking dish.

2. In medium saucepan, place ham cubes and Alfredo sauce; cook and stir over medium heat until sauce bubbles, about 4 to 6 minutes. Remove from heat and stir in cheese and thyme until cheese melts and mixture is smooth. Pour over asparagus in casserole.

3. Preheat broiler. In small bowl, combine bread crumbs and olive oil and toss to mix. Sprinkle over sauce mixture in casserole. Broil casserole 6 inches from heat for 4 to 6 minutes, until sauce is bubbly and bread crumbs are toasted. Serve immediately.

Menu Suggestions

Serve this rich and hearty casserole with Apple and Greens Salad (page 485) and Toasted Garlic Bread (page 341), with Chocolate Peanut Butter Pie (page 574) for dessert. Or choose Simple Spinach Salad (page 495) and Parmesan Crescents (page 331), with Raspberry Continental (page 564) for dessert.

Serves 4–6

1 pound bulk sweet Italian
    sausage
1 onion, chopped
1 24-ounce package frozen
    ravioli
1 28-ounce jar pasta sauce
1 teaspoon dried Italian
    seasoning
1½ cups shredded Italian
    blend cheese

Stovetop Lasagna

Serve this super-easy version of lasagna with a crisp green salad and some Cheese Breadsticks (page 338), with Fudgesicle Pie (page 580) for dessert.

1. Bring large pot of water to a boil. Meanwhile, in heavy skillet over medium heat, cook sausage and onion, stirring to break up sausage, until meat is browned. Drain sausage thoroughly, and wipe out skillet.

2. Add ravioli to boiling water; cook until almost tender, about 1 to 2 minutes. Drain well. In cleaned skillet, spread about 1 cup pasta sauce, then top with layers of sausage mixture, ravioli, and more pasta sauce. Sprinkle each layer with a bit of the dried Italian seasoning. Sprinkle with cheese. Cover and cook over medium heat, shaking pan occasionally, until sauce bubbles, cheese melts, and mixture is hot, about 5 to 8 minutes. Serve immediately.

Serves 6

1 tablespoon olive oil
1 onion, finely chopped
1½ pound cooked ham steak
½ cup orange marmalade
2 tablespoons reserved sweet
    potato liquid
¼ teaspoon nutmeg
1 15-ounce can sweet
    potatoes, drained,
    reserving 2 tablespoons
    liquid
1 15-ounce can mandarin
    oranges, drained

Ham and Sweet Potatoes

Sweet potatoes and oranges turn a ham steak into a real feast. This recipe is a good choice for smaller families for Thanksgiving or other holiday dinners.

1. In large skillet, heat olive oil over medium heat. Add onion; cook and stir until crisp-tender, about 3 to 4 minutes. Add steak to skillet along with marmalade, 2 tablespoons sweet potato liquid, and nutmeg. Cover and simmer for 10 minutes over medium-low heat.

2. Turn ham steak, then add sweet potatoes to skillet; cover and simmer for 5 minutes. Stir in mandarin oranges; cover and cook for 2 to 4 minutes longer, until hot. Serve immediately.

Pork and Apricot Skewers

This recipe is elegant enough for company. Serve with hot cooked rice and Toasted Garlic Bread (page 341), with a spinach salad on the side.

Serves 6

1½ pounds boneless pork
  tenderloin
1 cup apricot preserves
½ cup apricot nectar
12 dried whole apricots
2 onions
½ teaspoon dried thyme
  leaves

1. Prepare and heat grill. Cut pork into 1-inch cubes and place in medium bowl. Top with apricot preserves; let stand while preparing remaining ingredients. In small saucepan, combine apricot nectar and dried apricots; bring to a boil over high heat. Reduce heat and simmer for 3 minutes; remove apricots and set on wire rack to cool; pour hot nectar over pork cubes. Cut onions into 6 wedges each.

2. Drain pork, reserving marinade, and thread pork cubes, onion wedges, and apricots onto 6 metal skewers. Combine the reserved marinade with the thyme leaves in a small pan and bring to a boil over medium-high heat; reduce heat to low and simmer while skewers cook.

3. Grill skewers, covered, over medium coals for 5 minutes. Turn and brush with some of the simmering marinade. Cover and grill for 5 to 8 minutes longer, until pork is slightly pink in center and onions are crisp-tender; keep marinade simmering. Serve with the marinade on the side.

Kabobs

When you're making skewers or kabobs, there are different materials to choose from. Bamboo skewers must be soaked in water for at least 30 minutes before grilling so they won't burn while the food is cooking. Metal skewers are more durable, but use caution because they get very hot when on the grill.

Serves 4

1 cup Texmati rice
2 cups water
¾ cup orange marmalade
2 tablespoons frozen orange
    juice concentrate
2 tablespoons balsamic
    vinegar
2 tablespoons water
½ teaspoon dried marjoram
    leaves
½ teaspoon salt
⅛ teaspoon white pepper
1 1½-pound ham steak

Grilled Ham Steak

*Ham steak is a fully cooked slice of ham that may or may not contain a bone.
All you have to do is season it if you'd like and heat it.*

1. Prepare and heat grill. In large saucepan, combine rice and 2 cups water; bring to a boil over high heat. Reduce heat, cover, and simmer for 15 to 20 minutes. Meanwhile, in medium saucepan, combine all remaining ingredients except ham and bring to a boil. Reduce heat to low and simmer for about 4 minutes.

2. Place ham steak on grill and brush with some of the glaze. Cover and grill for 4 minutes; turn ham steak and brush with more of the glaze. Cover and grill for 3 to 5 minutes, until ham steak is thoroughly heated. Keep cooking marinade while ham is grilling. Serve with remaining marinade over rice.

Ham and Cheese Penne

This simple one-dish dinner recipe can be made with any frozen vegetable combo. You can even eliminate the pasta if you use a vegetable combo that includes pasta!

Serves 4

2 cups penne pasta
2 tablespoons olive oil
1½ cups frozen broccoli and cauliflower mixture
2 tablespoons water
2 cups cubed ham
1 10-ounce container refrigerated four-cheese Alfredo sauce
½ cup grated Parmesan cheese

1. Bring a large pot of water to boil; cook penne according to package directions. Meanwhile, heat olive oil in large saucepan over medium heat. Add frozen vegetables; sprinkle with 2 tablespoons water. Cover and cook over medium heat for 4 to 5 minutes until vegetables are almost hot, stirring once during cooking time. Add ham and Alfredo sauce; bring to a simmer.

2. Drain pasta when cooked and add to saucepan with ham mixture. Stir gently, then simmer for 2 to 3 minutes longer until vegetables and ham are hot. Sprinkle with Parmesan cheese and serve.

Al Dente

When cooking pasta, al dente *is a term used to indicate doneness. It means "to the tooth." Always test pasta by biting into it. When it's tender but still has a firmness to the center, it's done. Look at the pasta: you'll be able to see a small opaque line in the center after you bite it.*

2 pounds pork tenderloins
1 teaspoon salt
⅛ teaspoon pepper
⅓ cup frozen orange juice
    concentrate, thawed
¼ cup honey
¼ cup Dijon mustard
1 tablespoon lemon juice
½ teaspoon dried oregano
    leaves

Grilled Orange Pork Tenderloin

You can serve this elegant dish to company, along with Roasted Corn Salad (page 196), Herbed Couscous (page 222), Melty Cheese Bread (page 54), and Chocolate Raspberry Pie (page 275).

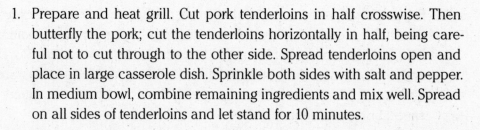

1. Prepare and heat grill. Cut pork tenderloins in half crosswise. Then butterfly the pork; cut the tenderloins horizontally in half, being careful not to cut through to the other side. Spread tenderloins open and place in large casserole dish. Sprinkle both sides with salt and pepper. In medium bowl, combine remaining ingredients and mix well. Spread on all sides of tenderloins and let stand for 10 minutes.

2. Grill tenderloins 6 inches from medium coals, covered, turning once, for 14 to 17 minutes, until a meat thermometer registers 160°F. Brush with any remaining marinade after turning. Discard remaining marinade. Slice tenderloins across the grain to serve.

Butterflying Meats

Butterflying meat cuts the cooking time almost in half. You can butterfly just about any cut of meat. Use a sharp knife and cut slowly, being sure not to cut all the way through to the other side. Spread the cut meat out, and if desired, use a meat mallet to gently pound it to flatten to an even thickness.

Sausage Stir-Fry

Serve this fresh-tasting stir-fry over hot cooked rice with chopped cashews on the side, along with a gelatin fruit salad.

Serves 4

1 pound sweet Italian
    sausages
¼ cup water
2 tablespoons olive oil
1 onion, chopped
2 yellow summer squash,
    sliced
1 cup frozen broccoli florets,
    thawed
¾ cup sweet-and-sour sauce

1. In large skillet, cook Italian sausage and water over medium heat for 6 to 8 minutes, turning frequently during cooking time, until water evaporates and sausages begin to brown. Remove sausages to plate and cut into 1-inch pieces.

2. Drain fat from skillet but do not rinse. Return to medium-high heat, add olive oil, then add onion. Stir-fry until onion is crisp-tender, 3 to 4 minutes. Add squash and broccoli; stir-fry for 4 to 5 minutes longer, until broccoli is hot and squash is tender. Return sausage pieces to skillet along with sweet-and-sour sauce. Stir-fry for 4 to 6 minutes, until sausage pieces are thoroughly cooked and sauce bubbles. Serve immediately.

Cooking Rice

Rice expands to three times its bulk when cooked. Each serving is about ½ cup, so if you want to serve six people, cook 1 cup of rice to make 3 cups. Combine 1 cup long-grain rice with 2 cups water and a pinch of salt in a saucepan. Cover, bring to a boil, reduce heat to low, and simmer for 15 to 20 minutes, until tender.

Serves 4

3 tablespoons olive oil
1 red onion, chopped
4 smoked pork chops
3 cups shredded red cabbage
1 Granny Smith apple, peeled
    and chopped
1 cup apple juice
½ teaspoon dried thyme
    leaves
½ teaspoon salt
⅛ teaspoon pepper

Skillet Pork Chops with Cabbage

Serve this hearty German feast with Smashed Potatoes (page 221) and a molded gelatin salad. For dessert, make Chocolate Peanut Butter Pie (page 286).

1. Heat olive oil in large skillet over medium heat. Add red onion; cook and stir for 3 to 4 minutes, until crisp-tender. Add pork chops; brown on both sides for about 3 minutes. Add cabbage and apple to the skillet; cook and stir for 3 minutes.

2. Pour apple juice over all and sprinkle with thyme leaves, salt, and pepper. Bring to a boil, then reduce heat, cover, and simmer for 10 to 15 minutes, until cabbage is crisp-tender and pork chops are hot and tender. Serve immediately.

Serves 4–6

1 16-ounce package seasoned
    pulled pork in BBQ sauce
2 tablespoons oil
2 cups frozen onion and bell
    pepper mixture
½ cup taco sauce
1 tablespoon chili powder
1 16-ounce can seasoned
    refried beans
8 crisp taco shells

Pork and Bean Tacos

Serve these easy tacos with lots of toppings: sour cream, guacamole, shredded cheese, chopped pickled jalapeño peppers, and chopped tomatoes

1. Preheat oven to 350°F. Heat pulled pork in BBQ sauce as directed on package. Meanwhile, heat oil in heavy saucepan over medium-high heat. Add frozen vegetables, pulled pork in BBQ sauce, taco sauce, chili powder, and refried beans. Bring to a simmer and cook for 6 to 8 minutes, until vegetables and meat are hot.

2. Meanwhile, place taco shells on cookie sheet and heat at 350°F for 4 to 6 minutes. Fill taco shells with pork mixture and serve.

Italian Crispy Pork Chops

Serve these delicious little pork chops with Lemon Pesto Pilaf (page 215), Toasted Garlic Bread (page 53), Greens with Basil Dressing (page 206), and Chocolate Velvet (page 293) for dessert.

~

Serves 6–8

8 thin-cut boneless pork
 chops
2 eggs, beaten
2 tablespoons water
½ cup grated Parmesan
 cheese
1 cup panko
1 teaspoon dried Italian
 seasoning
½ teaspoon dried basil leaves
2 tablespoons butter
3 tablespoons olive oil

1. Place pork chops between two pieces of plastic wrap and pound with a rolling pin or meat mallet until about ⅓ inch thick. In shallow bowl, combine eggs and water and beat until blended. On shallow plate, combine cheese, panko, Italian seasoning, and basil and mix well. Dip pork chops into egg mixture, then into cheese mixture, pressing the cheese mixture firmly onto the chops. Place on wire rack when coated. Let stand for 10 minutes.

2. Heat butter and olive oil in a large skillet over medium-high heat. Fry the pork chops, 2 to 4 minutes on each side, until brown and crisp and just slightly pink inside. Serve immediately.

Panko Bread Crumb Substitutions
Panko are Japanese bread crumbs that are very light, dry, and rough. If you can't find them, make your own soft bread crumbs from a fresh loaf of bread, spread crumbs on a baking sheet, and bake them in a 350°F oven for 5 to 8 minutes, until dry and crisp.

Serves 4

¾ pound bulk pork sausage
1 cup shredded carrots
1½ cups shredded Colby
    cheese
6 (12" × 18") sheets frozen filo
    dough, thawed
½ cup butter, melted

Sausage Filo Rolls

Serve these crisp little bundles for a brunch along with Scrambled Eggs with Pesto (page 58), Caramel Rolls (page 49), and fresh orange juice and hot coffee.

1. Preheat oven to 400°F. In heavy skillet over medium heat, cook sausage until partially done, stirring to break up sausage, about 3 to 4 minutes. Stir in carrots; continue cooking, stirring frequently, until sausage is done and carrots are crisp-tender, 2 to 3 minutes longer. Drain well if necessary. Remove from heat, sprinkle cheese over sausage mixture, and let stand while preparing filo dough.

2. Place 1 sheet filo dough on work surface and brush with some butter. Continue layering filo sheets with butter. Cut filo stack into four 6" × 9" rectangles. Stir sausage mixture and divide among rectangles, placing at one 9" edge. Roll up filo, enclosing filling and folding in ends. Brush with more butter.

3. Place on parchment paper–lined baking sheets. Bake at 400°F for 20 to 23 minutes, until golden brown.

Filo Dough

You can find filo, or phyllo, dough in the freezer section of your super-market near the frozen pie shells. Follow the thawing instructions care-fully, and cover the dough that you aren't using with a damp paper towel so it doesn't dry out.

Sausage Quesadillas

*These crisp little sandwiches are delicious served
with some fresh tomato salsa for dipping.*

Serves 4

1 pound bulk pork sausage
1 onion, chopped
1 red bell pepper, sliced
½ teaspoon paprika
½ teaspoon ground cumin
2 teaspoons chili powder
8 10-inch flour tortillas
2 cups shredded Co-Jack
    cheese
2 tablespoons olive oil

1. Preheat oven to 375°F. In heavy skillet, cook pork sausage with onion over medium heat, stirring to break up sausage, about 4 to 5 minutes. When browned, drain off most of the fat. Add red bell pepper; cook and stir for 2 to 3 minutes. Sprinkle with seasonings and remove from heat.

2. Lay four tortillas on work surface. Sprinkle each with ¼ cup cheese and top with one-fourth of the sausage mixture. Sprinkle with remaining cheese and top with remaining tortillas. Place on two cookie sheets and brush quesadillas with olive oil. Bake for 7 to 10 minutes, or until cheese is melted and tortillas are lightly browned. Cut into wedges and serve.

Tortillas

Tortillas are available in two types, corn and flour. Flour tortillas are usually larger, used for quesadillas and burritos. They can be flavored with spinach, red pepper, garlic, and tomato. Flavored corn tortillas are also available, as well as the traditional white, yellow, and blue corn varieties.

Serves 4–6

1 pound Polish sausage
1 green bell pepper, chopped
1 18-ounce jar pasta sauce
*1 16-ounce package
    refrigerated mashed
    potatoes*
*½ cup grated Parmesan
    cheese*

Knock Bockle

*This casserole is so hearty and comforting. Serve it with some steamed green
beans and a simple green salad, with a chocolate cake for dessert.*

1. Preheat oven to 425°F. Cut sausages into 1-inch slices; place in heavy skillet over medium heat and cook for 6 to 9 minutes, turning several times, until sausage is browned. Add green bell pepper; cook and stir for 2 minutes longer. Drain excess fat if necessary. Add pasta sauce and bring to a simmer.

2. Meanwhile, in medium bowl, combine potatoes and Parmesan cheese and mix well. Place sausage mixture into a 2-quart casserole dish and top with spoonfuls of the potato mixture. Bake for 15 to 20 minutes or until potatoes begin to turn light golden brown and sauce bubbles.

Serves 6

3 tablespoons olive oil
6 ½-inch boneless pork chops
1 teaspoon salt
⅛ teaspoon cayenne pepper
1 tablespoon chili powder
*1 chipotle chile in adobo
    sauce, minced*
2 tablespoons adobo sauce
½ cup salsa
1 8-ounce can tomato sauce

Southwest Pork Chops

*These spicy pork chops are coated with layers of Tex-Mex flavor.
Serve them with hot mashed potatoes, a cooling fruit salad,
and a lemon meringue pie for dessert.*

1. Place olive oil in heavy skillet and heat over medium heat. Meanwhile, sprinkle pork chops with salt, cayenne pepper, and chili powder and rub into meat. Add pork chops to skillet and cook for 4 minutes.

2. Meanwhile, combine chipotle chili, adobo sauce, salsa, and tomato sauce in a small bowl. Turn pork chops and cook for 2 minutes. Then add tomato sauce mixture to skillet, bring to a simmer, and simmer for 4 to 6 minutes, until chops are cooked and tender.

Pressure-Cooker Sausage Risotto

Your pressure cooker makes the most delicious risotto in less than half the time of traditional stovetop methods.

Serves 4

3 tablespoons olive oil, divided
1 pound bulk sweet Italian sausage
1 onion, finely chopped
2 cups Arborio rice
4 cups chicken stock, warmed
½ teaspoon dried Italian seasoning
½ cup grated Parmesan cheese

1. Turn the pressure cooker to high and add 2 tablespoons of the oil. Cook the sausage until almost done, stirring to break up meat, then add the onion and cook until the sausage is done and the onion is crisp-tender. Add remaining olive oil and the rice; cook and stir for 2 to 4 minutes, until the rice is coated and opaque.

2. Add ½ cup of the stock and cook, stirring constantly, for 2 to 4 minutes, until the liquid is absorbed by the rice. Add the remaining stock and Italian seasoning and lock the lid into place. Pressure cook on medium for 8 minutes. Let the pressure release, open the lid, and check the rice. If the rice isn't cooked al dente, lock the lid again and cook for 2 to 3 minutes longer. Release the pressure, open the lid, and stir in the Parmesan cheese until melted. Serve immediately.

Pressure Cookers
There are two kinds of pressure cookers: those that cook on the stove and those that are self-contained. You can brown food in either type of cooker before adding all the ingredients, sealing the cooker, and bringing it up to pressure. Regulate the heat on the stovetop models by adjusting the stove burners.

Ham Curry

Serves 4

2 tablespoons olive oil
1 onion, chopped
1–2 tablespoons curry powder
1 10-ounce container
    refrigerated Alfredo
    sauce
1½ cups chopped Grilled Ham
    Steak (page 130)
1 cup frozen baby peas

Serve this delicious, rich curry over hot cooked rice and pair it with Toasted Garlic Bread (page 53) and a crisp mixed-lettuce salad with a honey mustard salad dressing.

1. In large skillet, heat olive oil over medium heat. Add onion; cook and stir for 4 to 5 minutes, until onion is tender. Sprinkle curry powder over onions; cook and stir for 1 to 2 minutes, until fragrant. Stir in Alfredo sauce and bring to a simmer.

2. Add ham and frozen baby peas and stir gently. Continue to cook over medium heat, stirring frequently, until sauce bubbles and ham and peas are hot. Serve immediately.

Curry Powder
Curry powder combinations vary according to the cook, and in India, the spices included vary according to region. Some recipes call for simmering the curry in butter or oil before adding other ingredients. This technique really brings out the flavors and aromas of the complex mixture.

Ham and Cheese Fondue

Serves 4

2 tablespoons butter
1 onion, finely chopped
1 cup shredded ham
1 14-ounce package premade
    fondue
French bread cubes

You'll find packaged fondue in the deli section of your supermarket. Serve this excellent dish with sliced apples, breadsticks, vegetables, and crackers.

In a heavy saucepan, melt butter over medium heat. Add onion; cook and stir until tender, about 5 to 6 minutes. Add ham and stir. Add fondue and stir to break up. Cook and stir over medium-low heat for 15 minutes or until fondue is melted and smooth, stirring almost constantly. Pour into a fondue pot and place over burner. Serve with long forks to spear the bread cubes and dip them into the fondue.

Grilled Polish Sausages

Make extra Polish Sausages and save them for Easy Jambalaya (page 85). This easy recipe is perfect for a summer cookout; serve potato salad and melon wedges on the side.

Serves 6

6 Polish sausages
1 cup beer
3 cups coleslaw mix
¾ cup coleslaw dressing
6 whole wheat hot dog buns, split

1. Prepare and preheat grill. Prick sausages with fork and place in saucepan with beer. Bring to a boil over high heat, then reduce heat to low and simmer for 5 minutes, turning frequently. Drain sausages and place on grill over medium coals; grill until hot and crisp, turning occasionally, about 5 to 7 minutes.

2. Meanwhile, combine coleslaw mix and dressing in medium bowl and toss. Toast hot dog buns, cut-side down, on grill. Make sandwiches using sausages, coleslaw mix, and buns.

Sausages

Just about any sausage can be substituted for another. Just be sure to read the package to see if the sausages you choose are fully cooked or raw. The fully cooked sausages need only to be reheated, but the raw ones should be cooked until a meat thermometer registers 170°F.

Chapter 28

Vegetarian and Pasta Dishes

Serves 4–6

2 15-ounce cans spicy chili
    beans, undrained
1 14-ounce can diced
    tomatoes with green
    chilies, undrained
1 12-ounce jar tomato salsa
1 tablespoon chili powder
1 green bell pepper, chopped
1 cup water

Spicy Vegetarian Chili

You can use this chili in so many ways: from the topping for Taco Salad (page 64), to filled stuffed baked potatoes, and as the base for enchiladas and burritos.

In a heavy saucepan, combine all ingredients. Bring to a boil, then reduce heat and simmer for 15 to 20 minutes, stirring occasionally, until peppers are crisp-tender and mixture is heated and blended. Serve immediately, topped with sour cream, grated cheese, and chopped green onions, if desired.

Canned Tomatoes
There are several different types of flavored tomatoes in the market. Fire-roasted tomatoes are broiled or roasted until the skins blacken, then they are chopped or diced. Tomatoes can be packed with garlic, with green chilies; there are Mexican-seasoned tomatoes and Italian-seasoned tomatoes. Stock up on several kinds to add kick to your recipes.

Vegetarian Curry Stir-Fry

You can increase the amount of curry powder you use depending on your preferences. Serve this delicious curry over some hot cooked basmati rice.

Serves 4

2 tablespoons olive oil
1 onion, sliced
2 green bell peppers, sliced
2 teaspoons curry powder
3 tablespoons flour
½ teaspoon salt
¼ teaspoon red pepper flakes
1 pound firm tofu, cubed
1 14-ounce can coconut milk

1. In heavy saucepan over medium-high heat, add olive oil. Cook onion and green bell peppers for 4 to 5 minutes, stirring frequently, until crisp-tender.

2. In small bowl, combine curry powder, flour, salt, and red pepper flakes. Sprinkle over onion mixture. Cook and stir for 3 to 4 minutes, until bubbly. Add tofu and coconut milk to the saucepan. Cook, stirring occasionally, over medium heat for 5 to 8 minutes, until sauce is thickened and tofu is hot. Serve immediately.

About Tofu

There are two different types of tofu available in the supermarket: regular and silken. Regular tofu is firmer than silken tofu. Firm or extra-firm regular tofu can be sliced or cut into cubes; it's perfect for stir-fries and grilling. Silken tofu is usually used for dressings or puddings.

Serves 3–4

1 tablespoon olive oil

3 tablespoons butter

8 eggs

⅓ cup heavy cream

2 teaspoons chopped freeze-
dried chives

Salt and pepper to taste

1¼ cups shredded Fontina
cheese

¼ cup grated Parmesan
cheese

Cheese Omelet

*Add any of your favorite vegetables to this easy omelet recipe. Serve
it with a fresh fruit salad and some croissants from the bakery.*

1. Place olive oil and butter in a large nonstick skillet and heat over
   medium heat. Meanwhile, beat eggs, cream, chives, salt, and pepper
   in large bowl until foamy. Add eggs to skillet and cook over medium
   heat for 5 to 8 minutes, lifting edges of the omelet as it cooks to allow
   uncooked egg mixture to flow underneath.

2. When egg is cooked but still glossy, sprinkle cheeses on top. Cover and
   let stand for 2 to 3 minutes off the heat. Uncover pan and fold omelet
   out onto heated serving plate. Serve immediately.

Cream or Water?

*Believe it or not, a battle is raging over whether to add cream, milk, or
water to eggs when making an omelet or scrambled eggs. Cream
makes the eggs soft and fluffy; water makes the eggs fluffy but doesn't
add any fat, so the eggs are not as creamy. All three additions work well;
it's your choice.*

Vegetable Pancakes

You can make this recipe ahead of time and refrigerate. When ready to serve, microwave the crepes at 70 percent power for 4–7 minutes until hot.

⌐

1. Prepare crepes or defrost if frozen. In medium saucepan, heat olive oil over medium heat. Add potatoes and peas; cook and stir until vegetables are hot and potatoes begin to brown. Remove from heat and sprinkle with tarragon, salt, and pepper.

2. Add half of the sour cream and mix well. Fill crepes with this mixture; roll to enclose filling. Place in microwave-safe baking dish. Spread crepes with remaining sour cream and sprinkle with cheese.

3. Microwave, covered, for 3 to 6 minutes on 70 percent power, rotating once during cooking time, until cheese is melted and crepes are hot. Serve immediately.

Crepes

You can find prepared crepes in the supermarket's produce section. If not, they're easy to make. Combine 1 cup milk, 2 eggs, ½ cup flour, 3 tablespoons melted butter, and ½ teaspoon salt in a blender. Blend until smooth. Heat 8" pan over medium heat. Cook ¼ cup batter, rotating the pan so batter covers the bottom. Turn the crepes once, then cool on a kitchen towel.

Serves 4

8 crepes
2 tablespoons olive oil
1 cup refrigerated hash brown potatoes
1 cup frozen baby peas
½ teaspoon dried tarragon leaves
½ teaspoon salt
⅛ teaspoon pepper
1 cup sour cream, divided
1½ cups shredded Gruyère cheese

Serves 4

1 pound linguine
2 tomatoes, seeded and
    chopped
1 10-ounce container basil
    pesto
½ cup toasted pine nuts
½ cup grated Parmesan
    cheese

Pesto Pasta

*This simple recipe is bursting with the flavors of summer. You
must make it only when tomatoes are ripe, sweet, and tender.*

1. Bring large pot of water to a boil and cook linguine according to package directions.

2. Meanwhile, in serving bowl, place tomatoes and pesto. When linguine is cooked al dente, drain well and add to serving bowl. Toss gently to coat pasta with sauce. Sprinkle with pine nuts and cheese and serve.

Serves 4

1 cup vegetable broth
½ teaspoon dried thyme
    leaves
1 16-ounce package frozen
    pierogies
2 cups frozen baby peas
3 tomatoes, cut into wedges

Tomatoes and Pierogi

*You can use canned whole tomatoes in this recipe if the fresh ones are not in top
condition. Drain well and cut the tomatoes in half; add when directed in recipe.*

In heavy saucepan, combine vegetable broth and thyme. Bring to a boil over high heat. Add pierogies, bring to a simmer, lower heat to medium, and cover. Simmer for 5 to 7 minutes, until pierogies are almost hot. Add baby peas and tomatoes, cover, bring to a simmer, and cook for 3 to 5 minutes longer, or until pierogies are heated through and vegetables are hot. Serve immediately.

Pierogies

Pierogies are large pasta half rounds that are stuffed with mashed potatoes and seasonings, usually onion and cheese. They are a Polish or Hungarian specialty that is sold individually frozen. They cook in only a few minutes and can be dressed with any pasta sauce.

Broccoli Frittata

A frittata is an open-faced omelet that is usually finished under the broiler. Serve it with some orange juice, whole wheat toast, and grapefruit halves.

Serves 4

2 tablespoons olive oil
1 onion, finely chopped
1½ cups frozen broccoli florets, thawed
6 eggs, beaten
⅓ cup whole milk
½ teaspoon garlic salt
⅛ teaspoon white pepper
Dash red pepper flakes
1 cup shredded Gouda cheese

1. Preheat broiler. In large ovenproof skillet, heat olive oil over medium heat. Add onion; cook and stir for 3 to 4 minutes, until crisp-tender.

2. Meanwhile, drain broccoli thoroughly and press between paper towels to remove more liquid. Add broccoli to skillet; cook and stir for 2 to 3 minutes, until hot. In large bowl, beat eggs with milk, garlic salt, white pepper, and red pepper flakes to taste. Pour into skillet.

3. Cook over medium heat, covered, for 4 to 5 minutes. Remove cover and run spatula under eggs to loosen; cook until edges are puffed and center is almost set. Sprinkle with cheese. Place skillet under broiler and broil for 2 to 4 minutes, until eggs are set and cheese is melted.

Flavored Salt and Pepper
There are quite a few flavored salts and peppers that add great flavor with no extra work. Garlic salt, onion salt, seasoned salt, celery salt, and lemon-garlic salt are popular flavors. Lemon pepper, garlic pepper, and seasoned pepper are also good items to keep on hand in your pantry.

2 tablespoons olive oil
1 onion, chopped
½ teaspoon crushed red
*   pepper flakes*
2 cups frozen broccoli and
*   cauliflower combo,*
*   thawed*
1 15-ounce can black beans,
*   rinsed and drained*
1½ cups shredded Pepper
*   Jack cheese*
4 10-inch flour tortillas

Veggie Burritos

Burritos are made from flour tortillas rolled around a spicy
seasoned filling. Serve plain, or place in a baking pan,
cover with enchilada sauce, and bake until bubbly.

1. Heat large skillet over medium heat. Add olive oil and onion; cook and stir for 3 to 4 minutes, until crisp-tender. Sprinkle with red pepper flakes; cook and stir for a minute. Drain the vegetable combo well, then add to the skillet; cook and stir for 3 to 5 minutes, until hot. Stir in black beans, cover, and let simmer for 3 to 4 minutes.

2. Meanwhile, warm tortillas by layering in microwave-safe paper towels and microwaving on high for 1 to 2 minutes. Spread tortillas on work surface, divide vegetable mixture among them, sprinkle with cheese, and roll up, folding in sides. Serve immediately.

Frozen Vegetable Combos
Browse through your grocer's freezer aisle and you'll find almost endless combinations of frozen vegetables to add nutrition to your recipes in just one step. The combos range from broccoli, cauliflower, and carrots to baby corn, red peppers, and peas. They'll keep for a year in your freezer, so stock up!

Mushroom Risotto

Risotto is a creamy, rich dish of short grain rice and vegetables. Cooking constantly while stirring releases starch from the rice which makes the mixture thick.

Serves 4–6

3 tablespoons olive oil
1½ cups assorted fresh
   mushrooms, sliced
½ teaspoon dried thyme
   leaves
1 cup Arborio rice
4 cups vegetable stock
1 cup grated Parmesan
   cheese
2 tablespoons butter

1. Place olive oil in large saucepan over medium heat. When hot, add the mushrooms and thyme. Cook and stir until mushrooms give up their liquid and the liquid evaporates, about 6 to 8 minutes. Then stir in rice; cook and stir for 3 to 4 minutes, until rice is opaque.

2. Meanwhile, heat vegetable stock in another saucepan; keep over low heat while making risotto. Add the stock to the rice mixture about one cup at a time, stirring until the liquid is absorbed.

3. When all the stock is added and rice is tender, remove from the heat, stir in cheese and butter, cover, and let stand for 5 minutes. Stir and serve immediately.

Fresh Mushrooms
The variety of fresh mushrooms is staggering. In the regular grocery store, you can find portobello, cremini, button, chanterelle, shiitake, and porcini mushrooms. Use a combination for a rich, deep, earthy flavor in just about any recipe. Just brush them with a damp towel to clean, then slice and cook.

1 15-ounce package
    refrigerated hash brown
    potatoes
3 tablespoons olive oil
1 onion, chopped
3 cloves garlic, minced
1–2 tablespoons curry powder
1 teaspoon salt
⅛ teaspoon red pepper flakes
2 cups frozen baby peas
1 cup sour cream

Potato Curry

This rich dish uses refrigerated prepared potatoes to save time.
Serve it with a fruit salad and some whole wheat breadsticks.

1. Drain potatoes well, if necessary. Spread on paper towels to dry. Meanwhile, in large skillet, heat olive oil over medium heat. Add onion and garlic; cook and stir for 3 to 4 minutes, until crisp-tender. Sprinkle curry powder, salt, and red pepper flakes into skillet; cook and stir for 1 minute longer.

2. Add potatoes to skillet; cook and stir for 8 to 10 minutes, until potatoes are hot and tender and browning around the edges. Stir in peas and cook for 2 to 3 minutes longer.

3. Remove from heat and stir in sour cream. Cover and let stand for 3 minutes, then serve immediately.

Artichoke Stir-Fry

Be sure to purchase artichoke hearts that have been packed in water, not marinated. Serve this dish over hot cooked couscous with Roasted Sugar Snap Peas (page 227).

Serves 4

1 14-ounce can artichoke hearts

3 tablespoons olive oil

2 cups cremini mushrooms, sliced

3 cloves garlic, minced

½ teaspoon salt

⅛ teaspoon pepper

½ teaspoon dried thyme leaves

1 15-ounce can cannellini beans, rinsed and drained

¼ cup reserved artichoke liquid

¼ cup grated Romano cheese

1. Drain artichoke hearts, reserving ¼ cup liquid; cut artichoke hearts in thirds and set aside. In large skillet, heat olive oil over medium heat. Add mushrooms; cook and stir for 4 to 5 minutes, until tender. Sprinkle with garlic, salt, pepper, and thyme leaves; cook and stir for 1 minute longer.

2. Add drained artichoke hearts and cannellini beans along with reserved artichoke liquid. Cook and stir for 4 to 5 minutes, until ingredients are hot. Sprinkle with Romano cheese, cover pan, remove from heat, and let stand for 4 minutes. Stir and serve immediately.

Complete Proteins

When planning vegetarian menus, it's important to consider complete proteins. Your body needs complete proteins to heal injuries and keep your body healthy. Beans and grains are a common combination that provides these proteins. You don't need to fulfill all the requirements in one day; balancing over a two-day period is just fine.

*1 16-ounce package
    fettuccine*
3 tablespoons olive oil
1 onion, finely chopped
1 pound raw medium shrimp
½ teaspoon salt
¼ teaspoon lemon pepper
*1½ cups heavy cream or low-
    fat evaporated milk*
*1 cup grated Parmesan
    cheese*

Shrimp Fettuccine

*Low-fat evaporated milk is a good substitute for heavy cream
because it is as thick as cream but contains much less fat.*

1. Bring a large pot of water to a boil and cook fettuccine according to package directions.

2. Meanwhile, heat olive oil in a large saucepan and add onion. Cook and stir for 4 to 5 minutes, until tender. Sprinkle shrimp with salt and pepper and add to saucepan; cook over medium heat for 4 to 5 minutes, until shrimp curl and turn pink. Add cream and heat for 2 minutes.

3. When pasta is cooked al dente, drain well and stir into shrimp mixture, tossing gently to combine. Cook over medium heat for 3 to 4 minutes, until sauce is slightly thickened. Add cheese and stir gently to coat. Serve immediately.

Recipe Substitutions
You can substitute scallops, clams, oysters, or cubed fresh fish fillets for shrimp in just about any recipe. Scallops are cooked just until opaque, clams and oysters until they plump, and fish fillets until they turn opaque and flake when tested with a fork.

Pasta with Spinach Pesto

Adding spinach to prepared pesto turns the color a bright green and adds flavor and nutrition, in addition to lowering the fat content.

Serves 8

½ cup frozen cut spinach
¾ cup grated Parmesan
  cheese, divided
1 10-ounce container
  prepared basil pesto
2 tablespoons lemon juice
1 16-ounce package
  campanelle or farfalle
  pasta

1. Thaw spinach by running under hot water; drain well and squeeze with your hands to drain thoroughly. Combine in food processor or blender with ¼ cup Parmesan cheese, pesto, and lemon juice. Process or blend until mixture is smooth.

2. Meanwhile, cook pasta as directed on package until al dente. Drain well, reserving ½ cup pasta cooking water. Return pasta to pan and add pesto mixture and ¼ cup pasta cooking water. Toss gently to coat, adding more pasta cooking water if needed to make a smooth sauce. Serve with remaining ½ cup Parmesan cheese.

Pasta Shapes
There are hundreds of different pasta shapes on the market. Campanelle, which means "bellflowers," is a crimped and ruffled pasta that holds onto thick sauces. Farfalle, or butterfly-shaped pasta, is a good substitute, as is penne rigate or mostaccioli. Browse through the pasta aisle in your supermarket for more ideas.

Serves 4–6

5 large beefsteak tomatoes
⅓ cup olive oil
1 12-ounce box linguine pasta
½ teaspoon salt
¼ cup chopped fresh basil
1 6-ounce wedge Brie cheese

Linguine with Tomato Sauce

The combination of basil, tomatoes, and Brie cheese with hot pasta is simply sensational. This recipe can only be made when tomatoes are in season.

1. Cut tomatoes in half and squeeze out seeds. Coarsely chop tomatoes and combine in large bowl with olive oil.

2. Bring a large pot of water to a boil and cook linguine pasta as directed on package. Meanwhile, add salt and basil to tomatoes and toss gently. Cut Brie into small cubes and add to tomatoes.

3. Drain pasta and immediately add to tomato mixture. Toss, using tongs, until mixed. Serve immediately.

Soft Cheeses
Soft cheeses include Brie, Camembert, and Reblochon. These cheeses have a tangy flavor and very soft texture, making them difficult to work with. When you need to slice or grate these cheeses, place them in the freezer for about 15 minutes. The cheese will harden, making it easier to handle.

Creamy Tomato Sauce with Meatballs

This wonderful 20-minute recipe is great for a last-minute supper or to serve for unexpected company. Use freshly grated Parmesan cheese for the best flavor.

Serves 6–8

1 16-ounce package frozen
   meatballs
1 28-ounce jar pasta sauce
1 16-ounce package linguine
   pasta
1 cup whipping cream
1 cup grated Parmesan
   cheese

1. Bring a large pot of water to a boil. Bake meatballs as directed on package until hot and tender. Meanwhile, place pasta sauce in large saucepan; heat over medium heat until it comes to a simmer. Simmer for 4 to 5 minutes.

2. Cook pasta according to pasta directions until al dente; drain well. Meanwhile, remove meatballs from oven and add to pasta sauce in saucepan along with whipping cream. Bring back to a simmer and cook over medium heat for 4 to 6 minutes, stirring occasionally. Serve over cooked and drained pasta with Parmesan cheese on the side.

About Frozen Meatballs

There are several types of frozen meatballs in your grocer's freezer section. You can find plain meatballs, beef meatballs made with wild rice, chicken meatballs, and meatballs seasoned with Italian spices. Keep a selection in your freezer and you'll have the makings for dinner in minutes.

Serves 4

1 14-ounce package frozen
    cheese tortellini
2 tablespoons olive oil
3 cloves garlic, minced
½ cup white wine or
    vegetable broth
2 cups frozen baby peas
¼ teaspoon onion salt
¼ cup chopped flat-leaf
    parsley

Tortellini in Wine Sauce

*This elegant recipe is perfect for a spur of the moment dinner party.
You can keep all of these ingredients on hand and dinner
will be on the table in under 15 minutes.*

1. Bring a large pot of water to a boil and cook tortellini as directed on package. Meanwhile, in a large saucepan, heat olive oil over medium heat. Add garlic; cook and stir for 2 minutes, until garlic just begins to turn golden. Add wine, peas, and salt and bring to a simmer.

2. Drain tortellini and add to saucepan with wine. Cook over low heat for 4 to 5 minutes, until mixture is hot and slightly thickened. Add parsley, stir, and serve.

Serves 4–6

3 cups uncooked mostaccioli
    pasta
1 pound ground beef
1 onion, chopped
1 28-ounce jar pasta sauce
½ cup grated Parmesan
    cheese

Meaty Mostaccioli

*There are many varieties of jarred pasta sauce; you can find it with lots of vege-
tables, with meat, or just plain. Pick your favorite for this easy recipe.*

1. Bring a large pot of water to boil and cook pasta according to package directions. Meanwhile, in heavy saucepan, cook ground beef with onion until beef is browned, stirring frequently to break up meat. Drain well, if necessary.

2. Add pasta sauce to ground beef mixture and bring to a simmer. When pasta is cooked al dente, drain and place on serving plate. Cover with pasta sauce mixture, sprinkle with cheese, and serve.

Linguine with Peas

This recipe is so simple, yet packed full of flavor. You can make it with spaghetti or fettuccine as well; just make sure to serve it as soon as it's cooked.

Serves 4–6

1 pound linguine pasta
¼ cup olive oil
1 onion, chopped
3 cups frozen baby peas
½ cup toasted pine nuts
1 cup cubed Gouda cheese

1. Bring a large pot of salted water to a boil and cook pasta according to package directions.

2. Meanwhile, heat olive oil in a heavy saucepan over medium heat and add onion. Cook and stir for 5 to 7 minutes, until onions are tender. Add peas; cook and stir for 2 to 4 minutes longer, until peas are hot. Turn off heat and add pine nuts and Gouda cheese; cover and let stand while you drain pasta. Toss pasta with pea mixture and serve immediately.

Cooking Pasta
Pasta must be cooked in a large amount of salted, rapidly boiling water. The proportions are 1½ quarts of water for every 3 ounces of dried pasta. When finishing a dish by adding the pasta to a sauce, slightly undercook the pasta. Some of the residual heat from the sauce will continue to cook the pasta in the last few seconds.

Serves 4

1 pound spaghetti
3 tablespoons fermented
    black beans
1 15-ounce can black beans
¼ cup olive oil
5 cloves garlic, minced

Black-Bean Spaghetti

*A combination of salty fermented black beans and
canned black beans is a delicious topping for spaghetti.
Serve it with a simple green salad and a fresh fruit salad.*

1. Bring a large pot of water to a boil and add the spaghetti. Cook according to package directions until al dente.

2. Meanwhile, place fermented black beans in a strainer and rinse; drain on paper towels. Drain the black beans and rinse, then drain again. Heat olive oil in large skillet over medium heat. Add garlic; cook and stir for 3 to 4 minutes, until garlic is fragrant. Do not let it burn.

3. When pasta is cooked, drain thoroughly and add to skillet along with fermented black beans and plain black beans. Toss until heated and mixed and serve immediately.

About Fermented Black Beans
Fermented black beans are actually black soybeans that are marinated in a mixture of garlic, salt, and spices. They are very strongly flavored and add a nice spicy kick to Asian dishes. If using more than 1 tablespoon, rinse them briefly to cut down on the salt.

Pasta Frittata

Leftover pasta can be made into this simple main dish. Just reheat it in boiling water for about 30 seconds, drain well, then continue with the recipe.

⌒

Serves 4

1 handful linguine pasta
8 eggs, beaten
¼ cup heavy cream
½ teaspoon dried Italian seasoning
½ teaspoon garlic salt
⅛ teaspoon garlic pepper
2 tablespoons olive oil
1 cup chopped mushrooms
1 cup grated Cotija or Parmesan cheese

1. Heat a large stockpot filled with water until boiling. Break linguine in half and add to pot. Cook linguine until almost al dente, about 5 to 7 minutes; drain well. Meanwhile, in large bowl, beat eggs with cream, Italian seasoning, garlic salt, and garlic pepper.

2. Preheat broiler. Heat olive oil in heavy ovenproof skillet over medium heat. Add mushrooms; cook and stir for 3 to 4 minutes, until almost tender. Add egg mixture to skillet along with drained pasta; arrange in an even layer. Cook over medium heat for 4 to 7 minutes, until eggs are almost set, lifting egg mixture occasionally to let uncooked mixture flow to bottom.

3. Sprinkle frittata with cheese and place under broiler for 3 to 5 minutes, until eggs are cooked and cheese is melted and beginning to brown. Serve immediately.

Menu Ideas
A frittata is a wonderful dish for a late-night supper. Serve it with a spinach salad made with sliced red and yellow bell peppers, croutons, and a creamy Italian salad dressing, and some Toasted Garlic Bread (page 53). For dessert, try Peanut Cakes (page 291).

Serves 6–8

2 tablespoons olive oil

1 red bell pepper, chopped

1 28-ounce jar pasta sauce

½ cup water

1 24-ounce package frozen ravioli

1 15-ounce can black beans, rinsed and drained

1½ cups shredded pizza cheese

Black-Bean Unstructured Lasagna

Lasagna in under 15 minutes! Serve this wonderful dish with a fresh green salad drizzled with Italian dressing, some crisp breadsticks, and ice cream for dessert.

Preheat broiler. Heat olive oil in large ovenproof skillet over medium heat. Add bell pepper; cook and stir for 2 to 3 minutes, until crisp-tender. Add pasta sauce and water; bring to a boil. Add ravioli, stir, bring to a simmer, and cook for 4 to 8 minutes, until ravioli are hot. Add beans and stir. Sprinkle with cheese, place under the broiler, and broil until cheese is melted and begins to brown. Serve immediately.

Modifying Equipment

If you don't have ovenproof pans or skillets, use heavy-duty foil to protect the handles. Wrap two layers of the foil around the handles and you can use the pans under the broiler. Foil can also be used to make a large pan smaller; just use it to build walls for the size pan you want. Fill the empty space with dried beans.

Chapter 29

From the Deli

3 cups deli three-bean salad
1 cup cubed cooked ham
1 cup grape tomatoes
1 yellow bell pepper, seeded
    and chopped
1 cup mushrooms, sliced

Ham and Three-Bean Salad

Make sure that you taste (and like!) the three-bean salad from your deli before using it in this recipe. Most delis will offer you a taste if you ask.

Drain salad and reserve ½ cup of the dressing. Combine all ingredients in medium bowl and toss with enough reserved dressing to moisten. Serve immediately; refrigerate leftovers.

Serves 8

1 quart deli potato salad
1 tablespoon chili powder
2 red bell peppers, chopped
1 pint cherry or grape
    tomatoes
1 jalapeño pepper, minced
2 cups canned corn, drained

Southwest Potato Salad

If you like your food extra spicy, use more chili powder or add more jalapeño peppers. If you're really brave, try habañero peppers!

Place potato salad in serving bowl and sprinkle evenly with chili powder. Add remaining ingredients and gently stir to mix thoroughly. Serve immediately or cover and chill for 1 to 2 hours to blend flavors.

Dress Up Potato Salad

It's easy to dress up plain potato salad. To make a curried potato salad, mix curry powder with chutney and stir into potato salad along with sliced green onions and sliced celery. For an All-American potato salad, add grape tomatoes, some chopped dill pickles, and some yellow mustard.

Spicy Veggie Pizza

Boboli pizza crusts are available in any deli and you can usually find plain pizza crusts there too. This easy pizza is delicious served with some deli fruit salad and cold milk.

⌁

Serves 4

2 cups marinated deli vegetables
1 12- or 14-inch Boboli pizza crust
1 10-ounce container garlic and herb cream cheese
1 cup shredded provolone cheese
½ cup grated Parmesan cheese

1. Preheat oven to 400°F. Chop the marinated vegetables into smaller pieces and place in saucepan with the marinade. Bring to a simmer over medium heat; simmer for 3 to 4 minutes, until vegetables are tender. Drain thoroughly.

2. Place pizza crust on a cookie sheet and spread with the cream cheese. Arrange drained vegetables on top and sprinkle with provolone and Parmesan cheeses. Bake for 15 to 18 minutes, until crust is hot and crisp and cheese is melted and begins to brown.

Make Your Own Pizza Crust
Make your own crust by combining 2 cups flour, 1 cup cornmeal, 3 tablespoons oil, 1 package yeast, and 1⅓ cups water in a bowl. Knead thoroughly, let rise, punch down, divide in half, and roll out. Prebake the crust at 400°F for 8 to 10 minutes, then cool, wrap well, and freeze until ready to use.

Snickers Salad Éclairs

*In many delis, there is a fabulous sweet whipped cream
salad made with chopped candy bars. It stretches the
definition of "salad," but it makes a delicious dessert.*

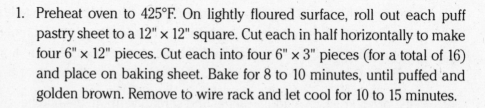

1. Preheat oven to 425°F. On lightly floured surface, roll out each puff pastry sheet to a 12" × 12" square. Cut each in half horizontally to make four 6" × 12" pieces. Cut each into four 6" × 3" pieces (for a total of 16) and place on baking sheet. Bake for 8 to 10 minutes, until puffed and golden brown. Remove to wire rack and let cool for 10 to 15 minutes.

2. Split each rectangle of pastry in half horizontally and put the halves together with some of the salad. Meanwhile, melt chocolate chips in microwave oven for 2 minutes on 50 percent power; stir until smooth. Drizzle chocolate over filled rectangles and sprinkle with walnuts. Cover and refrigerate, or serve immediately.

Re-creating Deli Salads
If you can't find certain deli salads, re-create them! Most salads use a combination of fruits with whipped cream or nondairy whipped topping. The Snickers-Bar Salad is made with vanilla pudding, chopped candy bars, chopped walnuts, nondairy whipped topping, and chopped apples.

Simple Fruit Parfaits

*Make these pretty parfaits ahead of time and keep them
in the refrigerator until you're ready to serve them.*

Serves 8
___

*2 cups frozen nondairy
   topping, thawed*
1 cup deli vanilla pudding
½ teaspoon cinnamon
2 cups deli fruit salad
1 cup granola

In medium bowl, combine topping, pudding, and cinnamon and fold together gently. Make parfaits by layering the fruit salad, topping mixture, and granola into tall parfait glasses, ending with granola. Serve immediately or cover and refrigerate for up to 4 hours.

Deli Fruit Salads

There are usually several kinds of deli fruit salads. You'll find plain mixed fruit with no dressing or a simple clear dressing, gelatin fruit salads, and fruit salads made with whipped cream or whipping topping. For this recipe, look for the plain mixed fruit salad.

Barbecued Roast Beef Sandwiches

*This recipe is great for using up leftover roast beef. The sauce
can also be used to make Sloppy Joe sandwiches; use 1½
pounds of cooked and drained ground beef for the roast beef.*

Serves 12
___

2 tablespoons olive oil
1 onion, chopped
½ cup steak sauce
1 8-ounce can tomato sauce
*1½ pounds thinly sliced
   cooked deli roast beef*
*12 sandwich buns, split and
   toasted*

1. In heavy skillet, heat olive oil over medium heat. Add onion and cook, stirring frequently, for 5 to 6 minutes, until onion is tender. Add steak sauce and tomato sauce and bring to a simmer. Stir in roast beef; simmer for 5 to 6 minutes, stirring frequently, until sauce thickens slightly and roast beef is heated through.

2. Make sandwiches using roast beef mixture and split and toasted sandwich buns. Serve immediately.

Serves 4–6

1 loaf Italian bread, unsliced
⅓ cup honey mustard/mayo
    combo
½ pound sliced deli ham
½ pound sliced deli turkey
½ pound sliced Muenster
    cheese

Hot Submarine Sandwiches

Use any combination of meats and cheeses for this easy and hearty sandwich recipe. Serve it with a deli fruit salad and a bakery pie for dessert.

⁓

Preheat oven to 400°F. Slice bread in half horizontally and place, cut sides up, on work surface. Spread cut surfaces with the honey mustard/mayo combo. Arrange ham, turkey, and Muenster cheese on bottom half of the bread, then top with second half. Wrap entire sandwich in foil. Bake for 20 to 23 minutes or until sandwich is hot, cheese is melted, and bread is toasted, opening foil for last 5 minutes of baking time to crisp bread. Slice into four to six portions and serve.

Mustard Combinations
There are many types and varieties of mustard combinations in the grocery store these days. From honey mustard to grainy mustard to mustard and mayonnaise blends, there's a large selection to choose from. Keep a supply on hand for making sandwiches from just about any leftover meat.

Corned Beef Sandwiches

These hearty sandwiches are perfect for a St. Patrick's Day celebration. Serve them with a deli fruit salad and Grasshopper Cookies (page 265) for dessert.

Serves 4

¼ cup mustard/mayonnaise combo
8 slices deli pumpernickel rye swirl bread
½ pound thinly sliced deli corned beef
2 cups deli coleslaw
4 slices deli Swiss cheese

Spread mustard/mayonnaise combo on the bread slices and make sandwiches with the corned beef, coleslaw, and Swiss cheese. Cut in half and serve with some deli dill pickles.

Salads in Sandwiches
When you're using any kind of prepared salads in sandwich recipes, you may need to drain the salad by placing it in a colander and letting it stand for a few minutes, or by using a slotted spoon to scoop the salad out of the container. If you're making sandwiches ahead of time, leave the salad out and add it just before serving.

Chicken Tortellini Salad

Most delis have a selection of prepared salads. Serve this gorgeous salad on some baby spinach leaves along with iced tea and bakery breadsticks.

Serves 4–6

1 quart deli tortellini salad
2 cups chopped deli chicken
1 red bell pepper, chopped
1 cup cubed Havarti cheese
½ cup mayonnaise

In large bowl, combine all ingredients and toss gently to coat. Serve immediately or cover and refrigerate up to 24 hours.

Salad Inspirations
Take some time to browse through your supermarket to find ideas for salads. In the produce section you'll find salad kits and lots of refrigerated dressings to inspire you. Many companies make salad kits that are placed in the meat aisle and some are in the grocery aisle near the bottled salad dressings.

*¼ pound thinly sliced deli
ham*
*¼ pound thinly sliced deli
turkey*
*¼ pound thinly sliced deli
Colby cheese*
8 slices whole grain bread
1 cup fish batter mix
⅓ cup oil

Monte Cristo Sandwiches

*Find fish batter mix near the fish in the supermarket's meat aisle.
It makes a wonderful crispy coating on these delicious sandwiches.*

1. Make sandwiches using ham, turkey, cheese, and bread. In shallow bowl, prepare batter mix as directed on package.

2. Pour oil into heavy saucepan and heat over medium heat until a drop of water sizzles and evaporates. Dip sandwiches into batter mixture and immediately place in oil in saucepan. Cook over medium heat, turning once, until bread is golden brown and cheese is melted, about 3 to 5 minutes per side. Cut sandwiches in half and serve immediately.

Monte Cristo Sandwich Dips
Serve these dips with Monte Cristo Sandwiches or any grilled sandwich. For a sweet dip, combine ½ cup sour cream with ¼ cup raspberry jam and mix well. For a spicy dip, combine ½ cup mayonnaise with 2 tablespoons honey Dijon mustard and a teaspoon of chili sauce and blend well.

Crispy Chicken Stir-Fry

Hot cooked rice is a must for this simple stir-fry recipe. Serve with chopsticks and some green tea for an authentic quick Asian meal.

~

Cut chicken meat off the bone; be sure to include some crisp skin on each piece. Set aside. If necessary, cut salad vegetables into uniform pieces. In large saucepan or wok, heat olive oil over medium high heat. Add onion and salad vegetables and stir-fry for 4 to 7 minutes, until crisp-tender. Add chicken pieces; stir-fry for 2 to 3 minutes, until hot. Add simmer sauce and stir-fry for 3 to 5 minutes, until hot. Serve immediately.

Serves 4

2 fried deli chicken breasts
2 cups mixed salad vegetables from deli salad bar
2 tablespoons olive oil
1 onion, chopped
⅔ cup sweet-and-sour simmer sauce

Roasted Chicken Penne

A tender baby spinach salad with a raspberry vinaigrette, some raspberries, and toasted slivered almonds is all you need to make this easy recipe a complete meal.

~

Serves 4

2 cups penne pasta
2 roasted deli chicken breasts
1 10-ounce jar garlic Alfredo sauce
½ cup chicken gravy (from deli or jar)
2 cups frozen mixed vegetables, thawed and drained

1. Bring a large pot of water to a boil and cook penne pasta according to package directions. Meanwhile, remove meat from chicken and shred. Combine with Alfredo sauce, chicken gravy, and vegetables in a large saucepan over medium heat. Cook, stirring occasionally, until sauce bubbles and chicken and vegetables are hot, about 8 to 10 minutes.

2. When pasta is cooked al dente, drain thoroughly and add to chicken mixture, stirring and tossing gently. Cook for another 1 to 2 minutes to heat through and serve.

Serves 6

1 package refrigerated pie
    crusts
1 7-ounce can artichoke
    hearts, drained
2 cups chopped deli roast
    beef
1½ cups diced Swiss cheese
⅓ cup sour cream

Roast Beef Calzones

*Calzones are a baked Italian sandwich, usually made with pizza dough.
This version, made with pie crusts, is more delicate and flaky.*

1. Preheat oven to 400°F. Let pie crusts stand at room temperature while preparing filling. Drain artichoke hearts, place on paper towels to drain further, and cut into smaller pieces. In medium bowl, combine artichoke hearts, chopped beef, cheese, and sour cream, and mix gently.

2. Place pie crusts on cookie sheet, placing the edges in the center of the cookie sheet, about 1 inch apart, and letting excess hang beyond the cookie sheet. Divide filling between pie crusts, placing on one half of each crust, leaving a 1-inch border. Fold the unfilled half of the pie crust (the part hanging beyond the cookie sheet) over the filling to form a half-moon shape. Press edges with a fork to firmly seal. Cut decorative shapes in the top of each crust. Bake for 18 to 24 minutes, until crust is golden brown and crisp and filling is hot. Let stand for 5 minutes, then cut into wedges to serve.

Pesto Potato Salad

This excellent salad is perfect for a picnic or cookout. Be sure to pack it in an insulated cooler with some ice packs, and discard leftovers after the picnic.

Serves 6–8

1 10-ounce container
  refrigerated pesto
½ cup mayonnaise
6 cups deli potato salad
½ cup grated Parmesan
  cheese
2 cups cubed Havarti cheese

In large bowl, combine pesto and mayonnaise; stir in potato salad until coated. Stir in cheeses and mix well. Serve immediately or cover and chill for up to 8 hours before serving.

Menu Ideas

Serve this potato salad along with Spicy Grilled Flank Steak (page 74), lots of tortilla chips and potato chips, and Grilled Asparagus (page 223). For dessert, make S'mores by toasting marshmallows over the coals and making sandwiches with the marshmallows, graham crackers, and chocolate bars.

Spinach and Fruit Ham Salad

For this recipe, purchase the deli fruit salad with a clear dressing, not the salad with the whipped cream dressing.

Serves 6

1 10-ounce bag baby spinach
2 cups (8 ounces) cubed deli
  ham
2 cups deli fruit salad
½ cup peach pie filling
1 cup pecan halves

In large serving bowl, arrange spinach. In medium bowl, combine ham with deli fruit salad and fold in pie filling. Add pecan halves and spoon salad over baby spinach; serve immediately.

Menu Suggestions

On hot summer days, serve cold main-dish salads on your back porch under a ceiling fan with some chewy bakery breadsticks on the side, some iced tea or Lemonade (page 36), and Oatmeal Cookie Parfaits (page 274) or Ice Cream with Mix-Ins (page 279) for dessert.

Serves 4

1 10- to 12-inch focaccia
  bread
¾ cup garlic Alfredo sauce
  (from 10-ounce jar)
8 ounces cold smoked
  salmon
1 8-ounce jar plain artichoke
  hearts, drained
1½ cups shredded Gouda
  cheese

Smoked Salmon Pizza

*If your deli makes a marinated vegetable salad that you like, cook it for
a few minutes over medium heat until tender, then drain thoroughly;
substitute it for the artichoke hearts in this simple recipe.*

Preheat oven to 400°F. Place focaccia on baking sheet. Spread with Alfredo
sauce. Arrange salmon and artichoke hearts on pizza, then sprinkle with
Gouda cheese. Bake for 18 to 22 minutes, until pizza is thoroughly heated
and cheese is melted and beginning to brown. Serve immediately.

Smoked Salmon

*Salmon is available hot-smoked or cold-smoked. Hot-smoked salmon, also
called kippered salmon, is usually hard and slightly chewy and is a deep red
color. Cold-smoked salmon, or lox, is pink and tender and is sliced very thin.
Either type of salmon will work in this easy pizza.*

Seafood Enchiladas

*Serve these easy enchiladas with Lemon Cucumber Salad
(page 204) and Garlicky Green Beans (page 226), with
Cereal Caramel Chews (page 262) for dessert.*

Serves 6

½ pound deli Muenster
  cheese
3 cups deli seafood salad
1 cup salsa
12 6-inch corn tortillas
1 10-ounce jar enchilada
  sauce

Preheat oven to 400°F. Shred cheese into large bowl or ask the deli to shred it. In another large bowl, combine seafood salad and salsa; stir in 1½ cups shredded cheese. Divide among corn tortillas and roll up. Place ½ cup enchilada sauce in bottom of 2-quart baking dish and lay filled tortillas on top. Drizzle with rest of enchilada sauce and sprinkle with remaining cheese. Bake for 20 to 23 minutes, until casserole is hot and bubbly. Serve immediately.

Asian Beef Rolls

*This cold entrée wraps tender roast beef around crunchy
coleslaw mix seasoned with Asian ingredients. Yum.*

Serves 6

3 tablespoons hoisin sauce
¼ cup plum sauce
1½ cups coleslaw mix
¼ cup chopped green onion
6 slices cooked deli roast beef

In medium bowl, combine hoisin sauce and plum sauce and mix well. Stir in coleslaw mix and green onion and mix gently. Place roast beef slices on work surface and divide coleslaw mixture among them. Roll up beef slices, enclosing filling. Serve immediately or cover and refrigerate up to 8 hours before serving.

Menu Suggestions
These spicy and crunchy rolls are delicious paired with Cold Pea Soup (page 245) and Pumpkin Bread (page 38) for lunch on the porch on a hot summer day. For dessert, serve Oatmeal Cookie Parfaits (page 274) topped with a dollop of nondairy frozen whipped topping.

½ cup tomato sauce
4 slices deli meatloaf
4 slices deli Cheddar cheese
8 slices deli pumpernickel
  bread
¼ cup butter, softened

Grilled Meatloaf Sandwiches

*These great sandwiches are also the perfect way to use up
leftover meatloaf. Serve with large dill pickles from the deli and some
deli coleslaw, along with root beer and ice cream for dessert.*

Preheat dual-contact indoor grill or large skillet over medium-high heat.
Spread tomato sauce onto meatloaf slices. Make sandwiches with coated
meatloaf, cheese, and pumpernickel bread. Spread outside of sandwiches
with softened butter and cook on grill or skillet, turning once, until bread is
hot and crisp and cheese begins to melt, about 4 to 6 minutes for dual contact grill, and 6 to 10 minutes for skillet. Serve immediately.

Dual-Contact Grills
*These grills are an easy way to grill just about any food. Just cut the cooking
time in half, because the food cooks on both sides at the same time. Be sure
to press the grill closed gently but firmly, to make good contact with the food.*

Chapter 30

Sandwiches and Pizza

4 pita breads, unsplit
4 slices Swiss cheese
1 avocado
1 6-ounce can tuna, drained
½ cup tartar sauce
¾ cup shredded Swiss cheese, divided
½ teaspoon dried dill weed

Tuna Melts

Tartar sauce is made of mayonnaise, pickles, and seasonings. It is delicious paired with mild canned tuna and Swiss cheese in these quick and easy sandwiches.

1. Preheat oven to 400°F. Toast pita breads in oven until crisp, about 5 minutes. Remove from oven and top each one with a slice of Swiss cheese.

2. Peel avocado and mash slightly, leaving some chunks. Spread this on top of the Swiss cheese. In small bowl, combine tuna and tartar sauce with ¼ cup shredded Swiss cheese. Spread on top of avocado.

3. Sprinkle sandwiches with remaining shredded Swiss cheese and the dill weed. Bake for 7 to 11 minutes, until cheese melts.

Sandwich Melts
Melts are open-faced sandwiches, or sandwiches without a "lid," that are usually grilled, baked, or broiled to heat the filling and melt the cheese. Serve them with a knife and fork, and with a simple fruit salad or green salad for a hearty, quick lunch or dinner.

Salmon Avocado Sandwiches

*Look for salmon packed in pouches in your supermarket.
The new varieties are boneless and skinless, eliminating the
step of discarding the bone and skins from canned salmon.*

Serves 4

1 7-ounce pouch pink salmon,
    drained
1 avocado, peeled and diced
½ cup mayonnaise
½ teaspoon dried basil leaves
½ cup chopped tomato
4 hamburger or hoagie buns,
    split, toasted if desired

In small bowl, combine all ingredients except hamburger or hoagie buns and mix gently but thoroughly. Divide mixture evenly between the hamburger or hoagie buns and serve.

Curried Chicken Sandwiches

*Keep this delicious sandwich spread in your refrigerator
and let hungry teenagers make their own sandwiches! You could
substitute pitted, halved cherries for the red grapes if you'd like.*

Serves 4–6

2 cups cubed, cooked chicken
½ cup plain yogurt
1/3 cup chutney
1 teaspoon curry powder
1 cup red grapes, cut in half
3 pita breads, cut in half

In medium bowl, combine all ingredients except pita breads and stir well to combine. Fill pita breads with chicken mixture and serve.

Cooking Chicken
To cook chicken breasts for use in any recipe, place boneless, skinless breasts in a pot and cover with half water and half canned chicken broth. Bring to a simmer, then reduce heat and poach chicken for 8 to 12 minutes, until chicken is thoroughly cooked. Let chicken cool in refrigerator, then chop. Reserve the broth for use in other recipes.

Serves 8

2 3-ounce packages cream
    cheese, softened
¼ cup sour cream
½ teaspoon dried dill weed
3 6-ounce cans small shrimp,
    drained
1½ cups chopped celery
    hearts
1 10-inch focaccia bread

Shrimp Sandwiches

*You can add some butter lettuce or watercress leaves to the
bottom half of the focaccia bread before adding the shrimp filling.
This is a good salad for a picnic because it's easy to carry.*

1. In medium bowl, beat cream cheese with sour cream and dill weed
   until smooth and fluffy. Stir in shrimp and chopped celery hearts.

2. Using serrated knife, cut focaccia bread in half horizontally. Spread bottom layer with cream cheese mixture and top with top layer. Cut into 8 wedges and serve.

Canned Seafood

Canned seafood can have a salty taste. You can rinse it before use, but be sure to drain it very well, and don't soak it. Canned salmon, crabmeat, and tuna, as well as surimi, or frozen faux crab, can all be substituted for canned shrimp in just about any recipe.

Stuffed Panini

You can stuff a hollowed-out loaf of bread with just about any combination of meats, cheeses, and salad dressings. Experiment, and have a taste-test party!

~

Serves 4

1 1-pound loaf round unsliced Italian bread
¼ cup creamy Italian salad dressing
¼ pound thinly sliced smoked turkey
¼ pound thinly sliced salami
½ pound sliced provolone cheese

1. Preheat oven to 400°F. Slice the top off the bread round and remove the center of the loaf, leaving a 1-inch border on the edges and the bottom. (Freeze the bread crumbs for another use or toast and use in Bread-Crumb Frittata, page 343.)

2. Spread half of the salad dressing in bottom and up sides of bread. Layer turkey, salami, and provolone cheese in the bread and drizzle with remaining salad dressing. Cover with top of bread round and place on baking sheet. Place an ovenproof skillet on top of sandwich to press it down as it bakes.

3. Bake sandwich for 15 to 20 minutes, until bread is toasted, filling is hot, and cheese is melted. Cut into wedges and serve.

Bacon Crisp Sandwiches

Serves 4

8 slices bacon

¾ cup grated Parmesan cheese, divided

½ teaspoon dried thyme leaves

¼ cup mayonnaise

4 hoagie buns, sliced

2 tomatoes, thickly sliced

This unusual way of cooking bacon makes these sandwiches simply superb. Be sure the tomatoes are ripe and juicy for best results. You could also add some fresh lettuce leaves or baby spinach.

1. Dip bacon slices in ½ cup Parmesan cheese and press to coat. Place 4 slices of the coated bacon on microwave-safe paper towels in a 12"×8" microwave-safe baking dish. Cover with another sheet of microwave-safe paper towels. Microwave on high for 3 to 4 minutes or until bacon is light golden brown. Repeat with remaining bacon slices.

2. Meanwhile, in small bowl, combine thyme, mayonnaise, and remaining ¼ cup Parmesan cheese and spread on cut sides of hoagie buns. Toast in toaster oven or under broiler until cheese mixture bubbles. Make sandwiches with the cooked bacon, tomatoes, and toasted buns and serve immediately.

Bacon Salmon Sandwich Spread

Yields 3 cups

8 slices bacon

1 8-ounce container cream cheese with herbs, softened

⅓ cup mayonnaise

1 7-ounce pouch pink salmon, drained

½ cup chopped green onions

This fabulous spread is perfect to keep in the fridge for lunch on the run. Have English muffins, pita breads, and whole wheat sandwich buns on hand and let your family make their own.

1. Cook bacon until crisp; drain on paper towels until cool enough to handle. Crumble bacon into small pieces.

2. In medium bowl, beat cream cheese until fluffy. Stir in mayonnaise and beat until smooth. Add reserved bacon, salmon, and green onions, and gently fold together. Cover and store in refrigerator up to 3 days. Make sandwiches using the spread.

Muffuletta

Muffuletta sandwiches are layered sandwiches that use olivada, or olive paste, as a spread between layers of meats and cheeses. Make them ahead of time and refrigerate until it's time to eat.

Serves 6

1 12-inch focaccia flatbread
⅓ cup bottled olivada, drained
½ pound thinly sliced Fontina cheese
¼ pound thinly sliced smoked turkey
¼ pound thinly sliced salami

1. Cut focaccia in half horizontally to make two thin round pieces. Spread cut side of both pieces with some of the olivada. Layer half of the Fontina cheese, a thin layer of olivada, smoked turkey, olivada, salami, olivada, and the rest of the Fontina cheese. Replace top of focaccia and press sandwich together gently.

2. Cut into wedges and serve immediately, or wrap whole sandwich in plastic wrap and chill for up to 8 hours.

Make Your Own Olivada
Combine 1 cup mixed olives (Kalamata, green, black, cracked) with ¼ cup olive oil, a few cloves of garlic, some thyme or marjoram, and a bit of pepper in a blender or food processor. Blend or process until olives are chopped. Store, covered, in the refrigerator and use it for sandwich spreads or as an appetizer dip.

Serves 4

½ cup bread crumbs
1 egg, beaten
½ teaspoon salt
¼ teaspoon cayenne pepper
¼ teaspoon cumin
1 teaspoon chili powder
1¼ pounds ground turkey
4 slices Pepper Jack cheese
4 whole wheat hamburger
    buns

Spicy Turkey Cheeseburgers

*Lots of spices make these burgers very flavorful. You could make a
Tex-Mex sandwich spread to put on the hamburger buns by combining
mayonnaise with some chopped chipotle peppers and adobo sauce.*

1. Prepare and preheat grill or broiler. In large bowl, combine bread
   crumbs, egg, salt, and seasonings and mix well. Add turkey and mix
   gently but thoroughly until combined. Form into 4 patties.

2. Cook patties, covered, 4 to 6 inches from medium heat for about 10
   minutes, turning once, until thoroughly cooked. Top each with a slice
   of cheese, cover grill, and cook for 1 minute longer, until cheese melts.
   Meanwhile, toast the cut sides of hamburger buns on the grill; make
   sandwiches with turkey patties and buns.

Make Recipes Your Own
*Once you get the hang of making a recipe quickly, think about varying
the ingredients to make it your own. For instance, Spicy Turkey
Cheeseburgers could be made with chutney, curry powder, and Havarti
or provolone cheese. Or make them Greek burgers with feta cheese,
chopped olives, and some dried oregano leaves.*

English Muffin Pizzas

These little pizzas can be topped with just about anything. Use cooked ground beef, drained chopped green chilies, and Pepper Jack cheese for Mexican pizzas; or chopped ham, drained pineapple tidbits, and Co-jack cheese for Hawaiian pizzas.

~

Preheat oven to broil. Place English muffin halves on baking sheet and top each one with pizza sauce. Layer mushrooms and pepperoni over pizza sauce. Sprinkle cheese over pizzas. Broil pizzas, 4 to 6 inches from heat source, for 2 to 4 minutes or until pizzas are hot and cheese is melted, bubbly, and beginning to brown. Serve immediately.

Serves 6–8

8 English muffins, split and toasted
1½ cups pizza sauce
1 6-ounce jar sliced mushrooms, drained
1 cup pepperoni, sliced
2 cups shredded mozzarella cheese

Mexican Chicken Pizzas

These individual pizzas are full of Tex-Mex flavor. Serve them with a simple fruit salad and an ice cream pie for dessert.

~

1. Preheat oven to 400°F. Place tortillas on two cookie sheets and bake for 5 to 8 minutes until tortillas are crisp, reversing the cookie sheets halfway through cooking time and turning tortillas over once.

2. In small bowl combine beans, taco sauce, oregano, and chili powder and mix well. Spread evenly over baked tortillas. Top with chicken strips and cheese. Bake for 12 to 18 minutes or until pizzas are hot and cheese is melted and beginning to brown, reversing cookie sheets halfway through cooking time. Cut into wedges and serve.

Serves 8

8 flour tortillas
1 16-ounce can refried beans
½ cup taco sauce
½ teaspoon dried oregano
1 tablespoon chili powder
2 9-ounce packages refrigerated grilled cooked chicken strips
2 cups shredded Pepper Jack cheese

1 16-ounce package frozen
   meatballs, thawed
1 15-ounce jar pasta sauce
1 cup frozen onion and
   pepper stir-fry combo,
   thawed and drained
4 hoagie rolls, sliced and
   toasted
1 6-ounce package sliced
   provolone cheese

Open-Faced Hoagies

*Thaw the meatballs by leaving the package in the refrigerator overnight,
or follow instructions on the package to thaw in the microwave.*

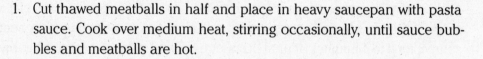

1. Cut thawed meatballs in half and place in heavy saucepan with pasta
   sauce. Cook over medium heat, stirring occasionally, until sauce bubbles and meatballs are hot.

2. Stir in onion and pepper stir-fry; cook and stir for 3 to 5 minutes, until
   vegetables are hot and tender. Preheat broiler.

3. Top each hoagie roll half with meatball mixture and place on broiler
   rack. Top each with a slice of cheese. Broil 6 inches from heat source for
   3 to 6 minutes, until cheese is melted and bubbly. Serve immediately.

Provolone Cheese
*Provolone cheese is a mild cheese with a slightly smoky taste that's
made from cow's milk. It is usually aged for a few months so the texture
is slightly firm. You can buy provolone aged for up to a year. This aged
cheese has a more intense flavor and firm texture, similar to Parmesan
cheese.*

Smashed Avocado Sandwiches

*Mashing avocados with salad dressing helps prevent
the avocados from turning brown. These rich sandwiches
must be made with juicy, ripe tomatoes and ripe avocados.*

Serves 4–6

3 avocados
⅓ cup creamy Italian salad
    dressing
4 hoagie buns, sliced and
    toasted
4 plum tomatoes, sliced
8 slices Muenster cheese

1. Preheat broiler. Peel and seed avocados; place in small bowl along with salad dressing. Mash, using a fork, until almost blended but there are still some pieces of avocado visible.

2. Place bottom halves of buns on broiler pan and spread with half of avocado mixture. Top with tomato slices and cover with cheese slices. Broil 6 inches from heat source for 2 to 5 minutes or until cheese is melted and begins to bubble. Spread top halves of buns with remaining avocado mixture and place on top of cheese. Serve immediately.

Tomatoes

Most tomatoes are full of seeds and liquid. This juiciness, desirable in salads, is less so in sandwiches and pizzas. Choose plum tomatoes for these recipes because there is more flesh and fewer seeds. Or you can seed tomatoes before use by cutting in half and gently squeezing them over the sink to remove seeds, jelly, and excess liquid.

4 pita pocket breads
3 tablespoons olive oil,
    divided
2 tablespoons mustard
6 ounces sliced cooked ham
6 ounces sliced Muenster
    cheese
½ cup sliced roasted red
    peppers, drained

Pita Paninis

*Roasted red peppers are sold in jars in the condiment aisle of the supermarket.
Drain them on paper towels before layering them in this sandwich.*

1. Heat dual-contact indoor grill. Using a sharp knife, split the pocket breads into 2 round pieces. In small bowl, combine 1 tablespoon olive oil and mustard and mix well. Spread this mixture on inside halves of the pita breads.

2. Layer ham, Muenster cheese, roasted red peppers, and more Muenster cheese on one side of each pita bread. Top with remaining pita bread sides. Spread outside of sandwiches with remaining 2 tablespoons olive oil.

3. Place each sandwich on dual-contact indoor grill and close the cover. Grill for 2 to 4 minutes, until cheese is melted and bread is golden brown and toasted. Cut sandwiches in half and serve.

Indoor Grills
If you like to make a lot of grilled sandwiches, buying a dual-contact indoor grill or panini grill is a good investment. They come in many different sizes, are nonstick for easy cleanup, and they heat up quickly. You can find some grills that are equipped with different surfaces to make patterns on the bread as it cooks.

Spinach Cheese Pizzas

Nutmeg really helps to bring out spinach's rich flavor. This may seem like a strange addition to pizza, but try it—you'll like it!

Serves 6–8

6 bagels, split and toasted
2 tablespoons olive oil
1 onion, chopped
1 8-ounce can pizza sauce
Pinch ground nutmeg
1 cup frozen chopped spinach, thawed
1½ cups shredded mozzarella cheese

1. Preheat broiler. Place bagels on a cookie sheet. In heavy saucepan, heat olive oil over medium heat and add onion; cook and stir for 4 to 6 minutes, until onion is tender. Add pizza sauce and nutmeg; bring to a simmer.

2. Meanwhile, drain the thawed spinach in a colander or strainer, then drain again by pressing between paper towels. Spread bagel halves with pizza sauce mixture and top evenly with the spinach. Sprinkle with cheese. Broil 6 inches from heat for 4 to 7 minutes, until cheese melts and sandwiches are hot.

Smoked Salmon Pizza

Cold-cured smoked salmon is a better choice than hot-cured for this recipe because the salmon is softer and sliced much thinner. Ask your grocer or butcher if you aren't sure about the salmon you buy.

Serves 4

1 10- or 12-inch Boboli pizza crust
1 8-ounce package garlic and herb soft cream cheese
½ pound thinly sliced smoked salmon
1 red or orange bell pepper, thinly sliced
1½ cups shredded provolone cheese

1. Heat oven to 400°F. Place pizza crust on cookie sheet. Spread with cream cheese and arrange smoked salmon and bell pepper slices on top. Sprinkle evenly with provolone cheese.

2. Bake for 18 to 22 minutes or until crust is hot and crisp and cheese is melted. Serve immediately.

1 10- or 12-inch Boboli pizza
crust
1 cup pizza sauce
½ teaspoon dried oregano
leaves
1 cup crumbled feta cheese
with garlic and herbs
½ cup sliced black olives
2 cups shredded mozzarella
cheese

Greek Pizza

Feta cheese, tomatoes, garlic, and olives give this pizza a Greek flair.
Serve it with a simple spinach salad and Grape and Melon Salad (page 200).

1. Preheat oven to 400°F. Place pizza crust on a cookie sheet and spread evenly with pizza sauce. Sprinkle with oregano. Arrange feta cheese and olives over sauce and top with mozzarella cheese.

2. Bake for 10 to 16 minutes or until crust is hot and crisp and cheese is melted and beginning to brown. Serve immediately.

Feta Cheese
Feta cheese usually comes cut into small blocks and packed in a brine solution. You can find several different varieties of flavored cheese, including garlic and herbs, sun-dried tomato, plain, peppercorn, basil and tomato, and low fat. Don't drain the brine before you use the cheese, because it helps preserve the cheese.

Meatball Pizza

This simple pizza can be made with cooked and drained ground beef or sausage instead of the meatballs. Serve with a green salad and carrot sticks.

———

Serves 4

1 14-inch prepared pizza crust
1½ cups pizza sauce
½ teaspoon dried oregano
    leaves
½ teaspoon dry mustard
½ 16-ounce bag frozen
    meatballs, thawed
1 cup frozen onion and bell
    pepper stir-fry combo
2 cups shredded pizza cheese

1. Preheat oven to 400°F. Place pizza crust on a cookie sheet. In small bowl, combine pizza sauce with oregano and dry mustard and mix well. Spread over pizza crust.

2. Cut meatballs in half, and arrange, cut-side down, on pizza sauce. Sprinkle with onion and bell pepper stir-fry combo, then with pizza cheese. Bake at 400°F for 18 to 23 minutes or until crust is golden brown and cheese has melted and begins to brown. Serve immediately.

Pizza Cheese
Pizza cheese is usually a blend of Cheddar, mozzarella, and provolone or Monterey Jack cheeses, and sometimes Parmesan or Romano. It's available preshredded in the dairy section of your supermarket. You can substitute Co-Jack cheese for the pizza cheese blend—it is a blend of Colby and Monterey Jack cheeses.

1 10-ounce container
    refrigerated pizza dough
2 tablespoons olive oil
½ teaspoon dried oregano
    leaves
2 cups cubed cooked Grilled
    Turkey Tenderloin (page
    112)
½ cup sour cream
2 tablespoons orange juice
1 green bell pepper, chopped
¼ teaspoon salt
⅛ teaspoon pepper

Orange Turkey Focaccia Sandwiches

*The combination of warm, freshly baked focaccia and
cold turkey filling is really wonderful. Serve with some
carrots sticks and potato chips for a great lunch.*

1. Preheat oven to 350°F. To make focaccia, unroll pizza dough and place
   on cookie sheet. Gently stretch to a 10" × 12" rectangle. Cut into eight
   5" × 3" rectangles and separate slightly. Press fingers into dough to
   dimple. In small bowl combine olive oil and oregano leaves and drizzle
   over dough. Bake for 14 to 18 minutes or until the focaccia pieces are
   light golden brown. Remove to wire racks.

2. Meanwhile, in medium bowl, combine turkey with remaining ingredients and blend well. Store in refrigerator while dough is baking, if necessary. When dough is baked, make sandwiches with the turkey filling
   and two rectangles of the baked focaccia. Serve immediately.

Focaccia Substitutions

*You can substitute any type of bread for the focaccia in this easy recipe.
Split croissants; toast split English muffins; use whole grain bread slices,
toasted or not; or try crusty French bread slices. The sandwiches made
with bread slices can be grilled on a dual-contact indoor grill until crisp
and brown.*

Seafood Pizza

You could add some vegetables like sliced mushrooms and chopped red or orange bell peppers to this elegant pizza.

Serves 4

1 14-inch prepared pizza crust
1 cup bottled four-cheese Alfredo sauce
½ teaspoon dried dill weed
1 cup cooked shrimp
1 cup lump crabmeat
1½ cups shredded mozzarella cheese

1. Preheat oven to 400°F. Place pizza crust on cookie sheet. Spread with Alfredo sauce and sprinkle with dill weed. Arrange shrimp and crabmeat on sauce, and sprinkle with mozzarella cheese.

2. Bake for 18 to 23 minutes or until crust is golden brown and cheese is melted and begins to brown. Serve immediately.

Open-Faced Chicken Sandwiches

These easy sandwiches can be made with any leftover meat: roast beef, ham, cooked turkey, or even shrimp.

Serves 4

4 whole wheat English muffins, split
2 cooked Mustard-Glazed Chicken Breasts (page 120)
¾ cup double Cheddar Alfredo sauce (from 10-ounce jar)
½ cup shredded carrots
¾ cup grated Parmesan cheese, divided

Preheat broiler. Toast English muffins under broiler and set on cookie sheet. Chop chicken breasts. In medium bowl, combine chicken with Alfredo sauce, shredded carrots, and ½ cup Parmesan cheese. Divide among English muffins and sprinkle with remaining ¼ cup Parmesan cheese. Broil 6 inches from heat source for 4 to 7 minutes, until sandwiches are hot and sauce is bubbling and begins to brown. Serve immediately.

Serves 4

1 cooked Herbed Steak
   (page 75)
1 cup jarred roasted red
   peppers, drained
8 slices French bread
2 cups shredded Muenster
   cheese
¼ cup butter

Grilled Steak Sandwiches

*Not only does this recipe stretch one steak to feed four people,
the combinations of flavors and textures are simply superb!*

Cut steak into ¼-inch-thick pieces against the grain. Slice the red peppers into strips. Place four bread slices on work surface and top each with ¼ cup cheese. Arrange one-fourth of the steak strips and red peppers on top of each. Top each with another ¼ cup cheese, then top with remaining bread slices. Spread butter on the outsides of the sandwiches. Grill on a dual-contact grill for 2 to 4 minutes, until sandwiches are hot and cheese is melted, or cook on a preheated griddle or skillet, turning once, about 5 to 6 minutes.

Slicing Bread for Sandwiches

When you're slicing French or Italian bread for sandwiches, be sure to cut the bread on the diagonal. That way there's more surface area and you get larger pieces to hold more filling ingredients. Use a serrated bread knife and grasp the bread firmly with your nondominant hand.

Chapter 31

Salads

Serves 6

2 tablespoons oil
1 10-ounce package frozen
    corn
1 green bell pepper, chopped
1 red bell pepper, chopped
2 tomatoes, chopped
¾ cup creamy garlic salad
    dressing
½ teaspoon dried Italian
    seasoning
½ teaspoon salt
⅛ teaspoon pepper

Roasted Corn Salad

Roasting corn helps concentrate the sweetness of this vegetable, and makes the kernels slightly chewy. It's delicious mixed with crisp peppers and ripe tomatoes.

1. Preheat oven to 400°F. Brush baking sheet with oil and set aside. Thaw corn under running water and drain well; dry with paper towels and spread onto prepared baking sheet. Roast at 400°F for 10 to 15 minutes, stirring once during cooking, until corn browns slightly around edges. Remove to serving bowl.

2. Add bell peppers and tomatoes and toss to mix. In small bowl, combine salad dressing, Italian seasoning, salt, and pepper and mix well. Drizzle over corn mixture and toss to coat. Serve immediately or cover and chill up to 8 hours.

Apple and Greens Salad

You can make the dressing ahead of time, but be sure to prepare the apples just before serving, or they will darken.

Serves 4

⅓ cup oil
3 tablespoons apple cider
    vinegar
¼ cup sugar
½ teaspoon celery seed
¼ teaspoon salt
⅛ teaspoon pepper
2 apples, cored and sliced
4 cups butter lettuce, torn
    into bite-sized pieces
1 cup curly endive

In small bowl, combine oil, vinegar, sugar, celery seed, salt, and pepper and mix well with wire whisk to blend. Place apples, lettuce, and endive in serving bowl and pour dressing over salad; toss gently to coat. Serve immediately.

Apple Varieties
Choose apple varieties according to whether you want a sweet or tart taste. Granny Smith apples are generally tart, while Golden Delicious and Red Delicious apples are sweeter. Gala apples have a sweet and honeylike taste, while Jonathans, McIntosh apples, and Cortlands are more tart.

1 pound fresh broccoli

1 cup sliced fresh mushrooms

3 strips bacon, cooked and crumbled

½ cup honey mustard salad dressing

½ cup cubed Swiss cheese

Broccoli Swiss Cheese Salad

This salad is similar to a popular deli salad; to make it identical, add some golden raisins.

1. Cut florets from broccoli, and cut stems into 2-inch pieces. Place in heavy saucepan, cover with water, and bring to a boil. Simmer for 6 to 8 minutes, until broccoli is crisp-tender. Drain well and place in serving bowl.

2. Add mushrooms and bacon; toss gently. Drizzle with salad dressing and toss again. Sprinkle with cheese and serve.

Salad Substitutions

Salad recipes are made for substituting! Just about any vegetable can be substituted for another. Crumble cauliflower florets into a salad in place of mushrooms, slice crisp jicama as a substitute for bell peppers, and use blanched asparagus in place of green or wax beans (and vice versa!).

Greek Lentil Salad

This salad is a great choice for a light lunch or brunch. It's a vegetarian salad that offers complete protein with the combination of cracked wheat and lentils. Top it with some crumbled feta cheese for even more flavor.

~

1. Place cracked wheat in medium bowl and cover with boiling water. Set aside. In heavy skillet, combine lentils and 2 cups water and bring to a boil. Cover and simmer for 20 minutes, until tender; drain if necessary. Drain cracked wheat, if necessary. In small bowl, combine salad dressing and oregano.

2. Meanwhile, cut tomatoes in half, gently squeeze out the seeds, and chop. Peel cucumber, cut in half, remove seeds, and slice.

3. In serving bowl, combine cracked wheat, lentils, vegetables, and salad dressing; toss gently to coat and serve immediately.

Serves 6

¾ cup cracked wheat
1½ cups boiling water
¾ cup lentils
2 cups water
½ cup red wine vinaigrette
    salad dressing
¼ teaspoon dried oregano
    leaves
2 tomatoes
1 cucumber

Bacon and Spinach Salad

Baby spinach is wonderfully tender, with a rich and mild taste. It's perfect in this salad, accented with crisp bacon and creamy Havarti cheese.

~

1. In medium saucepan, cook bacon until crisp. Drain on paper towels until cool enough to handle, then crumble. Combine cooked bacon, spinach, and cheese in serving bowl.

2. In small bowl, combine mayonnaise, buttermilk, salt, and pepper and mix well with wire whisk to blend. Drizzle half of dressing over spinach mixture and toss to coat. Serve with remaining dressing.

Serves 6–8

4 strips bacon
1 pound baby spinach leaves
1 cup cubed Havarti cheese
½ cup mayonnaise
½ cup buttermilk
½ teaspoon seasoned salt
⅛ teaspoon white pepper

Serves 8
_____

1 cantaloupe
2 cups green grapes
¼ cup honey
2 tablespoons lime juice
¼ teaspoon salt

Grape and Melon Salad

*This simple salad is the perfect accompaniment to a grilled steak,
or serve it for breakfast along with frozen waffles and maple syrup.*

1. Cut cantaloupe in half and scoop out seeds. Using a melon baller, remove the flesh from the rind. Place cantaloupe balls in a serving dish along with the grapes.

2. In small bowl, combine honey, lime juice, and salt and stir well with a wire whisk until combined. Drizzle over fruit mixture and serve.

About Cantaloupe
Cantaloupe flesh does not turn brown when exposed to air, so you can make this salad ahead of time. Ripe cantaloupes smell ripe, and they give slightly when pressed with the fingers. They should be firm and heavy for their size, with an even webbing over a greenish-gold skin.

Paella Rice Salad

Paella is a Spanish dish that combines rice with shrimp, sausages, chicken, peas, and saffron. This salad is a simplified version of the classic recipe.

———

Serves 4

1 cup uncooked long-grain rice

2 cups water

¼ teaspoon saffron threads (or ½ teaspoon turmeric)

1 cup frozen baby peas

1 cup sliced celery

½ pound cooked, shelled shrimp

⅔ cup creamy Italian salad dressing

1. In medium saucepan over high heat, combine rice, water, and saffron. Cover and bring to a boil; lower heat and cook for 15 to 20 minutes, until rice is tender. Stir in baby peas during final 3 minutes of cooking time. Remove from heat and let stand for 5 minutes, then fluff rice mixture with fork.

2. Place rice mixture in serving bowl and add celery and shrimp; toss gently. Drizzle with salad dressing and toss again, then serve, or cover and refrigerate up to 8 hours.

Refrigerated Salad Dressings
Browse through your grocery store's produce aisle and you'll find many flavors of refrigerated salad dressings. These dressings are usually richer than shelf-stable bottled dressings, and are made with fresh ingredients. They must be stored in the refrigerator; keep a supply of your favorites on hand.

Serves 4–6

2 cups cubed cooked chicken
    breast
1½ cups blueberries
3 nectarines, sliced
¾ cup mayonnaise
¼ cup mango chutney
½ teaspoon curry powder

Chicken Salad with Nectarines

*Use any combination of fresh fruit in this simple and elegant salad.
You can also try different flavors of chutney to vary the taste.*

In serving bowl, combine chicken, blueberries, and nectarines and toss gently. In small bowl, combine mayonnaise, chutney, and curry powder and mix well. Spoon over chicken mixture and toss gently to coat. Serve immediately.

Chutney
Chutney is a cooked sauce made of fruit juices, dried fruits, and spices. You can usually find pineapple chutney, mango chutney, or cranberry chutney in the condiment aisle of your grocery store. There are also many recipes for making your own chutney; blueberry is a homemade favorite.

Serves 6

2 nectarines
2 cups sliced strawberries
2 cups blueberries
1 cup cubed Havarti cheese
½ cup poppy seed salad
    dressing

Fruit and Cheese Salad

The fruits of summer—strawberries, raspberries, melons, peaches, and blackberries—can all be used in this refreshing and beautiful salad.

Slice nectarines and discard pits. Combine with remaining ingredients in a serving bowl and toss gently to coat. Serve immediately or cover and refrigerate up to 2 hours before serving.

Wilted Lettuce Salad

This warm salad can be a meal in itself. Serve it with some Melty Cheese Bread (page 54) and fresh fruit for a light lunch or late-night supper.

Serve it with some Melty Cheese Bread (page 54)

∼

Serves 4–6

1 head romaine lettuce
1 head butter lettuce
1 cup sliced cremini
   mushrooms
5 slices bacon
3 tablespoons apple cider
   vinegar
1 teaspoon sugar
½ teaspoon dry mustard
¼ teaspoon salt
⅛ teaspoon pepper

1. Wash lettuces, dry, and tear into bite-size pieces; place in serving bowl along with mushrooms. Cook bacon in heavy skillet over medium heat, turning frequently, until crisp. Remove bacon to paper towels to drain; crumble when cool enough to handle.

2. Remove pan from heat; drain all but ¼ cup bacon drippings from pan. Carefully add remaining ingredients and stir with wire whisk; return to medium heat and bring to a boil. Immediately pour over lettuces and mushrooms in salad bowl; toss to wilt lettuce. Sprinkle with bacon and serve immediately.

Cremini Mushrooms
Cremini mushrooms can be found in most supermarkets in the produce section. They are actually small portobello mushrooms, those large, dark mushrooms that are so perfect for grilling or stuffing. Creminis have more flavor than button mushrooms do; wipe them with damp paper towels, cut off the stem, and slice.

Serves 6

3 cucumbers
1 teaspoon salt
2 tablespoons sugar
1 6-ounce container lemon-
    flavored yogurt
⅓ cup sour cream
2 tablespoons lemon juice
1 teaspoon sugar
½ teaspoon dried thyme
    leaves
⅛ teaspoon white pepper

Lemon Cucumber Salad

The cucumbers are sprinkled with salt and sugar before dressing to draw out any sour taste and to reduce their high water content, so the salad dressing isn't diluted.

1. Peel cucumbers and slice thinly. Place in colander and sprinkle with salt and 2 tablespoons sugar. Let stand for 15 minutes, then toss cucumbers and press to drain out excess liquid. Rinse cucumbers, drain again, and press between paper towels to dry.

2. Meanwhile, in large bowl, combine yogurt, sour cream, lemon juice, 1 teaspoon sugar, thyme, and pepper and mix well to blend. Gently stir in drained cucumbers, then serve.

Summer Squashes
Summer squashes, like zucchini and yellow squash, are thin skinned and excellent eaten raw. They can be substituted for cucumbers or mushrooms in most salads. Unless the skins are waxed, they don't need to be peeled, just cut into sticks, julienne, cubes, or slices.

Turkey Waldorf Salad

Waldorf Salad is traditionally made of chopped apples and walnuts in a creamy dressing. Adding turkey to this salad elevates it to a main dish delight.

Serves 6

3 Granny Smith apples
1 cup golden raisins
1 cup coarsely chopped
   toasted walnuts
2 cups chopped cooked
   turkey breast
1½ cups mayonnaise
⅛ teaspoon allspice
⅛ teaspoon white pepper

Core apples and coarsely chop. Combine in medium bowl with raisins, walnuts, and turkey. In small bowl, combine mayonnaise, allspice, and pepper and blend well. Spoon over turkey mixture and toss to coat. Cover and refrigerate for 10 to 15 minutes to blend flavors. Store leftovers in refrigerator.

Toasting Walnuts

Toasting walnuts concentrates and brings out the flavor. To toast them, spread on a shallow baking sheet and bake in a 350°F oven for 10 to 15 minutes, stirring twice during baking time. Or microwave the nuts: place in a single layer on microwave-safe plate and heat at 100 percent power for 2 to 4 minutes, until fragrant.

8 cups salad greens
½ cup yogurt
½ cup mayonnaise
¼ cup buttermilk
⅓ cup chopped fresh basil
   leaves
½ teaspoon dried basil leaves
½ teaspoon salt
⅛ teaspoon white pepper

Greens with Basil Dressing

The dressing can be served with any green or vegetable salad. It will keep, well covered, in the refrigerator for about 3 to 4 days.

Place salad greens in a serving bowl. In a food processor or blender container, combine remaining ingredients. Process or blend until the basil leaves are very finely chopped. Drizzle dressing over the salad, toss, and serve.

Fresh and Dried Herbs

Using fresh and dried herbs in the same recipe is an easy way to increase the depth of flavor. Many dried herbs taste different than their fresh counterparts. Dried basil, for instance, has a smokier flavor than fresh. And dried thyme has a more intense mint flavor, while the fresh tends to be more lemony.

Simple Spinach Salad

This beautiful salad can be served with some Corn Bread (page 39) or hot biscuits for a simple lunch, or as a side dish for a casserole, soup, or stew.

Serves 4

4 cups baby spinach leaves
½ cup toasted pine nuts
1 cup frozen baby peas
1 cup grape tomatoes
½ cup basil vinaigrette salad
    dressing

Toss together spinach and pine nuts in serving bowl. Place peas in a colander and run hot water over them for 1 to 2 minutes to thaw. Drain well and add to spinach mixture along with grape tomatoes. Drizzle with half of the salad dressing and toss gently. Serve immediately with remaining dressing on the side.

Tiny Tomatoes

There are some new small tomatoes on the market. Grape tomatoes are about the size of grapes; they are sweet, tender, and juicy. Cherry tomatoes are less popular since grape tomatoes burst onto the scene, but they are still available; they come in red and yellow varieties. And sweet currant tomatoes are about half the size of cherry tomatoes.

Yields 6 cups

2 cups frozen soybeans
1 15-ounce can green beans,
  drained
1 15-ounce can wax beans,
  drained
¾ cup red wine vinaigrette
  salad dressing
2 tablespoons red wine
  vinegar
⅓ cup sugar
¼ teaspoon dried tarragon
  leaves
Dash black pepper

Three-Bean Salad

Three-Bean Salad is typically marinated in a sweet and sour salad dressing. You can use any combination of beans you'd like, selecting from green beans, wax beans, kidney beans, chick peas, black beans, red beans, and soybeans.

1. Bring large pot of water to a boil and cook frozen soybeans for 2 to 3 minutes, until tender. Drain and rinse with cold water. Combine in serving bowl with green beans and wax beans.

2. In small saucepan combine salad dressing, vinegar, sugar, tarragon, and pepper; whisk over low heat until sugar is dissolved. Pour over bean mixture and stir gently. Let stand for 10 minutes, then serve. Store leftovers in refrigerator.

Serves 6

1 10-ounce container basil
  pesto
½ cup mayonnaise
1 cup cubed smoked Gouda
  cheese
2 red bell peppers, chopped
1 18-ounce package frozen
  cheese tortellini

Pasta and Cheese Salad

Of course, you can add any number of fresh vegetables to this simple salad. Sliced mushrooms, yellow summer squash, cucumbers, and spring onions would all be nice additions.

Bring large pot of salted water to a boil. Meanwhile, in large bowl, combine pesto and mayonnaise and blend well. Stir in cheese and chopped peppers. Add tortellini to pot of water and cook according to package directions until done. Drain well and stir into cheese mixture. Serve immediately or cover and chill for 2 to 3 hours.

Smoked Turkey Fruit Salad

This delicious dressing, made by puréeing ripe strawberries with yogurt and minty thyme leaves, makes this salad simply spectacular.

Serves 6–8

1 quart strawberries
½ cup vanilla yogurt
¼ teaspoon salt
¼ teaspoon dried thyme
　leaves
1 ripe cantaloupe
2 cups chopped smoked
　turkey
1 pint raspberries

1. Wash and hull the strawberries and cut in half. In food processor or blender, combine yogurt, salt, thyme, and ½ cup of the sliced strawberries. Process or blend until smooth.

2. Cut cantaloupe in half and remove seeds. Cut flesh into chunks.

3. In serving bowl, combine remaining strawberries, cantaloupe, and turkey. Drizzle dressing over and toss gently to coat. Top with raspberries and serve.

Raspberries

Raspberries are a very delicate fruit. They must be used within a day or two of purchase. Do not rinse raspberries before you are ready to use them because they develop mold very easily. Never toss them with a salad; use them as a garnish on top.

2 tablespoons olive oil
2 cups chopped ham, divided
2 cups frozen bell pepper and
    onion stir-fry combo
1 head romaine lettuce
1 cup mayonnaise
1 tablespoon brown sugar
2 tablespoons grated
    Parmesan cheese

Layered Ham Salad

*Layered salads were big in the 1970s and 1980s.
They are a great choice for a buffet. Be sure to use a clear
glass serving dish so all the beautiful layers are visible.*

1. In heavy skillet, heat olive oil over medium heat. Add ¼ cup of the chopped ham; cook and stir until ham pieces are crisp around the edges. Remove ham to paper towel to drain. Add bell pepper and onion combo; cook and stir for 3 to 5 minutes, until vegetables are hot and tender.

2. Clean and chop romaine lettuce. In large bowl, layer half of the lettuce followed by half the bell pepper mixture and half the remaining 1¾ cups ham. Repeat layers.

3. In small bowl combine mayonnaise with sugar and cheese. Spread over top of salad and sprinkle with the fried ham bits. Serve immediately or cover and refrigerate for 2 to 3 hours before serving.

Sugared Almond Green Salad

Sugared almonds add wonderful crunch and flavor to this simple salad made with tender salad greens and sweet mandarin oranges.

1. In small heavy saucepan, melt butter over medium heat until foaming. Stir in almonds; cook and stir for 2 to 4 minutes, until almonds begin to show color. Sprinkle sugar over almonds; cook and stir for another minute. Remove to paper towel to drain and cool.

2. In serving bowl, combine salad greens and drained oranges and toss gently. In small bowl, combine 2 tablespoons reserved orange juice and the salad dressing and whisk to blend. Drizzle over salad and top with sugared almonds.

Sugared Almonds
Sugared almonds are easy to make, but you must make sure to watch them carefully as they cook, and never leave the stove. They burn easily! Make a large batch and store them in an airtight container in a cool place. You can sprinkle them over many salads; try them on Ambrosia (page 212). They'll keep up to 3 weeks.

Serves 4–6

2 tablespoons butter
½ cup sliced almonds
3 tablespoons sugar
6 cups mixed salad greens
1 15-ounce can mandarin oranges, drained, juice reserved
2 tablespoons reserved juice from oranges
½ cup honey mustard salad dressing

Serves 6

1 8-ounce container frozen
whipped topping,
thawed

⅓ cup reserved pineapple
juice

1 cup cottage cheese

2 14-ounce cans mandarin
oranges, drained

1 15-ounce can crushed
pineapple, drained,
reserving juice

1 cup shredded coconut

Ambrosia

*Ambrosia is an old-fashioned salad that is sweet and
delicious. It always includes oranges and coconut along
with a sweet whipped dressing; the rest is up to you!*

In serving bowl, combine whipped topping, reserved pineapple juice, and cottage cheese; stir with wire whisk until blended. Fold in remaining ingredients. Cover and chill for 15 minutes before serving. Store leftovers in refrigerator.

Whipped Cream or Frozen Topping?

You can use heavy cream, whipped until stiff with a few spoonfuls of powdered sugar, for the frozen whipped topping in this simple salad. If you are watching fat and calories, look for low-fat nondairy frozen whipped toppings in your grocery store's frozen-food aisle. Any frozen topping must thaw in the refrigerator for 6 to 8 hours.

Chapter 32

Side Dishes

Serves 8

1 12-ounce package
   refrigerated mashed
   potatoes
1 egg, beaten
¼ cup grated Parmesan
   cheese
2 tablespoons sour cream
½ teaspoon dried basil leaves
2 tablespoons milk
2 tablespoons grated
   Parmesan cheese

Duchess Potatoes

This recipe is a great way to use up leftover mashed or riced potatoes. You may need to add some more milk if you use leftover homemade potatoes, since they can dry out when refrigerated.

1. Preheat oven to 375°F. In large bowl, combine all ingredients except milk and 2 tablespoons Parmesan cheese and beat well until combined. Spoon or pipe mixture into 16 mounds onto parchment paper–lined cookie sheets. Brush with milk and sprinkle with 2 tablespoons Parmesan cheese.

2. Bake potatoes for 15 to 20 minutes or until tops are beginning to brown and potatoes are hot. Serve immediately.

Prepared Potatoes
You can find prepared refrigerated mashed potatoes in your supermarket's dairy aisle, or perhaps in one of the refrigerated endcaps at the end of the aisles. There are many different types of refrigerated prepared potatoes; look for hash brown potatoes and scalloped potatoes, too.

Risi Bisi

*This Italian version of rice with peas is simple and
delicious, the perfect side dish for a grilled steak.*

Serves 6

2 tablespoons olive oil
1 onion, finely chopped
1½ cups long-grain rice
2 10-ounce cans chicken
    broth
½ cup water
1 cup frozen baby green peas
½ cup grated Parmesan
    cheese

1. In heavy saucepan, heat olive oil over medium heat. Add onion; cook
    and stir until onion is translucent. Add rice; cook and stir for 2 minutes.
    Add chicken broth and water and bring to a boil. Cover pan, reduce
    heat, and simmer mixture for 15 to 20 minutes, until rice is almost
    tender.

2. Add peas, cover, and cook over medium-low heat until peas are hot
    and rice is tender, 3 to 5 minutes. Stir in cheese and serve.

Lemon Pesto Pilaf

*This simple pilaf has so much flavor and the most beautiful color.
You can find prepared pesto in the refrigerated section
of your supermarket, near the cheeses and eggs.*

Serves 4–6

1 tablespoon butter
1 cup long-grain white rice
2 cups chicken or vegetable
    broth, heated
2 tablespoons lemon juice
½ teaspoon lemon zest
¼ cup prepared pesto

In heavy saucepan, melt butter over medium heat. Add rice; cook and stir for
3 to 4 minutes, until rice is opaque. Add broth, stir well, cover, bring to a boil,
reduce heat to low, and simmer for about 15 to 20 minutes, until rice is tender.
Stir in lemon juice, zest, and pesto; remove from heat and cover; and let stand
for 3 to 4 minutes. Fluff rice with fork and serve.

Lemon Zest
*Lemon zest is the outer skin of the lemon; use just the yellow part, because
the white pith can be bitter. Lemon zesters and microplane graters are the best
tools to use since they only remove the yellow part of the skin.*

Serves 6

2 tablespoons olive oil
1 onion, finely chopped
3 cups frozen green beans
1 red bell pepper, cut into
   strips
1 tablespoon lemon juice
½ teaspoon salt
½ teaspoon dried thyme
   leaves

Green Beans with Red Peppers

*You can buy frozen julienned green beans or frozen cut green beans.
For this recipe, frozen cut green beans work best. The color combination
of the deep green beans and the bright red pepper is very festive.*

1. In heavy saucepan, heat olive oil over medium heat. Add onion; cook until onion is tender, stirring frequently.

2. Meanwhile, prepare green beans as directed on package and drain well. Add red bell pepper to saucepan with onions; cook and stir for 2 to 4 minutes, until tender. Add beans, lemon juice, salt, and thyme leaves; stir gently and cook until hot, about 2 to 3 minutes longer. Serve immediately.

How to Julienne Bell Peppers

To julienne bell peppers, hold them upright on a cutting board. Cut off the four sides of the pepper from the stem and core. Remove any extra seeds or ribs. Place each piece skin-side down on the cutting board and cut the peppers into thin strips. Discard stem and core.

Honey-Orange Carrots

*These sweet-and-tart little carrots are perfect for a dinner party.
You can easily double or triple the recipe for a larger crowd.*

Serves 4–6

1 16-ounce package baby
    carrots
2 cups water
2 tablespoons orange juice
    concentrate
2 tablespoons honey
2 tablespoons butter
¼ teaspoon dried thyme
    leaves

1. Rinse carrots and place in medium saucepan with water. Bring to a boil over high heat, then lower heat to medium and simmer carrots for 5 to 8 minutes, until just tender.

2. Drain carrots and return to pan. Stir in orange juice concentrate, honey, and butter; cook and stir over medium heat until sauce thickens and coats carrots, 2 to 4 minutes. Add thyme leaves and simmer for a minute, then serve.

Baby Carrots

Baby carrots are actually large carrots that have been carefully trimmed and shaped. They are sweeter than the carrots you remember from your childhood because they are a different variety that is bred to grow faster, longer, and with a higher sugar content.

2 16-ounce cans sweet
   potatoes in syrup
½ cup brown sugar, divided
½ cup butter, divided
¼ cup reserved sweet potato
   liquid
½ cup chopped cashews
3 tablespoons flour
⅛ teaspoon nutmeg

Praline Sweet Potatoes

This recipe is excellent for an easy side dish for Thanksgiving. Since it takes only about 20 minutes to make, you can prepare it just before serving.

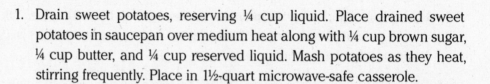

1. Drain sweet potatoes, reserving ¼ cup liquid. Place drained sweet potatoes in saucepan over medium heat along with ¼ cup brown sugar, ¼ cup butter, and ¼ cup reserved liquid. Mash potatoes as they heat, stirring frequently. Place in 1½-quart microwave-safe casserole.

2. In small bowl, combine cashews, remaining ¼ cup brown sugar, flour, and nutmeg and mix well. Melt remaining ¼ cup butter and add to cashew mixture; mix until crumbly and set aside.

3. Microwave potatoes on high power for 2 minutes, then stir well. Sprinkle with cashew mixture and microwave on high 5 to 7 minutes longer or until potatoes are hot.

Sweet Potatoes

Sweet potatoes are usually canned in a sweet syrup, but some are canned in plain water; be sure to read the labels carefully. Sweet potatoes, whether canned or fresh, are a wonderful source of vitamins A and C; in fact, one serving can provide more than 400 percent of the recommended daily allowance of vitamin A.

Glazed Squash

Acorn squash are green globes with scalloped sides. This dish is an excellent accompaniment to Cuban Pork Chops (page 124).

Serves 4

1 acorn squash
2 tablespoons water
2 tablespoons butter
2 tablespoons brown sugar
1 tablespoon honey
½ teaspoon dried tarragon
    leaves
½ teaspoon salt
⅛ teaspoon white pepper

1. Cut squash in half lengthwise and remove seeds and fibers from center. Place the squash halves cut side down on work surface and cut crosswise into 1-inch pieces. Place, skin-side down, in a microwave-safe 12" × 8" baking dish; sprinkle with 2 tablespoons water.

2. Cover with microwave-safe plastic wrap, vent one corner, and microwave on high power for 12 to 15 minutes, until flesh is almost tender when tested with fork. Uncover, drain if necessary, and let stand while assembling sauce.

3. In small microwave-safe bowl, combine remaining ingredients and microwave on high power for 2 minutes, then stir until sauce is smooth. Pour sauce over squash and microwave, uncovered, on high power for 3 to 4 minutes, until squash is tender, spooning sauce over squash twice during cooking time.

Winter Squash
Winter squash are hard-sided squashes that require cooking before they are edible. Acorn, butternut, delicata, buttercup, and pumpkin will all work in this easy microwave recipe. Any winter squash variety stores very well and will last up to 3 months if kept in a cool, dry place.

¼ cup olive oil

½ red onion, chopped

½ head red cabbage, chopped

2 tablespoons balsamic vinegar

½ teaspoon salt

⅛ teaspoon white pepper

2 Granny Smith apples, cored and sliced

Cabbage and Apples

This dish is a perfect accompaniment to roasted pork loin or smoked pork chops for a wonderful fall dinner.

In heavy skillet, heat olive oil over medium heat. Add onion; cook and stir for 5 minutes, until crisp-tender. Add cabbage and vinegar; stir well. Cover and cook over medium heat for 7 to 10 minutes, until cabbage is tender, stirring once during cooking time. Sprinkle with salt and pepper and add apples. Cover and cook for 3 to 4 minutes longer, until apples are hot and crisp tender. Serve immediately.

Preparing Cabbage

To prepare cabbage, remove some of the tough or blemished outer leaves. Using a large knife, cut cabbage in half through the center. Cut out the core on both halves. Turn cabbage cut-side down and cut lengthwise. Cut crosswise, and cabbage will fall into bite-size pieces.

Smashed Potatoes

When you cube potatoes they will cook in much less time.
This side dish is perfect to serve with a classic meatloaf.

⁓

Serves 6–8

6 russet potatoes
¼ cup butter
4 cloves garlic, minced
⅓ cup whole milk
½ teaspoon salt
1 tablespoon chopped fresh
basil leaves

1. Peel potatoes and cut into 1-inch cubes; as you work, place the potatoes in a large saucepan filled with cold water. When all the potatoes are prepared, bring to a boil over high heat. Cover pan, lower heat, and simmer potatoes for 15 to 20 minutes, until potatoes are tender when pierced with fork.

2. Meanwhile, combine butter and garlic in small saucepan and cook over medium heat, stirring frequently, until garlic is fragrant and tender, about 2 minutes. Remove from heat. In another small saucepan, combine milk, salt, and basil and heat until steam forms.

3. When potatoes are tender, drain thoroughly, then return potatoes to hot pan and shake for 1 minute over medium heat. Add butter mixture and mash with a potato masher. Then add milk mixture and stir gently. Serve immediately.

The Fluffiest Mashed Potatoes

Adding butter to the potatoes before adding liquid helps ensure that the potatoes will be fluffy. The fat in the butter helps coat the starch granules in the potatoes so they don't absorb too much liquid and become sticky or gluey. Use this rule every time you make mashed or smashed potatoes for best results.

Serves 8

2 16-ounce packages frozen
    broccoli and cauliflower
    combo
1 16-ounce jar four-cheese
    Alfredo sauce
1 cup shredded Cheddar
    cheese
1½ cups soft bread crumbs
¼ cup butter, melted

Crispy Broccoli Casserole

This casserole is so good even your kids will like it!
Any vegetable is improved by being smothered in cheese
sauce and topped with crisp buttered bread crumbs.

Thaw vegetables according to package directions and drain thoroughly.
Place in 13" × 9" glass baking dish. Top with the Alfredo sauce and sprinkle
with the cheese. In medium bowl, combine bread crumbs and butter and
toss to mix. Sprinkle over cheese. Bake casserole at 375°F for 20 to 23 minutes, until the sauce is bubbling, vegetables are hot, and bread crumbs
begin to brown. Serve immediately.

Serves 6

2 tablespoons olive oil
1 onion, finely chopped
2 cups chicken or vegetable
    broth
½ teaspoon dried oregano
    leaves
½ teaspoon dried marjoram
    leaves
1 cup couscous

Herbed Couscous

Couscous actually isn't a grain; it is ground semolina pasta
that is usually precooked, so all you have to do is combine it
with boiling liquid and let stand until the liquid is absorbed.

In heavy skillet, heat olive oil over medium heat. Add onion; cook and stir
until tender, about 5 minutes. Add chicken broth and herbs and bring to
a rolling boil. Stir in couscous, then cover pan and remove from heat. Let
stand for 5 to 10 minutes, or according to package directions, until liquid is
absorbed. Fluff couscous mixture with fork and serve.

Grilled Asparagus

Grilling makes asparagus smoky and crisp tender. The combination of butter and olive oil adds extra richness.

Serves 6

*1 pound asparagus
2 tablespoons butter
1 tablespoon garlic-flavored olive oil
1 teaspoon seasoned salt
⅛ teaspoon pepper*

⌐⌐⌐

1. Hold asparagus spears between your hands and bend until they snap; discard the tough ends.

2. Prepare and preheat grill. In small saucepan, melt butter with oil, salt, and pepper. Brush asparagus with this mixture, then place on grill 6 inches from medium coals. Cover and grill asparagus, brushing frequently with butter mixture, for 5 to 9 minutes, until tender. Serve immediately.

Flavored Olive Oils

You can find flavored olive oils at gourmet and specialty shops, and in the regular supermarket. Garlic oil, lemon oil, and herb oils are a great way to add complex flavor with just one ingredient. Please do not make your own flavored oils; the risk of food poisoning is just too great because of the oil's anaerobic (oxygen-free) environment.

Serves 8

1 8-ounce package orzo
pasta
2 tablespoons butter
1 onion, finely chopped
3 cloves garlic, minced
½ teaspoon dried thyme
leaves
½ teaspoon salt
Dash pepper
½ cup grated Parmesan
cheese

Pasta Pilaf

*Orzo, or rosamarina pasta, is shaped like grains of rice. This recipe
is an excellent choice for people who have trouble cooking rice.*

1. Bring large pot of water to a boil and cook pasta according to package
   directions.

2. Meanwhile, melt butter in heavy saucepan and cook onion and garlic
   over medium heat for 4 to 5 minutes, until tender. Add thyme, salt, and
   pepper; cover; and remove from heat.

3. Drain the pasta thoroughly and add to onion mixture. Cook and stir
   over medium heat for 2 to 3 minutes, until hot and blended. Stir in Parmesan cheese and serve.

Orange Cauliflower

Tender cooked cauliflower florets are accented with orange juice that has been reduced to a syrupy sauce and flavored with marjoram. This is a great side dish to serve with roast chicken.

~

Serves 6

4 cups water
1 16-ounce package prepared
    cauliflower florets
2 tablespoons olive oil
1 onion, finely chopped
2 cloves garlic, minced
½ cup orange juice
½ teaspoon dried marjoram
    leaves
½ teaspoon salt
⅛ teaspoon white pepper

1. In large saucepan, place water and cauliflower florets. Bring to a boil over high heat, then cover, reduce heat to medium, and simmer for 6 to 7 minutes, until cauliflower is almost tender.

2. Meanwhile, in heavy skillet, heat olive oil over medium heat. Add onion and garlic and cook until tender. Add orange juice and seasonings and bring to a boil. Boil for a few minutes until slightly thickened.

3. When cauliflower is almost tender, drain well and add to orange juice mixture. Simmer for 2 to 4 minutes, spooning sauce over cauliflower, until sauce thickens and cauliflower is tender. Serve immediately.

About Cauliflower

Cauliflower is a cruciferous vegetable, related to broccoli. It is white because it grows wrapped in leaves that shield it from sunlight. The tender florets are creamy and mild when cooked, and crisp and tart when eaten raw. Look for cauliflower that is a creamy white color, with no discolored spots. It will keep in the refrigerator for 4 to 6 days.

Serves 6

1 pound green beans
4 cups water
1 tablespoon olive oil
1 tablespoon butter
6 cloves garlic, peeled and
    chopped
1 shallot, peeled and chopped
½ teaspoon salt

Garlicky Green Beans

You can add more garlic to this simple and flavorful side dish if you'd like. Just be sure to stir constantly while the garlic and shallots are browning so they don't burn.

1. Trim the ends off the green beans and cut each bean in half crosswise. Place in heavy saucepan and cover with water. Bring to a boil over high heat, then lower heat to medium and simmer for 5 to 8 minutes, until beans are crisp-tender.

2. Meanwhile, combine olive oil and butter in heavy saucepan and add garlic and shallot. Cook and stir over medium heat until the garlic is fragrant and turns light brown around the edges.

3. Drain beans and add to garlic mixture in pan along with salt. Cook and stir over medium heat for 2 to 3 minutes, until beans are coated. Serve immediately.

Types of Garlic
There are several forms of garlic that you can buy. Garlic powder is powdered dried garlic; ⅛ teaspoon is equal to one clove. Garlic salt is garlic powder combined with salt; ¼ teaspoon is equal to one clove. And garlic paste in a tube is puréed, concentrated garlic. One teaspoon is equal to one clove of garlic.

Roasted Sugar Snap Peas

You can sometimes find stringless sugar snap peas in the market. If you can't, to remove the string, cut off the very end of the pea, pull the string off and discard.

～

Serves 6

3 cups sugar snap peas
2 tablespoons olive oil
½ teaspoon dried marjoram
   leaves
½ teaspoon garlic salt
⅛ teaspoon pepper

1. Preheat oven to 425°F. Remove strings from sugar snap peas, if desired. Place on baking sheet and sprinkle with remaining ingredients. Mix with your hands until the peas are coated.

2. Roast for 4 to 6 minutes, until peas just begin to brown in spots and are crisp-tender. Serve immediately.

About Sugar Snap Peas
Sugar snap peas are very sweet peas that are totally edible, including the pod. when purchasing, look for a bright green color with no dark or light spots and buy peas that are plump and crisp. Don't cook them too long; 2 to 3 minutes in boiling water is enough.

1 pound carrots
¾ cup water
¼ cup orange juice
1 tablespoon sugar
½ teaspoon salt
⅛ teaspoon white pepper
¼ teaspoon dried marjoram
    leaves
2 tablespoons butter

Braised Carrots

*Braising means cooking food covered in a small amount of liquid until tender.
The liquid is then reduced to a syrup and poured over the food to serve.*

1. Peel carrots and cut diagonally into 1½-inch chunks; set aside. In a heavy saucepan, combine remaining ingredients. Bring to a boil over medium heat.

2. Add carrots to the pan and cover. Reduce heat to low and simmer carrots, covered, for 5 to 8 minutes, until carrots are soft when pierced with a knife. Remove the carrots from the pan and place on serving plate. Increase heat to high and bring liquid to a boil. Boil for 3 to 5 minutes, until liquid is reduced and syrupy. Pour over carrots and serve.

Three-Bean Medley

This combination of beans is flavorful and delicious. And the sweet-and-sour salad dressing adds a nice punch of flavor. Serve it with a grilled steak and a mixed lettuce salad, with breadsticks on the side.

Serves 4–6

1 cup frozen green beans
1 cup frozen soybeans
1 cup frozen lima beans
½ cup sweet-and-sour salad dressing
¼ cup toasted pine nuts

1. Place the frozen green beans, soybeans, and lima beans in a heavy saucepan and cover with cold water. Bring to a boil, then reduce heat and simmer for 4 to 6 minutes, until all the beans are tender.

2. Drain beans thoroughly and return to saucepan. Add salad dressing and cook over medium heat until liquid comes to a boil and beans are glazed. Sprinkle with pine nuts and serve.

About Soybeans

Soybeans, also known as edamame, are grown in hairy pods; they are often served as a snack in the pod. The beans are high in complete protein and fiber and contain lots of isoflavones, which may help reduce the risk of cancer. And they taste great—nutty and sweet, with a buttery texture.

*1 head broccoli, broken into
  florets*
4 cups water
2 tablespoons olive oil
1 tablespoon butter
1 onion, chopped
3 cloves garlic, minced
*2 tablespoons toasted
  sesame seeds*

Broccoli Toss

*When broccoli is properly prepared, the florets are bright
green, tender, and mildly flavored. Serve this simple
side dish with a pasta casserole and a fresh fruit salad.*

1. Place broccoli florets in large saucepan and cover with water. Bring to a boil, then reduce heat and simmer, uncovered, for 5 to 7 minutes, until crisp-tender.

2. Meanwhile, place olive oil and butter in a skillet over medium heat. Add onion and garlic; cook and stir for 4 to 6 minutes, until crisp-tender.

3. Drain broccoli thoroughly and add to skillet with onion and garlic. Toss to coat broccoli with onion mixture. Sprinkle with sesame seeds, toss gently, and serve.

About Broccoli
*The trick to cooking broccoli is to use a large amount of water and cook
it, uncovered, very quickly. Use at least four cups of water for each head
of broccoli. Follow these steps and your broccoli will be crisp-tender and
mildly flavored.*

Roasted Baby Beets

You can find baby beets in gourmet stores and farmer's markets. Look for candy cane beets, which are red and white striped, golden beets, or white beets.

～

Preheat oven to 400°F. Cut off beet tops and root, if attached; scrub beets thoroughly. Cut beets in half. Place beets in large roasting pan and drizzle with olive oil; sprinkle with salt and pepper. Toss to coat. Roast for 20 to 25 minutes or until beets are tender when pierced with a fork. Place in serving bowl and toss with butter and oregano leaves until butter is melted. Serve warm.

Serves 4–6

1 pound baby beets
2 tablespoons olive oil
½ teaspoon salt
⅛ teaspoon pepper
3 tablespoons butter
1 tablespoon fresh oregano leaves

Crunchy Puréed Squash

Frozen puréed squash is a fabulous convenience food that saves, literally, hours of work in the kitchen. This hearty side dish is perfect for Thanksgiving.

～

In large saucepan, combine the frozen squash with orange juice and bring to a simmer. Cook for 6 to 8 minutes, until the squash begins to thaw. Stir in maple syrup, salt, and pepper; continue cooking for 3 to 4 minutes longer, until squash is hot and smooth. Place in 2-quart casserole dish and sprinkle with granola. Bake at 400°F for 12 to 15 minutes, until hot and granola browns slightly.

Serves 6

1 12-ounce package frozen puréed winter squash
¼ cup orange juice
2 tablespoons maple syrup
½ teaspoon salt
Dash white pepper
1 cup granola

Herbed Baby Potatoes

Serves 6

1 pound baby red-skinned
   potatoes
¼ cup butter
3 cloves garlic, minced
2 tablespoons fresh thyme
   leaves
2 tablespoons chopped fresh
   parsley
½ teaspoon salt
⅛ teaspoon white pepper

*Baby potatoes cook quickly because they are so small. Removing a strip
of skin from the middle of the potatoes prevents splitting as they cook.*

1. Peel a strip of skin from the middle of each potato. Place in large pot
   and cover with cold water. Cover and bring to a boil over high heat.
   Uncover, lower heat, and cook potatoes until tender when pierced with
   a fork, about 12 to 14 minutes.

2. Meanwhile, combine butter and garlic in a small saucepan. Cook over
   medium heat for 2 to 3 minutes, until garlic is fragrant. Remove from
   heat.

3. When potatoes are done, drain thoroughly, then return potatoes to the
   hot pot. Let stand off the heat for 2 to 3 minutes, shaking occasionally.
   Place pot over medium heat and pour butter mixture over potatoes.
   Sprinkle with remaining ingredients, toss gently, then serve.

Preparing Fresh Herbs
*To prepare herbs with tiny leaves, like oregano, rosemary, marjoram,
and thyme, simply pull the leaves backward off the stem; chop if desired.
Herbs with larger leaves, like sage, mint, and basil, should be rolled into
a log and julienned.*

Chapter 33

Soup Recipes

1 tablespoon olive oil
1 onion, finely chopped
1 10-ounce container
   refrigerated Alfredo
   sauce
1½ cups chicken or vegetable
   broth
1½ cups whole milk
2 14-ounce cans diced
   tomatoes, undrained
½ teaspoon dried basil leaves
¼ teaspoon dried marjoram
   leaves

Tomato Bisque

A bisque is a rich soup that combines vegetables, stock, and milk or cream. Serve for lunch with some chewy breadsticks and a mixed fruit salad.

~~~~~~

1. In heavy saucepan, heat olive oil over medium heat and add onion. Cook and stir until onion is tender, about 4 minutes. Add Alfredo sauce and chicken broth; cook and stir with wire whisk until mixture is smooth. Add milk and stir; cook over medium heat for 2 to 3 minutes.

2. Meanwhile, purée undrained tomatoes in food processor or blender until smooth. Add to saucepan along with seasonings and stir well. Heat soup over medium heat, stirring frequently, until mixture just comes to a simmer. Serve immediately.

Alfredo Sauce
Alfredo sauce is basically a white sauce, usually with some cheese added. You can find it in the refrigerated dairy section of your supermarket. It can also be found on the pasta aisle. In addition to Alfredo sauce, four-cheese sauce, cheddar pasta sauce, and roasted garlic Parmesan pasta sauce are available.

Super-Quick Beef Vegetable Stew

*There are so many types of fully prepared meat entrées in
your grocery store; browse the selection and stock up!*

Serves 6

3 tablespoons olive oil
1 onion, chopped
3 cloves garlic, minced
1 16-ounce package prepared
    roast beef in gravy
1 16-ounce package frozen
    mixed vegetables
1 10-ounce can cream of
    mushroom soup
2 cups water
½ teaspoon dried thyme
    leaves

1. In heavy large saucepan, heat olive oil over medium heat. Add onion
    and garlic; cook and stir until tender, 4 to 5 minutes. Meanwhile, cut
    the cooked roast beef into 1-inch chunks. Add to saucepan along with
    gravy, frozen mixed vegetables, soup, water, and thyme leaves.

2. Cook over medium-high heat until soup comes to a boil, about 7 to 9
    minutes. Reduce heat to low and simmer for 6 to 7 minutes longer, until
    vegetables and beef are hot and tender. Serve immediately.

Soup or Stew?

*The difference between soup and stew is the thickness of the liquid.
Soups are generally thin, sometimes made with just broth or stock.
Stews have ingredients that thicken the liquid, including potatoes, flour,
cornstarch, or puréed vegetables. You can make any soup into a stew
by adding some cornstarch dissolved in water.*

1 pound sweet Italian bulk
  sausage
1 8-ounce package sliced
  mushrooms
4 cloves garlic, minced
3 14-ounce cans beef broth
1½ cups water
1 teaspoon dried Italian
  seasoning
⅛ teaspoon pepper
1 24-ounce package frozen
  cheese tortellini

Tortellini Soup

*This rich soup is full of flavor. Serve it with some water crackers,
a chopped vegetable salad, and melon slices.*

1. In large saucepan over medium heat, brown sausage with mushrooms
   and garlic, stirring to break up sausage. When sausage is cooked, drain
   thoroughly. Add broth, water, Italian seasoning, and pepper to saucepan and bring to a boil over high heat. Reduce heat to low and simmer
   for 8 to 10 minutes.

2. Stir in frozen tortellini and cook, stirring frequently, over medium-high
   heat for 6 to 8 minutes or until tortellini are hot and tender. Serve immediately.

Frozen or Refrigerated Tortellini?

*Refrigerated, or fresh, tortellini is found in the dairy aisle of the regular
grocery store. It is generally more expensive than the frozen, and
package sizes are smaller. Frozen tortellini and tortelloni take a bit
longer to cook. Choose your favorite and stock up.*

Cheesy Clam Chowder

*This rich, thick, and super easy chowder can be made with
any other seafood too. Think about using canned oysters,
canned mussels, frozen cooked shrimp, or lump crabmeat.*

Serves 6–8

2 10-ounce cans condensed
    broccoli cheese soup
2 cups half-and-half
2 cups milk
3 cups refrigerated hash
    brown potatoes
½ teaspoon dried marjoram
2 8-ounce cans clams,
    undrained
⅛ teaspoon pepper

Combine soup, half-and-half, and milk in large heavy saucepan. Bring
to a boil, then add potatoes and marjoram. Bring to a boil again,
reduce heat, and simmer for 15 minutes. Add clams and pepper and
simmer for 5 to 10 minutes longer, until soup is hot and blended. Serve
immediately.

Cheesy Shrimp Chowder

*This rich chowder is very simple to make and has a
wonderful rich flavor. Serve it with tiny oyster crackers,
a baby spinach salad, and oatmeal cookies for dessert.*

Serves 6

2 tablespoons olive oil
1 onion, finely chopped
2 cups frozen hash brown
    potatoes
1½ cups water
2 6-ounce cans medium
    shrimp, drained
1 16-ounce jar four-cheese
    Alfredo sauce
1 15-ounce can evaporated
    milk

1. In large saucepan, heat olive oil over medium-high heat. Add onion;
   cook and stir until tender, about 4 to 5 minutes. Add potatoes and
   water; bring to a boil, cover, lower heat, and simmer for 5 minutes, until
   potatoes are hot and tender.

2. Add shrimp, Alfredo sauce, and evaporated milk to saucepan. Stir well
   and heat over medium heat until the soup comes to a simmer; do not
   boil. Serve immediately.

Serves 6

1 26-ounce jar double
    cheddar pasta sauce
2 14-ounce cans chicken
    broth
2 15-ounce cans corn, drained
2 9-ounce packages frozen
    cooked Southwest-style
    chicken strips
½ teaspoon dried Italian
    seasoning
2 cups shredded sharp
    Cheddar cheese

Chicken Corn Chowder

Open four packages and grate some cheese, and you'll have a hearty, hot soup on the table in about 15 minutes. Serve with some crackers and fresh fruit.

In large saucepan, combine all ingredients except cheese and bring to a boil over medium-high heat. Reduce heat to low, cover, and simmer for 6 to 8 minutes, until chicken is hot. Stir in Cheddar cheese, remove from heat, and let stand, covered, for 3 to 4 minutes. Stir thoroughly and serve.

Frozen Precooked Chicken
There are lots of varieties of frozen precooked chicken in your supermarket's meat aisle. You can find cooked grilled chicken, chicken strips, and chopped chicken in flavors that range from Southwest to plain grilled. Some varieties come with a sauce; be sure to read the label to make sure you're getting what you want.

Savory Minestrone

Minestrone is a rich vegetable soup made with beans and pasta. It's really a meal in one bowl; serve with some toasted garlic bread and tall glasses of milk.

———

Serves 6

4 cups chicken broth
1 16-ounce package frozen
    mixed vegetables
1 15-ounce can cannellini
    beans, drained
½ teaspoon dried basil leaves
½ teaspoon dried oregano
    leaves
1 14-ounce can diced
    tomatoes with garlic,
    undrained
1½ cups elbow macaroni

In large saucepan, combine chicken broth and vegetables; bring to a boil over medium-high heat. When broth boils, add beans, basil, oregano, and tomatoes. Bring to a simmer, lower heat, and cook for 5 minutes. Add macaroni; stir and simmer for 8 to 9 minutes, until pasta is tender, then serve.

Canned Beans

Canned beans are a great convenience food to have on hand, but they do tend to be high in sodium. To reduce sodium, drain the beans, place them in a strainer or colander, and run cold water over them. Drain well again and use in the recipe.

Serves 6

2 tablespoons olive oil
1 onion, chopped
1 16-ounce package cooked
   ground beef in taco sauce
2 15-ounce cans chili beans,
   undrained
2 cups frozen corn
1 14-ounce can Mexican-
   flavored chopped
   tomatoes, undrained
2 cups water
1 tablespoon chili powder
½ teaspoon cumin
⅛ teaspoon cayenne pepper

Mexican Beef Stew

Serve this rich stew topped with a dollop of sour cream and some chopped avocados or guacamole for a cooling contrast.

In large saucepan, heat olive oil over medium heat. Add onion; cook and stir until crisp-tender, about 3 to 4 minutes. Add remaining ingredients and stir well. Bring to a simmer, reduce heat to medium-low, and cook for 10 to 15 minutes, until corn is hot and soup has thickened slightly. Serve immediately.

Spices

Spices have a shelf life of about a year; after that time, they lose flavor and intensity and should be replaced. To keep track, write the purchase date on the can or bottle, using a permanent marker. Periodically, go through your spice drawer or rack and discard older spices; be sure to write the ones you need on your grocery list.

French Onion Soup

Because the onions need to sauté for a fairly long time to develop caramelization, this recipe starts with frozen chopped onions. You can chop fresh onions, but the recipe will take longer than 30 minutes.

Serves 6

2 tablespoons olive oil
2 tablespoons butter
2 10-ounce packages frozen
    chopped onions
2 tablespoons flour
2 16-ounce boxes beef stock
6 slices French bread
¼ cup butter, softened
1½ cups shredded Gruyère
    cheese

1. In large saucepan, combine olive oil and 2 tablespoons butter over medium heat until butter is foamy. Add onions; cook over medium heat for 10 to 12 minutes, stirring frequently, until onions brown around edges. Sprinkle flour over onions; cook and stir for 2 to 3 minutes.

2. Stir in stock, bring to a simmer, and cook for 10 minutes. Meanwhile, spread French bread slices with ¼ cup butter. In toaster oven, toast the bread until browned and crisp. Sprinkle with cheese and toast for 2 to 4 minutes, until cheese melts. Divide soup among soup bowls and float the toasted cheese bread on top.

Boxed Stocks

If your grocery store carries boxed stocks, buy them. These stocks tend to be richer and less salty than canned stocks. If you don't use all of the stock, these boxes come with a flip-top lid so you can close the box and store them in the refrigerator for a couple of weeks.

Serves 6

1 16-ounce package frozen
   meatballs
2 cups 8-vegetable juice
2 cups frozen mixed
   vegetables
1 10-ounce can beef broth
3 cups water
½ teaspoon dried Italian
   seasoning
⅛ teaspoon pepper
1½ cups mini penne pasta

Vegetable Meatball Soup

*Frozen cooked meatballs are available in several flavors;
choose plain or Italian-style for this super-easy recipe.*

In large saucepan or stockpot, combine all ingredients except pasta and mix gently. Bring to a boil over high heat, then stir in pasta, reduce heat to medium-high, and cook for 9 to 11 minutes, until meatballs are hot, vegetables are hot, and pasta is tender. Serve immediately.

Substituting Pasta
You can substitute one shape of pasta for another as long as they are about the same size and thickness. Whichever pasta you choose, be sure to cook it al dente; this means cooked through, but with a firm bite in the center.

Pressure-Cooker Beef Stew

*This stew tastes like it simmered for hours on your stove,
but the pressure cooker makes quick work of the recipe. Serve
with some crusty bread to soak up the wonderful sauce.*

Serves 8

2 pounds bottom-round
   steak
3 tablespoons flour
½ teaspoon garlic salt
⅛ teaspoon pepper
3 tablespoons olive oil
3 russet potatoes, cubed
1 16-ounce package baby
   carrots
½ teaspoon dried thyme
   leaves
½ teaspoon dried oregano
   leaves
4 cups beef stock, heated
1 14-ounce can diced
   tomatoes with garlic,
   undrained

Cut steak into 1-inch cubes. Sprinkle meat with flour, garlic salt, and pepper and toss to coat. Heat oil in the pressure cooker and brown the coated beef, stirring frequently, about 5 to 7 minutes. Add remaining ingredients and lock the lid. Bring up to high pressure and cook for 20 minutes. Release pressure using quick-release method and stir stew. Serve immediately.

Tex-Mex Cheese Soup

*As with all Tex-Mex foods, serve this hearty soup with salsa, sour cream,
chopped avocado or guacamole, and crumbled crisp tortilla chips.*

Serves 4

2 tablespoons olive oil
1 onion, chopped
1 1.25-ounce envelope taco
   seasoning mix
1 15-ounce can creamed corn
2 10-ounce cans condensed
   chicken broth
1½ cups water
2 cups shredded Pepper Jack
   cheese
2 tablespoons flour

1. In heavy saucepan, heat olive oil over medium heat. Add onion; sauté until crisp-tender, about 3 to 4 minutes. Sprinkle taco seasoning mix over the onions and stir, then add corn, chicken broth, and water. Bring to a simmer and cook for 10 minutes, stirring occasionally.

2. Meanwhile, in medium bowl, toss cheese with flour. Add to soup and lower heat; cook and stir for 2 to 3 minutes, until cheese is melted and soup is thickened. Serve immediately.

Serves 4–6

1 16-ounce package pork
   roast au jus
1 4-ounce can chopped green
   chilies, undrained
2 14-ounce cans chicken
   broth
1 tablespoon chili powder
1 teaspoon ground cumin
½ teaspoon dried oregano
   leaves
1 15-ounce can hominy,
   drained
2 cups frozen corn
3 tablespoons flour
½ cup water

Quick Posole

Posole is a Mexican stew made with hominy, green chilies, and cubes of tender pork. Serve it with some blue corn tortilla chips, guacamole, sour cream, and a green salad.

1. Remove pork from package and cut into 1-inch cubes. Combine in large saucepan along with juice from pork, chilies, broth, chili powder, cumin, oregano, hominy, and frozen corn. Bring to a boil over high heat, then reduce heat to low, cover, and simmer for 12 to 15 minutes, until pork is hot and tender.

2. In small jar, combine flour and water and shake well to blend. Stir into stew and raise heat to medium. Cook and stir until stew thickens, about 5 to 8 minutes. Serve immediately.

Hominy

Hominy is made by removing the bran and germ from kernels of corn. It can be made by soaking the corn kernels in a weak solution of lye and water, or by physically crushing the corn. Yellow hominy is generally sweeter than the white. You can substitute barley for it in any recipe if you'd like.

Cold Pea Soup

This elegant soup is perfect for a hot summer evening. Serve it with some crisp croutons, a fruit gelatin salad, and some popovers fresh from the oven.

Serves 4

1 16-ounce package frozen
    baby peas
1 avocado, peeled and
    chopped
1 tablespoon lemon juice
2 cups chicken broth
½ teaspoon salt
⅛ teaspoon white pepper
¼ cup chopped mint

Place frozen peas in a colander and run cold water over them for 2 to 3 minutes to thaw, tossing occasionally. Place in blender container or food processor along with avocado and sprinkle with lemon juice. Add chicken broth, salt, and pepper and process until smooth. Pour into serving bowl and sprinkle with chopped mint.

Baby Peas
Try to find baby peas in the frozen aisle of your supermarket. They are much more tender than regular peas and have a sweet, fresh flavor. Do not cook them before adding to recipes; when adding to a pasta recipe, drain the pasta over the peas in a colander, or add them to a soup at the very end of the cooking time.

Serves 6

2 tablespoons olive oil
1 onion, chopped
3 cloves garlic, minced
2 15-ounce cans black beans,
    drained and rinsed
1 14-ounce can diced
    tomatoes with green
    chilies
2 14-ounce cans chicken
    broth
½ teaspoon cumin
⅛ teaspoon white pepper

Black Bean Soup

*Serve this delicious soup with sour cream and chopped avocado
for toppings, a spinach salad, and crisp breadsticks.*

In heavy saucepan, heat olive oil over medium heat. Add onion and garlic; cook and stir for 3 to 4 minutes, until crisp-tender. Meanwhile, place black beans in a colander, rinse, and drain thoroughly. Using a potato masher, lightly mash some of the beans. Add all beans to saucepan along with remaining ingredients. Bring to a simmer; cook for 10 to 12 minutes, until blended.

Dried Beans

You can substitute dried beans for canned to reduce sodium. Rinse the beans and sort to remove any dirt or pebbles. Cover with cold water, bring to a boil, and boil for 1 minute. Cover and let stand for 1 hour. Drain the beans and cover with cold water. Simmer for about 2 hours, until beans are tender.

Potato Soup

This creamy and rich soup uses two kinds of potatoes for a nice depth of flavor. Serve with Green Beans with Red Peppers (page 216) and Cheese Crackers (page 40).

Serves 6

4 slices bacon
1 onion, chopped
1 5-ounce package cheese-scalloped potato mix
3 cups water
1 15-ounce can evaporated milk
2 cups frozen hash brown potatoes
½ teaspoon dried dill weed
⅛ teaspoon white pepper

In heavy saucepan, cook bacon until crisp. Remove bacon, drain on paper towels, crumble, and set aside. Cook onion in bacon drippings until tender, about 5 minutes. Add potato mix and seasoning packet from potato mix along with remaining ingredients. Bring to a boil and simmer for 17 to 20 minutes, until potatoes are tender. If desired, purée using an immersion blender. Sprinkle with bacon and serve.

Precooked Bacon?

When recipes call for crumbled bacon, you can use the precooked version. But if the recipe calls for cooking the bacon and using the bacon fat to sauté other ingredients, you must used uncooked bacon. Or you can use the precooked bacon and use butter or olive oil as a substitute for the bacon fat.

2 tablespoons olive oil

1 onion, chopped

1 1.25-ounce package taco
seasoning mix

1 15-ounce can kidney beans,
drained

1 15-ounce can black beans,
drained

2 14-ounce cans diced
tomatoes with green
chilies, undrained

1 cup water

Two-Bean Chili

This vegetarian chili can be varied so many ways. Add more beans, salsa, cooked ground beef or pork sausage, jalapeño peppers, or tomato sauce.

In heavy saucepan over medium heat, add olive oil and sauté onion until tender, about 4 to 5 minutes. Sprinkle taco seasoning mix over onions; cook and stir for 1 minute. Add drained but not rinsed beans, tomatoes, and water. Bring to a simmer; cook for 10 to 12 minutes, until thickened and blended.

Taco Seasoning Mix

You can make your own taco seasoning mix by combining 2 tablespoons chili powder, 2 teaspoons onion powder, 2 tablespoons cornstarch, 1 teaspoon dried oregano, 1 teaspoon dried red pepper flakes, 2 teaspoons salt, and ½ teaspoon cumin. Blend well and store in a cool dry place: 2 tablespoons equals one envelope mix.

Bean and Bacon Soup

This simple soup is great for kids' lunch boxes. Pack into an insulated thermos and provide some cheese crackers, baby carrots, and shredded Cheddar cheese for topping the soup.

Serves 4–6

1 8-ounce package bacon
1 onion, chopped
1 14-ounce can diced
    tomatoes, undrained
2 15-ounce cans pinto beans,
    drained
2 cups chicken broth

In large saucepan, cook bacon until crisp. Drain bacon on paper towels, crumble, and set aside. Drain off all but 2 tablespoons bacon drippings. Cook onion in drippings over medium heat for 3 to 4 minutes. Add remaining ingredients and bring to a simmer. Simmer for 10 to 12 minutes, then use a potato masher to mash some of the beans. Add reserved bacon, stir, and simmer for 5 minutes longer. Serve immediately or pour into warmed insulated thermoses and store up to 6 hours.

Sweet-and-Sour Pork Stew

Serve this delicious stew with a mixed lettuce salad, some crisp breadsticks, with a bakery layer cake for dessert.

Serves 4–6

2 tablespoons olive oil
1 onion, chopped
1 red bell pepper, chopped
1 8-ounce can pineapple
    tidbits, undrained
1 16-ounce package cooked
    sweet-and-sour pork
2½ cups water
½ cup long-grain rice
2 tablespoons cornstarch
⅓ cup water

1. In large saucepan, heat olive oil over medium heat. Add onion; cook and stir for 3 minutes until crisp-tender. Add red bell pepper; cook and stir for 2 to 3 minutes longer. Add undrained pineapple, pork with sauce, and 2½ cups water. Bring to a simmer, stir in rice, and cook for 10 minutes.

2. Meanwhile, in small bowl, combine cornstarch and ⅓ cup water and mix well. Stir into stew; cook and stir over medium heat for 5 to 8 minutes, until rice is tender and stew is thickened. Serve immediately.

Serves 4

5 cups chicken broth
1 cup shredded carrots
½ cup grated onion
2 eggs
1 egg yolk

Egg Drop Soup

Because this soup is so simple it demands the best chicken stock.
Try to find the boxed chicken stock at your grocery store,
or order it online. You can also make your own stock.

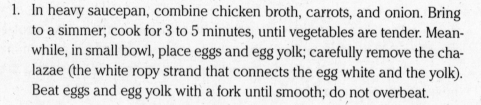

1. In heavy saucepan, combine chicken broth, carrots, and onion. Bring to a simmer; cook for 3 to 5 minutes, until vegetables are tender. Meanwhile, in small bowl, place eggs and egg yolk; carefully remove the chalazae (the white ropy strand that connects the egg white and the yolk). Beat eggs and egg yolk with a fork until smooth; do not overbeat.

2. Remove the saucepan from the heat. Using a fork, drizzle the egg mixture into the soup. When all the egg is added, stir the soup for 30 seconds, then serve immediately.

Make Your Own Chicken Stock
This recipe takes some time, but you can freeze it and it will add lots of flavor to your recipes. Cover one stewing chicken, some chopped onion, carrots, 1 bay leaf, some parsley, and celery with water and simmer for 3 to 4 hours. Strain broth, cool, pour into ice cube trays, and freeze, then package the cubes in freezer bags.

Chapter 34

Cookies and Candies

Serves 9

1 14-ounce package rich and
    fudgy brownie mix
⅓ cup sugar
1 egg
1 3-ounce package cream
    cheese, softened
1 cup semisweet chocolate
    chips

Layered Brownies

*Cream cheese and brownies are natural partners. This is a dual-use recipe;
you end up with layered brownies for tonight's dessert, and plain
brownies for this weekend's Brownie Parfait (page 281).*

1. Preheat oven to 375°F. Spray two 9" square pans with baking spray and
   set aside.

2. Prepare brownie mix as directed on package. Pour half of batter into
   one prepared pan and set aside. In small bowl, combine sugar, egg,
   and cream cheese and beat until smooth and blended.

3. Pour half of remaining brownie batter into second prepared pan. Top
   with cream cheese mixture, and pour last part of brownie batter over
   cream cheese mixture; marble with a knife.

4. Bake both pans of brownies for 19 to 22 minutes or until tops look dry
   and shiny. Remove from oven and immediately sprinkle cream cheese
   brownies with the chocolate chips; cover that pan with foil and let
   stand for a few minutes. Remove foil and spread chips evenly over
   brownies. Let cool completely. Cover and reserve plain brownies for
   the Brownie Parfait (page 281) or tuck into lunchboxes.

Low-Fat Products in Baking
*You can use low-fat cream cheese, low-fat milk, and low-fat sour cream
in baking, but do not use low-fat or whipped margarines or butter.
Those ingredients can contain a lot of water, which will ruin the struc-
ture of your baked products.*

No-Flour Peanut Butter Cookies

Believe it or not, these cookies turn out wonderfully with absolutely no flour of any kind! Do not use the refrigerated, or natural, type of peanut butter because the cookies will spread too much when they bake.

Yields 48 cookies

2 cups peanut butter
2 cups sugar
2 eggs
1 teaspoon vanilla
½ cup chopped peanuts
1 cup miniature semisweet chocolate chips

~

1. Preheat oven to 325°F. Line cookie sheets with parchment paper or Silpat silicon liners; set aside. In large bowl, combine peanut butter, sugar, eggs, and vanilla and mix well until blended. Stir in peanuts and chocolate chips.

2. Drop by teaspoonfuls onto prepared cookie sheets. Bake for 12 to 15 minutes, until cookies are just set. Cool for 5 minutes on cookie sheets, then carefully remove to wire racks to cool.

M&M's Cookies

You can use this basic formula to make an almost infinite variety of cookies. Use chocolate cake mix with walnuts, white cake mix with mini chocolate chips, or spice cake mix with raisins.

Yields 3 dozen cookies

1 18-ounce package yellow cake mix
1 cup quick-cooking oats
¼ cup butter, softened
2 eggs, beaten
1½ cups plain M&M's candies

~

Preheat oven to 350°F. In a large bowl, combine all ingredients except candies and beat until blended. Stir in candies, then drop mixture by tablespoons onto Silpat-lined cookie sheets. Bake for 12 to 15 minutes or until cookies are set. Let cool for 5 minutes on cookie sheets, then remove to wire racks to cool.

Yields 3 cups

1 cup brown sugar
½ cup sugar
⅓ cup orange juice
3 tablespoons butter, melted
1 teaspoon vanilla
3 cups mixed nuts

Candied Nuts

Candied nuts are a wonderful snack to have on hand for the holiday season; they also make great gifts packaged in decorative tins or glass jars.

1. Preheat oven to 350°F. Grease a large cookie sheet with butter and set aside. Grease 2 large sheets of foil with butter and set aside.

2. In large bowl, combine brown sugar, sugar, orange juice, melted butter, and vanilla and mix well. Add nuts and toss to coat. Spread onto prepared cookie sheet. Bake for 10 to 15 minutes or until nuts are dark golden brown and sugar mixture bubbles. Stir nuts twice during cooking time. Immediately place nuts onto buttered foil, spreading thinly. Let cool, then break nuts apart before storing in airtight container.

Storing Nuts
Many nuts should be stored in the freezer before use, because the oils they contain can turn rancid quickly at room temperature. Pour the nuts into a freezer container such as a heavy-duty resealable freezer bag or a hard-sided plastic container, label, and freeze up to 6 months.

Marshmallow Treats

This is a twist on the traditional combination of Rice Krispie bars. Peanut butter and chocolate are added to toasted rice flakes cereal and it is formed around large marshmallows; the finished cookies look like popcorn balls.

Yields 12 cookies

4 cups miniature
     marshmallows
¼ cup peanut butter
2 tablespoons butter
4 cups toasted rice flakes
     cereal
1 cup miniature chocolate
     chips
12 large marshmallows

1. Combine miniature marshmallows, peanut butter, and butter in large microwave-safe bowl. Microwave on high for 1 to 3 minutes or until marshmallows are melted, stirring once during cooking time. Stir well to combine. Add rice cereal and miniature chocolate chips and mix well.

2. Form a scant ½ cup cereal mixture around each large marshmallow and form a ball, using greased hands. Refrigerate about 10 to 15 minutes, until firm. Wrap in cellophane and store at room temperature.

Substitutions
For a nice treat, you can substitute many things for the large marshmallows in these easy cookies. You can use chocolate Kisses, either milk chocolate or dark; miniature candy bars; dates; or dried apricots. Or you don't need a filling at all! The cereal mixture can also be pressed into a 13" × 9" pan and cut into bars.

Yields 16 bars

1 cup flour
½ cup quick-cooking oats
½ cup brown sugar
⅛ teaspoon allspice
⅓ cup butter, melted
1 cup chopped red grapes
2 tablespoons grape jelly

Streusel Grape Bars

Grapes are a surprising and fresh filling for this rich oatmeal bar.
Serve them with a fork at the end of a company dinner,
or cut into small squares and tuck into lunchboxes.

1. Preheat oven to 350°F. In large bowl, combine flour, oats, brown sugar, and allspice and mix well. Add melted butter; stir until mixture forms crumbs. Press half of crumbs into 9" square pan and set aside.

2. In small bowl, combine grapes with jelly and mix well. Spoon over crust in pan and spread evenly. Sprinkle grapes with remaining crumb mixture. Bake for 15 to 20 minutes or until bars are light golden brown. Cool and cut into bars.

Grapes

Almost all the grapes sold in produce departments today are seedless. They are called "table grapes" to distinguish them from grapes used to make wine. You can buy red, green, or blue-black grapes. Varieties include Flame, Thompson Seedless, Red Globe, Autumn Royal, and Christmas Rose.

Graham Fudge Squares

These no-bake bars have the most wonderful rich flavor and texture from the cinnamon graham cracker crumbs.

Yields 36 squares

1 cup sugar
¾ cup flour
½ cup butter
1 15-ounce can sweetened
     condensed milk
2 cups semisweet chocolate
     chips, divided
1½ cups cinnamon graham
     cracker crumbs

1. Grease 9" square pan with butter and set aside. In heavy saucepan, mix sugar, flour, butter, and sweetened condensed milk. Bring to a boil over medium-high heat, stirring constantly. Let boil for 1 minute, stirring constantly. Remove from heat and add 1¼ cups of the chocolate chips. Stir until chocolate melts and mixture is smooth.

2. Add graham cracker crumbs and mix well. Spread in prepared pan and press down. In microwave-safe bowl, place remaining ¾ cup chocolate chips. Microwave on medium power (50 percent) for 1 minute. Remove and stir until smooth. Pour over bars and spread to cover. Chill in freezer for 10 to 15 minutes, then cut into bars to serve.

1 12-ounce package
  semisweet chocolate
  chips
⅓ cup peanut butter
1 cup cashews
1 cup mini marshmallows
1 cup crisp rice cereal

Choco-Peanut Crunchers

These little chocolate and peanut butter candies are very easy to make and fun to eat. Make them with your kids at holiday time.

1. Line cookie sheets with parchment paper or waxed paper and set aside. In microwave-safe bowl, place chocolate chips and peanut butter. Melt at 50 percent power for 2 minutes, remove from microwave, and stir until chips melt and mixture is smooth. It may be necessary to microwave the mixture for 1 to 2 minutes longer, until the chips melt.

2. Stir in remaining ingredients until coated. Drop mixture by spoonfuls onto prepared cookie sheets and refrigerate until set. Store in airtight container at room temperature.

About Semisweet Chocolate

Semisweet chocolate is made of cocoa butter (made from roasted, ground cocoa bean nibs), sugar, and vanilla. Semisweet chocolate chips are generally a bit sweeter than bar chocolate. You can substitute one for the other. Chop semisweet chocolate bars into small pieces to use in place of the chips.

Graham Cracker Crisps

These crisp and crunchy little bar cookies are very fun to make. They taste like English toffee, but they aren't quite as hard or crunchy.

⁓

Yields 24 cookies

24 graham cracker squares
1 cup butter
1 cup brown sugar
1 cup chopped cashews
1½ cups milk chocolate chips

1. Preheat oven to 350°F. Place graham crackers in an ungreased 15" × 10" jelly-roll pan and set aside.

2. In medium saucepan, combine butter and brown sugar. Bring to a boil, stirring frequently, and boil for 1 minute or until sauce comes together and blends. Slowly pour this mixture over the graham crackers and sprinkle with cashews.

3. Bake for 8 to 12 minutes or until entire surface bubbles. Remove from heat and sprinkle with milk chocolate chips. Let stand for 10 minutes, then swirl through chips with knife to marble. Let cool and cut into squares along the cracker lines.

Chopping Nuts
You can chop nuts by placing them on a work surface and using a chef's knife to rock back and forth over the nuts. There are specialty hand-turned nut choppers that do a good job. You can also place the nuts in a heavy-duty resealable plastic bag and roll over the bag with a rolling pin.

Serves 8–10

1 12-ounce package
    semisweet chocolate
    chips
½ cup milk chocolate chips
1 15-ounce can sweetened
    condensed milk
1 cup chopped cashews
1 cup miniature
    marshmallows

Easy Fudge

*Use just about anything as the additions in this easy candy—
candy-coated chocolate pieces, gumdrops, peanuts, chopped candy
bars, macadamia nuts, or toffee bits would all be wonderful.*

1. Grease an 8" square pan with butter and set aside. In medium microwave-safe bowl, combine semisweet chocolate chips, milk chocolate chips, and sweetened condensed milk. Microwave on 50 percent power for 2 to 4 minutes, stirring once during cooking time, until chocolate is almost melted. Remove from oven and stir until chocolate melts.

2. Stir in cashews until mixed, then stir in marshmallows. Spread into prepared pan and let stand until cool.

Sweetened Condensed Milk
Sweetened condensed milk was invented in the 1800s to prevent food poisoning in infants and children that was caused by lack of pasteurization and refrigeration. It's a combination of milk and sugar with 50 percent of the water removed. Keep a can or two on hand because it's a great ingredient for making fudge and candies.

Chocolate Cream Peppermints

These rich little peppermints are so fun to make. They make a wonderful gift at Christmas or Hanukah packaged into a red, green, or blue box tied with a bow.

Yields 24 candies

2 tablespoons light cream
1 tablespoon butter
1½ cups powdered sugar
¼ teaspoon peppermint
  extract
1½ cups milk chocolate chips

1. Place cream in microwave-safe bowl and heat at 50 percent power for 30 seconds. Stir in butter until melted, then blend in powdered sugar and peppermint extract. Work with hands until creamy. Shape into ¾-inch balls, place on parchment paper–lined cookie sheets, and flatten to ⅛-inch thickness.

2. Place 1¼ cups of the chocolate chips in a 2-cup glass measuring cup and microwave at 50 percent power for 2 minutes. Remove from oven and stir in remaining chips until mixture is melted and smooth.

3. Dip each peppermint center into the chocolate, shake off excess, and place back onto cookie sheets. Place in freezer for 10 minutes, until chocolate is hardened. Store in airtight container.

½ cup corn syrup
½ cup brown sugar
1 cup crunchy peanut butter
3 cups cornflakes
1 cup milk chocolate chips

Cereal Caramel Chews

These easy bars are crunchy and full of flavor, perfect for after-school munching or for a great treat in a lunch box. You could top them with butterscotch chips or semisweet chocolate chips instead.

1. Grease a 9" pan with butter and set aside. In heavy saucepan, combine corn syrup and brown sugar. Cook over medium heat until mixture boils, stirring frequently. Let boil for 2 minutes, stirring constantly.

2. Remove from heat and add peanut butter; stir until melted. Add cornflakes and stir gently, then spread into prepared pan. Press down with back of a greased spoon to form an even surface.

3. Place milk chocolate chips in small microwave-safe bowl. Microwave at 50 percent power for 1 to 1½ minutes, remove from oven, and stir until chips are melted. Pour over cereal mixture and spread; let cool. Cut into bars.

Storing Brown Sugar
Brown sugar can dry out and develop hard lumps if not stored properly. Decant the sugar from its plastic bag into a hard-sided container with a tightly sealing lid. You can put some foil on the sugar and place a bit of damp paper towel on the foil to keep the sugar moist. Change the paper towel when it dries out.

Crunchy Peanut Butter Sandwich Cookies

This rich chocolate peanut butter filling can be used as a frosting for brownies or cupcakes, or to fill any kind of cookie sandwich.

Yields 12 cookies

1 cup semisweet chocolate chips
¼ cup milk chocolate chips
¼ cup peanut butter
24 No-Flour Peanut Butter Cookies (page 253)
1 cup chopped salted peanuts

Place chocolate chips in medium microwave-safe bowl. Microwave on medium power for 1 minute, then remove and stir until chocolate is melted and smooth. Stir in peanut butter until smooth. Refrigerate for 10 minutes, stirring once. Make sandwiches using chocolate mixture and peanut butter cookies. Roll edges of cookie sandwiches in peanuts. Refrigerate for 10 to 15 minutes, until set. Store at room temperature.

Brown Sugar Bars

Be sure not to overbake these bars; watch them carefully while they are in the oven. They should be soft and chewy when cool.

Yields 9 bars

¾ cup brown sugar
¼ cup butter
1 teaspoon vanilla
1 egg
1 cup flour
1 teaspoon baking powder
½ cup candy-coated chocolate pieces
1 cup semisweet chocolate chips

1. Preheat oven to 350°F. Grease a 9" square pan and set aside. In saucepan, combine brown sugar and butter; cook and stir over medium heat until butter melts and mixture is smooth.

2. Remove from heat and add vanilla and egg; beat well. Stir in flour and baking powder. Then stir in candy-coated chocolate pieces. Spread into prepared pan. Bake for 12 to 16 minutes or until bars are very light golden brown and just set. Be careful not to overbake.

3. Immediately sprinkle bars with chocolate chips. Cover pan with foil and let stand for 1 to 2 minutes, until chips soften. Spread chips to cover bars, then cool on wire rack.

Yields 24 candies

3 cups milk chocolate chips,
    divided
½ cup cream of coconut
1 teaspoon vanilla
3 tablespoons butter, melted
1¾ cups powdered sugar
2 cups flaked coconut

Coconut Drops

These little candies taste just like the popular chocolate-covered coconut candy bar. You can use semisweet or dark chocolate instead of the milk chocolate if you'd like.

1. Set aside 2½ cups chocolate chips. Finely chop remaining ½ cup chocolate chips. Combine cream of coconut, vanilla, and butter in a large bowl and mix thoroughly. Add powdered sugar and mix well. Work in coconut and chopped chocolate with hands. Form mixture into 1-inch balls and place on waxed paper.

2. Place 2 cups milk chocolate chips in a microwave-safe glass measuring cup and heat at 50 percent power for 2 minutes. Stir chips until almost melted, then return to microwave. Heat at 50 percent power for 30 seconds. Remove from microwave and add remaining ½ cup chips. Stir until chocolate is melted and mixture is smooth.

3. Drop coconut balls, one at a time, into chocolate mixture and remove with a fork. Tap fork on side of glass measuring cup to shake off excess chocolate, then place coated candy on waxed paper. Refrigerate until set, then store at room temperature.

Cream of Coconut

Cream of coconut is not the same as coconut milk. Cream of coconut is smooth and quite thick, similar to sweetened condensed milk. It is made from fresh coconuts. Coconut milk is made by puréeing chopped coconut with water, and is often used in Thai and Asian main dishes.

Grasshopper Cookies

These easy cookies are based on the plain chocolate wafer cookies that are used to make the old-fashioned chocolate dessert of cookies layered with cream.

Yields 30 cookies

1 7-ounce jar marshmallow crème

½ teaspoon peppermint extract

3–5 drops green food color

1½ cups powdered sugar

1 12-ounce package semisweet chocolate chips, divided

1 10-ounce package chocolate wafer cookies

1. Place marshmallow crème in medium bowl and mix in peppermint extract and green food color. Stir in powdered sugar until blended, then stir in ¾ cup chocolate chips.

2. Place cookies on a wire rack and top each with a spoonful of the marshmallow crème mixture; spread to edges. Place in freezer for 10 minutes.

3. Meanwhile, place remaining 1¼ cups chocolate chips in glass measuring cup. Heat at 50 percent power in microwave oven until chips are almost melted, about 1½ minutes. Stir until chips are melted and mixture is smooth. Remove cookies from freezer. Spoon some of the chocolate mixture over each cookie to coat. Return to freezer for a few minutes to harden chocolate. Store in airtight container at room temperature.

Marshmallow Crème

Marshmallow crème, also known as marshmallow fluff, is a fat-free product usually made of corn syrup, sugar, egg whites, and vanilla. It will keep, unopened, in a cool place for about a year. To measure it, first oil the measuring cup and the crème will slip right out.

Yields 48 cookies

½ cup butter
1½ cups sugar
½ cup brown sugar
1 cup grated peeled Granny
   Smith apple
½ teaspoon cinnamon
3 cups quick-cooking
   oatmeal
1 cup chopped walnuts
½ cup powdered sugar

No-Bake Apple Cookies

The pectin in the apple helps thicken the cookie mixture without baking.
Store these cookies in an airtight container at room temperature.

1. In heavy saucepan, melt butter with sugars over medium heat, then stir in apple. Bring to a boil, then stir and boil for 1 minute. Remove from heat and add cinnamon, oatmeal, and walnuts; stir to combine. Let stand for 5 minutes.

2. Place powdered sugar on shallow pan. Drop apple mixture by teaspoons into powdered sugar and roll into balls. Place on waxed paper and let stand until the cookies are firm.

Yields 36 bars

2 cups crunchy peanut butter
2 cups sifted powdered sugar
½ cup butter, softened
2 cups crisp rice cereal
1 11.5-ounce package milk
   chocolate chips

Peanut Butter Bars

Make sure you sift the powdered sugar for this recipe,
or there will be little bits of unmixed sugar in the bars.

1. Butter bottom of 13" × 9" pan and set aside. In large bowl, combine peanut butter and sifted powdered sugar with butter; mix until well combined. Stir in rice cereal. Press in bottom of prepared pan.

2. In microwave-safe bowl, heat chips on 50 percent power for 2 minutes, then remove and stir until melted. Pour over peanut butter mixture in pan and spread to coat. Refrigerate until chocolate hardens.

Chocolate Date Balls

Dates and chocolate are a wonderful combination. These easy cookies are the perfect addition to a holiday cookie tray.

Yields 24 cookies

½ cup butter
¾ cup sugar
¼ cup brown sugar
1 cup chopped dates
1 egg
1 cup semisweet chocolate chips
½ teaspoon vanilla
1½ cups crisp rice cereal
1 cup powdered sugar

1. In heavy saucepan, melt butter, sugar, and brown sugar together over medium heat. Stir in dates and bring to a boil. Cook mixture, stirring constantly, for 3 to 4 minutes, until dates begin to melt. Add egg to mixture, beat well, and cook for 1 minute longer, stirring constantly. Add chocolate chips, remove pan from heat, cover, and let stand for 4 to 5 minutes. Add vanilla and stir until chocolate melts and mixture is blended.

2. Add rice cereal to date mixture. Spread powdered sugar onto shallow plate. Drop date mixture by tablespoons into powdered sugar and form into balls. Place on cookie sheet; let stand until cool and firm.

About Dates
You can buy dates in the baking aisle of the supermarket, and sometimes in the produce department. When choosing dates for baking and cooking, do not use the dates that are precut and rolled in sugar. They are often too dry and do not blend well in cookie dough.

Yields 36 bars

2 cups buttery round cracker
   crumbs
¾ cup butter, melted
1½ cups chopped macadamia
   nuts
1 14-ounce can sweetened
   condensed milk
1½ cups coconut

Macadamia Coconut Bars

The saltiness of the buttery round cracker crumbs helps temper the sweetness of the remaining ingredients in these easy bar cookies.

1. Preheat oven to 350°F. In medium bowl, combine cracker crumbs with melted butter. Press into 13" × 9" pan. Sprinkle nuts over the crust, then evenly drizzle with sweetened condensed milk. Sprinkle coconut over milk.

2. Bake for 22 to 26 minutes or until edges are golden brown and bars are almost set. Let cool, then cut into bars.

Don't Use Evaporated Milk!

Many cooks, especially beginning cooks, tend to confused sweetened condensed milk with evaporated milk. Doing so will ruin your recipes! Sweetened condensed milk is very thick and sweetened, while evaporated milk is simply milk with some water removed. Read labels!

Macaroonies

Ground almonds and chocolate chips add interest to these simple cookies that are great for Passover because they contain no flour.

⌐~

Yields 3 dozen cookies

¾ cup slivered almonds
1⅓ cups sugar, divided
2 cups coconut
3 egg whites
1 teaspoon vanilla
2 cups miniature chocolate
    chips

1. Preheat oven to 350°F. Line cookie sheets with Silpat liners and set aside. In food processor or blender, combine almonds with ⅓ cup sugar and process or blend until particles are fine. Stir in coconut and mix well.

2. In large bowl, beat egg whites until foamy. Gradually add remaining 1 cup sugar, beating until stiff peaks form. Fold in vanilla, coconut mixture, and chocolate chips.

3. Drop by tablespoons onto prepared cookie sheets. Bake for 8 to 12 minutes, until cookies are light golden brown around edges and are set. Cool on cookie sheets for 5 minutes, then remove to wire racks to cool.

Chapter 35

Desserts

½ cup sugar
1 teaspoon cinnamon
3 apples, peeled and chopped
½ cup butter
4 cups vanilla ice cream
8 shortbread cookies,
    crumbled
½ cup chopped toasted
    pecans

Caramel Apple Parfaits

*Choose crisp and tart apples for this simple fall dessert.
Granny Smith apples would be a good choice because
they hold their shape well even when cooked.*

1. In medium bowl, combine sugar, cinnamon, and apples and toss to coat. Melt butter in a heavy saucepan and add apple mixture. Cook over low heat for 10 to 12 minutes or until apples are tender and sauce is lightly caramelized. Remove from heat, pour mixture into a heat-proof bowl, and let stand for 10 minutes, stirring occasionally.

2. Make parfaits with apple mixture, ice cream, crumbled shortbread cookies, and pecans. Serve immediately.

Cooking Apples
There are apples that are best for eating out of hand, and those best for cooking. Cooking apples include McIntosh, Cortland, Rome Beauty, Jonathan, Haralson, and Granny Smith. The best apples for eating out of hand include Honeycrisp, Gala, Red Delicious, and new varieties including Sweet Sixteen and Honeygold.

Berry Cheese Cakes

*Use a combination of raspberries and blueberries, or raspberries
and sliced strawberries, or strawberries and blackberries
in this simple and elegant little dessert.*

⁓

Serves 8

1 8-ounce container soft
   cream cheese with
   pineapple
1½ cups powdered sugar
4 tablespoons pineapple
   preserves, divided
8 purchased individual
   sponge cake cups
2 cups mixed berries

1. In medium bowl, beat cream cheese until fluffy. Add powdered sugar and 2 tablespoons of the preserves and beat well until combined.

2. Carefully frost tops and sides of each sponge cake cup with the cream cheese mixture. In small saucepan over low heat, melt remaining preserves until thin. In small bowl combine the berries with the melted preserves and mix gently. Top each frosted sponge cake with some of the berry mixture and serve. You can prepare the cups ahead of time, refrigerate them, and top them with the berry mixture just before serving.

Recipe Substitution
You can use bakery or homemade cupcakes instead of the individual sponge cake cups if you'd like. Use a knife to cut a cone-shaped piece out of the top of the cupcakes, then frost as directed and spoon the berry mixture over the cupcakes before serving. Freeze the cupcake tops to use later in Raspberry Trifle (page 280).

Serves 4

1 3-ounce package instant
    chocolate pudding mix
1 cup chocolate milk
1 cup whipping cream
5 oatmeal cookies, broken
    into pieces
¼ cup toffee candy bits

Oatmeal Cookie Parfaits

You can vary this dessert any way you'd like! Use any type of cookie, like choco-late chip or peanut butter, vary the flavor of pudding mix, and use everything from M&M's candies to chocolate chips to toasted nuts for a garnish.

1. In medium bowl, combine pudding mix and chocolate milk and mix well with wire whisk until smooth and thickened. In small bowl beat cream until stiff peaks form; fold into pudding mixture.

2. Layer pudding mixture, cookies, and candy bits in parfait glasses. Serve immediately or cover and store in refrigerator up to 4 hours.

Desserts in an Instant
Keep the ingredients for several of these easy desserts on hand in the refrigerator and freezer and you can make dessert in an instant. For instance, keep nondairy whipped topping and cookies in the freezer, pudding mix and several types of candy in the pantry, and refrigerated prepared pudding in the fridge.

Mint Mousse

*This mousse must be served immediately for the best texture.
You can also pile it into a baked and cooled pie crust or
a chocolate cookie crumb pie crust and freeze it.*

In blender or food processor, combine vanilla ice cream and mint chip ice cream, peppermint extract, and whipping cream; blend or process until smooth and creamy. Quickly spoon into parfait glasses or custard cups and top with chopped candies. Serve immediately.

Serves 8

*2 cups vanilla ice cream
2 cups mint chip ice cream
¼ teaspoon peppermint
   extract
¼ cup whipping cream
16 chocolate-mint-layered
   rectangular candies,
   coarsely chopped*

Chocolate Raspberry Pie

*You can find prepared chocolate cookie pie crusts in the baking aisle of your
supermarket. Or make your own by combining 2 cups chocolate cookie
crumbs with 1/3 cup melted butter and pressing into a 9" pie pan.*

1. Put chocolate chips in a small microwave-safe bowl. Microwave at 50 percent power for 1½ minutes; stir until chips are melted. Cut cream cheese into cubes and add to melted chips; beat well until smooth. Place mixture in refrigerator for 10 minutes.

2. Spread cooled chocolate mixture in bottom of pie crust. Put jelly in medium saucepan over low heat; cook and stir just until jelly is almost melted. Remove from heat and gently fold in raspberries just until coated. Place on top of the chocolate mixture. Serve immediately or cover and refrigerate until serving time.

Serves 8

*1 cup semisweet chocolate
   chips
1 8-ounce package cream
   cheese, softened
1 9" chocolate cookie pie crust
¼ cup raspberry jelly
2 cups fresh raspberries*

Serves 9

1 9-inch round or square
    yellow cake layer
1½ cups powdered sugar
⅓ cup butter, softened
⅓ cup seedless raspberry jam
¾ cup whipping cream
3 tablespoons powdered
    sugar

Raspberry Continental

Using premade and convenience foods means you can make this elegant dessert in just minutes! This is an excellent cake for a birthday celebration.

1. Using a serrated knife, carefully cut the cake horizontally through the middle to make two thin layers.

2. In small bowl, combine 1½ cups powdered sugar with butter, beating until light and fluffy. Stir in raspberry jam. Spread this mixture on the bottom cake layer and carefully top with the top layer.

3. In small bowl combine whipping cream and 3 tablespoons powdered sugar; beat until stiff peaks form. Frost top and sides of cake with cream mixture. Serve immediately or cover and chill in refrigerator for 2 to 3 hours. Store leftovers in refrigerator.

Garnishes
Garnishes make even purchased desserts look homemade. Use one of the ingredients from the recipe to make a garnish. Grated chocolate works well on any chocolate dessert, place fresh raspberries or strawberries on a dessert made with fruit, and mint sprigs look beautiful on any dessert topped with whipped cream.

Crunchy Ice Cream Cupcakes

Ice cream contains sugar, eggs, and milk and is the secret ingredient in these simple little cupcakes. If you'd like, you can frost them after they have cooled with any canned frosting.

Yields 24 cupcakes

2 cups vanilla ice cream
1 tablespoon butter
1 18-ounce package yellow cake mix
3 eggs
1½ cups granola, slightly crushed

1. Preheat oven to 350°F. Line 24 muffin tins with paper liners and set aside.

2. In microwave-safe bowl, place ice cream and butter. Microwave on 50 percent power for 1 to 3 minutes, until ice cream and butter melt. Remove from microwave and stir in cake mix and eggs; beat at medium speed for 2 minutes.

3. Fill lined muffin tins two-thirds full with batter and top each with a tablespoon of the crushed granola. Bake for 18 to 23 minutes or until cupcakes are rounded and top springs back when lightly touched with finger. Cool on wire racks.

Recipe Variations
Use chocolate ice cream and chocolate cake mix in this easy recipe, and top the cupcake batter with chocolate chips and nuts. Or use caramel ice cream and spice cake mix, topping the cupcakes with toffee bits. Use your imagination and invent your own special flavor!

Serves 10–12

1 9-inch round angel food
     cake
4 1.4-ounce chocolate-
     covered toffee bars
2 cups whipping cream
⅔ cup powdered sugar
⅓ cup chocolate syrup
1 teaspoon vanilla

Chocolate Toffee Torte

*This elegant torte is a wonderful finish for a company meal
because you can make it up to 8 hours ahead of time.
Use a serrated knife for slicing for best results.*

1. Using serrated knife, cut angel food cake horizontally into four equal layers. Place toffee bars in resealable plastic bag and crush with a rolling pin.

2. In large bowl, combine cream, powdered sugar, chocolate syrup, and vanilla. Beat until stiff peaks form. Frost layers of cake as you reassemble it, sprinkling crushed toffee bars on each layer. Frost top and sides of cake and sprinkle with remaining crushed toffee bars. Serve immediately or cover and chill for 2 to 4 hours. Store leftovers in refrigerator.

Ice Cream with Mix-Ins

This new trend in ice cream lets you decide what to add: one or all of the toppings! Work on a marble surface and let your guests pick the additions.

⁓

Prepare all toppings. Let ice cream stand at room temperature for 10 minutes to soften slightly. Place ½ to ¾ cup ice cream on a cold marble or granite surface and sprinkle desired toppings over. Using two spatulas, chop the ice cream and the toppings together and fold until mixed. Scoop into a serving dish and continue with remaining ice cream and remaining toppings.

Marble Tiles

You can find inexpensive marble or granite tiles at discount stores and home improvement centers. It must be marble or granite to keep the ice cream cold while you work. Clean it thoroughly with soap and water and keep it in the freezer to make ice cream with mix-ins anytime.

Serves 4

2–3 cups vanilla ice cream

1 cup Candied Nuts (page 254), chopped

4 squares plain Brownies from Layered Brownies (page 252)

4 Choco-Peanut Crunchers (page 258), chopped

4 Graham Cracker Crisps (page 259), chopped

Serves 6

8 vanilla cupcakes
3 tablespoons raspberry
    liqueur
½ cup raspberry jam
1 8-ounce dark chocolate bar,
    chopped
1 8-ounce container nondairy
    whipped topping,
    thawed

Raspberry Trifle

*Ask at your bakery for cupcakes that are unfrosted. This easy dessert is delicious
served immediately, but you can cover and refrigerate it for 24 hours if you'd like.*

⟋⟍

Unwrap the cupcakes and break into small pieces. In glass serving dish,
place half of the cupcakes and sprinkle with half of the raspberry liqueur.
Top with half of the raspberry jam, half of the chopped chocolate bar, and
half of the whipped topping. Add remaining cupcakes, sprinkle with rest of
the liqueur, top with remaining jam, and the remaining whipped topping.
Sprinkle top with remaining chopped chocolate bar.

Liqueur Substitutions
*When you're making recipes for children and the ingredient list calls for liqueur,
substitute fruit juices or nectar like pear nectar or guava juice. Other substitutes include the liquid from maraschino cherries, thawed frozen fruit juice
concentrates, or fruit syrups like black currant syrup.*

Brownie Parfait

Use your favorite flavors of ice cream and toppings in this simple and indulgent dessert. You can use plain brownies from the Layered Brownies recipe (page 252) or purchase a pan of brownies from your supermarket or bakery.

Serves 8

5 plain brownies from Layered Brownies (page 252)
2 cups coffee ice cream
2 cups vanilla ice cream
1 cup chocolate fudge ice cream topping
½ cup English toffee bits

Cut brownies into 1-inch squares. Stir both flavors of ice cream until slightly softened. Layer brownies, ice cream, and fudge topping in 8 parfait glasses. Sprinkle with toffee bits. Serve immediately or freeze up to 8 hours; if frozen, let stand at room temperature for 10 to 15 minutes before serving.

Parfait Glasses

Parfait glasses and iced-tea spoons are the perfect utensils to use when making parfaits. The long and slender parfait glasses allow lots of beautiful layers to show through, and the iced-tea spoons are long enough to reach down to the bottom of the glasses.

24 frozen mini filo tart shells
½ cup apple jelly
½ teaspoon chopped fresh
  thyme leaves
½ cup blueberries
½ cup raspberries

Mini Fruit Tarts

Your grocer's freezer section is a gold mine of prepared pie and tart shells.
Stock up on a few different types to make pies and tarts in minutes.

1. Preheat oven to 375°F. Place tart shells on a cookie sheet and bake according to package directions. Remove to wire racks.

2. Meanwhile, heat apple jelly and thyme in a medium saucepan over low heat until jelly melts. Remove from heat and stir in berries. Put a couple of teaspoons of berry mixture into each tart shell and serve.

Herbs in Desserts
In the 1990s, using savory herbs in desserts became popular. Thyme, with its minty, lemony fragrance, is a natural partner with sweet and tart fruits. Rosemary is delicious with lemon desserts and in shortbreads, and lemon verbena is used in fruit jellies and cakes.

Blueberry Crisp

A crisp is a baked dessert that has a crumbly topping made of flour, sugar, butter, and usually oatmeal and nuts. Using canned pie filling streamlines this excellent recipe.

⁓

Serves 6

1 21-ounce can blueberry pie filling
½ cup flour
½ cup brown sugar
½ cup oatmeal
½ cup chopped walnuts
½ teaspoon cinnamon
¼ cup butter, melted

1. Preheat oven to 400°F. Pour blueberry pie filling into 9" square glass pan and set aside.

2. In medium bowl, combine flour, brown sugar, oatmeal, walnuts, and cinnamon and mix well. Pour butter into flour mixture and stir until mixture is crumbly. Sprinkle over blueberry pie filling. Bake for 20 to 25 minutes or until filling is bubbly and crust is light golden brown. Serve with ice cream or whipped cream.

Crisps, Crumbles, Grunts, and Cobblers
All of these old-fashioned, homey desserts are basically the same thing: fruits with some kind of topping. Crisps use oatmeal and nuts to form a crumbly topping; crumbles are the same thing. Grunts are more like a steamed pudding, sometimes cooked on top of the stove. Cobblers are similar to a deep-dish pie, with a thick biscuit-type crust.

Serves 6

1 14-ounce can sweetened
    condensed milk
1 8-ounce package cream
    cheese, softened
¼ cup lemon juice
1 9-inch graham cracker pie
    crust
1 18-ounce can cherry pie
    filling

Simple Cheesecake

*Use any flavor of canned pie filling in this easy pie. You could even
top it with some fresh berries mixed with a bit of jam or jelly.*

1. In large bowl, combine condensed milk, cream cheese, and lemon
   juice; beat on low speed until smooth and combined. Pour into graham
   cracker crust. Place in freezer for 10 minutes.

2. Using a slotted spoon, remove the cherries from the pie filling, leaving a lot of the gel behind. Place cherries on cream cheese filling and
   serve, or cover and chill the pie up to 8 hours. Store leftovers in the
   refrigerator.

Cheesecake Toppings
*There are many toppings that are delicious on cheesecake. Try mixing
fresh berries with preserves or jelly, drizzle the dessert with chocolate
and caramel ice cream toppings, beat whipping cream with chocolate
syrup, or combine chopped nuts with chopped chocolate bars and
marshmallows.*

Strawberries with Sour Cream

*There isn't an easier dessert on the planet, and this simple fruit recipe
has the most wonderful sweet-and-tart flavor. You can make it with
peaches, mangoes, grapes, or pears too; just use fruits that are acidic.*

Serves 6

2 pints strawberries, stemmed
    and sliced
1 cup sour cream
½ cup brown sugar
¼ cup toasted pecans

In glass serving bowl, place one-third of the strawberries. Top with one-third of the sour cream, and sprinkle with one-third of the brown sugar. Repeat layers, ending with brown sugar. Top with toasted pecans and serve, or cover and refrigerate up to 8 hours.

Grilled Peaches

*Grilling fruit makes the most wonderful dessert; the sugars
caramelize and the fruits become very tender and sweet.
Serve this after a cookout for a great finish.*

Serves 4

4 peaches, cut in half
3 tablespoons brown sugar
3 tablespoons maple syrup
½ teaspoon cinnamon
½ cup heavy cream

Remove pits from peaches. Prepare and preheat grill. In small bowl, combine sugar, syrup, and cinnamon. Brush this mixture over both sides of peaches. Place peaches, cut-side down, 4 to 6 inches from medium coals. Grill, uncovered, for 2 to 3 minutes, then turn peaches and top with remaining brown sugar mixture. Grill for 1 to 2 minutes longer, then remove. Drizzle with cream and serve.

30 fudge-covered graham
   crackers
⅓ cup butter, melted
3 pints chocolate ice cream
¾ cup peanut butter
5 ounces peanut butter cups,
   chopped

Chocolate Peanut Butter Pie

*This is such an indulgent dessert, it's hard to believe that it uses
only five ingredients! Take it out of the freezer 15 minutes
before serving for the best flavor and texture.*

1. Crush graham crackers and combine with butter; press crumbs into 9" pie pan and set aside.

2. In blender container or food processor, combine ice cream and peanut butter; blend or process until combined. Fold in chopped candies and place in pie crust. Freeze until firm.

Graham Crackers
There are many varieties of graham crackers on the market. You can find chocolate-covered crackers, low-fat crackers, and cinnamon-flavored and honey-flavored crackers. Choose any of them to make a wonderfully easy and quick pie crust by crushing the crackers and mixing the crumbs with some melted butter, then pressing into a pie pan.

Sherbet Roll

You can use any flavor sherbet, sorbet, or ice cream in this easy and colorful recipe. Think about using other flavors of ice cream and topping for unlimited dessert variations!

Serves 6

1 quart vanilla ice cream
1 cup granola
1 quart lemon sherbet
½ cup caramel ice cream topping

1. Line a jelly-roll pan with parchment paper. Let ice cream stand at room temperature for 5 minutes, then spread evenly in prepared pan. Sprinkle granola over ice cream and return to freezer.

2. Let sherbet stand at room temperature for 5 minutes, then spoon and spread over granola. Return to freezer for 5 minutes.

3. Lift narrow end of parchment paper and use it to roll the ice cream and sherbet together, peeling the paper away from the ice cream as you roll. Place on serving plate and freeze until firm. To serve, slice roll and place slices cut-side down on a spoonful of caramel ice cream topping.

Ice Cream Desserts
Keep several flavors of ice cream, sorbet, and sherbet on hand in your freezer to make easy desserts in a flash. Also, when you're making an ice cream dessert, make one or two extra and keep them in the freezer, well covered and labeled, for unexpected company.

2 pints raspberries
1½ cups whipping cream
½ cup powdered sugar
½ teaspoon vanilla
½ cup chopped pecans,
    toasted
½ cup grated semisweet
    chocolate

Raspberry Fool

A fool is a soft parfait usually made with a puréed fruit and flavored whipping cream. Top it with more sweetened whipped cream and some mint sprigs.

1. Place raspberries in medium bowl and mash some of them, leaving some whole. In large bowl, combine cream, powdered sugar, and vanilla and beat until stiff peaks form.

2. Layer raspberries with whipped cream mixture, pecans, and grated chocolate in 6 parfait glasses. Serve immediately or cover and refrigerate up to 6 hours.

Whipping Cream
Heavy whipping cream must contain at least 36 percent butterfat. To whip cream, chill the bowl and the beaters in the freezer for 10 to 15 minutes. Begin whipping slowly, and gradually increase speed as the cream thickens. The cream is done when peaks droop slightly when the beaters are lifted.

Flaky Peach Tarts

You should make these little mini tarts just before you plan to serve them for best flavor and texture. Top them with peach ice cream and some chopped cashews.

Serves 6

1 sheet frozen puff pastry, thawed
2 peaches
⅓ cup peach jam
3 tablespoons brown sugar
⅛ teaspoon cinnamon

⌐

1. Preheat oven to 375°F. Roll pastry into a 9" × 12" rectangle. Cut pastry into twelve 3-inch squares and place on parchment paper–lined cookie sheets; set aside.

2. Peel peaches, remove pit, and cut into thin slices. Arrange peach slices on pastry and brush each with some of the peach jam. Sprinkle with brown sugar and cinnamon. Bake for 10 to 14 minutes or until pastry is puffed and golden and fruit is tender.

Topping Tarts
Tarts can be topped with sweetened whipped cream, ice cream, or hard sauce. To make hard sauce, beat ½ cup softened butter with 1 cup powdered sugar and 1 teaspoon vanilla. Serve on hot desserts; the mixture will melt into the dessert and form a sweet sauce.

Serves 10–12

1 9-inch round angel food
    cake
1¼ cups whipping cream
2 tablespoons powdered
    sugar
1 cup lemon curd
1½ cups chopped Candied
    Nuts (page 254)

Lemon Angel Cake

*Bakeries always have angel food cake available; also look for
them in the bakery department of your supermarket. Lemon curd is
available near the pie fillings and also in the gourmet foods aisle.*

1. Using a serrated knife, cut cake horizontally into 3 layers. In a large bowl, combine cream and powdered sugar; beat until stiff peaks form. Fold in lemon curd until blended.

2. Spread mixture between layers, sprinkling each layer with some of the Candied Nuts, and then frost top and sides with lemon mixture. Sprinkle top with remaining Candied Nuts. Serve immediately or cover and refrigerate up to 8 hours; store leftovers in refrigerator.

Recipe Variation
You can use just about any well-flavored, smooth, creamy filling, pudding, or custard in place of the lemon curd in this easy recipe. Try chocolate pudding, caramel pudding, or cream cheese frosting. You can also sprinkle the layers with toasted coconut, nuts, or chopped or crushed candy bars as you frost them.

Peanut Cakes

You can find plain cake layers at most bakeries; in some cases you will have to ask for them. These little cakes are kind of fussy to make, but so delicious.

≈

Yields 9 cakes

1 9-inch square yellow cake
1 can vanilla frosting
¼ cup peanut butter
1–2 tablespoons milk
*2 cups chopped salted
    peanuts*

1. Cut cake into 9 squares and place on waxed paper–lined cookie sheets; set aside.

2. In medium bowl, combine frosting and peanut butter with enough milk to make a smooth spreading consistency. One at a time, frost all sides of the cake pieces with this frosting. When completely coated, drop cake pieces into the peanuts and roll to coat all sides. Serve immediately or cover and hold at room temperature for up to 8 hours.

Cake Layers

It's a good idea to keep some boxes of cake mix on hand, especially the single-layer-size mix. There are so many ways to use plain cake layers—frost them with canned frosting, layer them with pudding or ice cream for parfaits, and cut them into squares and frost individually.

Serves 6

1 21-ounce can apple pie
    filling
¾ cup brown sugar
1 teaspoon cinnamon
¼ teaspoon nutmeg
½ cup flour
½ cup oatmeal
⅓ cup butter, melted

Apple Crumble

*Use the crumbly topping with any flavor of canned pie filling;
peach would be very delicious. Top it with some vanilla
or caramel ice cream for extra decadence.*

1. Preheat oven to 400°F. Place pie filling into 1½-quart casserole. In medium bowl, combine sugar, cinnamon, nutmeg, flour, and oatmeal and mix well. Add melted butter and mix until crumbs form. Sprinkle crumbs over pie filling.

2. Bake for 15 to 20 minutes or until pie filling bubbles and crumb mixture is browned. Serve warm.

Serves 8

1 4-ounce package instant
    chocolate pudding mix
1 cup chocolate milk
2 cups vanilla ice cream
½ cup whipping cream
1 chocolate cookie crumb pie
    crust

Fudgesicle Pie

*This excellent recipe does taste just like a Fudgesicle in a pie crust. Garnish it
with chocolate-covered peanuts and some chocolate syrup.*

1. In large bowl, combine pudding mix with milk; mix with eggbeater or hand mixer for 1 minute until smooth and thickened. Using mixer on low speed, add vanilla ice cream and beat until combined.

2. In small bowl, beat cream until stiff peaks form. Add to ice cream mixture and beat just until combined. Pour into pie crust and freeze.

Chocolate Velvet

You can pile this mixture into a baked and cooled pie crust or a graham cracker crust and freeze to serve it as a pie; top wedges with some whipped cream and grated chocolate.

~

Serves 8

1 cup chocolate syrup
1 15-ounce can sweetened
    condensed milk
1 16-ounce container frozen
    whipped topping,
    thawed
½ teaspoon vanilla
⅓ cup sliced almonds, toasted

In large bowl, combine syrup and sweetened condensed milk and beat until smooth. Fold in whipped topping and vanilla. Sprinkle with almonds and serve immediately as a pudding, or place in 1-quart casserole dish, top with almonds, and freeze until solid.

Toasting Nuts

To toast nuts, place them on a shallow baking pan and bake at 350°F for 5 to 10 minutes, shaking pan frequently, until nuts are fragrant and just beginning to turn light golden brown. You can also microwave the nuts at 100 percent power for 3 to 5 minutes, until the nuts are fragrant. Let cool completely before chopping.

Standard U.S./Metric Measurement Conversions

VOLUME CONVERSIONS

U.S. Volume Measure	Metric Equivalent
⅛ teaspoon	0.5 milliliters
¼ teaspoon	1 milliliters
½ teaspoon	2 milliliters
1 teaspoon	5 milliliters
½ tablespoon	7 milliliters
1 tablespoon (3 teaspoons)	15 milliliters
2 tablespoons (1 fluid ounce)	30 milliliters
¼ cup (4 tablespoons)	60 milliliters
⅓ cup	90 milliliters
½ cup (4 fluid ounces)	125 milliliters
⅔ cup	160 milliliters
¾ cup (6 fluid ounces)	180 milliliters
1 cup (16 tablespoons)	250 milliliters
1 pint (2 cups)	500 milliliters
1 quart (4 cups)	1 liter (about)

WEIGHT CONVERSIONS

U.S. Weight Measure	Metric Equivalent
½ ounce	15 grams
1 ounce	30 grams
2 ounces	60 grams
3 ounces	85 grams
¼ pound (4 ounces)	115 grams
½ pound (8 ounces)	225 grams
¾ pound (12 ounces)	340 grams
1 pound (16 ounces)	454 grams

OVEN TEMPERATURE CONVERSIONS

Degrees Fahrenheit	Degrees Celsius
200 degrees F	100 degrees C
250 degrees F	120 degrees C
275 degrees F	140 degrees C
300 degrees F	150 degrees C
325 degrees F	160 degrees C
350 degrees F	180 degrees C
375 degrees F	190 degrees C
400 degrees F	200 degrees C
425 degrees F	220 degrees C
450 degrees F	230 degrees C

BAKING PAN SIZES

American	Metric
8 x 1½ inch round baking pan	20 x 4 cm cake tin
9 x 1½ inch round baking pan	23 x 3.5 cm cake tin
1 x 7 x 1½ inch baking pan	28 x 18 x 4 cm baking tin
113 x 9 x 2 inch baking pan	30 x 20 x 5 cm baking tin
2 quart rectangular baking dish	30 x 20 x 3 cm baking tin
15 x 10 x 2 inch baking pan	30 x 25 x 2 cm baking tin (Swiss roll tin)
9 inch pie plate	22 x 4 or 23 x 4 cm pie plate
7 or 8 inch springform pan	18 or 20 cm springform or loose bottom cake tin
9 x 5 x 3 inch loaf pan	23 x 13 x 7 cm or 2 lb narrow loaf or pate tin
1½ quart casserole	1.5 litre casserole
2 quart casserole	2 litre casserole